ŚRĪMAD BHĀGAVATAM

Seventh Canto

"The Science of God"

(Part Three—Chapters 10-15)

With the Original Sanskrit Text,
Its Roman Transliteration, Synonyms,
Translation and Elaborate Purports

by

His Divine Grace
A.C. Bhaktivedanta Swami Prabhupāda
Founder-*Ācārya* of the International Society for Krishna Consciousness

THE BHAKTIVEDANTA BOOK TRUST
New York · Los Angeles · London · Bombay

Readers interested in the subject matter of this book
are invited by the International Society for Krishna Consciousness
to correspond with its Secretary.

International Society for Krishna Consciousness
3764 Watseka Avenue
Los Angeles, California 90034

Library of Congress Catalogue Card Number: 73-169353
International Standard Book Number: 0-912776-89-7

First printing, 1976: 20,000 copies

Printed in the United States of America

ALL GLORY TO ŚRĪ GURU AND GAURĀṄGA

ŚRĪMAD BHĀGAVATAM

of

KṚṢṆA-DVAIPĀYANA VYĀSA

पात्रं त्वत्र निरुक्तं वै कविभिः पात्रवित्तमैः ।
हरिरेवैक उर्वीश यन्मयं वै चराचरम् ॥

pātraṁ tv atra niruktaṁ vai
kavibhiḥ pātra-vittamaiḥ
harir evaika urvīśa
yan-mayaṁ vai carācaram (p. 181)

BOOKS by
His Divine Grace A. C. Bhaktivedanta Swami Prabhupāda

Bhagavad-gītā As It Is
Śrīmad-Bhāgavatam, Cantos 1–8 (24 Vols.)
Śrī Caitanya-caritāmṛta (17 Vols.)
Teachings of Lord Caitanya
The Nectar of Devotion
The Nectar of Instruction
Śrī Īśopaniṣad
Easy Journey to Other Planets
Kṛṣṇa Consciousness: The Topmost Yoga System
Kṛṣṇa, the Supreme Personality of Godhead (3 Vols.)
Perfect Questions, Perfect Answers
Dialectic Spiritualism—A Vedic View of Western Philosophy (3 Vols.)
Transcendental Teachings of Prāhlad Mahārāja
Kṛṣṇa, the Reservoir of Pleasure
Life Comes from Life
The Perfection of Yoga
Beyond Birth and Death
On the Way to Kṛṣṇa
Rāja-vidyā: The King of Knowledge
Elevation to Kṛṣṇa Consciousness
Kṛṣṇa Consciousness: The Matchless Gift
Back to Godhead Magazine (Founder)

A complete catalogue is available upon request

The Bhaktivedanta Book Trust
3764 Watseka Avenue
Los Angeles, California 90034

Table of Contents

Preface *ix*
Introduction *xiii*

CHAPTER TEN
Prahlāda, the Best Among Exalted Devotees (Part II) **1**
Chapter Summary 1
The Absolute Truth Is a Person 3
The Demoniac Genius, Maya Dānava 8
Man Proposes, Kṛṣṇa Disposes 14

CHAPTER ELEVEN
The Perfect Society: Four Social Classes **21**
Chapter Summary 21
Our Eternal Occupational Duty 24
The Qualifications of a Human Being 32
The Intellectual, Administrative, Mercantile and Worker Classes 36
Chaste Women: A Social Necessity 46
How to Divide Society 55

CHAPTER TWELVE
The Perfect Society: Four Spiritual Classes **57**
Chapter Summary 57
Brahmacārī Life: Living under the Care of a Guru 59
Women Are like Fire, Men Are the Butter 65
Understanding Vedic Knowledge Is Real Education 70
Vānaprastha Life: Preparing to Meet Death 74

CHAPTER THIRTEEN
The Behavior of a Perfect Person **85**
Chapter Summary 85
The Renounced Order of Life 87
Avoid Reading Mundane Literature 92
Prahlāda's Conversation with a Perfect Sage 97
Only Humans Can Choose Their Next Body 108
Sense Enjoyment Is Simply Imaginary 113
The Threefold Miseries 119
The Bee and Python Are Excellent Teachers 126
Those Who Know Retire from the Illusion 135

CHAPTER FOURTEEN
Ideal Family Life **139**
Chapter Summary 139
How Householders Can Obtain Liberation 141
Plain Living, High Thinking 147
Treat Animals like Your Own Children 154
The Real Value of the Wife's Body 160
Distributing Prasāda, Spiritual Food 166
ISKCON Centers Benefit Everyone 175
Everything Must Be Given to Kṛṣṇa 181

CHAPTER FIFTEEN
Instructions for Civilized Human Beings **195**
Chapter Summary 195
Offering Food to the Lord and His Devotees 203
Slaughtering Animals for Religion and Food 207
The Five Branches of Pseudoreligion 209
How to Transcend Economic Endeavor 213
Greed: The Merciless Taskmaster 217

The Guru Is Life's Greatest Asset 223
The Yoga Process 229
Breaking Spiritual Regulations Is Intolerable 240
The Mercy of the Spiritual Master 249
Why You Cannot Remain in the Heavenly Planets 258
What Is Reality? 267
The Ultimate Self-interest 276
Nārada Muni's Previous Lives 281
Kṛṣṇa Lived with the Pāṇḍavas Just like an Ordinary Human Being 288

Appendixes

The Author 297
References 299
Glossary 301
Sanskrit Pronunciation Guide 307
Index of Sanskrit Verses 309
General Index 317

Preface

We must know the present need of human society. And what is that need? Human society is no longer bounded by geographical limits to particular countries or communities. Human society is broader than in the Middle Ages, and the world tendency is toward one state or one human society. The ideals of spiritual communism, according to *Śrīmad-Bhāgavatam*, are based more or less on the oneness of the entire human society, nay, on the entire energy of living beings. The need is felt by great thinkers to make this a successful ideology. *Śrīmad-Bhāgavatam* will fill this need in human society. It begins, therefore, with the aphorism of Vedānta philosophy (*janmādy asya yataḥ*) to establish the ideal of a common cause.

Human society, at the present moment, is not in the darkness of oblivion. It has made rapid progress in the field of material comforts, education and economic development throughout the entire world. But there is a pinprick somewhere in the social body at large, and therefore there are large-scale quarrels, even over less important issues. There is need of a clue as to how humanity can become one in peace, friendship and prosperity with a common cause. *Śrīmad-Bhāgavatam* will fill this need, for it is a cultural presentation for the re-spiritualization of the entire human society.

Śrīmad-Bhāgavatam should be introduced also in the schools and colleges, for it is recommended by the great student devotee Prahlāda Mahārāja in order to change the demonic face of society.

kaumāra ācaret prājño
dharmān bhāgavatān iha
durlabhaṁ mānuṣaṁ janma
tad apy adhruvam arthadam
(*Bhāg.* 7.6.1)

Disparity in human society is due to lack of principles in a godless civilization. There is God, or the Almighty One, from whom everything emanates, by whom everything is maintained and in whom everything is merged to rest. Material science has tried to find the ultimate source of creation very insufficiently, but it is a fact that there is one ultimate source of everything that be. This ultimate source is explained rationally and authoritatively in the beautiful *Bhāgavatam* or *Śrīmad-Bhāgavatam.*

Śrīmad-Bhāgavatam is the transcendental science not only for knowing the ultimate source of everything but also for knowing our relation with Him and our duty towards perfection of the human society on the basis of this perfect knowledge. It is powerful reading matter in the Sanskrit language, and it is now rendered into English elaborately so that simply by a careful reading one will know God perfectly well, so much so that the reader will be sufficiently educated to defend himself from the onslaught of atheists. Over and above this, the reader will be able to convert others to accept God as a concrete principle.

Śrīmad-Bhāgavatam begins with the definition of the ultimate source. It is a bona fide commentary on the *Vedānta-sūtra* by the same author, Śrīla Vyāsadeva, and gradually it develops into nine cantos up to the highest state of God realization. The only qualification one needs to study this great book of transcendental knowledge is to proceed step by step cautiously and not jump forward haphazardly as with an ordinary book. It should be gone through chapter by chapter, one after another. The reading matter is so arranged with its original Sanskrit text, its English transliteration, synonyms, translation and purports so that one is sure to become a God realized soul at the end of finishing the first nine cantos.

The Tenth Canto is distinct from the first nine cantos, because it deals directly with the transcendental activities of the Personality of Godhead Śrī Kṛṣṇa. One will be unable to capture the effects of the Tenth Canto without going through the first nine cantos. The book is complete in twelve cantos, each independent, but it is good for all to read them in small installments one after another.

I must admit my frailties in presenting *Śrīmad-Bhāgavatam*, but still I am hopeful of its good reception by the thinkers and leaders of society on the strength of the following statement of *Śrīmad-Bhāgavatam.*

tad-vāg-visargo janatāgha-viplavo
yasmin pratiślokam abaddhavaty api

nāmāny anantasya yaśo 'ṅkitāni yac
chṛṇvanti gāyanti gṛṇanti sādhavaḥ
(*Bhāg.* 1.5.11)

"On the other hand, that literature which is full with descriptions of the transcendental glories of the name, fame, form and pastimes of the unlimited Supreme Lord is a transcendental creation meant to bring about a revolution in the impious life of a misdirected civilization. Such transcendental literatures, even though irregularly composed, are heard, sung and accepted by purified men who are thoroughly honest."

Oṁ tat sat

A. C. Bhaktivedanta Swami

Introduction

"This *Bhāgavata Purāṇa* is as brilliant as the sun, and it has arisen just after the departure of Lord Kṛṣṇa to His own abode, accompanied by religion, knowledge, etc. Persons who have lost their vision due to the dense darkness of ignorance in the age of Kali shall get light from this *Purāṇa.*" (*Śrīmad-Bhāgavatam* 1.3.43)

The timeless wisdom of India is expressed in the *Vedas,* ancient Sanskrit texts that touch upon all fields of human knowledge. Originally preserved through oral tradition, the *Vedas* were first put into writing five thousand years ago by Śrīla Vyāsadeva, the "literary incarnation of God." After compiling the *Vedas,* Vyāsadeva set forth their essence in the aphorisms known as *Vedānta-sūtras. Śrīmad-Bhāgavatam* is Vyāsadeva's commentary on his own *Vedānta-sūtras.* It was written in the maturity of his spiritual life under the direction of Nārada Muni, his spiritual master. Referred to as "the ripened fruit of the tree of Vedic literature," *Śrīmad-Bhāgavatam* is the most complete and authoritative exposition of Vedic knowledge.

After compiling the *Bhāgavatam,* Vyāsa impressed the synopsis of it upon his son, the sage Śukadeva Gosvāmī. Śukadeva Gosvāmī subsequently recited the entire *Bhāgavatam* to Mahārāja Parīkṣit in an assembly of learned saints on the bank of the Ganges at Hastināpura (now Delhi). Mahārāja Parīkṣit was the emperor of the world and was a great *rājarṣi* (saintly king). Having received a warning that he would die within a week, he renounced his entire kingdom and retired to the bank of the Ganges to fast until death and receive spiritual enlightenment. The *Bhāgavatam* begins with Emperor Parīkṣit's sober inquiry to Śukadeva Gosvāmī:

> "You are the spiritual master of great saints and devotees. I am therefore begging you to show the way of perfection for all persons, and especially for one who is about to die. Please let me know what a man should hear, chant, remember and worship, and also what he should not do. Please explain all this to me."

Śukadeva Gosvāmī's answer to this question, and numerous other questions posed by Mahārāja Parīkṣit, concerning everything from the nature of the self to the origin of the universe, held the assembled sages in rapt attention continuously for the seven days leading to the King's death. The sage Sūta Gosvāmī, who was present on the bank of the Ganges when Śukadeva Gosvāmī first recited *Śrīmad-Bhāgavatam,* later repeated the *Bhāgavatam* before a gathering of sages in the forest of Naimiṣāraṇya. Those sages, concerned about the spiritual welfare of the people in general, had gathered to perform a long, continuous chain of sacrifices to counteract the degrading influence of the incipient age of Kali. In response to the sages' request that he speak the essence of Vedic wisdom, Sūta Gosvāmī repeated from memory the entire eighteen thousand verses of *Śrīmad-Bhāgavatam,* as spoken by Śukadeva Gosvāmī to Mahārāja Parīkṣit.

The reader of *Śrīmad-Bhāgavatam* hears Sūta Gosvāmī relate the questions of Mahārāja Parīkṣit and the answers of Śukadeva Gosvāmī. Also, Sūta Gosvāmī sometimes responds directly to questions put by Śaunaka Ṛṣi, the spokesman for the sages gathered at Naimiṣāraṇya. One therefore simultaneously hears two dialogues: one between Mahārāja Parīkṣit and Śukadeva Gosvāmī on the bank of the Ganges, and another at Naimiṣāraṇya between Sūta Gosvāmī and the sages at Naimiṣāraṇya Forest, headed by Śaunaka Ṛṣi. Furthermore, while instructing King Parīkṣit, Śukadeva Gosvāmī often relates historical episodes and gives accounts of lengthy philosophical discussions between such great souls as the saint Maitreya and his disciple Vidura. With this understanding of the history of the *Bhāgavatam,* the reader will easily be able to follow its intermingling of dialogues and events from various sources. Since philosophical wisdom, not chronological order, is most important in the text, one need only be attentive to the subject matter of *Śrīmad-Bhāgavatam* to appreciate fully its profound message.

The translator of this edition compares the *Bhāgavatam* to sugar candy—wherever you taste it, you will find it equally sweet and relishable. Therefore, to taste the sweetness of the *Bhāgavatam,* one may begin by reading any of its volumes. After such an introductory taste, however, the serious reader is best advised to go back to Volume One of the First Canto and then proceed through the *Bhāgavatam,* volume after volume, in its natural order.

This edition of the *Bhāgavatam* is the first complete English translation of this important text with an elaborate commentary, and it is the first widely available to the English-speaking public. It is the product of the scholarly and devotional effort of His Divine Grace A. C. Bhaktivedanta Swami Prabhupāda, the world's most distinguished teacher of Indian religious and philosophical thought. His consummate Sanskrit scholarship and intimate familiarity with Vedic culture and thought as well as the modern way of life combine to reveal to the West a magnificent exposition of this important classic.

Readers will find this work of value for many reasons. For those interested in the classical roots of Indian civilization, it serves as a vast reservoir of detailed information on virtually every one of its aspects. For students of comparative philosophy and religion, the *Bhāgavatam* offers a penetrating view into the meaning of India's profound spiritual heritage. To sociologists and anthropologists, the *Bhāgavatam* reveals the practical workings of a peaceful and scientifically organized Vedic culture, whose institutions were integrated on the basis of a highly developed spiritual world view. Students of literature will discover the *Bhāgavatam* to be a masterpiece of majestic poetry. For students of psychology, the text provides important perspectives on the nature of consciousness, human behavior and the philosophical study of identity. Finally, to those seeking spiritual insight, the *Bhāgavatam* offers simple and practical guidance for attainment of the highest self-knowledge and realization of the Absolute Truth. The entire multivolume text, presented by the Bhaktivedanta Book Trust, promises to occupy a significant place in the intellectual, cultural and spiritual life of modern man for a long time to come.

—The Publishers

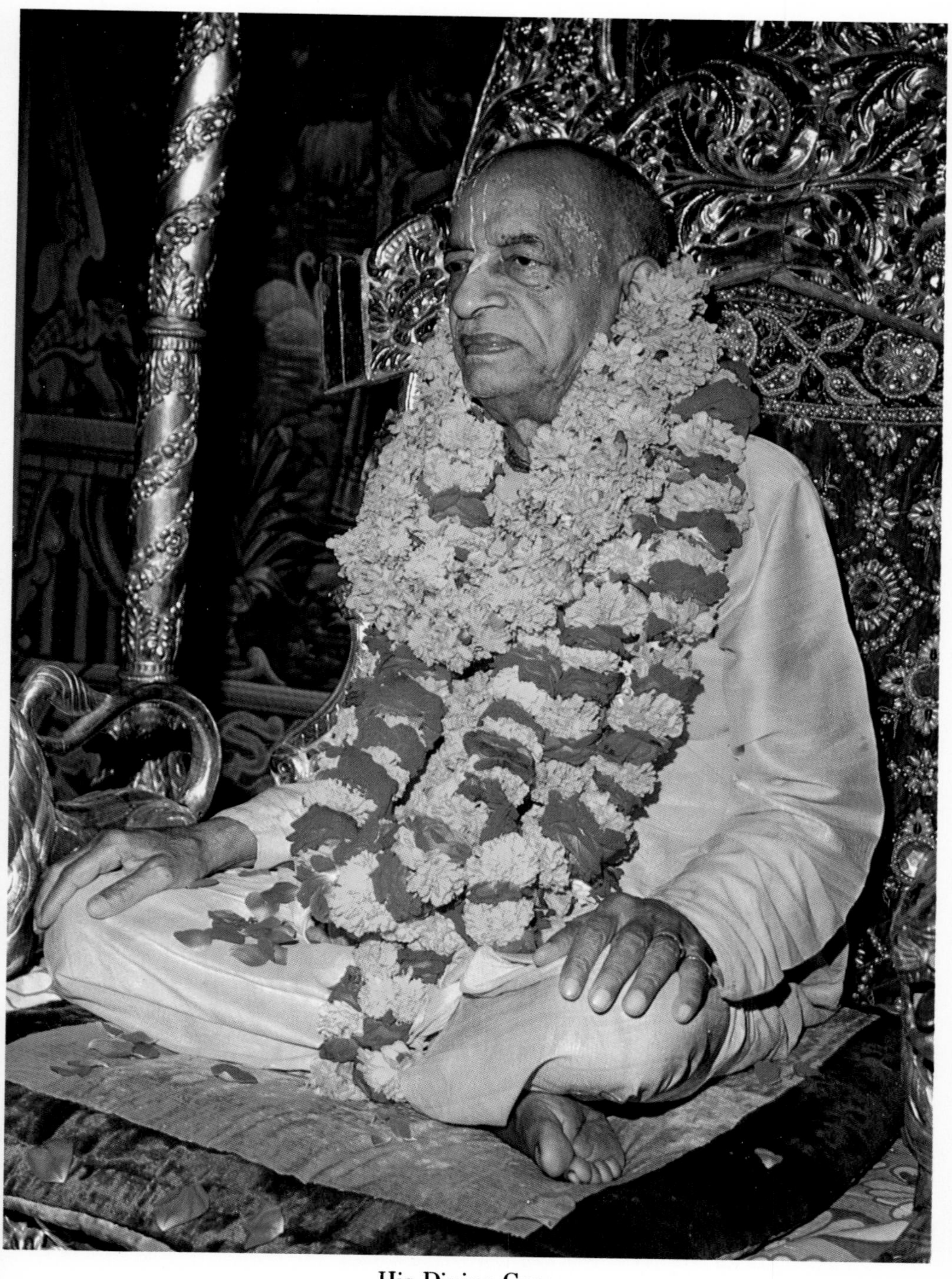

His Divine Grace
A. C. Bhaktivedanta Swami Prabhupāda
Founder-Ācārya of the International Society for Krishna Consciousness

PLATE ONE

Thousands of years ago, Yudhiṣṭhira Mahārāja was the most exalted and respected king of India. During a great gathering of sages, he took the opportunity to inquire from the exalted saint Nārada Muni about the principles of the eternal religious system, by which one can attain the ultimate goal of life. Nārada Muni, the supreme spiritual master of human society, instructed King Yudhiṣṭhira on the behavior of perfect persons, the organization of the perfect society, and ideal family life. He taught the path of spiritual liberation leading to the understanding of the Supreme Personality of Godhead, Śrī Kṛṣṇa. Mahārāja Yudhiṣṭhira thus learned everything from the descriptions of Nārada Muni. After hearing these instructions, he felt great pleasure from within his heart, and in great ecstasy, love and affection, he worshiped Lord Kṛṣṇa. *(pp. 23–292)*

PLATE TWO

When the planets of the demigods were attacked by the demoniac soldiers of Maya Dānava, the rulers of those planets appealed to Lord Śiva for protection. "Do not be afraid," Lord Śiva assured the demigods, and then he attacked and killed the demons with a barrage of fiery arrows. But Maya Dānava, who was extremely powerful by dint of his mystic *yoga* practice, brought the demons back to life by dropping them into a nectar-filled well he had created. When the dead bodies of the demons came in touch with the nectar, their bodies became invincible to thunderbolts. Endowed with great strength, they got up like lightning penetrating clouds. *(pp. 9–12)*

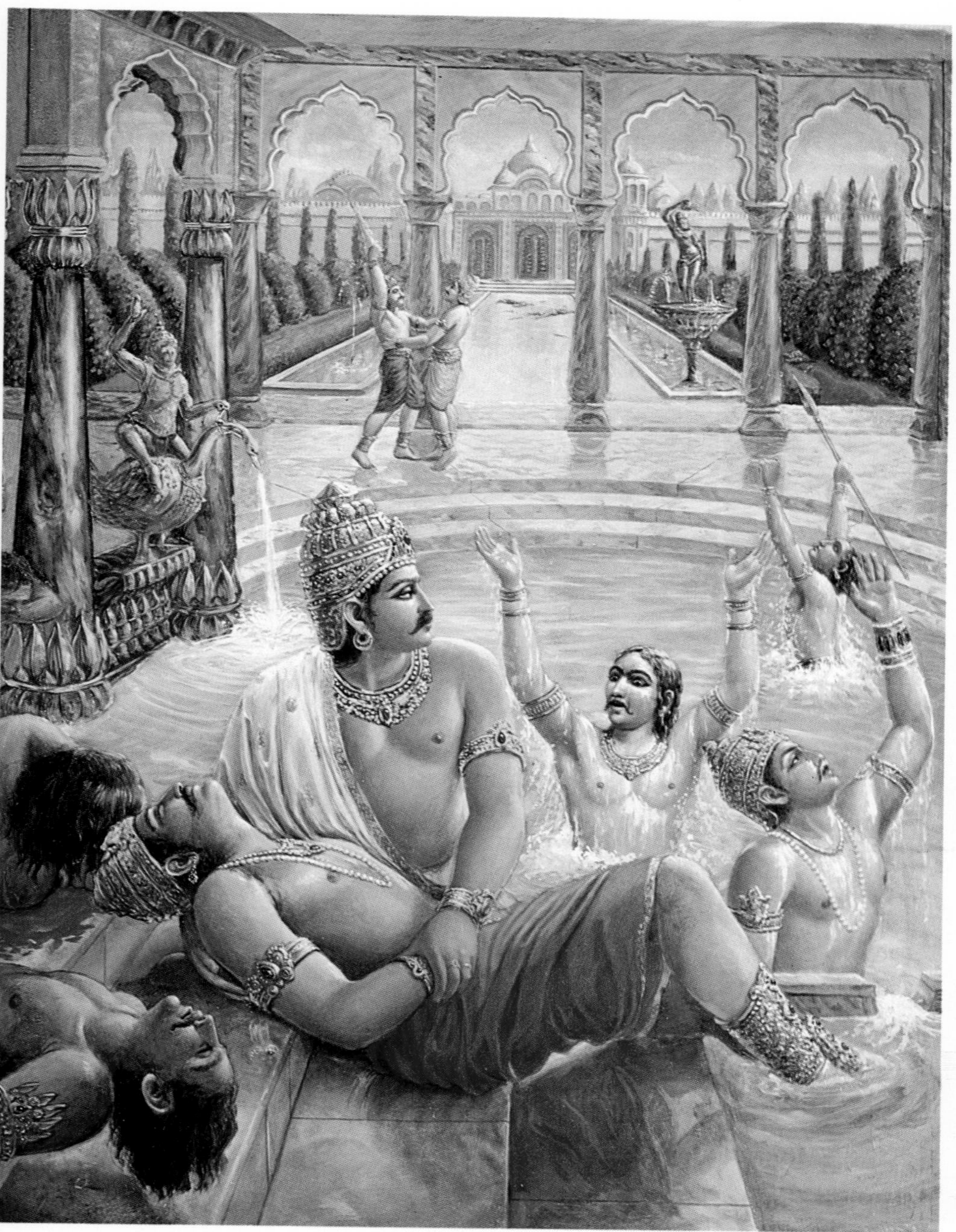

PLATE THREE

Maya Dānava, the great leader of the demons, prepared three invisible residences and gave them to the demons. These dwellings resembled airplanes made of gold, silver and iron, and they contained uncommon paraphernalia, which enabled the demons to remain invisible. Taking advantage of this opportunity, the demons began to attack the three planetary systems. Seeing this great disturbance, the Supreme Lord Kṛṣṇa, by His own personal potency (consisting of religion, knowledge, renunciation, opulence, austerity, education and activities) equipped Lord Śiva with all the necessary paraphernalia, such as a chariot, a charioteer, a flag, horses, elephants, a bow, a shield and an arrow. When Lord Śiva was fully equipped in this way, he sat down on the chariot with his arrows and bow to fight with the demons. The most powerful Lord Śiva then joined the arrows to his bow, and at noon he set fire to all three residences of the demons and thus destroyed them. *(pp. 8–17)*

PLATE FOUR

The Supreme Personality of Godhead has created many residential places like the bodies of human beings, animals, birds, saints and demigods. In all of these innumerable bodily forms, the Lord resides with the living beings as Paramātmā, the Supersoul. The Supersoul in every body gives intelligence to the individual soul according to his capacity for understanding. Therefore, the Supersoul is the chief within the body. The Supersoul is manifested to the individual soul according to the individual's comparative development, knowledge, austerity, penance and so on. The Supreme Lord is situated in everyone's heart, and is directing the wanderings of all living entities, who are seated as on a machine, made of the material energy. One who sees the Supersoul, Lord Viṣṇu, accompanying the individual soul in all bodies and who understands that neither the soul nor the Supersoul is ever destroyed, actually sees, and he therefore gradually advances toward spiritual perfection. *(pp. 185–188)*

PLATE FIVE

Prahlāda Mahārāja, the most dear servitor of the Supreme Personality of Godhead, once went out touring the universe with some of his confidential associates just to study the nature of saintly persons. Thus he arrived at the bank of the Kāverī, where there was a mountain known as Sahya. There he found a great saintly person who was lying on the ground, covered with dirt and dust, but who was deeply spiritually advanced. Neither by that saintly person's activities, by his bodily features, by his words, nor by the symptoms of his cultural status could people understand whether he was the same person they had known. The great devotee Prahlāda Mahārāja, in order to understand him, inquired why he had ceased taking part in all materialistic activities. The sage explained that material existence is illusory and that real happiness can be achieved by retiring from materialistic activities and absorbing oneself in self-realization. *(pp. 98–137)*

PLATE SIX

The Supreme Personality of Godhead, Lord Kṛṣṇa, is the master of all other living entities and of the material nature. Kṛṣṇa, who is known as Govinda, is the supreme controller. He has an eternal, blissful, spiritual body. He is the origin of all. He has no other origin, but He is the prime cause of all causes. One can understand the Supreme Personality as He is only by devotional service. And when one is in full consciousness of the Supreme Lord Kṛṣṇa by such devotion, he can enter into the kingdom of God. (*p. 267*)

PLATE SEVEN

Long, long ago, Nārada Muni existed as the Gandharva known as Upabarhaṇa. With his beautiful face, pleasing, attractive bodily structure, and decorations of flower garlands and sandalwood pulp, he was most pleasing to the women in his city, and thus he was bewildered, always feeling lusty desires. Once there was a *saṅkīrtana* festival to glorify the Supreme Lord in an assembly of the demigods, and the Gandharvas and Apsarās were invited by the *prajāpatis* to take part in it. At that festival, Upabarhaṇa, surrounded by lusty women, began singing ordinary songs. Because of this, the *prajāpatis*, the great demigods in charge of the affairs of the universe, forcefully cursed him with these words: "Because you have committed an offense, may you immediately become a *śūdra*, devoid of beauty." *(pp. 281–285)*

CHAPTER TEN

Prahlāda, the Best Among Exalted Devotees

(continued from the previous volume)

TEXT 48

यूयं नृलोके बत भूरिभागा
लोकं पुनाना मुनयोऽभियन्ति ।
येषां गृहानावसतीति साक्षाद्
गूढं परं ब्रह्म मनुष्यलिङ्गम् ॥४८॥

yūyaṁ nṛ-loke bata bhūri-bhāgā
lokaṁ punānā munayo 'bhiyanti
yeṣāṁ gṛhān āvasatīti sākṣād
gūḍhaṁ paraṁ brahma manuṣya-liṅgam

yūyam—all of you (the Pāṇḍavas); *nṛ-loke*—within this material world; *bata*—however; *bhūri-bhāgāḥ*—extremely fortunate; *lokam*—all the planets; *punānāḥ*—who can purify; *munayaḥ*—great saintly persons; *abhiyanti*—almost always come to visit; *yeṣām*—of whom; *gṛhān*—the house; *āvasati*—resides in; *iti*—thus; *sākṣāt*—directly; *gūḍham*—very confidential; *param brahma*—the Supreme Personality of Godhead; *manuṣya-liṅgam*—appearing just like a human being.

TRANSLATION

Nārada Muni continued: My dear Mahārāja Yudhiṣṭhira, all of you [the Pāṇḍavas] are extremely fortunate, for the Supreme Personality of Godhead, Kṛṣṇa, lives in your palace just like a human being. Great saintly persons know this very well, and therefore they constantly visit this house.

PURPORT

After hearing about the activities of Prahlāda Mahārāja, a pure devotee should be very anxious to follow in his footsteps, but such a devotee might be disappointed, thinking that not every devotee can come to the standard of Prahlāda Mahārāja. This is the nature of a pure devotee; he always thinks himself to be the lowest, to be incompetent and unqualified. Thus after hearing the narration of Prahlāda Mahārāja's activities, Mahārāja Yudhiṣṭhira, who was on the same standard of devotional service as Prahlāda, might have been thinking of his own humble position. Nārada Muni, however, could understand Mahārāja Yudhiṣṭhira's mind, and therefore he immediately encouraged him by saying that the Pāṇḍavas were not less fortunate; they were as good as Prahlāda Mahārāja because although Lord Nṛsiṁhadeva appeared for Prahlāda, the Supreme Personality of Godhead in His original form as Kṛṣṇa was always living with the Pāṇḍavas. Although the Pāṇḍavas, because of the influence of Kṛṣṇa's *yogamāyā*, could not think of their fortunate position, every saintly person, including the great sage Nārada, could understand it, and therefore they constantly visited Mahārāja Yudhiṣṭhira.

Any pure devotee who is constantly conscious of Kṛṣṇa is naturally very fortunate. The word *nṛ-loke*, meaning "within the material world," indicates that before the Pāṇḍavas there had been many, many devotees, such as the descendants of the Yadu dynasty and Vasiṣṭha, Marīci, Kaśyapa, Lord Brahmā and Lord Śiva, who were all extremely fortunate. The Pāṇḍavas, however, were better than all of them because Kṛṣṇa Himself lived with them constantly. Nārada Muni therefore specifically mentioned that within this material world (*nṛ-loke*) the Pāṇḍavas were the most fortunate.

TEXT 49

स वा अयं ब्रह्म महद्विमृग्य-
कैवल्यनिर्वाणसुखानुभूतिः ।
प्रियः सुहृद् वः खलु मातुलेय
आत्मार्हणीयो विधिकृद् गुरुश्च ॥४९॥

sa vā ayaṁ brahma mahad-vimṛgya-
kaivalya-nirvāṇa-sukhānubhūtiḥ
priyaḥ suhṛd vaḥ khalu mātuleya
ātmārhaṇīyo vidhi-kṛd guruś ca

saḥ—that (Supreme Personality of Godhead, Kṛṣṇa); *vā*—also; *ayam*—this; *brahma*—the impersonal Brahman (which is an emanation from Kṛṣṇa); *mahat*—by great personalities; *vimṛgya*—searched for; *kaivalya*—oneness; *nirvāṇa-sukha*—of transcendental happiness; *anubhūtiḥ*—the source of practical experience; *priyaḥ*—very, very dear; *suhṛt*—well-wisher; *vaḥ*—of you; *khalu*—indeed; *mātuleyaḥ*—the son of a maternal uncle; *ātmā*—exactly like body and soul together; *arhaṇīyaḥ*—worshipable (because He is the Supreme Personality of Godhead); *vidhi-kṛt*—(yet He serves you as) an order carrier; *guruḥ*—your supreme advisor; *ca*—as well.

TRANSLATION

The impersonal Brahman is Kṛṣṇa Himself because Kṛṣṇa is the source of the impersonal Brahman. He is the origin of the transcendental bliss sought by great saintly persons, yet He, the Supreme Person, is your most dear friend and constant well-wisher and is intimately related to you as the son of your maternal uncle. Indeed, He is always like your body and soul. He is worshipable, yet He acts as your servant and sometimes as your spiritual master.

PURPORT

There is always a difference of opinion about the Absolute Truth. One class of transcendentalists concludes that the Absolute Truth is impersonal, and another class concludes that the Absolute Truth is a person. In *Bhagavad-gītā*, the Absolute Truth is accepted as the Supreme Person. Indeed, that Supreme Person Himself, Lord Kṛṣṇa, instructs in *Bhagavad-gītā, brahmaṇo hi pratiṣṭhāham, mattaḥ parataraṁ nānyat.* "The impersonal Brahman is My partial manifestation, and there is no truth superior to Me." That same Kṛṣṇa, the Supreme Personality of Godhead, acted as the supreme friend and relative of the Pāṇḍavas, and sometimes He even acted as their servant by carrying a letter from the Pāṇḍavas to Dhṛtarāṣṭra and Duryodhana. Because Kṛṣṇa was the well-wisher of the Pāṇḍavas, He also acted as *guru* by becoming the spiritual master of Arjuna. Arjuna accepted Kṛṣṇa as his spiritual master (*śiṣyas te 'haṁ śādhi māṁ tvāṁ prapannam*), and Kṛṣṇa sometimes chastised him. For example, the Lord said, *aśocyān anvaśocas tvaṁ prajñā-vādāṁś ca bhāṣase:* "While speaking learned words, you are mourning for what is not worthy of grief." The Lord also said, *kutas tvā kaśmalam idaṁ viṣame samupasthitam:* "My dear Arjuna, how have these impurities come upon you?" Such was the intimate relationship between the Pāṇḍavas and Kṛṣṇa. In the same way, a pure devotee of the Lord is always with Kṛṣṇa through thick and thin; his way of life is Kṛṣṇa. This is the statement of the authority Śrī Nārada Muni.

TEXT 50

न यस्य साक्षाद् भवपद्मजादिभी
रूपं धिया वस्तुतयोपवर्णितम् ।
मौनेन भक्त्योपशमेन पूजितः
प्रसीदतामेष स सात्वतां पतिः ॥५०॥

na yasya sākṣād bhava-padmajādibhī
rūpaṁ dhiyā vastutayopavarṇitam
maunena bhaktyopaśamena pūjitaḥ
prasīdatām eṣa sa sātvatāṁ patiḥ

na—not; *yasya*—of whom; *sākṣāt*—directly; *bhava*—Lord Śiva; *padma-ja*—Lord Brahmā (born from the lotus); *ādibhiḥ*—by them and others also; *rūpam*—the form; *dhiyā*—even by meditation; *vastutayā*—fundamentally; *upavarṇitam*—described and perceived; *maunena*—by *samādhi,* deep meditation; *bhaktyā*—by devotional service; *upaśamena*—by renunciation; *pūjitaḥ*—worshiped; *prasīdatām*—may He be pleased; *eṣaḥ*—this; *saḥ*—He; *sātvatām*—of the great devotees; *patiḥ*—the master.

TRANSLATION

Exalted persons like Lord Śiva and Lord Brahmā could not properly describe the truth of the Supreme Personality of God-

head, Kṛṣṇa. May the Lord, who is always worshiped as the protector of all devotees by great saints who observe vows of silence, meditation, devotional service and renunciation, be pleased with us.

PURPORT

The Absolute Truth is sought by different persons in different ways, yet He remains inconceivable. Nonetheless, devotees like the Pāṇḍavas, the *gopīs*, the cowherd boys, Mother Yaśodā, Nanda Mahārāja and all the inhabitants of Vṛndāvana do not need to practice conventional processes of meditation to attain the Supreme Personality of Godhead, for He remains with them through thick and thin. Therefore a saint like Nārada, understanding the difference between transcendentalists and pure devotees, always prays that the Lord will be pleased with him.

TEXT 51

स एष भगवान्राजन्व्यतनोद् विहतं यशः ।
पुरा रुद्रस्य देवस्य मयेनानन्तमायिना ॥५१॥

sa eṣa bhagavān rājan
vyatanod vihataṁ yaśaḥ
purā rudrasya devasya
mayenānanta-māyinā

saḥ eṣaḥ bhagavān—the same Personality of Godhead, Kṛṣṇa, who is Parabrahman; *rājan*—my dear King; *vyatanot*—expanded; *vihatam*—lost; *yaśaḥ*—reputation; *purā*—formerly in history; *rudrasya*—of Lord Śiva (the most powerful among the demigods); *devasya*—the demigod; *mayena*—by a demon named Maya; *ananta*—unlimited; *māyinā*—possessing technical knowledge.

TRANSLATION

My dear King Yudhiṣṭhira, long, long ago in history, a demon known as Maya Dānava, who was very expert in technical knowledge, reduced the reputation of Lord Śiva. In that situation, Kṛṣṇa, the Supreme Personality of Godhead, saved Lord Śiva.

PURPORT

Lord Śiva is known as Mahādeva, the most exalted demigod. Thus Viśvanātha Cakravartī Ṭhākura says that although Lord Brahmā did not know the glories of the Supreme Personality of Godhead, Lord Śiva could have known them. This historical incident proves that Lord Śiva derives power from Lord Kṛṣṇa, the Parabrahman.

TEXT 52

राजोवाच
कस्मिन् कर्मणि देवस्य मयोऽहञ्जगदीशितुः ।
यथा चोपचिता कीर्तिः कृष्णेनानेन कथ्यताम् ॥५२॥

rājovāca
kasmin karmaṇi devasya
mayo 'hañ jagad-īśituḥ
yathā copacitā kīrtiḥ
kṛṣṇenānena kathyatām

rājā uvāca—King Yudhiṣṭhira inquired; *kasmin*—for what reason; *karmaṇi*—by which activities; *devasya*—of Lord Mahādeva (Śiva); *mayaḥ*—the great demon Maya Dānava; *ahan*—vanquished; *jagat-īśituḥ*—of Lord Śiva, who controls the power of the material energy and is the husband of Durgādevī; *yathā*—just as; *ca*—and; *upacitā*—again expanded; *kīrtiḥ*—reputation; *kṛṣṇena*—by Lord Kṛṣṇa; *anena*—this; *kathyatām*—please describe.

TRANSLATION

Mahārāja Yudhiṣṭhira said: For what reason did the demon Maya Dānava vanquish Lord Śiva's reputation? How did Lord Kṛṣṇa save Lord Śiva and expand his reputation again? Kindly describe these incidents.

TEXT 53

श्रीनारद उवाच
निर्जिता असुरा देवैर्युध्यनेनोपबृंहितैः ।
मायिनां परमाचार्यं मयं शरणमाययुः ॥५३॥

śrī-nārada uvāca
nirjitā asurā devair
yudhy anenopabṛṁhitaiḥ
māyināṁ paramācāryaṁ
mayaṁ śaraṇam āyayuḥ

śrī-nāradaḥ uvāca—Śrī Nārada Muni said; *nirjitāḥ*—being defeated; *asurāḥ*—all the demons; *devaiḥ*—by the demigods; *yudhi*—in battle; *anena*—by Lord Kṛṣṇa; *upabṛṁhitaiḥ*—increased in power; *māyinām*—of all the demons; *parama-ācāryam*—the best and largest; *mayam*—unto Maya Dānava; *śaraṇam*—shelter; *āyayuḥ*—took.

TRANSLATION

Nārada Muni said: When the demigods, who are always powerful by the mercy of Lord Kṛṣṇa, fought with the asuras, the asuras were defeated, and therefore they took shelter of Maya Dānava, the greatest of the demons.

TEXTS 54–55

स निर्माय पुरस्तिस्रो हैमीरौप्यायसीर्विभुः ।
दुर्लक्ष्यापायसंयोगा दुर्वितर्क्यपरिच्छदाः ॥५४॥
ताभिस्तेऽसुरसेनान्यो लोकांस्त्रीन् सेश्वरान् नृप ।
स्मरन्तो नाशयाञ्चक्रुः पूर्ववैरमलक्षिताः ॥५५॥

sa nirmāya puras tisro
haimī-raupyāyasīr vibhuḥ
durlakṣyāpāya-saṁyogā
durvitarkya-paricchadāḥ

tābhis te 'sura-senānyo
lokāṁs trīn seśvarān nṛpa
smaranto nāśayāṁ cakruḥ
pūrva-vairam alakṣitāḥ

saḥ—that (great demon Maya Dānava); *nirmāya*—constructing; *puraḥ*—big residences; *tisraḥ*—three; *haimī*—made of gold; *raupyā*—

made of silver; *āyasīḥ*—made of iron; *vibhuḥ*—very great, powerful; *durlakṣya*—immeasurable; *apāya-saṁyogāḥ*—whose movements in coming and going; *durvitarkya*—uncommon; *paricchadāḥ*—possessing paraphernalia; *tābhiḥ*—by all of them (the three residences, which resembled airplanes); *te*—they; *asura-senā-anyaḥ*—the commanders of the *asuras; lokān trīn*—the three worlds; *sa-īśvarān*—with their chief rulers; *nṛpa*—my dear King Yudhiṣṭhira; *smarantaḥ*—remembering; *nāśayām cakruḥ*—began to annihilate; *pūrva*—former; *vairam*—enmity; *alakṣitāḥ*—unseen by anyone else.

TRANSLATION

Maya Dānava, the great leader of the demons, prepared three invisible residences and gave them to the demons. These dwellings resembled airplanes made of gold, silver and iron, and they contained uncommon paraphernalia. My dear King Yudhiṣṭhira, because of these three dwellings the commanders of the demons remained invisible to the demigods. Taking advantage of this opportunity, the demons, remembering their former enmity, began to vanquish the three worlds—the upper, middle and lower planetary systems.

TEXT 56

ततस्ते सेश्वरा लोका उपासाद्येश्वरं नताः ।
त्राहि नस्तावकान्देव विनष्टांस्त्रिपुरालयैः ॥५६॥

tatas te seśvarā lokā
upāsādyeśvaraṁ natāḥ
trāhi nas tāvakān deva
vinaṣṭāṁs tripurālayaiḥ

tataḥ—thereafter; *te*—they (the demigods); *sa-īśvarāḥ*—with their rulers; *lokāḥ*—the planets; *upāsādya*—approaching; *īśvaram*—Lord Śiva; *natāḥ*—fell down in surrender; *trāhi*—please save; *naḥ*—us; *tāvakān*—near and dear to you and very frightened; *deva*—O Lord; *vinaṣṭān*—almost finished; *tripura-ālayaiḥ*—by the demons dwelling in those three planes.

TRANSLATION

Thereafter, when the demons had begun to destroy the higher planetary systems, the rulers of those planets went to Lord Śiva, fully surrendered unto him and said: Dear Lord, we demigods living in the three worlds are about to be vanquished. We are your followers. Kindly save us.

TEXT 57

अथानुगृह्य भगवान्मा भैष्टेति सुरान्विभुः ।
शरं धनुषि सन्धाय पुरेष्वस्त्रं व्यमुञ्चत ॥५७॥

athānugṛhya bhagavān
mā bhaiṣṭeti surān vibhuḥ
śaraṁ dhanuṣi sandhāya
pureṣv astraṁ vyamuñcata

atha—thereafter; *anugṛhya*—just to show them favor; *bhagavān*—the most powerful; *mā*—do not; *bhaiṣṭa*—be afraid; *iti*—thus; *surān*—unto the demigods; *vibhuḥ*—Lord Śiva; *śaram*—arrows; *dhanuṣi*—on the bow; *sandhāya*—fixing; *pureṣu*—at those three residences occupied by the demons; *astram*—weapons; *vyamuñcata*—released.

TRANSLATION

The most powerful and able Lord Śiva reassured them and said, "Do not be afraid." He then fixed his arrows to his bow and released them toward the three residences occupied by the demons.

TEXT 58

ततोऽग्निवर्णा इषव उत्पेतुः सूर्यमण्डलात् ।
यथा मयूखसंदोहा नादृश्यन्त पुरो यतः ॥५८॥

tato 'gni-varṇā iṣava
utpetuḥ sūrya-maṇḍalāt
yathā mayūkha-sandohā
nādṛśyanta puro yataḥ

tataḥ—thereafter; *agni-varṇāḥ*—as brilliant as fire; *iṣavaḥ*—arrows; *utpetuḥ*—released; *sūrya-maṇḍalāt*—from the sun globe; *yathā*—just as; *mayūkha-sandohāḥ*—beams of light; *na adṛśyanta*—could not be seen; *puraḥ*—the three residences; *yataḥ*—because of this (being covered by the arrows of Lord Śiva).

TRANSLATION

The arrows released by Lord Śiva appeared like fiery beams emanating from the sun globe and covered the three residential airplanes, which could then no longer be seen.

TEXT 59

तैः स्पृष्टा व्यसवः सर्वे निपेतुः स्म पुरौकसः ।
तानानीय महायोगी मयः कूपरसेऽक्षिपत् ।।५९।।

taiḥ spṛṣṭā vyasavaḥ sarve
nipetuḥ sma puraukasaḥ
tān ānīya mahā-yogī
mayaḥ kūpa-rase 'kṣipat

taiḥ—by those (fiery arrows); *spṛṣṭāḥ*—being attacked or being touched; *vyasavaḥ*—without life; *sarve*—all the demons; *nipetuḥ*—fell down; *sma*—formerly; *pura-okasaḥ*—being the inhabitants of the above-mentioned three residential airplanes; *tān*—all of them; *ānīya*—bringing; *mahā-yogī*—the great mystic; *mayaḥ*—Maya Dānava; *kūpa-rase*—in the well of nectar (created by the great mystic Maya); *akṣipat*—put.

TRANSLATION

Attacked by Lord Śiva's golden arrows, all the demoniac inhabitants of those three dwellings lost their lives and fell down. Then the great mystic Maya Dānava dropped the demons into a nectarean well that he had created.

PURPORT

The *asuras* are generally extremely powerful because of their mystic yogic power. However, as Lord Kṛṣṇa says in *Bhagavad-gītā* (6.47):

yoginām api sarveṣāṁ
mad-gatenāntarātmanā
śraddhāvān bhajate yo māṁ
sa me yuktatamo mataḥ

"Of all *yogīs*, he who always abides in Me with great faith, worshiping Me in transcendental loving service, is most intimately united with Me in *yoga* and is the highest of all." The actual purpose of mystic *yoga* is to concentrate one's attention fully on the Personality of Godhead, Kṛṣṇa, and always think of Him (*mad-gatenāntarātmanā*). To attain such perfection, one must undergo a certain process—*haṭha-yoga*—and through this *yoga* system the practitioner achieves some uncommon mystic power. The *asuras*, however, instead of becoming devotees of Kṛṣṇa, utilize this mystic power for their personal sense gratification. Maya Dānava, for example, is mentioned here as *mahā-yogī*, a great mystic, but his business was to help the *asuras*. Nowadays we are actually seeing that there are some *yogīs* who cater to the senses of materialists, and there are imposters who advertise themselves as God. Maya Dānava was such a person, a god among the demons, and he could perform some wonderful feats, one of which is described here: he made a well filled with nectar and dipped the *asuras* into that nectarean well. This nectar was known as *mṛta-sanjīvayitari*, for it could bring a dead body to life. *Mṛta-sanjīvayitari* is also an Āyur-vedic preparation. It is a kind of liquor that invigorates even a person on the verge of death.

TEXT 60

सिद्धामृतरसस्पृष्टा वज्रसारा महौजसः ।
उत्तस्थुर्मेघदलना वैद्युता इव वह्नयः ॥६०॥

siddhāmṛta-rasa-spṛṣṭā
vajra-sārā mahaujasaḥ
uttasthur megha-dalanā
vaidyutā iva vahnayaḥ

siddha-amṛta-rasa-spṛṣṭāḥ—the demons, thus being touched by the powerful mystic nectarean liquid; *vajra-sārāḥ*—their bodies becoming invincible to thunderbolts; *mahā-ojasaḥ*—being extremely strong;

uttasthuḥ—again got up; *megha-dalanāḥ*—that which goes through the clouds; *vaidyutāḥ*—lightning (which penetrates the clouds); *iva*—like; *vahnayaḥ*—fiery.

TRANSLATION

When the dead bodies of the demons came in touch with the nectar, their bodies became invincible to thunderbolts. Endowed with great strength, they got up like lightning penetrating clouds.

TEXT 61

विलोक्य भग्नसङ्कल्पं विमनस्कं वृषध्वजम् ।
तदायं भगवान्विष्णुस्तत्रोपायमकल्पयत् ॥६१॥

vilokya bhagna-saṅkalpaṁ
vimanaskaṁ vṛṣa-dhvajam
tadāyaṁ bhagavān viṣṇus
tatropāyam akalpayat

vilokya—seeing; *bhagna-saṅkalpam*—disappointed; *vimanaskam*—extremely unhappy; *vṛṣa-dhvajam*—Lord Śiva; *tadā*—at that time; *ayam*—this; *bhagavān*—the Supreme Personality of Godhead; *viṣṇuḥ*—Lord Viṣṇu; *tatra*—about the well of nectar; *upāyam*—means (how to stop it); *akalpayat*—considered.

TRANSLATION

Seeing Lord Śiva very much aggrieved and disappointed, the Supreme Personality of Godhead, Lord Viṣṇu, considered how to stop this nuisance created by Maya Dānava.

TEXT 62

वत्सश्चासीत्तदा ब्रह्मा स्वयं विष्णुरयं हि गौः ।
प्रविश्य त्रिपुरं काले रसकूपामृतं पपौ ॥६२॥

vatsaś cāsīt tadā brahmā
svayaṁ viṣṇur ayaṁ hi gauḥ

praviśya tripuraṁ kāle
rasa-kūpāmṛtaṁ papau

vatsaḥ—a calf; *ca*—also; *āsīt*—became; *tadā*—at that time; *brahmā*—Lord Brahmā; *svayam*—personally; *viṣṇuḥ*—Lord Viṣṇu, the Supreme Personality of Godhead; *ayam*—this; *hi*—indeed; *gauḥ*—a cow; *praviśya*—entering; *tri-puram*—the three residences; *kāle*—at noon; *rasa-kūpa-amṛtam*—the nectar contained in that well; *papau*—drank.

TRANSLATION

Then Lord Brahmā became a calf and Lord Viṣṇu a cow, and at noon they entered the residences and drank all the nectar in the well.

TEXT 63

तेऽसुरा ह्यपि पश्यन्तो न न्यषेधन्विमोहिताः ।
तद् विज्ञाय महायोगी रसपालानिदं जगौ ।
स्मयं विशोकः शोकार्तान्स्मरन्दैवगतिं च ताम् ॥६३॥

te 'surā hy api paśyanto
na nyaṣedhan vimohitāḥ
tad vijñāya mahā-yogī
rasa-pālān idaṁ jagau
smayan viśokaḥ śokārtān
smaran daiva-gatiṁ ca tām

te—those; *asurāḥ*—demons; *hi*—indeed; *api*—although; *paśyantaḥ*—seeing (the calf and cow drinking the nectar); *na*—not; *nyaṣedhan*—forbade them; *vimohitāḥ*—being bewildered by illusion; *tat vijñāya*—knowing this fully; *mahā-yogī*—the great mystic Maya Dānava; *rasa-pālān*—unto the demons who guarded the nectar; *idam*—this; *jagau*—said; *smayan*—being bewildered; *viśokaḥ*—not being very unhappy; *śoka-ārtān*—greatly lamenting; *smaran*—remembering; *daiva-gatim*—spiritual power; *ca*—also; *tām*—that.

TRANSLATION

The demons could see the calf and cow, but because of the illusion created by the energy of the Supreme Personality of Godhead, the demons could not forbid them. The great mystic Maya Dānava became aware that the calf and cow were drinking the nectar, and he could understand this to be the unseen power of providence. Thus he spoke to the demons, who were grievously lamenting.

TEXT 64

देवोऽसुरो नरोऽन्यो वा नेश्वरोऽस्तीह कश्चन ।
आत्मनोऽन्यस्य वा दिष्टं दैवेनापोहितुं द्वयोः ॥६४॥

devo 'suro naro 'nyo vā
neśvaro 'stīha kaścana
ātmano 'nyasya vā diṣṭaṁ
daivenāpohituṁ dvayoḥ

devaḥ—the demigods; *asuraḥ*—the demons; *naraḥ*—humans; *anyaḥ*—or anyone else; *vā*—either; *na*—not; *īśvaraḥ*—the supreme controller; *asti*—is; *iha*—in this world; *kaścana*—anyone; *ātmanaḥ*—one's own; *anyasya*—another's; *vā*—either; *diṣṭam*—destiny; *daivena*—which is given by the Supreme Lord; *apohitum*—to undo; *dvayoḥ*—of both of them.

TRANSLATION

Maya Dānava said: What has been destined by the Supreme Lord for oneself, for others, or for both oneself and others cannot be undone anywhere or by anyone, whether one be a demigod, a demon, a human being or anyone else.

PURPORT

The Supreme Lord is one—Kṛṣṇa, the *viṣṇu-tattva.* Kṛṣṇa expands Himself into *viṣṇu-tattva* personal expansions (*svāṁśa*), who control everything. Maya Dānava said, "However I plan, you plan or both of us plan, the Lord has planned what is to happen. No one's plan will be successful without His sanction." We may make our own various plans, but unless they are sanctioned by the Supreme Personality of Godhead, Viṣṇu, they will never be successful. Hundreds and millions of plans are made by all kinds of living entities, but without the sanction of the Supreme Lord they are futile.

TEXT 65–66

अथासौ शक्तिभिःस्वाभिः शम्भोः प्राधानिकं व्यधात् ।
धर्मज्ञानविरक्त्यृद्धितपोविद्याक्रियादिभिः ॥६५॥
रथं सूतं ध्वजं वाहान्धनुर्वर्म शरादि यत् ।
सन्नद्धो रथमास्थाय शरं धनुरुपाददे ॥६६॥

athāsau śaktibhiḥ svābhiḥ
śambhoḥ prādhānikaṁ vyadhāt
dharma-jñāna-virakty-ṛddhi-
tapo-vidyā-kriyādibhiḥ

rathaṁ sūtaṁ dhvajaṁ vāhān
dhanur varma-śarādi yat
sannaddho ratham āsthāya
śaraṁ dhanur upādade

atha—thereafter; *asau*—He (Lord Kṛṣṇa); *śaktibhiḥ*—by His potencies; *svābhiḥ*—personal; *śambhoḥ*—of Lord Śiva; *prādhānikam*—ingredients; *vyadhāt*—created; *dharma*—religion; *jñāna*—knowledge; *virakti*—renunciation; *ṛddhi*—opulence; *tapaḥ*—austerity; *vidyā*—education; *kriyā*—activities; *ādibhiḥ*—by all these and other transcendental opulences; *ratham*—chariot; *sūtam*—charioteer; *dhvajam*—flag; *vāhān*—horses and elephants; *dhanuḥ*—bow; *varma*—shield; *śara-ādi*—arrows and so on; *yat*—everything that was required; *sannaddhaḥ*—equipped; *ratham*—on the chariot; *āsthāya*—seated; *śaram*—arrow; *dhanuḥ*—unto the bow; *upādade*—joined.

TRANSLATION

Nārada Muni continued: Thereafter, Lord Kṛṣṇa, by His own personal potency, consisting of religion, knowledge, renunciation,

opulence, austerity, education and activities, equipped Lord Śiva with all the necessary paraphernalia, such as a chariot, a charioteer, a flag, horses, elephants, a bow, a shield and arrows. When Lord Śiva was fully equipped in this way, he sat down on the chariot with his arrows and bow to fight with the demons.

PURPORT

As stated in *Śrīmad-Bhāgavatam* (12.13.16): *vaiṣṇavānāṁ yathā śambhuḥ:* Lord Śiva is the best of the Vaiṣṇavas, the devotees of Lord Kṛṣṇa. Indeed, he is one of the *mahājanas,* the twelve authorities on Vaiṣṇava philosophy (*svayambhūr nāradaḥ śambhuḥ kumāraḥ kapilo manuḥ,* etc.). Lord Kṛṣṇa is always prepared to help all the *mahājanas* and devotees in every respect (*kaunteya pratijānīhi na me bhaktaḥ praṇaśyati*). Although Lord Śiva is very powerful, he lost a battle to the *asuras,* and therefore he was morose and disappointed. However, because he is one of the chief devotees of the Lord, the Lord personally equipped him with all the paraphernalia for war. The devotee, therefore, must serve the Lord sincerely, and Kṛṣṇa is always in the background to protect him and, if need be, to equip him fully to fight with his enemy. For devotees there is no scarcity of knowledge or material requisites for spreading the Kṛṣṇa consciousness movement.

TEXT 67

शरं धनुषि सन्धाय मुहूर्तेऽभिजितीश्वरः ।
ददाह तेन दुर्भेद्या हरोऽथ त्रिपुरो नृप ॥६७॥

śaraṁ dhanuṣi sandhāya
muhūrte 'bhijitīśvaraḥ
dadāha tena durbhedyā
haro 'tha tripuro nṛpa

śaram—the arrows; *dhanuṣi*—on the bow; *sandhāya*—joining together; *muhūrte abhijiti*—at noon; *īśvaraḥ*—Lord Śiva; *dadāha*—set afire; *tena*—by them (the arrows); *durbhedyāḥ*—very difficult to pierce; *haraḥ*—Lord Śiva; *atha*—in this way; *tri-puraḥ*—the three residences of the demons; *nṛpa*—O King Yudhiṣṭhira.

TRANSLATION

My dear King Yudhiṣṭhira, the most powerful Lord Śiva joined the arrows to his bow, and at noon he set fire to all three residences of the demons and thus destroyed them.

TEXT 68

दिवि दुन्दुभयो नेदुर्विमानशतसङ्कुलाः ।
देवर्षिपितृसिद्धेशा जयेति कुसुमोत्करैः ।
अवाकिरञ्जगुर्हृष्टा ननृतुश्चाप्सरोगणाः ॥६८॥

divi dundubhayo nedur
vimāna-śata-saṅkulāḥ
devarṣi-pitṛ-siddheśā
jayeti kusumotkaraiḥ
avākirañ jagur hṛṣṭā
nanṛtuś cāpsaro-gaṇāḥ

divi—in the sky; *dundubhayaḥ*—kettledrums; *neduḥ*—vibrated; *vimāna*—of airplanes; *śata*—hundreds and thousands; *saṅkulāḥ*—endowed; *deva-ṛṣi*—all the demigods and saints; *pitṛ*—the residents of Pitṛloka; *siddha*—the residents of Siddhaloka; *īśāḥ*—all the great personalities; *jaya iti*—vibrated the chant "let there be victory"; *kusuma-utkaraiḥ*—various kinds of flowers; *avākiran*—showered on the head of Lord Śiva; *jaguḥ*—chanted; *hṛṣṭāḥ*—in great pleasure; *nanṛtuḥ*—danced; *ca*—and; *apsaraḥ-gaṇāḥ*—the beautiful women of the heavenly planets.

TRANSLATION

Seated in their airplanes in the sky, the inhabitants of the higher planetary systems beat many kettledrums. The demigods, saints, Pitās, Siddhas and various great personalities showered flowers on

the head of Lord Śiva, wishing him all victory, and the Apsarās began to chant and dance with great pleasure.

TEXT 69

एवं दग्ध्वा पुरस्तिस्रो भगवान्पुरहा नृप ।
ब्रह्मादिभिः स्तूयमानः स्वंधाम प्रत्यपद्यत ॥६९॥

evaṁ dagdhvā puras tisro
bhagavān pura-hā nṛpa
brahmādibhiḥ stūyamānaḥ
svaṁ dhāma pratyapadyata

evam—thus; *dagdhvā*—burning to ashes; *puraḥ tisraḥ*—the three residences of the demons; *bhagavān*—the supreme powerful; *pura-hā*—who annihilated the residences of the *asuras; nṛpa*—O King Yudhiṣṭhira; *brahma-ādibhiḥ*—by Lord Brahmā and other demigods; *stūyamānaḥ*—being worshiped; *svam*—to his own; *dhāma*—abode; *pratyapadyata*—returned.

TRANSLATION

O King Yudhiṣṭhira, thus Lord Śiva is known as Tripurāri, the annihilator of the three dwellings of the demons, because he burnt these dwellings to ashes. Being worshiped by the demigods, headed by Lord Brahmā, Lord Śiva returned to his own abode.

TEXT 70

एवंविधान्यस्य हरेः स्वमायया
विडम्बमानस्य नृलोकमात्मनः ।
वीर्याणि गीतान्यृषिभिर्जगद्गुरो-
र्लोकं पुनानान्यपरं वदामि किम् ॥७०॥

evaṁ vidhāny asya hareḥ sva-māyayā
viḍambamānasya nṛ-lokam ātmanaḥ
vīryāṇi gītāny ṛṣibhir jagad-guror
lokaṁ punānāny aparaṁ vadāmi kim

evam vidhāni—in this way; *asya*—of Kṛṣṇa; *hareḥ*—of the Supreme Personality of Godhead; *sva-māyayā*—by His transcendental potencies; *viḍambamānasya*—acting like an ordinary human being; *nṛ-lokam*—within human society; *ātmanaḥ*—of Him; *vīryāṇi*—transcendental activities; *gītāni*—narrations; *ṛṣibhiḥ*—by great saintly persons; *jagat-guroḥ*—of the supreme master; *lokam*—all the planetary systems; *punānāni*—purifying; *aparam*—what else; *vadāmi kim*—can I say.

TRANSLATION

The Lord, Śrī Kṛṣṇa, appeared as a human being, yet He performed many uncommon and wonderful pastimes by His own potency. How can I say more about His activities than what has already been said by great saintly persons? Everyone can be purified by His activities, simply by hearing about them from the right source.

PURPORT

Bhagavad-gītā and all the Vedic literatures fully explain that the Supreme Personality of Godhead, Kṛṣṇa, appears in human society as an ordinary human being but acts very uncommonly for the well-being of the entire world. One should not be influenced by the illusory energy and think Lord Kṛṣṇa to be an ordinary human being. Those who really seek the Absolute Truth come to the understanding that Kṛṣṇa is everything (*vāsudevaḥ sarvam iti*). Such great souls are very rare. Nonetheless, if one studies the entire *Bhagavad-gītā* as it is, Kṛṣṇa is very easy to understand. The Kṛṣṇa consciousness movement is just trying to make Kṛṣṇa known all over the world as the Supreme Personality of Godhead (*kṛṣṇas tu bhagavān svayam*). If people take this movement seriously, their lives as human beings will be successful.

Thus end the Bhaktivedanta purports of the Seventh Canto, Tenth Chapter, of the Śrīmad-Bhāgavatam, *entitled "Prahlāda, the Best Among Exalted Devotees."*

CHAPTER ELEVEN

The Perfect Society: Four Social Classes

This chapter describes the general principles by following which a human being, and specifically one who is interested in advancing in spiritual life, can become perfect.

By hearing about the characteristics of Prahlāda Mahārāja, Mahārāja Yudhiṣṭhira became extremely pleased. Now he inquired from Nārada Muni about the actual religion of a human being and about special characteristics of *varṇāśrama-dharma*, which marks the highest status of human civilization. When Mahārāja Yudhiṣṭhira asked Nārada Muni about these matters, Nārada Muni stopped giving his own statements and quoted statements by Lord Nārāyaṇa, for He is the supreme authority for giving religious codes (*dharmaṁ tu sākṣād bhagavat-praṇītam*). Every human being is expected to acquire thirty qualities, such as truthfulness, mercy and austerity. The process of following the principles of religion is known as *sanātana-dharma*, the eternal religious system.

The *varṇāśrama* system delineates the divisions of *brāhmaṇa*, *kṣatriya*, *vaiśya* and *śūdra*. It also sets forth the system of *saṁskāras*. The *garbhādhāna saṁskāra*, the ceremony for begetting a child, must be observed by the higher section of people, namely the *dvijas*. One who follows the *garbhādhāna saṁskāra* system is actually twiceborn, but those who do not, who deviate from the principles of *varṇāśrama-dharma*, are called *dvija-bandhus*. The principal occupations for a *brāhmaṇa* are worshiping the Deity, teaching others how to worship the Deity, studying the Vedic literatures, teaching the Vedic literatures, accepting charity from others and again giving charity to others. A *brāhmaṇa* should make his livelihood from these six occupational duties. The duty of a *kṣatriya* is to give protection to the citizens and levy taxes upon them, but he is forbidden to tax the *brāhmaṇas*. The members of the Kṛṣṇa consciousness movement should therefore be exempt from government taxation. *Kṣatriyas* may tax everyone but the *brāhmaṇas*. *Vaiśyas* should cultivate the land, produce food grains and protect the cows, whereas the *śūdras*, who by quality never become *brāhmaṇas*, *kṣatriyas* or *vaiśyas*, should serve the three higher classes and be satisfied. Other means of livelihood are also prescribed for the *brāhmaṇas*, and these are four—*śālīna*, *yāyāvara*, *śila*, and *uñchana*. Each of these occupational duties is successively better.

One who is in a lower grade of social life cannot accept the profession of a higher class unless necessary. In times of emergency, all the classes but the *kṣatriyas* may accept professional duties of others. The means of livelihood known as *ṛta* (*śiloñchana*), *amṛta* (*ayācita*), *mṛta* (*yācñā*), *pramṛta* (*karṣaṇa*), and *satyānṛta* (*vāṇijya*) may be accepted by everyone but the *kṣatriyas*. For a *brāhmaṇa* or a *kṣatriya*, engaging in the service of the *vaiśyas* or *śūdras* is considered the profession of dogs.

Nārada Muni also described that the symptom of a *brāhmaṇa* is controlled senses, the symptoms of a *kṣatriya* are power and fame, the symptom of a *vaiśya* is service to the *brāhmaṇas* and *kṣatriyas*, and the symptom of a *śūdra* is service to the three higher classes. The qualification for a woman is to be a very faithful and chaste wife. In this way, Nārada Muni described the characteristics of higher and lower grades of people and recommended that one follow the principles of his caste or his hereditary occupation. One cannot suddenly give up a profession to which he is accustomed, and therefore it is recommended that one gradually be awakened. The symptoms of *brāhmaṇas*, *kṣatriyas*, *vaiśyas*, and *śūdras* are very important, and therefore one should be designated only by these symptoms, and not by birth. Designation by birth is strictly forbidden by Nārada Muni and all great personalities.

TEXT 1

श्रीशुक उवाच

श्रुत्वेहितं साधुसभासभाजितं
महत्तमाग्रण्य उरुक्रमात्मनः ।
युधिष्ठिरो दैत्यपतेर्मुदान्वितः
पप्रच्छ भूयस्तनयं स्वयम्भुवः ॥ १ ॥

śrī-śuka uvāca
śrutvehitaṁ sādhu sabhā-sabhājitaṁ
mahattamāgraṇya urukramātmanaḥ

yudhiṣṭhiro daitya-pater mudānvitaḥ
papraccha bhūyas tanayaṁ svayambhuvaḥ

śrī-śukaḥ uvāca—Śrī Śukadeva Gosvāmī said; *śrutvā*—hearing; *īhitam*—the narration; *sādhu sabhā-sabhājitam*—which is discussed in assemblies of great devotees like Lord Brahmā and Lord Śiva; *mahat-tama-agraṇyaḥ*—the best of the saintly persons (Yudhiṣṭhira); *urukrama-ātmanaḥ*—of he (Prahlāda Mahārāja) whose mind is always engaged upon the Supreme Personality of Godhead, who always acts uncommonly; *yudhiṣṭhiraḥ*—King Yudhiṣṭhira; *daitya-pateḥ*—of the master of the demons; *mudā-anvitaḥ*—in a pleasing mood; *papraccha*—inquired; *bhūyaḥ*—again; *tanayam*—unto the son; *svayambhuvaḥ*—of Lord Brahmā.

TRANSLATION

Śukadeva Gosvāmī continued: After hearing about the activities and character of Prahlāda Mahārāja, which are adored and discussed among great personalities like Lord Brahmā and Lord Śiva, Yudhiṣṭhira Mahārāja, the most respectful king among exalted personalities, again inquired from the great saint Nārada Muni in a mood of great pleasure.

TEXT 2

श्रीयुधिष्ठिर उवाच
भगवन् श्रोतुमिच्छामि नृणां धर्मं सनातनम् ।
वर्णाश्रमाचारयुतं यत् पुमान्विन्दते परम् ॥ २ ॥

śrī-yudhiṣṭhira uvāca
bhagavan śrotum icchāmi
nṛṇāṁ dharmaṁ sanātanam
varṇāśramācāra-yutaṁ
yat pumān vindate param

śrī-yudhiṣṭhiraḥ uvāca—Mahārāja Yudhiṣṭhira inquired; *bhagavan*—O my lord; *śrotum*—to hear; *icchāmi*—I wish; *nṛṇām*—of human society; *dharmam*—the occupational duties; *sanātanam*—common and eternal (for everyone); *varṇa-āśrama-ācāra-yutam*—based on the principles of the four divisions of society and the four divisions of spiritual advancement; *yat*—from which; *pumān*—the people in general; *vindate*—can enjoy very peacefully; *param*—the supreme knowledge (by which one can attain devotional service).

TRANSLATION

Mahārāja Yudhiṣṭhira said: My dear lord, I wish to hear from you about the principles of religion by which one can attain the ultimate goal of life—devotional service. I wish to hear about the general occupational duties of human society and the system of social and spiritual advancement known as varṇāśrama-dharma.

PURPORT

Sanātana-dharma means devotional service. The word *sanātana* refers to that which is eternal, which does not change but continues in all circumstances. We have several times explained what the eternal occupational duty of the living being is. Indeed, it has been explained by Śrī Caitanya Mahāprabhu. *Jīvera 'svarūpa' haya—kṛṣṇera 'nitya-dāsa'*: the real occupational duty of the living entity is to serve the Supreme Personality of Godhead. Even if one prefers to deviate from this principle he remains a servant because that is his eternal position; but one serves *māyā*, the illusory, material energy. The Kṛṣṇa consciousness movement, therefore, is an attempt to guide human society to serving the Personality of Godhead instead of serving the material world with no real profit. Our actual experience is that every man, animal, bird and beast—indeed, every living entity—is engaged in rendering service. Even though one's body or one's superficial religion may change, every living entity is always engaged in the service of someone. Therefore, the mentality of service is called the eternal occupational duty. This eternal occupational duty can be organized through the institution of *varṇāśrama*, in which there are four *varṇas* (*brāhmaṇa*, *kṣatriya*, *vaiśya* and *śūdra*) and four *āśramas* (*brahmacarya*, *gṛhastha*, *vānaprastha* and *sannyāsa*). Thus, Yudhiṣṭhira Mahārāja inquired from Nārada Muni about the principles of *sanātana-dharma* for the benefit of human society.

TEXT 3

भवान्प्रजापतेः साक्षादात्मजः परमेष्ठिनः ।
सुतानां सम्मतो ब्रह्मंस्तपोयोगसमाधिभिः ॥ ३ ॥

bhavān prajāpateḥ sākṣād
ātmajaḥ parameṣṭhinaḥ
sutānāṁ sammato brahmaṁs
tapo-yoga-samādhibhiḥ

bhavān—Your Lordship; *prajāpateḥ*—of Prajāpati (Lord Brahmā); *sākṣāt*—directly; *ātma-jaḥ*—the son; *parameṣṭhinaḥ*—of the supreme person within this universe (Lord Brahmā); *sutānām*—of all the sons; *sammataḥ*—agreed upon as the best; *brahman*—O best of the *brāhmaṇas; tapaḥ*—by austerity; *yoga*—by mystic practice; *samādhibhiḥ*—and by trance or meditation (in all respects, you are the best).

TRANSLATION

O best of the brāhmaṇas, you are directly the son of Prajāpati [Lord Brahmā]. Because of your austerities, mystic yoga and trance, you are considered the best of all of Lord Brahmā's sons.

TEXT 4

नारायणपरा विप्रा धर्मं गुह्यं परं विदुः ।
करुणाः साधवः शान्तास्त्वद्विधा न तथापरे ॥ ४ ॥

nārāyaṇa-parā viprā
dharmaṁ guhyaṁ paraṁ viduḥ
karuṇāḥ sādhavaḥ śāntās
tvad-vidhā na tathāpare

nārāyaṇa-parāḥ—those who are always devoted to the Supreme Personality of Godhead, Nārāyaṇa; *viprāḥ*—the best of the *brāhmaṇas; dharmam*—religious principle; *guhyam*—the most confidential; *param*—supreme; *viduḥ*—know; *karuṇāḥ*—such persons are very merciful (being devotees); *sādhavaḥ*—whose behavior is very exalted; *śāntāḥ*—peaceful; *tvat-vidhāḥ*—like Your Honor; *na*—not; *tathā*—so; *apare*—others (followers of methods other than devotional service).

TRANSLATION

No one is superior to you in peaceful life and mercy, and no one knows better than you how to execute devotional service or how to become the best of the brāhmaṇas. Therefore, you know all the principles of confidential religious life, and no one knows them better than you.

PURPORT

Yudhiṣṭhira Mahārāja knew that Nārada Muni is the supreme spiritual master of human society who can teach the path of spiritual liberation leading to the understanding of the Supreme Personality of Godhead. Actually, it is for this purpose that Nārada Muni compiled his *Bhakti-sūtra* and gave directions in the *Nārada-pañcarātra.* To learn about religious principles and the perfection of life, one must take instruction from the disciplic succession of Nārada Muni. Our Kṛṣṇa consciousness movement is directly in the line of the Brahma-sampradāya. Nārada Muni received instructions from Lord Brahmā and in turn transmitted the instructions to Vyāsadeva. Vyāsadeva instructed his son Śukadeva Gosvāmī, who spoke *Śrīmad-Bhāgavatam.* The Kṛṣṇa consciousness movement is based on *Śrīmad-Bhāgavatam* and *Bhagavad-gītā.* Because *Śrīmad-Bhāgavatam* was spoken by Śukadeva Gosvāmī and *Bhagavad-gītā* was spoken by Kṛṣṇa, there is no difference between them. If we strictly follow the principle of disciplic succession, we are certainly on the right path of spiritual liberation, or eternal engagement in devotional service.

TEXT 5

श्रीनारद उवाच

नत्वा भगवतेऽजाय लोकानां धर्मसेतवे ।
वक्ष्ये सनातनं धर्मं नारायणमुखाच्छ्रुतम् ॥ ५ ॥

śrī-nārada uvāca
natvā bhagavate 'jāya
lokānāṁ dharma-setave
vakṣye sanātanaṁ dharmaṁ
nārāyaṇa-mukhāc chrutam

śrī-nāradaḥ uvāca—Śrī Nārada Muni said; *natvā*—offering my obeisances; *bhagavate*—unto the Supreme Personality of Godhead; *ajāya*—ever existing, never born; *lokānām*—throughout the entire universe; *dharma-setave*—who protects religious principles; *vakṣye*—I shall explain; *sanātanam*—eternal; *dharmam*—occupational duty; *nārāyaṇa-mukhāt*—from the mouth of Nārāyaṇa; *śrutam*—which I have heard.

TRANSLATION

Śrī Nārada Muni said: After first offering my obeisances unto Lord Kṛṣṇa, the protector of the religious principles of all living entities, let me explain the principles of the eternal religious system, of which I have heard from the mouth of Nārāyaṇa.

PURPORT

The word *aja* refers to Kṛṣṇa, who explains in *Bhagavad-gītā* (4.6), *ajo 'pi sann avyayātmā:* "I am ever existing, and thus I never take birth. There is no change in My existence."

TEXT 6

योऽवतीर्यात्मनोंऽशेन दाक्षायण्यां तु धर्मतः ।
लोकानां स्वस्तयेऽध्यास्ते तपो बदरिकाश्रमे ॥ ६ ॥

yo 'vatīryātmano 'ṁśena
dākṣāyaṇyāṁ tu dharmataḥ
lokānāṁ svastaye 'dhyāste
tapo badarikāśrame

yaḥ—He who (Lord Nārāyaṇa); *avatīrya*—adventing; *ātmanaḥ*—of Himself; *aṁśena*—with a part (Nara); *dākṣāyaṇyām*—in the womb of

Dākṣāyaṇī, the daughter of Mahārāja Dakṣa; *tu*—indeed; *dharmataḥ*—from Dharma Mahārāja; *lokānām*—of all people; *svastaye*—for the benefit of; *adhyāste*—executes; *tapaḥ*—austerity; *badarikāśrame*—in the place known as Badarikāśrama.

TRANSLATION

Lord Nārāyaṇa, along with His partial manifestation Nara, appeared in this world through the daughter of Dakṣa Mahārāja known as Mūrti. He was begotten by Dharma Mahārāja for the benefit of all living entities. Even now, He is still engaged in executing great austerities near the place known as Badarikāśrama.

TEXT 7

धर्ममूलं हि भगवान्सर्ववेदमयो हरिः ।
स्मृतं च तद्विदां राजन्येन चात्मा प्रसीदति ॥ ७ ॥

dharma-mūlaṁ hi bhagavān
sarva-vedamayo hariḥ
smṛtaṁ ca tad-vidāṁ rājan
yena cātmā prasīdati

dharma-mūlam—the root of religious principles; *hi*—indeed; *bhagavān*—the Supreme Personality of Godhead; *sarva-veda-mayaḥ*—the essence of all Vedic knowledge; *hariḥ*—the Supreme Being; *smṛtam ca*—and the scriptures; *tat-vidām*—of those who know the Supreme Lord; *rājan*—O King; *yena*—by which (religious principle); *ca*—also; *ātmā*—the soul, mind, body and everything; *prasīdati*—become fully satisfied.

TRANSLATION

The Supreme Being, the Personality of Godhead, is the essence of all Vedic knowledge, the root of all religious principles, and the memory of great authorities. O King Yudhiṣṭhira, this principle of religion is to be understood as evidence. On the basis of this religious principle, everything is satisfied, including one's mind, soul and even one's body.

PURPORT

As stated by Yamarāja, *dharmaṁ tu sākṣād bhagavat-praṇītam.* Yamarāja, the representative of the Lord who takes care of the living beings after their death, gives his verdict as to how and when the living being will change his body. He is the authority, and he says that the religious principles consist of the codes and laws given by God. No one can manufacture religion, and therefore manufactured religious systems are rejected by the followers of the Vedic principles. In *Bhagavad-gītā* (15.15) it is said, *vedaiś ca sarvair aham eva vedyaḥ:* Vedic knowledge means to understand the Supreme Personality of Godhead, Kṛṣṇa. Therefore, whether one speaks of the *Vedas*, scriptures, religion or the principles of everyone's occupational duty, all of them must aim at understanding Kṛṣṇa, the Supreme Personality of Godhead. *Śrīmad-Bhāgavatam* (1.2.6) therefore concludes:

sa vai puṁsāṁ paro dharmo
yato bhaktir adhokṣaje
ahaituky apratihatā
yayātmā suprasīdati

In other words, religious principles aim at learning how to render transcendental loving service to the Lord. That service must be unmotivated and unchecked by material conditions. Then human society will be happy in all respects.

The *smṛti*, the scriptures following the principles of Vedic knowledge, are considered the evidence of Vedic principles. There are twenty different types of scripture for following religious principles, and among them the scriptures of Manu and Yājñavalkya are considered to be all-pervading authorities. In the *Yājñavalkya-smṛti* it is said:

śruti-smṛti-sadācāraḥ
svasya ca priyam ātmanaḥ
samyak saṅkalpajaḥ kāmo
dharma-mūlam idaṁ smṛtam

One should learn human behavior from *śruti*, the *Vedas*, and from *smṛti*, the scriptures following the Vedic principles. Śrīla Rūpa Gosvāmī in his *Bhakti-rasāmṛta-sindhu* says:

śruti-smṛti-purāṇādi-
pañcarātra-vidhiṁ vinā
aikāntikī harer bhaktir
utpātāyaiva kalpate

The purport is that to become a devotee one must follow the principles laid down in *śruti* and *smṛti.* One must follow the codes of the *Purāṇas* and the *pāñcarātrikī-vidhi.* One cannot be a pure devotee without following the *śruti* and *smṛti,* and the *śruti* and *smṛti* without devotional service cannot lead one to the perfection of life.

Therefore, from all the evidence the conclusion is that without *bhakti,* devotional service, there is no question of religious principles. God is the central figure in the performance of religious principles. Almost everthing going on in this world as religion is devoid of any idea of devotional service and is therefore condemned by the verdict of *Śrīmad-Bhāgavatam.* Without devotional service, so-called religious principles are only cheating.

TEXTS 8–12

सत्यं दया तपः शौचं तितिक्षेक्षा शमो दमः ।
अहिंसा ब्रह्मचर्यं च त्यागः स्वाध्याय आर्जवम् ॥ ८ ॥
सन्तोषः समदृक् सेवा ग्राम्येहोपरमः शनैः ।
नृणां विपर्ययेहेक्षा मौनमात्मविमर्शनम् ॥ ९ ॥
अन्नाद्यादेः संविभागो भूतेभ्यश्च यथार्हतः ।
तेष्वात्मदेवताबुद्धिः सुतरां नृषु पाण्डव ॥१०॥
श्रवणं कीर्तनं चास्य स्मरणं महतां गतेः ।
सेवेज्यावनतिर्दास्यं सख्यमात्मसमर्पणम् ॥११॥
नृणामयं परो धर्मः सर्वेषां समुदाहृतः ।
त्रिंशल्लक्षणवान्राजन्सर्वात्मा येन तुष्यति ॥१२॥

satyaṁ dayā tapaḥ śaucaṁ
titikṣekṣā śamo damaḥ
ahiṁsā brahmacaryaṁ ca
tyāgaḥ svādhyāya ārjavam

santoṣaḥ samadṛk-sevā
grāmyehoparamaḥ śanaiḥ
nṛṇāṁ viparyayehekṣā
maunam ātma-vimarśanam

annādyādeḥ saṁvibhāgo
bhūtebhyaś ca yathārhataḥ
teṣv ātma-devatā-buddhiḥ
sutarāṁ nṛṣu pāṇḍava

śravaṇaṁ kīrtanaṁ cāsya
smaraṇaṁ mahatāṁ gateḥ
sevejyāvanatir dāsyaṁ
sakhyam ātma-samarpaṇam

nṛṇām ayaṁ paro dharmaḥ
sarveṣāṁ samudāhṛtaḥ
triṁśal-lakṣaṇavān rājan
sarvātmā yena tuṣyati

satyam—speaking the truth without distortion or deviation; *dayā*—sympathy to everyone suffering; *tapaḥ*—austerities (such as observing fasts at least twice in a month on the day of Ekādaśī); *śaucam*—cleanliness (bathing regularly at least twice a day, morning and evening, and remembering to chant the holy name of God); *titikṣā*—toleration (being unagitated by seasonal changes or inconvenient circumstances); *īkṣā*—distinguishing between good and bad; *śamaḥ*—control of the mind (not allowing the mind to act whimsically); *damaḥ*—control of the senses (not allowing the senses to act without control); *ahiṁsā*—nonviolence (not subjecting any living entity to the threefold miseries); *brahmacaryam*—continence or abstaining from misuse of one's semen (not indulging in sex with women other than one's own wife and not having sex with one's own wife when sex is forbidden, like during the period of menstruation); *ca*—and; *tyāgaḥ*—giving in charity at least fifty percent of one's income; *svādhyāyaḥ*—reading of transcendental literatures like *Bhagavad-gītā, Śrīmad-Bhāgavatam, Rāmāyaṇa* and *Mahābhārata* (or, for those not in Vedic culture, reading of the Bible or

Koran); *ārjavam*—simplicity (freedom from mental duplicity); *santoṣaḥ*—being satisfied with that which is available without severe endeavor; *samadṛk-sevā*—rendering service to saintly persons who make no distinctions between one living being and another and who see every living being as a spirit soul (*paṇḍitāḥ sama-darśinaḥ*); *grāmya-īhā-uparamaḥ*—not taking part in so-called philanthropic activities; *śanaiḥ*—gradually; *nṛṇām*—in human society; *viparyaya-īhā*—the unnecessary activities; *īkṣā*—discussing; *maunam*—being grave and silent; *ātma*—into the self; *vimarśanam*—research (as to whether one is the body or the soul); *anna-ādya-ādeḥ*—of food and drink, etc.; *saṁvibhāgaḥ*—equal distribution; *bhūtebhyaḥ*—to different living entities; *ca*—also; *yathā-arhataḥ*—as befitting; *teṣu*—all living entities; *ātma-devatā-buddhiḥ*—accepting as the self or the demigods; *sutarām*—preliminarily; *nṛṣu*—among all human beings; *pāṇḍava*—O Mahārāja Yudhiṣṭhira; *śravaṇam*—hearing; *kīrtanam*—chanting; *ca*—also; *asya*—of Him (the Lord); *smaraṇam*—remembering (His words and activities); *mahatām*—of great saintly persons; *gateḥ*—who is the shelter; *sevā*—service; *ijyā*—worship; *avanatiḥ*—offering obeisances; *dāsyam*—accepting the service; *sakhyam*—to consider as a friend; *ātma-samarpaṇam*—surrendering one's whole self; *nṛṇām*—of all human beings; *ayam*—this; *paraḥ*—the supermost; *dharmaḥ*—religious principle; *sarveṣām*—of all; *samudāhṛtaḥ*—described fully; *triṁśat-lakṣaṇa-vān*—possessing thirty characteristics; *rājan*—O King; *sarva-ātmā*—the Supreme Lord, the Supersoul of all; *yena*—by which; *tuṣyati*—is satisfied.

TRANSLATION

These are the general principles to be followed by all human beings: truthfulness, mercy, austerity (observing fasts on certain days of the month), bathing twice a day, tolerance, discrimination between right and wrong, control of the mind, control of the senses, nonviolence, celibacy, charity, reading of scripture, simplicity, satisfaction, rendering service to saintly persons, gradually taking leave of unnecessary engagements, observing the futility of the unnecessary activities of human society, remaining silent and grave and avoiding unnecessary talk, considering whether one is the body or the soul, distributing food equally to all living entities (both men and animals), seeing every soul

(especially in the human form) as a part of the Supreme Lord, hearing about the activities and instructions given by the Supreme Personality of Godhead (who is the shelter of the saintly persons), chanting about these activities and instructions, always remembering these activities and instructions, trying to render service, performing worship, offering obeisances, becoming a servant, becoming a friend, and surrendering one's whole self. O King Yudhiṣṭhira, these thirty qualifications must be acquired in the human form of life. Simply by acquiring these qualifications, one can satisfy the Supreme Personality of Godhead.

PURPORT

In order that human beings be distinct from the animals, the great saint Nārada recommends that every human being be educated in terms of the above-mentioned thirty qualifications. Nowadays there is propaganda everywhere, all over the world, for a secular state, a state interested only in mundane activities. But if the citizens of the state are not educated in the above-mentioned good qualities, how can there be happiness? For example, if the total populace is untruthful, how can the state be happy? Therefore, without consideration of one's belonging to a sectarian religion, whether Hindu, Muslim, Christian, Buddhist or any other sect, everyone should be taught to become truthful. Similarly, everyone should be taught to be merciful, and everyone should observe fasting on certain days of the month. Everyone should bathe twice a day, cleanse his teeth and body externally, and cleanse his mind internally by remembering the holy name of the Lord. The Lord is one, whether one is Hindu, Muslim or Christian. Therefore, one should chant the holy name of the Lord, regardless of differences in linguistic pronunciation. Also, everyone should be taught to be very careful not to discharge semen unnecessarily. This is very important for all human beings. If semen is not discharged unnecessarily, one becomes extremely strong in memory, determination, activity and the vitality of one's bodily energy. Everyone should also be taught to be simple in thought and feeling and satisfied in body and mind. These are the general qualifications of a human being. There is no question of a secular state or an ecclesiastical state. Unless one is educated in the above-mentioned thirty qualities, there cannot be any peace. Ultimately it is recommended:

śravaṇaṁ kīrtanaṁ cāsya
smaraṇaṁ mahatāṁ gateḥ
sevejyāvanatir dāsyaṁ
sakhyam ātma-samarpaṇam

Everyone should become a devotee of the Lord, because by becoming a devotee of the Lord one automatically acquires the other qualities.

yasyāsti bhaktir bhagavaty akiñcanā
sarvair guṇais tatra samāsate surāḥ
harāv abhaktasya kuto mahad-guṇā
manorathenāsati dhāvato bahiḥ

"In one who has unflinching devotional service to Kṛṣṇa, all the good qualities of Kṛṣṇa and the demigods are consistently manifest. However, he who has no devotion to the Supreme Personality of Godhead has no good qualifications because he is engaged by mental concoction in material existence, which is the external feature of the Lord." (*Bhāg.* 5.18.12) Our Kṛṣṇa consciousness movement, therefore, is all-embracing. Human civilization should take it very seriously and practice its principles for the peace of the world.

TEXT 13

संस्कारा यत्राविच्छिन्नाः स द्विजोऽजो जगाद यम् ।
इज्याध्ययनदानानि विहितानि द्विजन्मनाम् ।
जन्मकर्मावदातानां क्रियाश्चाश्रमचोदिताः ॥१३॥

saṁskārā yatrāvicchinnāḥ
sa dvijo 'jo jagāda yam
ijyādhyayana-dānāni
vihitāni dvijanmanām
janma-karmāvadātānāṁ
kriyāś cāśrama-coditāḥ

saṁskārāḥ—reformatory processes; *yatra*—wherein; *avicchinnāḥ*—without interruption; *saḥ*—such a person; *dvi-jaḥ*—twiceborn; *ajaḥ*—

Lord Brahmā; *jagāda*—sanctioned; *yam*—who; *ijyā*—worshiping; *adhyayana*—studies of the *Vedas; dānāni*—and charity; *vihitāni*—prescribed; *dvi-janmanām*—of persons who are called twiceborn; *janma*—by birth; *karma*—and activities; *avadātānām*—who are purified; *kriyāḥ*—activities; *ca*—also; *āśrama-coditāḥ*—recommended for the four *āśramas.*

TRANSLATION

Those who have been reformed by the garbhādhāna ceremony and other prescribed reformatory methods, performed with Vedic mantras and without interruption, and who have been approved by Lord Brahmā, are dvijas, or twiceborn. Such brāhmaṇas, kṣatriyas and vaiśyas, purified by their family traditions and by their behavior, should worship the Lord, study the Vedas and give charity. In this system, they should follow the principles of the four āśramas [brahmacarya, gṛhastha, vānaprastha and sannyāsa].

PURPORT

After giving a general list of thirty qualifications for one's behavior, Nārada Muni now describes the principles of the four *varṇas* and four *āśramas.* A human being must be trained in the above-mentioned thirty qualities; otherwise, he is not even a human being. Then, among such qualified persons, the *varṇāśrama* process should be introduced. In the *varṇāśrama* system, the first ceremony for purification is *garbhādhāna,* which is performed with *mantras* at the time of sex for propagating a good child. One who uses sex life not for sensual pleasures but only to beget children according to the reformatory method is also accepted as a *brahmacārī.* One should not waste semen on sensual pleasure, violating the principles of Vedic life. Restraint in sex is possible, however, only when the populace is trained in the above-mentioned thirty qualities; otherwise, it is not possible. Even if one is born in a family of *dvijas,* or twiceborn, if they have not followed the reformatory process he is called a *dvija-bandhu*—not one of the twiceborn, but a friend of the twiceborn. The whole purpose of this system is to create good population. As stated in *Bhagavad-gītā,* when women are polluted the populace is *varṇa-saṅkara,* and when the *varṇa-saṅkara* population increases, the situation of the entire world becomes hellish. Therefore, all the Vedic literatures strongly warn against creating *varṇa-saṅkara* population. When there is *varṇa-saṅkara* population, the people cannot be properly controlled for peace and prosperity, regardless of great legislative assemblies, parliaments and similar bodies.

TEXT 14

विप्रस्याध्ययनादीनि षडन्यस्याप्रतिग्रहः ।
राज्ञो वृत्तिः प्रजागोप्तुरविप्राद् वा करादिभिः ॥१४॥

viprasyādhyayanādīni
ṣaḍ-anyasyāpratigrahaḥ
rājño vṛttiḥ prajā-goptur
aviprād vā karādibhiḥ

viprasya—of the *brāhmaṇa; adhyayana-ādīni*—reading the *Vedas*, etc; *ṣaṭ*—six (to study the *Vedas*, to teach the *Vedas*, to worship the Deity, to teach others how to worship, to accept charity and to give charity); *anyasya*—of those other than the *brāhmaṇas* (the *kṣatriyas*); *apratigrahaḥ*—without accepting charity from others (the *kṣatriyas* may execute the five other occupational duties prescribed for the *brāhmaṇas*); *rājñaḥ*—of the *kṣatriya; vṛttiḥ*—the means of livelihood; *prajā-goptuḥ*—who maintain the subjects; *aviprāt*—from those who are not *brāhmaṇas; vā*—or; *kara-ādibhiḥ*—by levying revenue taxes, customs duties, fines for punishment, etc.

TRANSLATION

For a brāhmaṇa there are six occupational duties. A kṣatriya should not accept charity, but he may perform the other five of these duties. A king or kṣatriya is not allowed to levy taxes on brāhmaṇas, but he may make his livelihood by levying minimal taxes, customs duties, and penalty fines upon his other subjects.

PURPORT

Viśvanātha Cakravartī Ṭhākura explains the position of *brāhmaṇas* and *kṣatriyas* as follows. *Brāhmaṇas* have six occupational duties, of which three are compulsory—namely, studying the *Vedas*, worshiping the Deity and giving charity. By teaching, by inducing others to worship the Deity, and by accepting gifts, the *brāhmaṇas* receive the necessities of life. This is also confirmed in the *Manu-saṁhitā:*

ṣaṇṇāṁ tu karmaṇām asya
trīṇi karmāṇi jīvikā
yajanādhyāpane caiva
viśuddhāc ca pratigrahaḥ

Of the six occupational duties of the *brāhmaṇas*, three are compulsory—namely, worship of the Deity, study of the *Vedas* and the giving of charity. In exchange, a *brāhmaṇa* should receive charity, and this should be his means of livelihood. A *brāhmaṇa* cannot take up any professional occupational duty for his livelihood. The *śāstras* especially stress that if one claims to be a *brāhmaṇa*, he cannot engage in the service of anyone else; otherwise he at once falls from his position and becomes a *śūdra.* Śrīla Rūpa Gosvāmī and Sanātana Gosvāmī belonged to a very respectful family, but because they engaged in the service of Nawab Hussain Shah—not even as ordinary clerks, but as ministers—they were ostracized from brahminical society. Indeed, they became like Mohammedans and even changed their names. Unless a *brāhmaṇa* is very pure, he cannot accept charity from others. Charity should be given to those who are pure. Even if one is born in a family of *brāhmaṇas*, if one acts as a *śūdra* one cannot accept charity, for this is strictly prohibited. Although the *kṣatriyas* are almost as qualified as the *brāhmaṇas*, even they cannot accept charity. This is strictly prohibited in this verse by the word *apratigraha.* What to speak of the lower social orders, even the *kṣatriyas* must not accept charity. The king or government may levy taxes upon the citizens in various ways—by revenue duties, customs duties, realization of fines, and so on—provided the king is able to give full protection to his subjects to assure the security of their life and property. Unless he is able to give protection, he cannot levy taxes. However, a king must not levy any tax upon the *brāhmaṇas* and the Vaiṣṇavas fully engaged in Kṛṣṇa consciousness.

TEXT 15

वैश्यस्तु वार्तावृत्तिः स्यान् नित्यं ब्रह्मकुलानुगः ।
शूद्रस्य द्विजशुश्रूषा वृत्तिश्च स्वामिनो भवेत् ॥१५॥

vaiśyas tu vārtā-vṛttiḥ syān
nityaṁ brahma-kulānugaḥ
śūdrasya dvija-śuśrūṣā
vṛttiś ca svāmino bhavet

vaiśyaḥ—the mercantile community; *tu*—indeed; *vārtā-vṛttiḥ*—engaged in agriculture, cow protection, and trade; *syāt*—must be; *nityam*—always; *brahma-kula-anugaḥ*—following the directions of the *brāhmaṇas; śūdrasya*—of the fourth-grade persons, the workers; *dvija-śuśrūṣā*—the service of the three higher sections (the *brāhmaṇas, kṣatriyas* and *vaiśyas*); *vṛttiḥ*—means of livelihood; *ca*—and; *svāminaḥ*—of the master; *bhavet*—he must be.

TRANSLATION

The mercantile community should always follow the directions of the brāhmaṇas and engage in such occupational duties as agriculture, trade, and protection of cows. For the śūdras the only duty is to accept a master from a higher social order and engage in his service.

TEXT 16

वार्ता विचित्रा शालीनयायावरशिलोञ्छनम् ।
विप्रवृत्तिश्चतुर्धेयं श्रेयसी चोत्तरोत्तरा ॥१६॥

vārtā vicitrā śālīna-
yāyāvara-śiloñchanam
vipra-vṛttiś caturdheyaṁ
śreyasī cottarottarā

vārtā—the occupational means of livelihood for the *vaiśya* (agriculture, cow protection, and trade); *vicitrā*—various types; *śālīna*—livelihood achieved without effort; *yāyāvara*—going to the field to beg for some paddy; *śila*—picking up the grains left in the field by the proprietor; *uñchanam*—picking up the grains that have fallen from bags in shops; *vipra-vṛttiḥ*—the means of livelihood for the *brāhmaṇas; caturdhā*—four different kinds; *iyam*—this; *śreyasī*—better; *ca*—also; *uttara-uttarā*—the latter compared to the former.

TRANSLATION

As an alternative, a brāhmaṇa may also take to the vaiśya's occupational duty of agriculture, cow protection, or trade. He may depend on that which he has received without begging, he may beg in the paddy field every day, he may collect paddy left in a field by its proprietor, or he may collect food grains left here and there in the shops of grain dealers. These are four means of livelihood that may also be adopted by brāhmaṇas. Among these four, each of them in succession is better than the one preceding it.

PURPORT

A *brāhmaṇa* is sometimes offered land and cows in charity, and thus for his livelihood he may act in the same way as a *vaiśya*, by cultivating land, giving protection to cows and trading off his surpluses. A better process, however, is to pick up grains from a field or from a dealer's shop without begging.

TEXT 17

जघन्यो नोत्तमां वृत्तिमनापदि भजेन्नरः ।
ऋते राजन्यमापत्सु सर्वेषामपि सर्वशः ॥१७॥

jaghanyo nottamāṁ vṛttim
anāpadi bhajen naraḥ
ṛte rājanyam āpatsu
sarveṣām api sarvaśaḥ

jaghanyaḥ—low (person); *na*—not; *uttamām*—high; *vṛttim*—means of livelihood; *anāpadi*—when there is no social upheaval; *bhajet*—may accept; *naraḥ*—a man; *ṛte*—except; *rājanyam*—the profession of the *kṣatriyas; āpatsu*—at times of emergency; *sarveṣām*—of everyone in every status of life; *api*—certainly; *sarvaśaḥ*—all professions or occupational duties.

TRANSLATION

Except in a time of emergency, lower persons should not accept the occupational duties of those who are higher. When there is such an emergency, of course, everyone but the kṣatriya may accept the means of livelihood of others.

PURPORT

The occupational duty of a *brāhmaṇa* should not be accepted by persons in lower social orders, especially *vaiśyas* and *śūdras*. For example, an occupational duty of the *brāhmaṇa* is to teach Vedic knowledge, but unless there is an emergency, this professional duty should not be accepted by the *kṣatriyas, vaiśyas* or *śūdras*. Even a *kṣatriya* cannot accept the duties of a *brāhmaṇa* unless there is an emergency, and then even if he does so he should not accept charity from anyone else. Sometimes *brāhmaṇas* protest against our Kṛṣṇa consciousness movement for creating *brāhmaṇas* from Europeans, or, in other words, from *mlecchas* and *yavanas*. This movement, however, is here supported in *Śrīmad-Bhāgavatam*. At the present moment, society is in a chaotic condition, and everyone has given up the cultivation of spiritual life, which is especially meant for the *brāhmaṇas*. Because spiritual culture has been stopped all over the world, there is now an emergency, and therefore it is now time to train those who are considered lower and condemned, so that they may become *brāhmaṇas* and take up the work of spiritual progress. The spiritual progress of human society has been stopped, and this should be considered an emergency. Here is solid support from Nārada Muni of the movement known as Kṛṣṇa consciousness.

TEXTS 18–20

ऋतामृताभ्यां जीवेत मृतेन प्रमृतेन वा ।
सत्यानृताभ्यामपि वा न श्ववृत्त्या कदाचन ॥१८॥
ऋतमुञ्छशिलं प्रोक्तममृतं यद्याचितम् ।
मृतं तु नित्ययाच्ञा स्यात् प्रमृतं कर्षणं स्मृतम् ॥१९॥
सत्यानृतं च वाणिज्यं श्ववृत्तिर्नीचसेवनम् ।
वर्जयेत् तां सदा विप्रो राजन्यश्च जुगुप्सिताम् ।
सर्ववेदमयो विप्रः सर्वदेवमयो नृपः ॥२०॥

ṛtāmṛtābhyāṁ jīveta
mṛtena pramṛtena vā
satyānṛtābhyām api vā
na śva-vṛttyā kadācana

ṛtam uñchaśilaṁ proktam
amṛtaṁ yad ayācitam
mṛtaṁ tu nitya-yācñā syāt
pramṛtaṁ karṣaṇaṁ smṛtam

satyānṛtaṁ ca vāṇijyaṁ
śva-vṛttir nīca-sevanam
varjayet tāṁ sadā vipro
rājanyaś ca jugupsitām
sarva-vedamayo vipraḥ
sarva-devamayo nṛpaḥ

ṛta-amṛtābhyām—of the means of livelihood known as *ṛta* and *amṛta; jīveta*—one may live; *mṛtena*—by the profession of *mṛta; pramṛtena vā*—or by the profession of *pramṛta; satyānṛtābhyām api*—even by the profession of *satyānṛta; vā*—or; *na*—never; *śva-vṛttyā*—by the profession of the dogs; *kadācana*—at any time; *ṛtam*—*ṛta; uñchaśilam*—the livelihood of collecting grains left in the field or marketplace; *proktam*—it is said; *amṛtam*—the profession of *amṛta; yat*—which; *ayācitam*—obtained without begging from anyone else; *mṛtam*—the profession of *mṛta; tu*—but; *nitya-yācñā*—begging grains every day from the farmers; *syāt*—should be; *pramṛtam*—the *pramṛta* means of livelihood; *karṣaṇam*—tilling the field; *smṛtam*—it is so remembered; *satyānṛtam*—the occupation of *satyānṛta; ca*—and; *vāṇijyam*—trade; *śva-vṛttiḥ*—the occupation of the dogs; *nīca-sevanam*—the service of low persons (the *vaiśyas* and *śūdras*); *varjayet*—should give up; *tām*—that (the profession of the dogs);*sadā*—always; *vipraḥ*—the *brāhmaṇa; rājanyaḥ ca*—and the *kṣatriya; jugupsitām*—very abominable; *sarva-veda-mayaḥ*—learned in all the Vedic understandings; *vipraḥ*—the *brāhmaṇa; sarva-deva-mayaḥ*—the embodiment of all the demigods; *nṛpaḥ*—the *kṣatriya* or king.

TRANSLATION

In time of emergency, one may accept any of the various types of professions known as ṛta, amṛta, mṛta, pramṛta and satyānṛta, but one should not at any time accept the profession of a dog. The profession of uñchaśila, collecting grains from the field, is called

ṛta. Collecting without begging is called amṛta, begging grains is called mṛta, tilling the ground is called pramṛta, and trade is called satyānṛta. Engaging in the service of low-grade persons, however, is called śva-vṛtti, the profession of the dogs. Specifically, brāhmaṇas and kṣatriyas should not engage in the low and abominable service of śūdras. Brāhmaṇas should be well acquainted with all the Vedic knowledge, and kṣatriyas should be well acquainted with the worship of demigods.

PURPORT

As stated in *Bhagavad-gītā* (4.13), *cātur-varṇyaṁ mayā sṛṣṭaṁ guṇa-karma-vibhāgaśaḥ:* the four divisions of human society were created by the Supreme Lord according to the three modes of material nature and the work ascribed to them. Formerly, the principle of dividing human society into four sections—*brāhmaṇa, kṣatriya, vaiśya* and *śūdra*—was strictly followed, but because of gradual neglect of the *varṇāśrama* principles, *varṇa-saṅkara* population developed, and the entire institution has now been lost. In this age of Kali, practically everyone is a *śūdra* (*kalau śūdra-sambhavāḥ*), and finding anyone who is a *brāhmaṇa, kṣatriya* or *vaiśya* is very difficult. Although the Kṛṣṇa consciousness movement is a movement of *brāhmaṇas* and Vaiṣṇavas, it is trying to re-establish the divine *varṇāśrama* institution, for without this division of society there cannot be peace and prosperity anywhere.

TEXT 21

शमो दमस्तपः शौचं संतोषः क्षान्तिरार्जवम् ।
ज्ञानं दयाच्युतात्मत्वं सत्यं च ब्रह्मलक्षणम् ॥२१॥

śamo damas tapaḥ śaucaṁ
santoṣaḥ kṣāntir ārjavam
jñānaṁ dayācyutātmatvaṁ
satyaṁ ca brahma-lakṣaṇam

śamaḥ—control of the mind; *damaḥ*—control of the senses; *tapaḥ*—austerity and penance; *śaucam*—cleanliness; *santoṣaḥ*—satisfaction;

kṣāntiḥ—forgiveness (being unagitated by anger); *ārjavam*—simplicity; *jñānam*—knowledge; *dayā*—mercy; *acyuta-ātmatvam*—accepting oneself as an eternal servant of the Lord; *satyam*—truthfulness; *ca*—also; *brahma-lakṣaṇam*—the symptoms of a *brāhmaṇa.*

TRANSLATION

The symptoms of a brāhmaṇa are control of the mind, control of the senses, austerity and penance, cleanliness, satisfaction, forgiveness, simplicity, knowledge, mercy, truthfulness, and complete surrender to the Supreme Personality of Godhead.

PURPORT

In the institution of *varṇāśrama-dharma,* the symptoms of a *brāhmaṇa, kṣatriya, vaiśya, śūdra, brahmacārī, gṛhastha, vānaprastha,* and *sannyāsī* are all described. The ultimate aim is *acyutātmatvam*—to think always of the Supreme Personality of Godhead, Kṛṣṇa, or Viṣṇu. To make advancement in Kṛṣṇa consciousness, one has to become a *brāhmaṇa,* with the above-mentioned symptoms.

TEXT 22

शौर्यं वीर्यं धृतिस्तेजस्त्यागश्चात्मजयः क्षमा ।
ब्रह्मण्यता प्रसादश्च सत्यं च क्षत्रलक्षणम् ॥२२॥

śauryaṁ vīryaṁ dhṛtis tejas
tyāgaś cātmajayaḥ kṣamā
brahmaṇyatā prasādaś ca
satyaṁ ca kṣatra-lakṣaṇam

śauryam—power in battle; *vīryam*—being unconquerable; *dhṛtiḥ*—patience (even in reverses, a *kṣatriya* is very grave); *tejaḥ*—ability to defeat others; *tyāgaḥ*—giving charity; *ca*—and; *ātma-jayaḥ*—not being overwhelmed by bodily necessities; *kṣamā*—forgiveness; *brahmaṇyatā*—faithfulness to the brahminical principles; *prasādaḥ*—jolliness in any condition of life; *ca*—and; *satyam ca*—and truthfulness; *kṣatra-lakṣaṇam*—these are the symptoms of a *kṣatriya.*

TRANSLATION

To be influential in battle, unconquerable, patient, challenging and charitable, to control the bodily necessities, to be forgiving, to be attached to the brahminical nature and to be always jolly and truthful—these are the symptoms of the kṣatriya.

TEXT 23

देवगुर्वच्युते भक्तिस्त्रिवर्गपरिपोषणम् ।
आस्तिक्यमुद्यमो नित्यं नैपुण्यं वैश्यलक्षणम् ॥२३॥

deva-gurv-acyute bhaktis
tri-varga-paripoṣaṇam
āstikyam udyamo nityaṁ
naipuṇyaṁ vaiśya-lakṣaṇam

deva-guru-acyute—unto the demigods, the spiritual master and Lord Viṣṇu; *bhaktiḥ*—engagement in devotional service; *tri-varga*—of the three principles of pious life (religion, economic development and sense gratification); *paripoṣaṇam*—execution; *āstikyam*—faith in the scriptures, the spiritual master and the Supreme Lord; *udyamaḥ*—active; *nityam*—without cessation, continuously; *naipuṇyam*—expertise; *vaiśya-lakṣaṇam*—the symptoms of a *vaiśya.*

TRANSLATION

Being always devoted to the demigods, the spiritual master and the Supreme Lord, Viṣṇu; endeavoring for advancement in religious principles, economic development and sense gratification [dharma, artha and kāma]; believing in the words of the spiritual master and scripture; and always endeavoring with expertise in earning money—these are the symptoms of the vaiśya.

TEXT 24

शूद्रस्य संनतिः शौचं सेवा स्वामिन्यमायया ।
अमन्त्रयज्ञो ह्यस्तेयं सत्यं गोविप्ररक्षणम् ॥२४॥

śūdrasya sannatiḥ śaucaṁ
sevā svāminy amāyayā
amantra-yajño hy asteyaṁ
satyaṁ go-vipra-rakṣaṇam

śūdrasya—of the *śūdra* (the fourth grade of man in society, the worker); *sannatiḥ*—obedience to the higher classes (the *brāhmaṇas, kṣatriyas* and *vaiśyas*); *śaucam*—cleanliness; *sevā*—service; *svāmini*—to the master who maintains him; *amāyayā*—without duplicity; *amantra-yajñaḥ*—performance of sacrifices simply by offering obeisances (without *mantras*); *hi*—certainly; *asteyam*—practicing not to steal; *satyam*—truthfulness; *go*—cows; *vipra*—*brāhmaṇas; rakṣaṇam*—protecting.

TRANSLATION

Offering obeisances to the higher sections of society [the brāhmaṇas, kṣatriyas and vaiśyas], being always very clean, being free from duplicity, serving one's master, performing sacrifices without uttering mantras, not stealing, always speaking the truth and giving all protection to the cows and brāhmaṇas—these are the symptoms of the śūdra.

PURPORT

It is everyone's experience that workers or servants are generally accustomed to stealing. A first-class servant is one who does not steal. Here it is recommended that a first-class *śūdra* must remain very clean, must not steal or speak lies, and must always render service to his master. A *śūdra* may attend sacrifices and Vedic ritualistic ceremonies along with his master, but he should not utter the *mantras*, for these may be uttered only by the members of the higher sections of society. Unless one is completely pure and has been raised to the standard of a *brāhmaṇa, kṣatriya* or *vaiśya*—in other words, unless one is *dvija*, twiceborn—the chanting of *mantras* will not be fruitful.

TEXT 25

स्त्रीणां च पतिदेवानां तच्छुश्रूषानुकूलता ।
तद्बन्धुष्वनुवृत्तिश्च नित्यं तद्व्रतधारणम् ॥२५॥

strīṇāṁ ca pati-devānāṁ
tac-chuśrūṣānukūlatā
tad-bandhuṣv anuvṛttiś ca
nityaṁ tad-vrata-dhāraṇam

strīṇām—of women; *ca*—also; *pati-devānām*—who have accepted their husbands as worshipable; *tat-śuśrūṣā*—readiness to render service to her husband; *anukūlatā*—being favorably disposed towards her husband; *tat-bandhuṣu*—unto the friends and relatives of the husband; *anuvṛttiḥ*—being similarly disposed (to treat them well for the satisfaction of the husband); *ca*—and; *nityam*—regularly; *tat-vrata-dhāraṇam*—accepting the vows of the husband or acting exactly as the husband acts.

TRANSLATION

To render service to the husband, to be always favorably disposed toward the husband, to be equally well disposed toward the husband's relatives and friends, and to follow the vows of the husband—these are the four principles to be followed by women described as chaste.

PURPORT

It is very important for peaceful householder life that a woman follow the vow of her husband. Any disagreement with the husband's vow will disrupt family life. In this regard, Cāṇakya Paṇḍita gives a very valuable instruction: *dampatyoḥ kalaho nāsti tatra śrīḥ svayam āgatāḥ.* When there are no fights between husband and wife, the goddess of fortune automatically comes to the home. A woman's education should be conducted along the lines indicated in this verse. The basic principle for a chaste woman is to be always favorably disposed toward her husband. In *Bhagavad-gītā* (1.40) it is said, *strīṣu duṣṭāsu vārṣṇeya jāyate varṇa-saṅkaraḥ:* if the women are polluted, there will be *varṇa-saṅkara* population. In modern terms, the *varṇa-saṅkara* are the hippies, who do not follow any regulative injunctions. Another explanation is that when the population is *varṇa-saṅkara,* no one can know who is on what platform. The *varṇāśrama* system scientifically divides society into four *varṇas* and four *āśramas*, but in *varṇa-saṅkara* society there are no such distinctions, and no one can know who is who. In such a society, no one can distinguish between a *brāhmaṇa*, a *kṣatriya*, a *vaiśya* and a *śūdra*. For peace and happiness in the material world, the *varṇāśrama* institution must be introduced. The symptoms of one's activities must be defined, and one must be educated accordingly. Then spiritual advancement will automatically be possible.

TEXTS 26–27

संमार्जनोपलेपाभ्यां गृहमण्डनवर्तनैः ।
स्वयं च मण्डिता नित्यं परिमृष्टपरिच्छदा ॥२६॥
कामैरुच्चावचैः साध्वी प्रश्रयेण दमेन च ।
वाक्यैःसत्यैः प्रियैः प्रेम्णा काले काले भजेत् पतिम् ॥ २७॥

sammārjanopalepābhyāṁ
gṛha-maṇḍana-vartanaiḥ
svayaṁ ca maṇḍitā nityaṁ
parimṛṣṭa-paricchadā

kāmair uccāvacaiḥ sādhvī
praśrayeṇa damena ca
vākyaiḥ satyaiḥ priyaiḥ premṇā
kāle kāle bhajet patim

sammārjana—by cleaning; *upalepābhyām*—by smearing with water or other cleansing liquids; *gṛha*—the household; *maṇḍana*—decorating; *vartanaiḥ*—remaining at home and engaged in such duties; *svayam*—personally; *ca*—also; *maṇḍitā*—finely dressed; *nityam*—always; *parimṛṣṭa*—cleansed; *paricchadā*—garments and household utensils; *kāmaiḥ*—according to the desires of the husband; *ucca-avacaiḥ*—both great and small; *sādhvī*—a chaste woman; *praśrayeṇa*—with modesty; *damena*—by controlling the senses; *ca*—also; *vākyaiḥ*—by speech; *satyaiḥ*—truthful; *priyaiḥ*—very pleasing; *premṇā*—with love; *kāle kāle*—at appropriate times; *bhajet*—should worship; *patim*—her husband.

TRANSLATION

A chaste woman must dress nicely and decorate herself with golden ornaments for the pleasure of her husband. Always wearing clean and attractive garments, she should sweep and clean the household with water and other liquids so that the entire house is always pure and clean. She should collect the household paraphernalia and keep the house always aromatic with incense and flowers and must be ready to execute the desires of her husband. Being modest and truthful, controlling her senses, and speaking in sweet words, a chaste woman should engage in the service of her husband with love, according to time and circumstances.

TEXT 28

संतुष्टालोलुपा दक्षा धर्मज्ञा प्रियसत्यवाक् ।
अप्रमत्ता शुचिः स्निग्धा पतिं त्वपतितं भजेत् ॥२८॥

santuṣṭālolupā dakṣā
dharma-jñā priya-satya-vāk
apramattā śuciḥ snigdhā
patiṁ tv apatitaṁ bhajet

santuṣṭā—always satisfied; *alolupā*—without being greedy; *dakṣā*—very expert in serving; *dharma-jñā*—fully conversant with religious principles; *priya*—pleasing; *satya*—truthful; *vāk*—in speaking; *apramattā*—attentive in service to her husband; *śuciḥ*—always clean and pure; *snigdhā*—affectionate; *patim*—the husband; *tu*—but; *apatitam*—who is not fallen; *bhajet*—should worship.

TRANSLATION

A chaste woman should not be greedy, but satisfied in all circumstances. She must be very expert in handling household affairs and should be fully conversant with religious principles. She should speak pleasingly and truthfully and should be very careful and always clean and pure. Thus a chaste woman should engage with affection in the service of a husband who is not fallen.

PURPORT

According to the injunction of Yājñavalkya, an authority on religious principles, *āśuddheḥ sampratikṣyo hi mahāpātaka-dūṣitaḥ*. One is considered contaminated by the reactions of great sinful activities when one has not been purified according to the methods of the *daśa-vidhā-saṁskāra*. In *Bhagavad-gītā*, however, the Lord says, *na māṁ duṣkṛtino mūḍhāḥ prapadyante narādhamāḥ:* "Those miscreants who do not surrender unto Me are the lowest of mankind." The word *narādhama* means "nondevotee." Śrī Caitanya Mahāprabhu also said, *yei bhaje sei baḍa, abhakta—hīna, chāra*. Anyone who is a devotee is sinless. One who is not a devotee, however, is the most fallen and condemned. It is recommended, therefore, that a chaste wife not associate with a fallen husband. A fallen husband is one who is addicted to the four principles of sinful activity—namely illicit sex, meat-eating, gambling and intoxication. Specifically, if one is not a soul surrendered to the Supreme Personality of Godhead, he is understood to be contaminated. Thus a chaste woman is advised not to agree to serve such a husband. It is not that a chaste woman should be like a slave while her husband is *narādhama*, the lowest of men. Although the duties of a woman are different from those of a man, a chaste woman is not meant to serve a fallen husband. If her husband is fallen, it is recommended that she give up his association. Giving up the association of her husband does not mean, however, that a woman should marry again and thus indulge in prostitution. If a chaste woman unfortunately marries a husband who is fallen, she should live separately from him. Similarly, a husband can separate himself from a woman who is not chaste according to the description of the *śāstra*. The conclusion is that a husband should be a pure Vaiṣṇava and that a woman should be a chaste wife with all the symptoms described in this regard. Then both of them will be happy and make spiritual progress in Kṛṣṇa consciousness.

TEXT 29

या पतिं हरिभावेन भजेत् श्रीरिव तत्परा ।
हर्यात्मना हरेर्लोके पत्या श्रीरिव मोदते ॥२९॥

yā patiṁ hari-bhāvena
bhajet śrīr iva tat-parā

hary-ātmanā harer loke
patyā śrīr iva modate

yā—any woman who; *patim*—her husband; *hari-bhāvena*—mentally accepting him as equal to Hari, the Supreme Personality of Godhead; *bhajet*—worships or renders service to; *śrīḥ iva*—exactly like the goddess of fortune; *tat-parā*—being devoted; *hari-ātmanā*—completely absorbed in thoughts of Hari; *hareḥ loke*—in the spiritual world, the Vaikuṇṭha planets; *patyā*—with her husband; *śrīḥ iva*—exactly like the goddess of fortune; *modate*—enjoys spiritual, eternal life.

TRANSLATION

The woman who engages in the service of her husband, following strictly in the footsteps of the goddess of fortune, surely returns home, back to Godhead, with her devotee husband, and lives very happily in the Vaikuṇṭha planets.

PURPORT

The faithfulness of the goddess of fortune is the ideal for a chaste woman. The *Brahma-saṁhitā* (5.29) says, *lakṣmī-sahasra-śata-sambhrama-sevyamānam.* In the Vaikuṇṭha planets, Lord Viṣṇu is worshiped by many, many thousands of goddesses of fortune, and in Goloka Vṛndāvana, Lord Kṛṣṇa is worshiped by many, many thousands of *gopīs,* all of whom are goddesses of fortune. A woman should serve her husband as faithfully as the goddess of fortune. A man should be an ideal servant of the Lord, and a woman should be an ideal wife like the goddess of fortune. Then both husband and wife will be so faithful and strong that by acting together they will return home, back to Godhead, without a doubt. In this regard, Śrīla Madhvācārya gives this opinion:

harir asmin sthita iti
strīṇāṁ bhartari bhāvanā
śiṣyāṇāṁ ca gurau nityaṁ
śūdrāṇāṁ brāhmaṇādiṣu
bhṛtyānāṁ svāmini tathā
hari-bhāva udīritaḥ

A woman should think of her husband as the Supreme Lord. Similarly, a disciple should think of the spiritual master as the Supreme Personality of Godhead, a *śūdra* should think of a *brāhmaṇa* as the Supreme Personality of Godhead, and a servant should think of his master as the Supreme Personality of Godhead. In this way, all of them will automatically become devotees of the Lord. In other words, by thinking this way, all of them will become Kṛṣṇa conscious.

TEXT 30

वृत्तिः सङ्करजातीनां तत्तत्कुलकृता भवेत् ।
अचौराणामपापानामन्त्यजान्तेवसायिनाम् ॥३०॥

vṛttiḥ saṅkara-jātīnāṁ
tat-tat-kula-kṛtā bhavet
acaurāṇām apāpānām
antyajāntevasāyinām

vṛttiḥ—occupational duty; *saṅkara-jātīnām*—of the mixed classes of men (those other than the four divisions); *tat-tat*—according to their respective; *kula-kṛtā*—family tradition; *bhavet*—should be; *acaurāṇām*—not thieves by profession; *apāpānām*—not sinful; *antyaja*—lower classes; *antevasāyinām*—known as *antevasāyī* or *caṇḍāla.*

TRANSLATION

Among the mixed classes known as saṅkara, those who are not thieves are known as antevasāyī or caṇḍālas [dog-eaters], and they also have their hereditary customs.

PURPORT

The four principal divisions of society—*brāhmaṇa, kṣatriya, vaiśya* and *śūdra*—have been defined, and now there is a description of the *antyaja,* the mixed classes. Among the mixed classes, there are two divisions—*pratilomaja* and *anulomaja.* If a woman of a high caste marries a man of a lower caste, their union is called *pratilo.* If a woman of a low caste, however, marries a man of a higher caste, their union is called *anulo.* The members of such dynasties have their traditional duties as barbers, washermen and so on. Among the *antyajas,* those who are still somewhat pure in that they do not steal and are not addicted to meat-eating, drinking, illicit sex and gambling are called *antevasāyī.* Among people of the lower classes, intermarriage and the drinking of wine are allowed, for these people do not recognize such conduct as sinful among themselves.

TEXT 31

प्रायः स्वभावविहितो नृणां धर्मो युगे युगे ।
वेददृग्भिः स्मृतो राजन्प्रेत्य चेह च शर्मकृत् ॥३१॥

prāyaḥ sva-bhāva-vihito
nṛṇāṁ dharmo yuge yuge
veda-dṛgbhiḥ smṛto rājan
pretya ceha ca śarma-kṛt

prāyaḥ—generally; *sva-bhāva-vihitaḥ*—prescribed, according to one's material modes of nature; *nṛṇām*—of human society; *dharmaḥ*—the occupational duty; *yuge yuge*—in every age; *veda-dṛgbhiḥ*—by *brāhmaṇas* well conversant in the Vedic knowledge; *smṛtaḥ*—recognized; *rājan*—O King; *pretya*—after death; *ca*—and; *iha*—here (in this body); *ca*—also; *śarma-kṛt*—auspicious.

TRANSLATION

My dear King, brāhmaṇas well conversant in Vedic knowledge have given their verdict that in every age [yuga] the conduct of different sections of people according to their material modes of nature is auspicious both in this life and after death.

PURPORT

In *Bhagavad-gītā* (3.35) it is said, *śreyān sva-dharmo viguṇaḥ para-dharmāt svanuṣṭhitāt:* "It is far better to discharge one's prescribed duties, even though they may be faulty, than another's duties." The *antyajas,* the men of the lower classes, are accustomed to stealing, drinking and illicit sex, but that is not considered sinful. For example, if a tiger kills a man, this is not sinful but if a man kills another man, this is considered sinful, and the killer is hanged. What is a daily affair among the animals is a sinful act in human society. Thus according to the symptoms of higher and lower sections of society, there are different varieties of occupational duties. According to the experts in Vedic knowledge, these duties are prescribed in terms of the age concerned.

TEXT 32

वृत्त्या स्वभावकृतया वर्तमानः स्वकर्मकृत् ।
हित्वा स्वभावजं कर्म शनैर्निर्गुणतामियात् ॥३२॥

vṛttyā sva-bhāva-kṛtayā
vartamānaḥ sva-karma-kṛt
hitvā sva-bhāva-jaṁ karma
śanair nirguṇatām iyāt

vṛttyā—with the profession; *sva-bhāva-kṛtayā*—performed according to one's modes of material nature; *vartamānaḥ*—existing; *sva-karma-kṛt*—executing his own work; *hitvā*—giving up; *sva-bhāva-jam*—born from one's own modes of nature; *karma*—activities; *śanaiḥ*—gradually; *nirguṇatām*—transcendental position; *iyāt*—may attain.

TRANSLATION

If one acts in his profession according to his position in the modes of nature and gradually gives up these activities, he attains the niṣkāma stage.

PURPORT

If one gradually gives up his hereditary customs and duties and tries to serve the Supreme Personality of Godhead in his natural position, he is gradually able to become free from these activities, and he attains the stage of *niṣkāma*, freedom from material desires.

TEXTS 33–34

उप्यमानं मुहुः क्षेत्रं स्वयं निर्वीर्यतामियात् ।
न कल्पते पुनः सूत्यै उप्तं बीजं च नश्यति ॥३३॥

एवं कामाशयं चित्तं कामानामतिसेवया ।
विरज्येत यथा राजन्नग्निवत् कामबिन्दुभिः ॥३४॥

upyamānaṁ muhuḥ kṣetraṁ
svayaṁ nirvīryatām iyāt
na kalpate punaḥ sūtyai
uptaṁ bījaṁ ca naśyati

evaṁ kāmāśayaṁ cittaṁ
kāmānām atisevayā
virajyeta yathā rājann
agnivat kāma-bindubhiḥ

upyamānam—being cultivated; *muhuḥ*—again and again; *kṣetram*—a field; *svayam*—itself; *nirvīryatām*—barrenness; *iyāt*—may obtain; *na kalpate*—is not suitable; *punaḥ*—again; *sūtyai*—for growing further harvests; *uptam*—sown; *bījam*—the seed; *ca*—and; *naśyati*—is spoiled; *evam*—in this way; *kāma-āśayam*—full of lusty desires; *cittam*—the core of the heart; *kāmānām*—of the desirable objects; *ati-sevayā*—by enjoyment over and over again; *virajyeta*—may become detached; *yathā*—just as; *rājan*—O King; *agni-vat*—a fire; *kāma-bindubhiḥ*—by small drops of clarified butter.

TRANSLATION

My dear King, if an agricultural field is cultivated again and again, the power of its production decreases, and whatever seeds are sown there are lost. Just as drops of ghee on a fire never extinguish the fire but a flood of ghee will, similarly, overindulgence in lusty desires mitigates such desires entirely.

PURPORT

If one continuously sprinkles drops of ghee on a fire, the fire will not be extinguished, but if one suddenly puts a lump of ghee on a fire, the fire may possibly be extinguished entirely. Similarly, those who are too sinful and have thus been born in the lower classes are allowed to enjoy sinful activities fully, for thus there is a chance that these activities will become detestful to them, and they will get the opportunity to be purified.

TEXT 35

यस्य यल्लक्षणं प्रोक्तं पुंसो वर्णाभिव्यञ्जकम् ।
यदन्यत्रापि दृश्येत तत् तेनैव विनिर्दिशेत् ॥३५॥

yasya yal lakṣaṇaṁ proktaṁ
puṁso varṇābhivyañjakam
yad anyatrāpi dṛśyeta
tat tenaiva vinirdiśet

yasya—of whom; *yat*—which; *lakṣaṇam*—symptom; *proktam*—described (above); *puṁsaḥ*—of a person; *varṇa-abhivyañjakam*—indicating the classification (*brāhmaṇa, kṣatriya, vaiśya, śūdra*, etc.); *yat*—if; *anyatra*—elsewhere; *api*—also; *dṛśyeta*—is seen; *tat*—that; *tena*—by that symptom; *eva*—certainly; *vinirdiśet*—one should designate.

TRANSLATION

If one shows the symptoms of being a brāhmaṇa, kṣatriya, vaiśya or śūdra, as described above, even if he has appeared in a different class, he should be accepted according to those symptoms of classification.

PURPORT

Herein it is clearly stated by Nārada Muni that one should not be accepted as a *brāhmaṇa, kṣatriya, vaiśya* or *śūdra* according to birth, for although this is going on now, it is not accepted by the *śāstras*. As stated in *Bhagavad-gītā* (4.13), *cātur-varṇyaṁ mayā sṛṣṭaṁ guṇa-karma-vibhāgaśaḥ*. Thus the four divisions of society—*brāhmaṇa, kṣatriya, vaiśya* and *śūdra*—are to be ascertained according to qualities and activities. If one was born in a *brāhmaṇa* family and has acquired the brahminical qualifications, he is to be accepted as a *brāhmaṇa;* otherwise, he should be considered a *brahma-bandhu.* Similarly, if a *śūdra* acquires the qualities of a *brāhmaṇa*, although he was born in a *śūdra* family, he is not a *śūdra;* because he has developed the qualities of a *brāhmaṇa*, he should be accepted as a *brāhmaṇa.* The Kṛṣṇa consciousness movement is meant to develop these brahminical qualities. Regardless of the community in which one was born, if one develops the qualities of a *brāhmaṇa* he should be accepted as a *brāhmaṇa*, and he then may be offered the order of *sannyāsa.* Unless one is qualified in terms of the brahminical symptoms, one cannot take *sannyāsa.* In designating a person a *brāhmaṇa, kṣatriya, vaiśya* or *śūdra,* birth is not the essential symptom. This understanding is very important. Herein Nārada Muni distinctly says that one may be accepted according to the caste of his birth if he has the corresponding qualifications, but otherwise he should not. One who has attained the qualifications of a *brāhmaṇa,* regardless of where he was born, should be accepted as a *brāhmaṇa.* Similarly, if one has developed the qualities of a *śūdra* or a *caṇḍāla,* regardless of where he was born, he should be accepted in terms of those symptoms.

Thus end the Bhaktivedanta purports of the Seventh Canto, Eleventh Chapter, of the Śrīmad-Bhāgavatam, *entitled "The Perfect Society: Four Social Classes."*

CHAPTER TWELVE

The Perfect Society: Four Spiritual Classes

This chapter particularly describes the *brahmacārī* and the person in the *vānaprastha* stage, and it also gives a general description of the four *āśramas—brahmacarya, gṛhastha, vānaprastha* and *sannyāsa.* In the previous chapter, the great saint Nārada Muni has described the *varṇa* institution of society, and now, in this chapter, he will describe the stages of spiritual advancement in the four *āśramas,* which are known as *brahmacarya, gṛhastha, vānaprastha* and *sannyāsa.*

The *brahmacārī* should live under the care of the true spiritual master, giving him sincere respect and obeisances, acting as his menial servant, and always carrying out his order. The *brahmacārī* should engage himself in spiritual activities and study the Vedic literature under the direction of the spiritual master. According to the *brahmacarya* system, he should dress with a belt, deerskin, and matted hair and should bear a *daṇḍa,* waterpot and sacred thread. He should collect alms daily in the morning, and in the evening whatever alms he has collected he should offer to the spiritual master. A *brahmacārī* should accept *prasāda* upon the order of the spiritual master, and if the spiritual master sometimes forgets to order the disciple to eat, the disciple should not take *prasāda* on his own initiative; rather, he should fast. The *brahmacārī* should be trained to be satisfied with eating what is absolutely necessary, he should be very expert in executing responsibilities, he should be faithful, and he should control his senses and try to avoid the association of women as far as possible. A *brahmacārī* should very strictly abstain from living with women and should not meet with *gṛhasthas* and those too addicted to women. Nor should a *brahmacārī* speak in a lonely place with a woman.

After completing one's education as a *brahmacārī* in this way, one should give *dakṣiṇā,* an offering of gratitude, to one's *guru,* and then one may leave for home and accept the next *āśrama*—the *gṛhastha-āśrama*—or else one may continue in the *brahmacarya-āśrama* without adulteration. The duties for the *gṛhastha-āśrama* and *brahmacarya-*

āśrama, as well as the duties for *sannyāsīs*, are prescribed in the *śāstras*. A *gṛhastha* is not meant to enjoy sex life without restriction. Indeed, the whole purpose of Vedic life is to become free from sexual indulgence. All the *āśramas* are recognized for spiritual progress, and therefore although the *gṛhastha-āśrama* gives a kind of license for sex life for a certain time, it does not allow unrestricted sex life. Therefore, in *gṛhastha* life also, there is no illicit sex. A *gṛhastha* should not accept a woman for sexual enjoyment. Wasting semen is also illicit sex.

After the *gṛhastha-āśrama* is another *āśrama*, known as *vānaprastha*, which is midway between *gṛhastha* and *sannyāsa*. A person in the *vānaprastha* order is restricted in eating food grains and forbidden to eat fruits that have not ripened on the tree. Nor should he cook food with fire, although he is allowed to eat *caru*, grains that have been offered in a sacrificial fire. He may also eat fruits and grains that have grown naturally. Living in a thatched cottage, the *vānaprastha* should endure all kinds of heat and cold. He should not cut his nails or hair, and he should give up cleaning his body and teeth. He should wear tree bark, accept a *daṇḍa*, and practice life in the forest, taking a vow to live there for twelve years, eight years, four years, two years or at least one year. At last, when because of old age he can no longer perform the activities of a *vānaprastha*, he should gradually stop everything and in this way give up his body.

TEXT 1

श्रीनारद उवाच

ब्रह्मचारी गुरुकुले वसन्दान्तो गुरोर्हितम् ।
आचरन्दासवन्नीचो गुरौ सुदृढसौहृदः ॥ १ ॥

śrī-nārada uvāca
brahmacārī guru-kule
vasan dānto guror hitam
ācaran dāsavan nīco
gurau sudṛḍha-sauhṛdaḥ

śrī-nāradaḥ uvāca—Śrī Nārada Muni said; *brahmacārī*—a *brahmacārī*, a student living at the residence of the *guru; guru-kule*—at the residence of the *guru; vasan*—by living; *dāntaḥ*—continuously practicing control of the senses; *guroḥ hitam*—only for the benefit of the *guru* (not for one's personal benefit); *ācaran*—practicing; *dāsa-vat*—very humbly, like a slave; *nīcaḥ*—submissive, obedient; *gurau*—unto the spiritual master; *su-dṛḍha*—firmly; *sauhṛdaḥ*—in friendship or good will.

TRANSLATION

Nārada Muni said: A student should practice completely controlling his senses. He should be submissive and should have an attitude of firm friendship for the spiritual master. With a great vow, the brahmacārī should live at the guru-kula, only for the benefit of the guru.

TEXT 2

सायं प्रातरुपासीत गुर्वग्न्यर्कसुरोत्तमान् ।
सन्ध्ये उभे च यतवाग् जपन्ब्रह्म समाहितः ॥ २ ॥

sāyaṁ prātar upāsīta
gurv-agny-arka-surottamān
sandhye ubhe ca yata-vāg
japan brahma samāhitaḥ

sāyam—in the evening; *prātaḥ*—in the morning; *upāsīta*—he should worship; *guru*—the spiritual master; *agni*—the fire (by a fire sacrifice); *arka*—the sun; *sura-uttamān*—and Lord Viṣṇu, Puruṣottama, the best of personalities; *sandhye*—morning and evening; *ubhe*—both; *ca*—also; *yata-vāk*—without talking, being silent; *japan*—murmuring; *brahma*—the Gāyatrī *mantra; samāhitaḥ*—being fully absorbed.

TRANSLATION

At both junctions of day and night, namely, in the early morning and in the evening, he should be fully absorbed in thoughts of the spiritual master, fire, the sun-god and Lord Viṣṇu and by chanting the Gāyatrī mantra he should worship them.

TEXT 3

छन्दांस्यधीयीत गुरोराहूतश्चेत् सुयन्त्रितः ।
उपक्रमेऽवसाने च चरणौ शिरसा नमेत् ॥ ३ ॥

chandāṁsy adhīyīta guror
āhūtaś cet suyantritaḥ
upakrame 'vasāne ca
caraṇau śirasā namet

chandāṁsi—*mantras* in the *Vedas,* like the Hare Kṛṣṇa *mahā-mantra* and the Gāyatrī *mantra; adhīyīta*—one should chant or read regularly; *guroḥ*—from the spiritual master; *āhūtaḥ*—being addressed or called (by him); *cet*—if; *su-yantritaḥ*—faithful, well behaved; *upakrame*—in the beginning; *avasāne*—at the end (of reading Vedic *mantras*); *ca*—also; *caraṇau*—at the lotus feet; *śirasā*—by the head; *namet*—one should offer obeisances.

TRANSLATION

Being called by the spiritual master, the student should study the Vedic mantras regularly. Every day, before beginning his studies and at the end of his studies, the disciple should respectfully offer obeisances unto the spiritual master.

TEXT 4

मेखलाजिनवासांसि जटादण्डकमण्डलून् ।
बिभृयादुपवीतं च दर्भपाणिर्यथोदितम् ॥ ४ ॥

mekhalājina-vāsāṁsi
jaṭā-daṇḍa-kamaṇḍalūn
bibhṛyād upavītaṁ ca
darbha-pāṇir yathoditam

mekhalā—a belt made of straw; *ajina-vāsāṁsi*—garments made of deerskin; *jaṭā*—matted hair; *daṇḍa*—a rod; *kamaṇḍalūn*—and a waterpot known as a *kamaṇḍalu; bibhṛyāt*—he (the *brahmacārī*) should regularly carry or wear; *upavītam ca*—and a sacred thread; *darbha-pāṇiḥ*—taking purified *kuśa* in his hand; *yathā uditam*—as recommended in the *śāstras.*

TRANSLATION

Carrying pure kuśa grass in his hand, the brahmacārī should dress regularly with a belt of straw and with deerskin garments. He

should wear matted hair, carry a rod and waterpot and be decorated with a sacred thread, as recommended in the śāstras.

TEXT 5

सायं प्रातश्चरेद्भैक्ष्यं गुरवे तन्निवेदयेत् ।
भुञ्जीत यद्यनुज्ञातो नो चेदुपवसेत् क्वचित् ॥ ५ ॥

sāyaṁ prātaś cared bhaikṣyaṁ
gurave tan nivedayet
bhuñjīta yady anujñāto
no ced upavaset kvacit

sāyam—in the evening; *prātaḥ*—in the morning; *caret*—should go out; *bhaikṣyam*—to collect alms; *gurave*—unto the spiritual master; *tat*—all that he collects; *nivedayet*—should offer; *bhuñjīta*—he should eat; *yadi*—if; *anujñātaḥ*—ordered (by the spiritual master); *no*—otherwise; *cet*—if; *upavaset*—should observe fasting; *kvacit*—sometimes.

TRANSLATION

The brahmacārī should go out morning and evening to collect alms, and he should offer all that he collects to the spiritual master. He should eat only if ordered to take food by the spiritual master; otherwise, if the spiritual master does not give this order, he may sometimes have to fast.

TEXT 6

सुशीलो मितभुग् दक्षः श्रद्दधानो जितेन्द्रियः ।
यावदर्थं व्यवहरेत् स्त्रीषु स्त्रीनिर्जितेषु च ॥ ६ ॥

suśīlo mita-bhug dakṣaḥ
śraddadhāno jitendriyaḥ
yāvad-arthaṁ vyavaharet
strīṣu strī-nirjiteṣu ca

su-śīlaḥ—very polite and well behaved; *mita-bhuk*—eating only exactly what he needs, neither more nor less; *dakṣaḥ*—expert or without laziness, always busy; *śraddadhānaḥ*—possessing full faith in the instructions of the *śāstra* and the spiritual master; *jita-indriyaḥ*—having full control over the senses; *yāvat-artham*—as much as necessary; *vyavaharet*—should behave externally; *strīṣu*—unto women; *strī-nirjiteṣu*—men who are henpecked, controlled by women; *ca*—also.

TRANSLATION

A brahmacārī should be quite well behaved and gentle and should not eat or collect more than necessary. He must always be active and expert, fully believing in the instructions of the spiritual master and the śāstra. Fully controlling his senses, he should associate only as much as necessary with women or those controlled by women.

PURPORT

A *brahmacārī* should be very careful not to mix with women or with men addicted to women. Although when he goes out to beg alms it is necessary to talk with women and with men very much attached to women, this association should be very short, and he should talk with them only about begging alms, and not more. A *brahmacārī* should be very careful in associating with men who are attached to women.

TEXT 7

वर्जयेत् प्रमदागाथामगृहस्थो बृहद्व्रतः ।
इन्द्रियाणि प्रमाथीनि हरन्त्यपि यतेर्मनः ॥ ७ ॥

varjayet pramadā-gāthām
agṛhastho bṛhad-vrataḥ
indriyāṇi pramāthīni
haranty api yater manaḥ

varjayet—must give up; *pramadā-gāthām*—talking with women; *agṛhasthaḥ*—a person who has not accepted the *gṛhastha-āśrama* (a *brahmacārī* or *sannyāsī*); *bṛhat-vrataḥ*—invariably observing the vow of celibacy; *indriyāṇi*—the senses; *pramāthīni*—almost always unconquerable; *haranti*—take away; *api*—even; *yateḥ*—of the *sannyāsī;* *manaḥ*—the mind.

TRANSLATION

A brahmacārī, or one who has not accepted the gṛhastha-āśrama [family life], must rigidly avoid talking with women or about women, for the senses are so powerful that they may agitate even the mind of a sannyāsī, a member of the renounced order of life.

PURPORT

Brahmacarya essentially means the vow not to marry but to observe strict celibacy (*bṛhad-vrata*). A *brahmacārī* or *sannyāsī* should avoid talking with women or reading literature concerning talks between man and woman. The injunction restricting association with women is the basic principle of spiritual life. Associating or talking with women is never advised in any of the Vedic literatures. The entire Vedic system teaches one to avoid sex life so that one may gradually progress from *brahmacarya* to *gṛhastha*, from *gṛhastha* to *vānaprastha*, and from *vānaprastha* to *sannyāsa* and thus give up material enjoyment, which is the original cause of bondage to this material world. The word *bṛhad-vrata* refers to one who has decided not to marry, or in other words, not to indulge in sex life throughout his entire life.

TEXT 8

केशप्रसाधनोन्मर्दस्नपनाभ्यञ्जनादिकम् ।
गुरुस्त्रीभिर्युवतिभिः कारयेन्नात्मनो युवा ॥ ८ ॥

keśa-prasādhanonmarda-
snapanābhyañjanādikam
guru-strībhir yuvatibhiḥ
kārayen nātmano yuvā

keśa-prasādhana—brushing the hair; *unmarda*—massaging the body; *snapana*—bathing; *abhyañjana-ādikam*—massaging the body with oil and so on; *guru-strībhiḥ*—by the wife of the spiritual master; *yuvatibhiḥ*—very young; *kārayet*—should allow to do; *na*—never; *ātmanaḥ*—for personal service; *yuvā*—if the student is a young man.

TRANSLATION

If the wife of the spiritual master is young, a young brahmacārī should not allow her to care for his hair, massage his body with oil, or bathe him with affection like a mother.

PURPORT

The relationship between the student or disciple and the wife of the spiritual master or teacher is like that between son and mother. A mother sometimes cares for her son by combing his hair, massaging his body with oil, or bathing him. Similarly, the wife of the teacher is also a mother (*guru-patnī*), and therefore she may also care for the disciple in a motherly way. If the wife of the teacher is a young woman, however, a young *brahmacārī* should not allow such a mother to touch him. This is strictly prohibited. There are seven kinds of mothers:

ātma-mātā guroḥ patnī
brāhmaṇī rāja-patnikā
dhenur dhātrī tathā pṛthvī
saptaitā mātaraḥ smṛtāḥ

These mothers are the original mother, the wife of the teacher or spiritual master, the wife of a *brāhmaṇa*, the king's wife, the cow, the nurse and the earth. Unnecessary association with women, even with one's mother, sister or daughter, is strictly prohibited. This is human civilization. A civilization that allows men to mix unrestrictedly with women is an animal civilization. In Kali-yuga, people are extremely liberal, but mixing with women and talking with them as equals actually constitutes an uncivilized way of life.

TEXT 9

नन्वग्निः प्रमदा नाम घृतकुम्भसमः पुमान् ।
सुतामपि रहो जह्यादन्यदा यावदर्थकृत् ॥ ९ ॥

nanv agniḥ pramadā nāma
ghṛta-kumbha-samaḥ pumān
sutām api raho jahyād
anyadā yāvad-artha-kṛt

nanu—certainly; *agniḥ*—the fire; *pramadā*—the woman (one who bewilders the mind of man); *nāma*—the very name; *ghṛta-kumbha*—a pot of butter; *samaḥ*—like; *pumān*—a man; *sutām api*—even one's daughter; *rahaḥ*—in a secluded place; *jahyāt*—one must not associate with; *anyadā*—with other women also; *yāvat*—as much as; *artha-kṛt*—required.

TRANSLATION

Woman is compared to fire, and man is compared to a butter pot. Therefore a man should avoid associating even with his own daughter in a secluded place. Similarly, he should also avoid association with other women. One should associate with women only for important business and not otherwise.

PURPORT

If a butter pot and fire are kept together, the butter within the pot will certainly melt. Woman is compared to fire, and man is compared to a butter pot. However advanced one may be in restraining the senses, it is almost impossible for a man to keep himself controlled in the presence of a woman, even if she is his own daughter, mother or sister. Indeed, his mind is agitated even if one is in the renounced order of life. Therefore, Vedic civilization carefully restricts mingling between men and women. If one cannot understand the basic principle of restraining association between man and woman, he is to be considered an animal. That is the purport of this verse.

TEXT 10

कल्पयित्वात्मना यावदाभासमिदमीश्वरः ।
द्वैतं तावन्न विरमेत् ततो ह्यस्य विपर्ययः ॥१०॥

kalpayitvātmanā yāvad
ābhāsam idam īśvaraḥ
dvaitaṁ tāvan na viramet
tato hy asya viparyayaḥ

kalpayitvā—ascertaining positively; *ātmanā*—by self-realization; *yāvat*—as long as; *ābhāsam*—reflection (of the original body and senses); *idam*—this (the body and senses); *īśvaraḥ*—completely independent of illusion; *dvaitam*—duality; *tāvat*—for that long; *na*—does not; *viramet*—see; *tataḥ*—by such duality; *hi*—indeed; *asya*—of the person; *viparyayaḥ*—counteraction.

TRANSLATION

As long as a living entity is not completely self-realized—as long as he is not independent of the misconception of identifying with his body, which is nothing but a reflection of the original body and senses—he cannot be relieved of the conception of duality, which is epitomized by the duality between man and woman. Thus there is every chance that he will fall down because his intelligence is bewildered.

PURPORT

Here is another important warning that a man must save himself from attraction to woman. Until one is self-realized, fully independent of the illusory conception of the material body, the duality of man and woman must undoubtedly continue, but when one is actually self-realized this distinction ceases.

vidyā-vinaya-sampanne
brāhmaṇe gavi hastini
śuni caiva śvapāke ca
paṇḍitāḥ sama-darśinaḥ

"The humble sage, by virtue of true knowledge, sees with equal vision a learned and gentle *brāhmaṇa*, a cow, an elephant, a dog and a dog-eater [outcaste]." (Bg. 5.18) On the spiritual platform, the learned person not only gives up the duality of man and woman, but also gives up the duality of man and animal. This is the test of self-realization. One must realize perfectly that the living being is spirit soul but is tasting various types of material bodies. One may theoretically understand this, but when one has practical realization, then he actually becomes a *paṇḍita*, one who knows. Until that time, the duality continues, and the conception of man and woman also continues. In this stage, one should be extremely careful about mixing with women. No one should think himself perfect and forget the śāstric instruction that one should be very careful about associating even with his daughter, mother or sister, not to speak of other women. Śrīla Madhvācārya cites the following *ślokas* in this regard:

bahutvenaiva vastūnāṁ
yathārtha-jñānam ucyate
advaita-jñānam ity etad
dvaita-jñānaṁ tad-anyathā

yathā jñānaṁ tathā vastu
yathā vastus tathā matiḥ
naiva jñānārthayor bhedas
tata ekatva-vedanam

Unity in variety is real knowledge, and therefore giving up variety artificially does not reflect perfect knowledge of monism. According to the *acintya-bhedābheda* philosophy of Śrī Caitanya Mahāprabhu, there are varieties, but all of them constitute one unit. Such knowledge is knowledge of perfect oneness.

TEXT 11

एतत् सर्वं गृहस्थस्य समाम्नातं यतेरपि ।
गुरुवृत्तिर्विकल्पेन गृहस्थस्यर्तुगामिनः ॥११॥

etat sarvaṁ gṛhasthasya
samāmnātaṁ yater api
guru-vṛttir vikalpena
gṛhasthasyartu-gāminaḥ

etat—this; *sarvam*—all; *gṛhasthasya*—of a householder; *samāmnātam*—described; *yateḥ api*—even of the person in the renounced order; *guru-vṛttiḥ vikalpena*—to follow the orders of the spiritual master; *gṛhasthasya*—of the householder; *ṛtu-gāminaḥ*—accepting sex only during the period favorable for procreation.

TRANSLATION

All the rules and regulations apply equally to the householder and the sannyāsī, the member of the renounced order of life. The

gṛhastha, however, is given permission by the spiritual master to indulge in sex during the period favorable for procreation.

PURPORT

It is sometimes misunderstood that a *gṛhastha,* a householder, is permitted to indulge in sex at any time. This is a wrong conception of *gṛhastha* life. In spiritual life, whether one is a *gṛhastha, vānaprastha, sannyāsī* or *brahmacārī,* everyone is under the control of the spiritual master. For *brahmacārīs* and *sannyāsīs* there are strong restrictions on sexual indulgence. Similarly, there are strong restrictions for *gṛhasthas. Gṛhasthas* should indulge in sex life only in accordance with the order of the *guru.* Therefore it is mentioned here that one must follow the orders of the spiritual master (*guru-vṛttir vikalpena*). When the spiritual master orders, the *gṛhastha* may accept sex life. This is confirmed in *Bhagavad-gītā* (7.11). *Dharmāviruddho bhūteṣu kāmo 'smi:* indulgence in sex life without disobedience to the religious rules and regulations constitutes a religious principle. The *gṛhastha* is allowed to indulge in sex life during the period favorable for procreation and in accordance with the spiritual master's order. If the spiritual master's orders allow a *gṛhastha* to engage in sex life at a particular time, then the *gṛhastha* may do so; otherwise, if the spiritual master orders against it, the *gṛhastha* should abstain. The *gṛhastha* must obtain permission from the spiritual master to observe the ritualistic ceremony of *garbhādhāna-saṁskāra.* Then he may approach his wife to beget children, otherwise not. A *brāhmaṇa* generally remains a *brahmacārī* throughout his entire life, but although some *brāhmaṇas* become *gṛhasthas* and indulge in sex life, they do so under the complete control of the spiritual master. The *kṣatriya* is allowed to marry more than one wife, but this also must be in accordance with the instructions of the spiritual master. It is not that because one is a *gṛhastha* he may marry as many times as he likes and indulge in sex life as he likes. This is not spiritual life. In spiritual life, one must conduct one's whole life under the guidance of the *guru.* Only one who executes his spiritual life under the direction of the spiritual master can achieve the mercy of Kṛṣṇa. *Yasya prasādād bhagavat-prasādaḥ.* If one desires to advance in spiritual life but he acts whimsically, not following the orders of the spiritual master, he has no shelter. *Yasyāprasādān na gatiḥ kuto 'pi.*

Without the spiritual master's order, even the *gṛhastha* should not indulge in sex life.

TEXT 12

अञ्जनाभ्यञ्जनोन्मर्दस्त्र्यवलेखामिषं मधु ।
स्रग्गन्धलेपालंकारांस्त्यजेयुर्ये बृहद्व्रताः ॥१२॥

añjanābhyañjanonmarda-
stry-avalekhāmiṣaṁ madhu
srag-gandha-lepālankārāṁs
tyajeyur ye bṛhad-vratāḥ

añjana—ointment or powder for decorating the eyes; *abhyañjana*—massaging the head; *unmarda*—massaging the body; *strī-avalekha*—to glance over a woman or to paint a woman's picture; *āmiṣam*—meat-eating; *madhu*—drinking liquor or honey; *srak*—decorating the body with garlands of flowers; *gandha-lepa*—smearing the body with scented ointment; *alaṅkārān*—decorating the body with ornaments; *tyajeyuḥ*—must give up; *ye*—those who; *bṛhat-vratāḥ*—have taken the vow of celibacy.

TRANSLATION

Brahmacārīs or gṛhasthas who have taken the vow of celibacy as described above should not indulge in the following: applying powder or ointment to the eyes, massaging the head with oil, massaging the body with the hands, seeing a woman or painting a woman's picture, eating meat, drinking wine, decorating the body with flower garlands, smearing scented ointment on the body, or decorating the body with ornaments. These they should give up.

TEXTS 13–14

उषित्वैवं गुरुकुले द्विजोऽधीत्यावबुध्य च ।
त्रयीं साङ्गोपनिषदं यावदर्थं यथाबलम् ॥१३॥
दत्त्वा वरमनुज्ञातो गुरोः कामं यदीश्वरः ।
गृहं वनं वा प्रविशेत् प्रव्रजेत् तत्र वा वसेत् ॥१४॥

uṣitvaivaṁ guru-kule
dvijo 'dhītyāvabudhya ca
trayīṁ sāṅgopaniṣadaṁ
yāvad-arthaṁ yathā-balam

dattvā varam anujñāto
guroḥ kāmaṁ yadīśvaraḥ
gṛhaṁ vanaṁ vā praviśet
pravrajet tatra vā vaset

uṣitvā—residing; *evam*—in this way; *guru-kule*—under the care of the spiritual master; *dvi-jaḥ*—the twiceborn, namely the *brāhmaṇas, kṣatriyas* and *vaiśyas; adhītya*—studying Vedic literature; *avabudhya*—understanding it properly; *ca*—and; *trayīm*—the Vedic literatures; *sa-aṅga*—along with supplementary parts; *upaniṣadam*—as well as the *Upaniṣads; yāvat-artham*—as far as possible; *yathā-balam*—as far as one can, according to one's ability; *dattvā*—giving; *varam*—remuneration; *anujñātaḥ*—being asked; *guroḥ*—of the spiritual master; *kāmam*—desires; *yadi*—if; *īśvaraḥ*—capable; *gṛham*—household life; *vanam*—retired life; *vā*—either; *praviśet*—one should enter; *pravrajet*—or get out of; *tatra*—there; *vā*—either; *vaset*—should reside.

TRANSLATION

According to the rules and regulations mentioned above, one who is twiceborn, namely a brāhmaṇa, kṣatriya or vaiśya, should reside in the guru-kula under the care of the spiritual master. There he should study and learn all the Vedic literatures along with their supplements and the Upaniṣads, according to his ability and power to study. If possible, the student or disciple should reward the spiritual master with the remuneration the spiritual master requests, and then, following the master's order, the disciple should leave and accept one of the other āśramas, namely the gṛhastha-āśrama, vānaprastha-āśrama or sannyāsa-āśrama, as he desires.

PURPORT

To study the *Vedas* and understand them, of course, requires some special intelligence, but the members of the three higher sections of society—namely the *brāhmaṇas, kṣatriyas* and *vaiśyas*—must learn the Vedic literatures according to their capability and power to understand. In other words, studying the Vedic literatures is compulsory for everyone but the *śūdras* and *antyajas*. The Vedic literature gives the knowledge that can lead one to understand the Absolute Truth—Brahman, Paramātmā or Bhagavān. *Guru-kula*, or the reformatory educational institution, should be used only to understand Vedic knowledge. At the present time there are many educational institutions for training and technology, but such knowledge has nothing to do with understanding of the Absolute Truth. Technology, therefore, is meant for the *śūdras*, whereas the *Vedas* are meant for the *dvijas*. Consequently this verse states, *dvijo 'dhītyāvabudhya ca trayīṁ sāṅgopaniṣadam*. At the present time, in the age of Kali, practically everyone is a *śūdra*, and no one is a *dvija*. Therefore the condition of society has very much deteriorated.

Another point to be observed from this verse is that from the *brahmacārī-āśrama* one may accept the *sannyāsa-āśrama, vānaprastha-āśrama* or *gṛhastha-āśrama*. It is not compulsory for a *brahmacārī* to become a *gṛhastha*. Because the ultimate aim is to understand the Absolute Truth, there is no necessity of going through all the different *āśramas*. Thus one may proceed to the *sannyāsa-āśrama* directly from the *brahmacārī-āśrama*. Śrīla Bhaktisiddhānta Sarasvatī Ṭhākura accepted the *sannyāsa-āśrama* directly from the *brahmacārī-āśrama*. In other words, His Divine Grace Bhaktisiddhānta Sarasvatī Ṭhākura did not think it compulsory to accept the *gṛhastha-āśrama* or *vānaprastha-āśrama*.

TEXT 15

अग्नौ गुरावात्मनि च सर्वभूतेष्वधोक्षजम् ।
भूतैः स्वधामभिः पश्येदप्रविष्टं प्रविष्टवत् ॥१५॥

agnau gurāv ātmani ca
sarva-bhūteṣv adhokṣajam
bhūtaiḥ sva-dhāmabhiḥ paśyed
apraviṣṭaṁ praviṣṭavat

agnau—in the fire; *gurau*—in the spiritual master; *ātmani*—in one's self; *ca*—also; *sarva-bhūteṣu*—in every living entity; *adhokṣajam*—the

Supreme Personality of Godhead, who cannot be seen or perceived with the material eyes or other material senses; *bhūtaiḥ*—with all living entities; *sva-dhāmabhiḥ*—along with His Lordship's paraphernalia; *paśyet*—one should see; *apraviṣṭam*—not entered; *praviṣṭa-vat*—also entered.

TRANSLATION

One should realize that in the fire, in the spiritual master, in one's self and in all living entities—in all circumstances and conditions—the Supreme Personality of Godhead, Viṣṇu, has simultaneously entered and not entered. He is situated externally and internally as the full controller of everything.

PURPORT

Realization of the Supreme Personality of Godhead's omnipresence is the perfect realization of the Absolute Truth to be attained through the study of the Vedic literatures. As stated in the *Brahma-saṁhitā* (5.35), *aṇḍāntara-stha-paramāṇu-cayāntara-stham:* the Lord is situated within the universe, within the heart of every living entity and also within the atom. We should understand that whenever the Supreme Personality of Godhead is present, He is present with all His paraphernalia, including His name, form, associates and servants. The living entity is part and parcel of the Supreme Personality of Godhead, and thus one should understand that since the Supreme Lord has entered the atom, the living entities are also there. One must accept the inconceivable quality of the Supreme Personality of Godhead, for no one can understand from the material point of view how the Lord is all-pervasive and yet is situated in His own abode, Goloka Vṛndāvana. This realization is possible if one strictly follows the regulative principles of *āśrama* (*brahmacārī, gṛhastha, vānaprastha* and *sannyāsa*). Śrīla Madhvācārya says in this regard:

apraviṣṭaḥ sarva-gataḥ
praviṣṭas tv anurūpavān
evaṁ dvi-rūpo bhagavān
harir eko janārdanaḥ

The Supreme Personality of Godhead, in His original form, has not entered everything (*apraviṣṭaḥ*), but in His impersonal form He has entered (*praviṣṭaḥ*). Thus He has entered and not entered simultaneously. This is also explained in *Bhagavad-gītā* (9.4), wherein the Lord says:

mayā tatam idaṁ sarvaṁ
jagad avyakta-mūrtinā
mat-sthāni sarva-bhūtāni
na cāhaṁ teṣv avasthitaḥ

"By Me, in My unmanifested form, this entire universe is pervaded. All beings are in Me, but I am not in them." The Lord can defy Himself. Thus there is variety in unity (*ekatvaṁ bahutvam*).

TEXT 16

एवंविधो ब्रह्मचारी वानप्रस्थो यतिर्गृही ।
चरन्विदितविज्ञानः परं ब्रह्माधिगच्छति ॥१६॥

evaṁ vidho brahmacārī
vānaprastho yatir gṛhī
caran vidita-vijñānaḥ
paraṁ brahmādhigacchati

evam vidhaḥ—in this way; *brahmacārī*—whether one is a *brahmacārī; vānaprasthaḥ*—or one is in the *vānaprastha-āśrama; yatiḥ*—or in the *sannyāsa-āśrama; gṛhī*—or in the *gṛhastha-āśrama; caran*—by practice of self-realization and understanding of the Absolute Truth; *vidita-vijñānaḥ*—fully conversant with the science of the Absolute Truth; *param*—the Supreme; *brahma*—the Absolute Truth; *adhigacchati*—one can understand.

TRANSLATION

By practicing in this way, whether one be in the brahmacārī-āśrama, gṛhastha-āśrama, vānaprastha-āśrama or sannyāsa-āśrama, one must always realize the all-pervading presence of the Supreme

Lord, for in this way it is possible to understand the Absolute Truth.

PURPORT

This is the beginning of self-realization. One must first understand how Brahman is present everywhere and how He is acting. This education is called *brahma-jijñāsā* and is the real concern of human life. Without such knowledge, one cannot claim to be a human being; rather, he remains in the animal kingdom. As it is said, *sa eva go-kharaḥ:* without such knowledge, one is no better than a cow or an ass.

TEXT 17

वानप्रस्थस्य वक्ष्यामि नियमान्मुनिसम्मतान् ।
यानास्थाय मुनिर्गच्छेदृषिलोकमुहाञ्जसा ॥१७॥

vānaprasthasya vakṣyāmi
niyamān muni-sammatān
yān āsthāya munir gacched
ṛṣi-lokam uhāñjasā

vānaprasthasya—of a person in the *vānaprastha-āśrama* (retired life); *vakṣyāmi*—I shall now explain; *niyamān*—the rules and regulations; *muni-sammatān*—which are recognized by great *munis*, philosophers and saintly persons; *yān*—which; *āsthāya*—being situated in, or practicing; *muniḥ*—a saintly person; *gacchet*—is promoted; *ṛṣi-lokam*—to the planetary system where the seers and *munis* go (Maharloka); *uha*—O King; *añjasā*—without difficulty.

TRANSLATION

O King, I shall now describe the qualifications for a vānaprastha, one who has retired from family life. By rigidly following the rules and regulations for the vānaprastha, one can easily be elevated to the upper planetary system known as Maharloka.

TEXT 18

न कृष्टपच्यमश्नीयादकृष्टं चाप्यकालतः ।
अग्निपक्वमथामं वा अर्कपक्वमुताहरेत् ॥१८॥

na kṛṣṭa-pacyam aśnīyād
akṛṣṭaṁ cāpy akālataḥ
agni-pakvam athāmaṁ vā
arka-pakvam utāharet

na—not; *kṛṣṭa-pacyam*—grains grown by tilling of the field; *aśnīyāt*—one should eat; *akṛṣṭam*—grains that have grown without tilling of the field; *ca*—and; *api*—also; *akālataḥ*—ripened untimely; *agni-pakvam*—grains prepared by being cooked in fire; *atha*—as well as; *āmam*—mango; *vā*—either; *arka-pakvam*—food ripened naturally by the sunshine; *uta*—it is so enjoined; *āharet*—the *vānaprastha* should eat.

TRANSLATION

A person in vānaprastha life should not eat grains grown by tilling of the fields. He should also not eat grains that have grown without tilling of the field but are not fully ripe. Nor should a vānaprastha eat grains cooked in fire. Indeed, he should eat only fruit ripened by the sunshine.

TEXT 19

वन्यैश्चरुपुरोडाशान् निर्वपेत् कालचोदितान् ।
लब्धे नवे नवेऽन्नाद्ये पुराणं च परित्यजेत् ॥१९॥

vanyaiś caru-puroḍāśān
nirvapet kāla-coditān
labdhe nave nave 'nnādye
purāṇaṁ ca parityajet

vanyaiḥ—by fruits and grains produced in the forest without cultivation; *caru*—grains to be offered in a fire sacrifice; *puroḍāśān*—the cakes prepared from *caru; nirvapet*—one should execute; *kāla-coditān*—that which has grown naturally; *labdhe*—on obtaining; *nave*—new; *nave anna-ādye*—newly produced food grains; *purāṇam*—the stock of old grains; *ca*—and; *parityajet*—one should give up.

TRANSLATION

A vānaprastha should prepare cakes to be offered in sacrifice from fruits and grains grown naturally in the forest. When he obtains some new grains, he should give up his old stock of grains.

TEXT 20

अग्न्यर्थमेव शरणमुटजं वाद्रिकन्दरम् ।
श्रयेत हिमवाय्वग्निवर्षार्कातपषाट् स्वयम् ॥२०॥

agny-artham eva śaraṇam
uṭajaṁ vādri-kandaram
śrayeta hima-vāyv-agni-
varṣārkātapa-ṣāṭ svayam

agni—the fire; *artham*—to keep; *eva*—only; *śaraṇam*—a cottage; *uṭa-jam*—made of grass; *vā*—or; *adri-kandaram*—a cave in a mountain; *śrayeta*—the *vānaprastha* should take shelter of; *hima*—snow; *vāyu*—wind; *agni*—fire; *varṣa*—rain; *arka*—of the sun; *ātapa*—shining; *ṣāṭ*—enduring; *svayam*—personally.

TRANSLATION

A vānaprastha should prepare a thatched cottage or take shelter of a cave in a mountain only to keep the sacred fire, but he should personally practice enduring snowfall, wind, fire, rain and the shining of the sun.

TEXT 21

केशरोमनखश्मश्रुमलानि जटिलो दधत् ।
कमण्डल्वजिने दण्डवल्कलाग्निपरिच्छदान् ॥२१॥

keśa-roma-nakha-śmaśru-
malāni jaṭilo dadhat
kamaṇḍalv-ajine daṇḍa-
valkalāgni-paricchadān

keśa—hair on the head; *roma*—hair on the body; *nakha*—nails; *śmaśru*—moustache; *malāni*—and dirt on the body; *jaṭilaḥ*—with matted locks of hair; *dadhat*—one should keep; *kamaṇḍalu*—a waterpot; *ajine*—and a deerskin; *daṇḍa*—rod; *valkala*—the bark of a tree; *agni*—fire; *paricchadān*—garments.

TRANSLATION

The vānaprastha should wear matted locks of hair on his head and let his body hair, nails and moustache grow. He should not cleanse his body of dirt. He should keep a waterpot, deerskin and rod, wear the bark of a tree as a covering, and use garments colored like fire.

TEXT 22

चरेद् वने द्वादशाब्दानष्टौ वा चतुरो मुनिः ।
द्वावेकं वा यथा बुद्धिर्न विपद्येत कृच्छ्रतः ॥२२॥

cared vane dvādaśābdān
aṣṭau vā caturo muniḥ
dvāv ekaṁ vā yathā buddhir
na vipadyeta kṛcchrataḥ

caret—should remain; *vane*—in the forest; *dvādaśa-abdān*—twelve years; *aṣṭau*—for eight years; *vā*—either; *caturaḥ*—four years; *muniḥ*—a saintly, thoughtful man; *dvau*—two; *ekam*—one; *vā*—either; *yathā*—as well as; *buddhiḥ*—intelligence; *na*—not; *vipadyeta*—bewildered; *kṛcchrataḥ*—because of hard austerities.

TRANSLATION

Being very thoughtful, a vānaprastha should remain in the forest for twelve years, eight years, four years, two years or at least one year. He should behave in such a way that he will not be disturbed or troubled by too much austerity.

TEXT 23

यदाकल्पः स्वक्रियायां व्याधिभिर्जरयाथवा ।
आन्वीक्षिक्यां वा विद्यायां कुर्यादनशनादिकम् ॥२३॥

yadākalpaḥ sva-kriyāyāṁ
vyādhibhir jarayāthavā
ānvīkṣikyāṁ vā vidyāyāṁ
kuryād anaśanādikam

yadā—when; *akalpaḥ*—unable to act; *sva-kriyāyām*—in one's own prescribed duties; *vyādhibhiḥ*—because of disease; *jarayā*—or because of old age; *athavā*—either; *ānvīkṣikyām*—in spiritual advancement; *vā*—or; *vidyāyām*—in the advancement of knowledge; *kuryāt*—one must do; *anaśana-ādikam*—not take sufficient food.

TRANSLATION

When because of disease or old age one is unable to perform his prescribed duties for advancement in spiritual consciousness or study of the Vedas, he should practice fasting, not taking any food.

TEXT 24

आत्मन्यग्नीन् समारोप्य संन्यस्याहंममात्मताम् ।
कारणेषु न्यसेत् सम्यक् संघातं तु यथार्हतः ॥२४॥

ātmany agnīn samāropya
sannyasyāhaṁ mamātmatām
kāraṇeṣu nyaset samyak
saṅghātaṁ tu yathārhataḥ

ātmani—in one's self; *agnīn*—the fire elements within the body; *samāropya*—properly placing; *sannyasya*—giving up; *aham*—false identity; *mama*—false conception; *ātmatām*—of the body's being one's self or one's own; *kāraṇeṣu*—in the five elements that cause the material body; *nyaset*—one should merge; *samyak*—completely; *saṅghātam*—combination; *tu*—but; *yathā-arhataḥ*—as it befits.

TRANSLATION

He should properly place the fire element in his own self and in this way give up bodily affinity, by which one thinks the body to be

one's self or one's own. One should gradually merge the material body into the five elements [earth, water, fire, air and sky].

PURPORT

The body is an effect of a cause, namely the five material elements (earth, water, fire, air and sky). In other words, one should know perfectly well that the material body is nothing but a combination of the five elements. This knowledge constitutes merging of the material body and the five material elements. Merging into Brahman in perfect knowledge means understanding perfectly that one is not the body but a spiritual soul.

TEXT 25

खे खानि वायौ निश्वासांस्तेजःसूष्माणमात्मवान् ।
अप्स्वसृक्श्लेष्मपूयानि क्षितौ शेषं यथोद्भवम् ॥२५॥

khe khāni vāyau niśvāsāṁs
tejaḥsūṣmāṇam ātmavān
apsv asṛk-śleṣma-pūyāni
kṣitau śeṣaṁ yathodbhavam

khe—in the sky; *khāni*—all the holes of the body; *vāyau*—in the air; *niśvāsān*—all the different airs moving within the body (*prāṇa, apāna,* etc.); *tejaḥsu*—in fire; *uṣmāṇam*—the heat of the body; *ātma-vān*—a person who knows the self; *apsu*—in water; *asṛk*—blood; *śleṣma*—mucus; *pūyāni*—and urine; *kṣitau*—in the earth; *śeṣam*—the remaining (namely skin, bones and the other hard things in the body); *yathā-udbhavam*—wherefrom all of them grew.

TRANSLATION

A sober, self-realized person who has full knowledge should merge the various parts of the body in their original sources. The holes in the body are caused by the sky, the process of breathing is caused by the air, the heat of the body is caused by fire, and semen, blood and mucus are caused by water. The hard substances, like skin, muscle and bone, are caused by earth. In this way all the

constituents of the body are caused by various elements, and they should be merged again into those elements.

PURPORT

To be self-realized, one must understand the original sources of the various elements of the body. The body is a combination of skin, bone, muscle, blood, semen, urine, stool, heat, breath and so on, which all come from earth, water, fire, air and sky. One must be well conversant with the sources of all the bodily constituents. Then one becomes a self-realized person, or *ātmavān*, one who knows the self.

TEXTS 26–28

वाचमग्नौ सवक्तव्यामिन्द्रे शिल्पं करावपि ।
पदानि गत्या वयसि रत्योपस्थं प्रजापतौ ॥२६॥
मृत्यौ पायुं विसर्गं च यथास्थानं विनिर्दिशेत् ।
दिक्षु श्रोत्रं सनादेन स्पर्शेनाध्यात्मनि त्वचम् ॥२७॥
रूपाणि चक्षुषा राजन् ज्योतिष्यभिनिवेशयेत् ।
अप्सु प्रचेतसा जिह्वां घ्रेयैर्घ्राणं क्षितौ न्यसेत् ॥२८॥

vācam agnau savaktavyām
indre śilpaṁ karāv api
padāni gatyā vayasi
ratyopasthaṁ prajāpatau

mṛtyau pāyuṁ visargaṁ ca
yathā-sthānaṁ vinirdiśet
dikṣu śrotraṁ sa-nādena
sparśenādhyātmani tvacam

rūpāṇi cakṣuṣā rājan
jyotiṣy abhiniveśayet
apsu pracetasā jihvāṁ
ghreyair ghrāṇaṁ kṣitau nyaset

vācam—speech; *agnau*—in the fire-god (the personified god controlling fire); *sa-vaktavyām*—with the subject matter of speaking; *indre*—

unto King Indra; *śilpam*—craftsmanship or the capacity to work with the hands; *karau*—as well as the hands; *api*—indeed; *padāni*—the legs; *gatyā*—with the power to move; *vayasi*—unto Lord Viṣṇu; *ratyā*—sexual desire; *upastham*—with the genitals; *prajāpatau*—unto Prajāpati; *mṛtyau*—unto the demigod known as Mṛtyu; *pāyum*—the rectum; *visargam*—with its activity, evacuation; *ca*—also; *yathā-sthānam*—in the proper place; *vinirdiśet*—one should indicate; *dikṣu*—unto different directions; *śrotram*—the aural sense; *sa-nādena*—with sound vibration; *sparśena*—with touch; *adhyātmani*—unto the wind-god; *tvacam*—the sense of touch; *rūpāṇi*—form; *cakṣuṣā*—with eyesight; *rājan*—O King; *jyotiṣi*—in the sun; *abhiniveśayet*—one should endow; *apsu*—unto water; *pracetasā*—with the demigod known as Varuṇa; *jihvām*—the tongue; *ghreyaiḥ*—with the object of smell; *ghrāṇam*—the power to smell; *kṣitau*—in the earth; *nyaset*—one should give.

TRANSLATION

Thereafter, the object of speech, along with the sense of speech [the tongue], should be bestowed upon fire. Craftsmanship and the two hands should be given to the demigod Indra. The power of movement and the legs should be given to Lord Viṣṇu. Sensual pleasure, along with the genitals, should be bestowed upon Prajāpati. The rectum, with the power of evacuation, should be bestowed, in its proper place, unto Mṛtyu. The aural instrument, along with sound vibration, should be given to the deities presiding over the directions. The instrument of touch, along with the sense objects of touch, should be given to Vāyu. Form, with the power of sight, should be bestowed upon the sun. The tongue, along with the demigod Varuṇa, should be bestowed upon water, and the power of smell, along with the two Aśvinī-kumāra demigods, should be bestowed upon the earth.

TEXTS 29–30

मनो मनोरथैश्चन्द्रे बुद्धिं बोध्यैः कवौ परे ।
कर्माण्यध्यात्मना रुद्रे यदहंममताक्रिया ।
सत्त्वेन चित्तं क्षेत्रज्ञे गुणैर्वैकारिकं परे ॥२९॥

अप्सु क्षितिमपो ज्योतिष्यदो वायौ नभस्यमुम् ।
कूटस्थे तच्च महति तदव्यक्तेऽक्षरे च तत् ॥३०॥

mano manorathaiś candre
buddhiṁ bodhyaiḥ kavau pare
karmāṇy adhyātmanā rudre
yad-ahaṁ mamatā-kriyā
sattvena cittaṁ kṣetra-jñe
guṇair vaikārikaṁ pare

apsu kṣitim apo jyotiṣy
ado vāyau nabhasy amum
kūṭasthe tac ca mahati
tad avyakte 'kṣare ca tat

manaḥ—the mind; *manorathaiḥ*—along with material desires; *candre*—unto Candra, the mood demigod; *buddhim*—intelligence; *bodhyaiḥ*—with the subject matter of intelligence; *kavau pare*—unto the supreme learned person, Lord Brahmā; *karmāṇi*—material activities; *adhyātmanā*—with false ego; *rudre*—unto Lord Śiva (Rudra); *yat*—wherein; *aham*—I am the material body; *mamatā*—everything belonging to the material body is mine; *kriyā*—such activities; *sattvena*—along with the existential conception; *cittam*—consciousness; *kṣetra-jñe*—unto the individual soul; *guṇaiḥ*—along with the material activities conducted by the material qualities; *vaikārikam*—the living entities under the influence of the material modes; *pare*—in the Supreme Being; *apsu*—in the water; *kṣitim*—the earth; *apaḥ*—the water; *jyotiṣi*—in the luminaries, specifically in the sun; *adaḥ*—brightness; *vāyau*—in the air; *nabhasi*—in the sky; *amum*—that; *kūṭasthe*—in the materialistic conception of life; *tat*—that; *ca*—also; *mahati*—in the *mahat-tattva*, the total material energy; *tat*—that; *avyakte*—in the nonmanifested; *akṣare*—in the Supersoul; *ca*—also; *tat*—that.

TRANSLATION

The mind, along with all material desires, should be merged in the moon demigod. All the subject matters of intelligence, along with the intelligence itself, should be placed in Lord Brahmā. False

ego, which is under the influence of the material modes of nature and which induces one to think, "I am this body, and everything connected with this body is mine," should be merged, along with material activities, in Rudra, the predominating deity of false ego. Material consciousness, along with the goal of thought, should be merged in the individual living being, and the demigods acting under the modes of material nature should be merged, along with the perverted living being, into the Supreme Being. The earth should be merged in water, water in the brightness of the sun, this brightness into the air, the air into the sky, the sky into the false ego, the false ego into the total material energy, the total material energy into the unmanifested ingredients [the pradhāna feature of the material energy], and at last the ingredient feature of material manifestation into the Supersoul.

TEXT 31

इत्यक्षरतयात्मानं चिन्मात्रमवशेषितम् ।
ज्ञात्वाद्वयोऽथ विरमेद् दग्धयोनिरिवानलः ॥३१॥

ity akṣaratayātmānaṁ
cin-mātram avaśeṣitam
jñātvādvayo 'tha viramed
dagdha-yonir ivānalaḥ

iti—thus; *akṣaratayā*—because of being spiritual; *ātmānam*—oneself (the individual soul); *cit-mātram*—completely spiritual; *avaśeṣitam*—the remaining balance (after the material elements are merged, one after another, into the original Supersoul); *jñātvā*—understanding; *advayaḥ*—without differentiation, or of the same quality as the Paramātmā; *atha*—thus; *viramet*—one should cease from material existence; *dagdha-yoniḥ*—whose source (the wood) has burnt up; *iva*—like; *analaḥ*—flames.

TRANSLATION

When all the material designations have thus merged into their respective material elements, the living beings, who are all ultimately completely spiritual, being one in quality with the

Supreme Being, should cease from material existence, as flames cease when the wood in which they are burning is consumed. When the material body is returned to its various material elements, only the spiritual being remains. This spiritual being is Brahman and is equal in quality with Parabrahman.

Thus end the Bhaktivedanta purports of the Seventh Canto, Twelfth Chapter, of the Śrīmad-Bhāgavatam, *entitled "The Perfect Society: Four Spiritual Classes."*

CHAPTER THIRTEEN

The Behavior of a Perfect Person

This Thirteenth Chapter describes the regulative principles for *sannyāsīs* and also describes the history of an *avadhūta.* It concludes with a description of perfection for the student in spiritual advancement.

Śrī Nārada Muni has been describing the symptoms of various *āśramas* and *varṇas.* Now, in this chapter, he specifically describes the regulative principles to be followed by *sannyāsīs.* After retiring from family life, one should accept the status of *vānaprastha,* in which he must formally accept the body as his means of existence but gradually forget the bodily necessities of life. After *vānaprastha* life, having left home, one should travel to different places as a *sannyāsī.* Without bodily comforts and free from dependence on anyone with respect to bodily necessities, one should travel everywhere, wearing almost nothing or actually walking naked. Without association with ordinary human society, one should beg alms and always be satisfied in himself. One should be a friend to every living entity and be very peaceful in Kṛṣṇa consciousness. A *sannyāsī* should travel alone in this way, not caring for life or death, waiting for the time when he will leave his material body. He should not indulge in unnecessary books or adopt professions like astrology, nor should he try to become a great orator. He should also give up the path of unnecessary argument and should not depend on anyone under any circumstances. He should not try to allure people into becoming his disciples just so that the number of his disciples may increase. He should give up the habit of reading many books as a means of livelihood, and he should not attempt to increase the number of temples and *maṭhas,* or monasteries. When a *sannyāsī* thus becomes completely independent, peaceful and equipoised, he can select the destination he desires after death and follow the principles by which to reach that destination. Although fully learned, he should always remain silent, like a dumb person, and travel like a restless child.

In this regard, Nārada Muni described a meeting between Prahlāda and a saintly person who had adopted the mode of life of a python. In this way he described the symptoms of a *paramahaṁsa.* A person who has attained the *paramahaṁsa* stage knows very well the distinction between matter and spirit. He is not at all interested in gratifying the material senses, for he is always deriving pleasure from devotional service to the Lord. He is not very anxious to protect his material body. Being satisfied with whatever he attains by the grace of the Lord, he is completely independent of material happiness and distress, and thus he is transcendental to all regulative principles. Sometimes he accepts severe austerities, and sometimes he accepts material opulence. His only concern is to satisfy Kṛṣṇa, and for that purpose he can do anything and everything, without reference to the regulative principles. He is never to be equated with materialistic men, nor is he subject to the judgments of such men.

TEXT 1

श्रीनारद उवाच

कल्पस्त्वेवं परिव्रज्य देहमात्रावशेषितः ।
ग्रामैकरात्रविधिना निरपेक्षश्चरेन्महीम् ॥ १ ॥

śrī-nārada uvāca
kalpas tv evaṁ parivrajya
deha-mātrāvaśeṣitaḥ
grāmaika-rātra-vidhinā
nirapekṣaś caren mahīm

śrī-nāradaḥ uvāca—Śrī Nārada Muni said; *kalpaḥ*—a person who is competent to undergo the austerities of *sannyāsa,* the renounced order of life, or to prosecute studies in transcendental knowledge; *tu*—but; *evam*—in this way (as described previously); *parivrajya*—fully understanding his spiritual identity and thus traveling from one place to another; *deha-mātra*—keeping only the body; *avaśeṣitaḥ*—at last; *grāma*—in a village; *eka*—one only; *rātra*—of passing a night; *vidhinā*—in the process; *nirapekṣaḥ*—without dependence on any material thing; *caret*—should move from one place to another; *mahīm*—on the earth.

TRANSLATION

Śrī Nārada Muni said: A person able to cultivate spiritual knowledge should renounce all material connections, and merely keeping the body inhabitable, he should travel from one place to another, passing only one night in each village. In this way, without dependence in regard to the needs of the body, the sannyāsī should travel all over the world.

TEXT 2

बिभृयाद्‌ यद्यसौ वासः कौपीनाच्छादनं परम्‌ ।
त्यक्तं न लिङ्गाद्‌ दण्डादेरन्यत्‌ किञ्चिदनापदि ॥ २ ॥

bibhṛyād yady asau vāsaḥ
kaupīnācchādanaṁ param
tyaktaṁ na liṅgād daṇḍāder
anyat kiñcid anāpadi

bibhṛyāt—one should use; *yadi*—if; *asau*—a person in the renounced order; *vāsaḥ*—a garment or covering; *kaupīna*—a loincloth (just to cover the private parts); *ācchādanam*—for covering; *param*—that much only; *tyaktam*—given up; *na*—not; *liṅgāt*—than the distinguishing marks of a *sannyāsī; daṇḍa-ādeḥ*—like the rod (*tridaṇḍa*); *anyat*—other; *kiñcit*—anything; *anāpadi*—in ordinary undisturbed times.

TRANSLATION

A person in the renounced order of life may try to avoid even a dress to cover himself. If he wears anything at all, it should be only a loincloth, and when there is no necessity, a sannyāsī should not even accept a daṇḍa. A sannyāsī should avoid carrying anything but a daṇḍa and kamaṇḍalu.

TEXT 3

एक एव चरेद्‌ भिक्षुरात्मारामोऽनपाश्रयः ।
सर्वभूतसुहृच्छान्तो नारायणपरायणः ॥ ३ ॥

eka eva cared bhikṣur
ātmārāmo 'napāśrayaḥ
sarva-bhūta-suhṛc-chānto
nārāyaṇa-parāyaṇaḥ

ekaḥ—alone; *eva*—only; *caret*—can move; *bhikṣuḥ*—a *sannyāsī* taking alms; *ātma-ārāmaḥ*—fully satisfied in the self; *anapāśrayaḥ*—without depending on anything; *sarva-bhūta-suhṛt*—becoming a well-wisher of all living entities; *śāntaḥ*—completely peaceful; *nārāyaṇa-parāyaṇaḥ*—becoming absolutely dependent on Nārāyaṇa and becoming His devotee.

TRANSLATION

The sannyāsī, completely satisfied in the self, should live on alms begged from door to door. Not being dependent on any person or any place, he should always be a friendly well-wisher to all living beings and be a peaceful, unalloyed devotee of Nārāyaṇa. In this way he should move from one place to another.

TEXT 4

पश्येदात्मन्यदो विश्वं परे सदसतोऽव्यये ।
आत्मानं च परं ब्रह्म सर्वत्र सदसन्मये ॥ ४ ॥

paśyed ātmany ado viśvaṁ
pare sad-asato 'vyaye
ātmānaṁ ca paraṁ brahma
sarvatra sad-asan-maye

paśyet—one should see; *ātmani*—in the Supreme Soul; *adaḥ*—this; *viśvam*—universe; *pare*—beyond; *sat-asataḥ*—the creation or cause of creation; *avyaye*—in the Absolute, which is free from deterioration; *ātmānam*—himself; *ca*—also; *param*—the supreme; *brahma*—absolute; *sarvatra*—everywhere; *sat-asat*—in the cause and in the effect; *maye*—all-pervading.

TRANSLATION

The sannyāsī should always try to see the Supreme pervading everything and see everything, including this universe, resting on the Supreme.

TEXT 5

सुप्तिप्रबोधयोः सन्धावात्मनो गतिमात्मदृक् ।
पश्यन्बन्धं च मोक्षं च मायामात्रं न वस्तुतः ॥ ५ ॥

supti-prabodhayoḥ sandhāv
ātmano gatim ātma-dṛk
paśyan bandhaṁ ca mokṣaṁ ca
māyā-mātraṁ na vastutaḥ

supti—in the state of unconsciousness; *prabodhayoḥ*—and in the state of consciousness; *sandhau*—in the state of marginal existence; *ātmanaḥ*—of oneself; *gatim*—the movement; *ātma-dṛk*—one who can actually see the self; *paśyan*—always trying to see or understand; *bandham*—the conditional state of life; *ca*—and; *mokṣam*—the liberated state of life; *ca*—also; *māyā-mātram*—only illusion; *na*—not; *vastutaḥ*—in fact.

TRANSLATION

During unconsciousness and consciousness, and between the two, he should try to understand the self and be fully situated in the self. In this way, he should realize that the conditional and liberated stages of life are only illusory and not actually factual. With such a higher understanding, he should see only the Absolute Truth pervading everything.

PURPORT

The unconscious state is nothing but ignorance, darkness or material existence, and in the conscious state one is awake. The marginal state, between consciousness and unconsciousness, has no permanent existence. Therefore one who is advanced in understanding the self should understand that unconsciousness and consciousness are but illusions, for they fundamentally do not exist. Only the Supreme Absolute Truth exists. As confirmed by the Lord in *Bhagavad-gītā* (9.4):

mayā tatam idaṁ sarvaṁ
jagad avyakta-mūrtinā

mat-sthāni sarva-bhūtāni
na cāhaṁ teṣv avasthitaḥ

"By Me, in My unmanifested form, this entire universe is pervaded. All beings are in Me, but I am not in them." Everything exists on the basis of Kṛṣṇa's impersonal feature; nothing can exist without Kṛṣṇa. Therefore the advanced devotee of Kṛṣṇa can see the Lord everywhere, without illusion.

TEXT 6

नाभिनन्देद् ध्रुवं मृत्युमध्रुवं वास्य जीवितम् ।
कालं परं प्रतीक्षेत भूतानां प्रभवाप्ययम् ॥ ६ ॥

nābhinanded dhruvaṁ mṛtyum
adhruvaṁ vāsya jīvitam
kālaṁ paraṁ pratīkṣeta
bhūtānāṁ prabhavāpyayam

na—not; *abhinandet*—one should praise; *dhruvam*—sure; *mṛtyum*—death; *adhruvam*—not sure; *vā*—either; *asya*—of this body; *jīvitam*—the duration of life; *kālam*—eternal time; *param*—supreme; *pratīkṣeta*—one must observe; *bhūtānām*—of the living entities; *prabhava*—manifestation; *apyayam*—disappearance.

TRANSLATION

Since the material body is sure to be vanquished and the duration of one's life is not fixed, neither death nor life is to be praised. Rather, one should observe the eternal time factor, in which the living entity manifests himself and disappears.

PURPORT

The living entities in the material world, not only at the present but also in the past, have been involved in trying to solve the problem of birth and death. Some stress death and point to the illusory existence of everything material, whereas others stress life, trying to preserve it perpetually and enjoy it to the best of their ability. Both of them are fools and rascals. It is advised that one observe the eternal time factor, which is the cause of the material body's appearance and disappearance, and that one observe the living entity's entanglement in this time factor. Śrīla Bhaktivinoda Ṭhākura therefore sings in his *Gītāvalī:*

anādi karama-phale, padi 'bhavārṇava-jale,
taribāre nā dekhi upāya

One should observe the activities of eternal time, which is the cause of birth and death. Before the creation of the present millennium, the living entities were under the influence of the time factor, and within the time factor the material world comes into existence and is again annihilated. *Bhūtvā bhūtvā pralīyate.* Being under the control of the time factor, the living entities appear and die, life after life. This time factor is the impersonal representation of the Supreme Personality of Godhead, who gives the living entities conditioned by material nature a chance to emerge from this nature by surrendering to Him.

TEXT 7

नासच्छास्त्रेषु सज्जेत नोपजीवेत जीविकाम् ।
वादवादांस्त्यजेत् तर्कान्पक्षं कं च न संश्रयेत् ॥ ७ ॥

nāsac-chāstreṣu sajjeta
nopajīveta jīvikām
vāda-vādāṁs tyajet tarkān
pakṣaṁ kaṁca na saṁśrayet

na—not; *asat-śāstreṣu*—literature like newspapers, novels, dramas and fiction; *sajjeta*—one should be attached or should indulge in reading; *na*—nor; *upajīveta*—one should try to live; *jīvikām*—upon some professional literary career; *vāda-vādān*—unnecessary arguments on different aspects of philosophy; *tyajet*—one should give up; *tarkān*—arguments and counterarguments; *pakṣam*—faction; *kaṁca*—any; *na*—not; *saṁśrayet*—should take shelter of.

TRANSLATION

Literature that is a useless waste of time—in other words, literature without spiritual benefit—should be rejected. One should not become a professional teacher as a means of earning one's livelihood, nor should one indulge in arguments and counterarguments. Nor should one take shelter of any cause or faction.

PURPORT

A person desiring to advance in spiritual understanding should be extremely careful to avoid reading ordinary literature. The world is full of ordinary literature that creates unnecessary agitation in the mind. Such literature, including newspapers, dramas, novels and magazines, is factually not meant for advancement in spiritual knowledge. Indeed, it has been described as a place of enjoyment for crows (*tad vāyasaṁ tīrtham*). Anyone advancing in spiritual knowledge must reject such literature. Furthermore, one should not concern oneself with the conclusions of various logicians or philosophers. Of course, those who preach sometimes need to argue with the contentions of opponents, but as much as possible one should avoid an argumentative attitude. In this connection, Śrīla Madhvācārya says:

aprayojana-pakṣaṁ na saṁśrayet
nāprayojana-pakṣī syān
na vṛthā śiṣya-bandha-kṛt
na codāsīnaḥ śāstrāṇi
na viruddhāni cābhyaset

na vyākhyayopajīveta
na niṣiddhān samācaret
evam-bhūto yatir yāti
tad-eka-śaraṇo harim

"There is no need to take shelter of unnecessary literature or concern oneself with many so-called philosophers and thinkers who are useless for spiritual advancement. Nor should one accept a disciple for the sake of fashion or popularity. One should be callous to these so-called *śāstras*, neither opposing nor favoring them, and one should not earn one's livelihood by taking money for explaining *śāstra*. A *sannyāsī* must always be neutral and seek the means to advance in spiritual life, taking full shelter under the lotus feet of the Lord."

TEXT 8

न शिष्याननुबध्नीत ग्रन्थान्नैवाभ्यसेद् बहून् ।
न व्याख्यामुपयुञ्जीत नारम्भानारभेत् क्वचित् ॥८॥

na śiṣyān anubadhnīta
granthān naivābhyased bahūn
na vyākhyām upayuñjīta
nārambhān ārabhet kvacit

na—not; *śiṣyān*—disciples; *anubadhnīta*—one should induce for material benefit; *granthān*—unnecessary literatures; *na*—not; *eva*—certainly; *abhyaset*—should try to understand or cultivate; *bahūn*—many; *na*—nor; *vyākhyām*—discourses; *upayuñjīta*—should make as a means of livelihood; *na*—nor; *ārambhān*—unnecessary opulences; *ārabhet*—should attempt to increase; *kvacit*—at any time.

TRANSLATION

A sannyāsī must not present allurements of material benefits to gather many disciples, nor should he unnecessarily read many books or give discourses as a means of livelihood. He must never attempt to increase material opulences unnecessarily.

PURPORT

So-called *svāmīs* and *yogīs* generally make disciples by alluring them with material benefits. There are many so-called *gurus* who attract disciples by promising to cure their diseases or increase their material opulence by manufacturing gold. These are lucrative allurements for unintelligent men. A *sannyāsī* is prohibited from making disciples through such material allurements. *Sannyāsīs* sometimes indulge in material opulence by unnecessarily constructing many temples and monasteries, but actually such endeavors should be avoided. Temples and monasteries should be constructed for the preaching of spiritual consciousness or Kṛṣṇa consciousness, not to provide free hotels for persons who are useful for neither material nor spiritual purposes. Temples and monasteries should be strictly off limits to worthless clubs of crazy men. In the Kṛṣṇa consciousness movement we welcome everyone who agrees at least to follow the movement's regulative principles—no illicit sex, no intoxication, no meat-eating and no gambling. In the temples and monasteries, gatherings of unnecessary, rejected, lazy fellows should be strictly disallowed. The temples and monasteries should be used exclusively by devotees who are serious about spiritual advancement in Kṛṣṇa consciousness. Śrīla Viśvanātha Cakravartī Ṭhākura explains the word *ārambhān* as meaning *maṭhādi-vyāpārān,* which means "attempts to construct temples and monasteries." The first business of the *sannyāsī* is to preach Kṛṣṇa consciousness, but if, by the grace of Kṛṣṇa, facilities are available, then he may construct temples and monasteries to give shelter to the serious students of Kṛṣṇa consciousness. Otherwise such temples and monasteries are not needed.

TEXT 9

न यतेराश्रमः प्रायो धर्महेतुर्महात्मनः ।
शान्तस्य समचित्तस्य बिभृयादुत वा त्यजेत् ॥ ९ ॥

na yater āśramaḥ prāyo
dharma-hetur mahātmanaḥ
śāntasya sama-cittasya
bibhṛyād uta vā tyajet

na—not; *yateḥ*—of the *sannyāsī; āśramaḥ*—the symbolic dress (with *daṇḍa* and *kamaṇḍalu*); *prāyaḥ*—almost always; *dharma-hetuḥ*—the cause of advancement in spiritual life; *mahā-ātmanaḥ*—who is factually exalted and advanced; *śāntasya*—who is peaceful; *sama-cittasya*—who has attained the stage of being equipoised; *bibhṛyāt*—one may accept (such symbolic signs); *uta*—indeed; *vā*—or; *tyajet*—one may give up.

TRANSLATION

A peaceful, equipoised person who is factually advanced in spiritual consciousness does not need to accept the symbols of a

sannyāsī, such as the tridaṇḍa and kamaṇḍalu. According to necessity, he may sometimes accept those symbols and sometimes reject them.

PURPORT

There are four stages of the renounced order of life—*kuṭīcaka, bahūdaka, parivrājakācārya* and *paramahaṁsa*. Herein, *Śrīmad-Bhāgavatam* considers the *paramahaṁsas* among the *sannyāsīs*. The Māyāvādī impersonalist *sannyāsīs* cannot attain the *paramahaṁsa* stage. This is because of their impersonal conception of the Absolute Truth. *Brahmeti paramātmeti bhagavān iti śabdyate.* The Absolute Truth is perceived in three stages, of which *bhagavān*, or realization of the Supreme Personality of Godhead, is meant for the *paramahaṁsas*. Indeed, *Śrīmad-Bhāgavatam* itself is meant for the *paramahaṁsas* (*paramo nirmatsarāṇāṁ satām*). Unless one is in the *paramahaṁsa* stage, he is not eligible to understand the *Śrīmad-Bhāgavatam*. For *paramahaṁsas*, or *sannyāsīs* in the Vaiṣṇava order, preaching is the first duty. To preach, such *sannyāsīs* may accept the symbols of *sannyāsa*, such as the *daṇḍa* and *kamaṇḍalu*, or sometimes they may not. Generally the Vaiṣṇava *sannyāsīs*, being *paramahaṁsas*, are automatically called *bābājīs*, and they do not carry a *kamaṇḍalu* or *daṇḍa*. Such a *sannyāsī* is free to accept or reject the marks of *sannyāsa*. His only thought is "Where is there an opportunity to spread Kṛṣṇa consciousness?" Sometimes the Kṛṣṇa consciousness movement sends its representative *sannyāsīs* to foreign countries where the *daṇḍa* and *kamaṇḍalu* are not very much appreciated. We send our preachers in ordinary dress to introduce our books and philosophy. Our only concern is to attract people to Kṛṣṇa consciousness. We may do this in the dress of *sannyāsīs* or in the regular dress of gentlemen. Our only concern is to spread interest in Kṛṣṇa consciousness.

TEXT 10

अव्यक्तलिङ्गो व्यक्तार्थो मनीष्युन्मत्तबालवत् ।
कविर्मूकवदात्मानं स दृष्ट्या दर्शयेन्नृणाम् ॥१०॥

avyakta-liṅgo vyaktārtho
manīṣy unmatta-bālavat

kavir mūkavad ātmānaṁ
sa dṛṣṭyā darśayen nṛṇām

avyakta-liṅgaḥ—whose symptoms of *sannyāsa* are unmanifested; *vyakta-arthaḥ*—whose purpose is manifested; *manīṣī*—such a great saintly person; *unmatta*—restless; *bāla-vat*—like a boy; *kaviḥ*—a great poet or orator; *mūka-vat*—like a dumb man; *ātmānam*—himself; *saḥ*—he; *dṛṣṭyā*—by example; *darśayet*—should present; *nṛṇām*—to human society.

TRANSLATION

Although a saintly person may not expose himself to the vision of human society, by his behavior his purpose is disclosed. To human society he should present himself like a restless child, and although he is the greatest thoughtful orator, he should present himself like a dumb man.

PURPORT

A great personality very much advanced in Kṛṣṇa consciousness may not expose himself by the signs of a *sannyāsī.* To cover himself, he may live like a restless child or a dumb person, although he is the greatest orator or poet.

TEXT 11

अत्राप्युदाहरन्तीममितिहासं पुरातनम् ।
प्रह्रादस्य च संवादं मुनेराजगरस्य च ॥११॥

atrāpy udāharantīmam
itihāsaṁ purātanam
prahrādasya ca saṁvādaṁ
muner ājagarasya ca

atra—herein; *api*—although not exposed to common eyes; *udāharanti*—the learned sages recite as an example; *imam*—this; *itihāsam*—historical incident; *purātanam*—very, very old; *prahrādasya*—of Prahlāda Mahārāja; *ca*—also; *saṁvādam*—conversation; *muneḥ*—of the great saintly person; *ājagarasya*—who took the profession of a python; *ca*—also.

TRANSLATION

As a historical example of this, learned sages recite the story of an ancient discussion between Prahlāda Mahārāja and a great saintly person who was feeding himself like a python.

PURPORT

The saintly person met by Prahlāda Mahārāja was undergoing *ājagara-vṛtti*, the living conditions of a python, which does not go anywhere but sits in one place for years and eats whatever is automatically available. Prahlāda Mahārāja, along with his associates, met this great saint and spoke to him as follows.

TEXTS 12–13

तं शयानं धरोपस्थे कावेर्यां सह्यसानुनि ।
रजस्वलैस्तनूदेशैर्निगूढामलतेजसम् ॥१२॥
ददर्श लोकान्विचरन् लोकतत्त्वविवित्सया ।
वृतोऽमात्यैः कतिपयैः प्रह्रादो भगवत्प्रियः ॥१३॥

taṁ śayānaṁ dharopasthe
kāveryāṁ sahya-sānuni
rajas-valais tanū-deśair
nigūḍhāmala-tejasam

dadarśa lokān vicaran
loka-tattva-vivitsayā
vṛto 'mātyaiḥ katipayaiḥ
prahrādo bhagavat-priyaḥ

tam—that (saintly person); *śayānam*—lying down; *dharā-upasthe*—on the ground; *kāveryām*—on the bank of the River Kāverī; *sahya-sānuni*—on a ridge of the mountain known as Sahya; *rajaḥ-valaiḥ*—covered with dust and dirt; *tanū-deśaiḥ*—with all the parts of the body; *nigūḍha*—very grave and deep; *amala*—spotless; *tejasam*—whose spiritual power; *dadarśa*—he saw; *lokān*—to all the different planets; *vicaran*—traveling; *loka-tattva*—the nature of the living beings (especially those who are trying to advance in Kṛṣṇa consciousness); *vivitsayā*—to try to understand; *vṛtaḥ*—surrounded; *amātyaiḥ*—by royal associates; *katipayaiḥ*—a few; *prahrādaḥ*—Mahārāja Prahlāda; *bhagavat-priyaḥ*—who is always very, very dear to the Supreme Personality of Godhead.

TRANSLATION

Prahlāda Mahārāja, the most dear servitor of the Supreme Personality of Godhead, once went out touring the universe with some of his confidential associates just to study the nature of saintly persons. Thus he arrived at the bank of the Kāverī, where there was a mountain known as Sahya. There he found a great saintly person who was lying on the ground, covered with dirt and dust, but who was deeply spiritually advanced.

TEXT 14

कर्मणाकृतिभिर्वाचा लिङ्गैर्वर्णाश्रमादिभिः ।
न विदन्ति जना यं वै सोऽसाविति न वेति च ॥१४॥

karmaṇākṛtibhir vācā
liṅgair varṇāśramādibhiḥ
na vidanti janā yaṁ vai
so 'sāv iti na veti ca

karmaṇā—by activities; *ākṛtibhiḥ*—by bodily features; *vācā*—by words; *liṅgaiḥ*—by symptoms; *varṇa-āśrama*—pertaining to the particular material and spiritual divisions of *varṇa* and *āśrama*; *ādibhiḥ*—and by other symptoms; *na vidanti*—could not understand; *janāḥ*—people in general; *yam*—whom; *vai*—indeed; *saḥ*—whether that person; *asau*—was the same person; *iti*—thus; *na*—not; *vā*—or; *iti*—thus; *ca*—also.

TRANSLATION

Neither by that saintly person's activities, by his bodily features, by his words nor by the symptoms of his varṇāśrama status could

people understand whether he was the same person they had known.

PURPORT

The inhabitants of that particular place on the bank of the Kāverī in the valley of the mountain known as Sahya were unable to understand whether that saint was the same man they had known. It is therefore said, *vaiṣṇavera kriyā mudrā vijñe nā bhujhaya.* A highly advanced Vaiṣṇava lives in such a way that no one can understand what he is or what he was. Nor should attempts be made to understand the past of a Vaiṣṇava. Without asking the saintly person about his previous life, Prahlāda Mahārāja immediately offered him respectful obeisances.

TEXT 15

तं नत्वाभ्यर्च्य विधिवत् पादयोः शिरसा स्पृशन् ।
विवित्सुरिदमप्राक्षीन्महाभागवतोऽसुरः ॥१५॥

taṁ natvābhyarcya vidhivat
pādayoḥ śirasā spṛśan
vivitsur idam aprākṣīn
mahā-bhāgavato 'suraḥ

tam—him (the saintly person); *natvā*—after offering obeisances unto; *abhyarcya*—and worshiping; *vidhi-vat*—in terms of the rules and regulations of etiquette; *pādayoḥ*—the lotus feet of the saintly person; *śirasā*—with the head; *spṛśan*—touching; *vivitsuḥ*—desiring to know about him (the saintly person); *idam*—the following words; *aprākṣīt*—inquired; *mahā-bhāgavataḥ*—the very advanced devotee of the Lord; *asuraḥ*—although born in an *asura* family.

TRANSLATION

The advanced devotee Prahlāda Mahārāja duly worshiped and offered obeisances to the saintly person who had adopted a python's means of livelihood. After thus worshiping the saintly person and touching his own head to the saint's lotus feet, Prahlāda Mahārāja, in order to understand him, inquired very submissively as follows.

TEXTS 16–17

बिभर्षि कायं पीवानं सोद्यमो भोगवान्यथा ॥१६॥
वित्तं चैवोद्यमवतां भोगो वित्तवतामिह ।
भोगिनां खलु देहोऽयं पीवा भवति नान्यथा ॥१७॥

bibharṣi kāyaṁ pīvānaṁ
sodyamo bhogavān yathā

vittaṁ caivodyamavatāṁ
bhogo vittavatām iha
bhogināṁ khalu deho 'yaṁ
pīvā bhavati nānyathā

bibharṣi—you are maintaining; *kāyam*—a body; *pīvānam*—fat; *sa-udyamaḥ*—one who endeavors; *bhogavān*—one who enjoys; *yathā*—as; *vittam*—money; *ca*—also; *eva*—certainly; *udyama-vatām*—of persons always engaged in economic development; *bhogaḥ*—sense gratification; *vitta-vatām*—for persons who possess considerable wealth; *iha*—in this world; *bhoginām*—of the enjoyers, *karmīs; khalu*—indeed; *dehaḥ*—body; *ayam*—this; *pīvā*—very fat; *bhavati*—becomes; *na*—not; *anyathā*—otherwise.

TRANSLATION

Seeing the saintly person to be quite fat, Prahlāda Mahārāja said: My dear sir, you undergo no endeavor to earn your livelihood, but you have a stout body, exactly like that of a materialistic enjoyer. I know that if one is very rich and has nothing to do, he becomes extremely fat by eating and sleeping and performing no work.

PURPORT

Śrīla Bhaktisiddhānta Sarasvatī Ṭhākura did not like his disciples to become very fat in the course of time. He would become very anxious upon seeing his fat disciples becoming *bhogīs*, or enjoyers of the senses. This attitude is herewith confirmed by Prahlāda Mahārāja, who was surprised to see a saintly person adopting *ājagara-vṛtti* and becoming very fat. In the material world also, we generally see that when a man who is poor and skinny gradually endeavors to earn money through business or some other means and he then gets the money, he enjoys the senses to his satisfaction. By enjoying the senses one becomes fat. Therefore in spiritual advancement becoming fat is not at all satisfactory.

TEXT 18

न ते शयानस्य निरुद्यमस्य
ब्रह्मन् नु हार्थो यत एव भोगः ।
अभोगिनोऽयं तव विप्र देहः
पीवा यतस्तद्वद नः क्षमं चेत् ॥१८॥

na te śayānasya nirudyamasya
brahman nu hārtho yata eva bhogaḥ
abhogino 'yaṁ tava vipra dehaḥ
pīvā yatas tad vada naḥ kṣamaṁ cet

na—not; *te*—of you; *śayānasya*—lying down; *nirudyamasya*—without activities; *brahman*—O saintly person; *nu*—indeed; *ha*—it is evident; *arthaḥ*—money; *yataḥ*—from which; *eva*—indeed; *bhogaḥ*—sense enjoyment; *abhoginaḥ*—of one who is not engaged in sense enjoyment; *ayam*—this; *tava*—your; *vipra*—O learned *brāhmaṇa; dehaḥ*—body; *pīvā*—fat; *yataḥ*—how is it; *tat*—that fact; *vada*—kindly tell; *naḥ*—us; *kṣamam*—excuse; *cet*—if I have asked an impudent question.

TRANSLATION

O brāhmaṇa, fully in knowledge of transcendence, you have nothing to do, and therefore you are lying down. It is also understood that you have no money for sense enjoyment. How then has your body become so fat? Under the circumstances, if you do not consider my question impudent, kindly explain how this has happened.

PURPORT

Generally those engaged in spiritual advancement take food only once, either in the afternoon or in the evening. If one takes food only once, naturally he does not become fat. The learned sage, however, was quite fat, and therefore Prahlāda Mahārāja was very much surprised. Because of being experienced in self-realization, a transcendentalist certainly becomes bright-faced. And one who is advanced in self-realization must be considered to possess the body of a *brāhmaṇa.* Because the bright-faced saintly person was lying down and not working and yet was quite fat, Prahlāda Mahārāja was puzzled and wanted to question him about this.

TEXT 19

कविः कल्पो निपुणदृक् चित्रप्रियकथः समः ।
लोकस्य कुर्वतः कर्म शेषे तद्वीक्षितापि वा ॥१९॥

kaviḥ kalpo nipuṇa-dṛk
citra-priya-kathaḥ samaḥ
lokasya kurvataḥ karma
śeṣe tad-vīkṣitāpi vā

kaviḥ—very learned; *kalpaḥ*—expert; *nipuṇa-dṛk*—intelligent; *citra-priya-kathaḥ*—able to speak palatable words that are pleasing to the heart; *samaḥ*—equipoised; *lokasya*—of the people in general; *kurvataḥ*—engaged in; *karma*—fruitive work; *śeṣe*—you lie down; *tat-vīkṣitā*—seeing them all; *api*—although; *vā*—either.

TRANSLATION

Your Honor appears learned, expert and intelligent in every way. You can speak very well, saying things that are pleasing to the heart. You see that people in general are engaged in fruitive activities, yet you are lying here inactive.

PURPORT

Prahlāda Mahārāja studied the bodily features of the saintly person, and through the saint's physiognomy Prahlāda Mahārāja could understand that he was intelligent and expert, although he was lying down and not doing anything. Prahlāda was naturally inquisitive about why he was lying there inactive.

TEXT 20

श्रीनारद उवाच

स इत्थं दैत्यपतिना परिपृष्टो महामुनिः ।
स्मयमानस्तमभ्याह तद्वागमृतयन्त्रितः ॥२०॥

śrī-nārada uvāca
sa itthaṁ daitya-patinā
paripṛṣṭo mahā-muniḥ
smayamānas tam abhyāha
tad-vāg-amṛta-yantritaḥ

śrī-nāradaḥ uvāca—the great saint Nārada Muni said; *saḥ*—that saintly person (lying down); *ittham*—in this way; *daitya-patinā*—by the King of the Daityas (Prahlāda Mahārāja); *paripṛṣṭaḥ*—being sufficiently questioned; *mahā-muniḥ*—the great saintly person; *smayamānaḥ*—smiling; *tam*—unto him (Prahlāda Mahārāja); *abhyāha*—prepared to give answers; *tat-vāk*—of his words; *amṛta-yantritaḥ*—being captivated by the nectar.

TRANSLATION

Nārada Muni continued: When the saintly person was thus questioned by Prahlāda Mahārāja, the King of the Daityas, he was captivated by this shower of nectarean words, and he replied to the inquisitiveness of Prahlāda Mahārāja with a smiling face.

TEXT 21

श्रीब्राह्मण उवाच

वेदेदमसुरश्रेष्ठ भवान् नन्वार्यसम्मतः ।
ईहोपरमयोर्नृणां पदान्यध्यात्मचक्षुषा ॥२१॥

śrī-brāhmaṇa uvāca
vededam asura-śreṣṭha
bhavān nanv ārya-sammataḥ
īhoparamayor nṛṇāṁ
padāny adhyātma-cakṣuṣā

śrī-brāhmaṇaḥ uvāca—the *brāhmaṇa* replied; *veda*—know very well; *idam*—all these things; *asura-śreṣṭha*—O best of the *asuras; bhavān*—you; *nanu*—indeed; *ārya-sammataḥ*—whose activities are approved by civilized men; *īhā*—of inclination; *uparamayoḥ*—of decreasing; *nṛṇām*—of the people in general; *padāni*—different stages; *adhyātma-cakṣuṣā*—by transcendental eyes.

TRANSLATION

The saintly brāhmaṇa said: O best of the asuras, Prahlāda Mahārāja, who are recognized by advanced and civilized men, you are aware of the different stages of life because of your inherent transcendental eyes, with which you can see a man's character and thus know clearly the results of acceptance and rejection of things as they are.

PURPORT

A pure devotee like Prahlāda Mahārāja can understand the minds of others because of his pure vision in devotional service. A devotee like Prahlāda Mahārāja can study another man's character without difficulty.

TEXT 22

यस्य नारायणो देवो भगवान्हृद्गतः सदा ।
भक्त्या केवलयाज्ञानं धुनोति ध्वान्तमर्कवत् ॥२२॥

yasya nārāyaṇo devo
bhagavān hṛd-gataḥ sadā
bhaktyā kevalayājñānaṁ
dhunoti dhvāntam arkavat

yasya—of whom; *nārāyaṇaḥ devaḥ*—the Supreme Personality of Godhead, Nārāyaṇa; *bhagavān*—the Lord; *hṛt-gataḥ*—in the core of the heart; *sadā*—always; *bhaktyā*—by devotional service; *kevalayā*—alone; *ajñānam*—ignorance; *dhunoti*—cleans; *dhvāntam*—darkness; *arkavat*—as the sun.

TRANSLATION

Nārāyaṇa, the Supreme Personality of Godhead, who is full of all opulences, is predominant within the core of your heart be-

cause of your being a pure devotee. He always drives away all the darkness of ignorance, as the sun drives away the darkness of the universe.

PURPORT

The words *bhaktyā kevalayā* indicate that simply by executing devotional service one can become full of all knowledge. Kṛṣṇa is the master of all knowledge (*aiśvaryasya samagrasya vīryasya yaśasaḥ śriyaḥ*). The Lord is situated in everyone's heart (*īśvaraḥ sarva-bhūtānāṁ hṛd-deśe 'rjuna tiṣṭhati*), and when the Lord is pleased with a devotee, the Lord instructs him. Only to the devotees, however, does the Lord give instructions by which to advance further and further in devotional service. To others, the nondevotees, the Lord gives instructions according to the manner of their surrender. The pure devotee is described by the words *bhaktyā kevalayā*. Śrīla Viśvanātha Cakravartī Ṭhākura explains that *bhaktyā kevalayā* means *jñāna-karmādy-amiśrayā*, "unmixed with fruitive activities or speculative knowledge." Simply surrendering at the lotus feet is the cause of all a devotee's enlightenment and awareness.

TEXT 23

तथापि ब्रूमहे प्रश्नांस्तव राजन्यथाश्रुतम् ।
सम्भाषणीयो हि भवानात्मनः शुद्धिमिच्छता ॥२३॥

tathāpi brūmahe praśnāṁs
tava rājan yathā-śrutam
sambhāṣaṇīyo hi bhavān
ātmanaḥ śuddhim icchatā

tathāpi—still; *brūmahe*—I shall answer; *praśnān*—all the questions; *tava*—your; *rājan*—O King; *yathā-śrutam*—as I have learned by hearing from the authorities; *sambhāṣaṇīyaḥ*—fit for being addressed; *hi*—indeed; *bhavān*—you; *ātmanaḥ*—of the self; *śuddhim*—purification; *icchatā*—by one who desires.

TRANSLATION

My dear King, although you know everything, you have posed some questions, which I shall try to answer according to what I

have learned by hearing from authorities. I cannot remain silent in this regard, for a personality like you is just fit to be spoken to by one who desires self-purification.

PURPORT

A saintly person doesn't wish to speak to anyone and everyone, and he is therefore grave and silent. Generally a common man does not need to be advised. Unless one is prepared to take instructions, it is said that a saintly person should not address him, although sometimes, because of great kindness, a saintly person speaks to ordinary men. As for Prahlāda Mahārāja, however, since he was not a common, ordinary man, whatever questions he posed would have to be answered, even by a great and exalted personality. Therefore the saintly *brāhmaṇa* did not remain silent, but began to answer. These answers, however, were not concocted by him. This is indicated by the words *yathā-śrutam*, meaning "as I have heard from the authorities." In the *paramparā* system, when the questions are bona fide the answers are bona fide. No one should attempt to create or manufacture answers. One must refer to the *śāstras* and give answers according to Vedic understanding. The words *yathā-śrutam* refer to Vedic knowledge. The *Vedas* are known as *śruti* because this knowledge is received from authorities. The statements of the *Vedas* are known as *śruti-pramāṇa.* One should quote evidence from the *śruti*—the *Vedas* or Vedic literature—and then one's statements will be correct. Otherwise one's words will proceed from mental concoction.

TEXT 24

तृष्णया भववाहिन्या योग्यैः कामैरपूर्यया ।
कर्माणि कार्यमाणोऽहं नानायोनिषु योजितः ॥२४॥

tṛṣṇayā bhava-vāhinyā
yogyaiḥ kāmair apūryayā
karmāṇi kāryamāṇo 'haṁ
nānā-yoniṣu yojitaḥ

tṛṣṇayā—because of material desires; *bhava-vāhinyā*—under the sway of the material laws of nature; *yogyaiḥ*—as it is befitting;

kāmaiḥ—by material desires; *apūryayā*—without end, one after another; *karmāṇi*—activities; *kāryamāṇaḥ*—constantly being compelled to perform; *aham*—I; *nānā-yoniṣu*—in various forms of life; *yojitaḥ*—engaged in the struggle for existence.

TRANSLATION

Because of insatiable material desires, I was being carried away by the waves of material nature's laws, and thus I was engaging in different activities, struggling for existence in various forms of life.

PURPORT

As long as a living entity wants to fulfill various types of material desire, he must continuously change from one body to accept another. Śrīla Viśvanātha Cakravartī Ṭhākura explains that as a small piece of grass falls in a river and is tossed about with different types of wood and tree branches, the living entity floats in the ocean of material existence and is dashed and tossed amidst material conditions. This is called the struggle for existence. One kind of fruitive activity causes the living being to take one form of body, and because of actions performed in that body, another body is created. One must therefore stop these material activities, and the chance to do so is given in the human form of life. Specifically, our energy to act should be engaged in the service of the Lord, for then materialistic activities will automatically stop. One must fulfill one's desires by surrendering unto the Supreme Lord, for He knows how to fulfill them. Even though one may have material desires, one should therefore engage in the devotional service of the Lord. That will purify one's struggle for existence.

akāmaḥ sarva-kāmo vā
mokṣa-kāma udāra-dhīḥ
tīvreṇa bhakti-yogena
yajeta puruṣaṁ param

"A person who has broader intelligence, whether he be full of all material desire, without any material desire, or desiring liberation, must by all means worship the supreme whole, the Personality of Godhead." (*Bhāg.* 2.3.10)

anyābhilāṣitā-śūnyaṁ
jñāna-karmādy-anāvṛtam
ānukūlyena kṛṣṇānu-
śīlanaṁ bhaktir uttamā

"One should render transcendental loving service to the Supreme Lord Kṛṣṇa favorably and without desire for material profit or gain through fruitive activities or philosophical speculation. That is called pure devotional service." (*Bhakti-rasāmṛta-sindhu* 1.1.11)

TEXT 25

यदृच्छया लोकमिमं प्रापितः कर्मभिर्भ्रमन् ।
स्वर्गापवर्गयोर्द्वारं तिरश्चां पुनरस्य च ॥२५॥

yadṛcchayā lokam imaṁ
prāpitaḥ karmabhir bhraman
svargāpavargayor dvāraṁ
tiraścāṁ punar asya ca

yadṛcchayā—carried by the waves of material nature; *lokam*—human form; *imam*—this; *prāpitaḥ*—achieved; *karmabhiḥ*—by the influence of different fruitive activities; *bhraman*—wandering from one form of life to another; *svarga*—to the heavenly planets; *apavargayoḥ*—to liberation; *dvāram*—the gate; *tiraścām*—lower species of life; *punaḥ*—again; *asya*—of the human beings; *ca*—and.

TRANSLATION

In the course of the evolutionary process, which is caused by fruitive activities due to undesirable material sense gratification, I have received this human form of life, which can lead to the heavenly planets, to liberation, to the lower species, or to rebirth among human beings.

PURPORT

All living entities within this material world are undergoing the cycle of birth and death according to the laws of nature. This struggle of birth and death in different species may be called the evolutionary process, but in the Western world it has been wrongly explained. Darwin's theory of evolution from animal to man is incomplete because the theory does not present the reverse condition, namely evolution from man to animal. In this verse, however, evolution has been very well explained on the strength of Vedic authority. Human life, which is obtained in the course of the evolutionary process, is a chance for elevation (*svargāpavarga*) or for degradation (*tiraścām punar asya ca*). If one uses this human form of life properly, he can elevate himself to the higher planetary systems, where material happiness is many thousands of times better than on this planet, or one may cultivate knowledge by which to become free from the evolutionary process and be reinstated in one's original spiritual life. This is called *apavarga*, or liberation.

Material life is called *pavarga* because here we are subject to five different states of suffering, represented by the letters *pa, pha, ba, bha* and *ma. Pa* means *pariśrama,* very hard labor. *Pha* means *phena,* or foam from the mouth. For example, sometimes we see a horse foaming at the mouth with heavy labor. *Ba* means *byarthatā,* disappointment. In spite of so much hard labor, at the end we find disappointment. *Bha* means *bhaya,* or fear. In material life, one is always in the blazing fire of fear, since no one knows what will happen next. Finally, *ma* means *mṛtyu,* or death. When one attempts to nullify these five different statuses of life—*pa, pha, ba, bha* and *ma*—one achieves *apavarga,* or liberation from the punishment of material existence.

The word *tiraścām* refers to degraded life. Human life, of course, provides an opportunity for the best living conditions. As Western people think, from the monkeys come the human beings, who are more comfortably situated. However, if one does not utilize his human life for *svarga* or *apavarga,* he falls again to the degraded life of animals like dogs and hogs. Therefore a sane human being must consider whether he will elevate himself to the higher planets, prepare to free himself from the evolutionary process, or travel again through the evolutionary process in higher and lower grades of life. If one works piously one may be elevated to the higher planetary systems or achieve liberation and return home, back to Godhead, but otherwise one may be degraded to a life as a dog, a hog and so on. As explained in *Bhagavad-gītā* (9.25), *yānti deva-vratā devān.* Those interested in being elevated to the higher planetary systems (Devaloka or Svargaloka) must prepare to do so. Similarly, if one wants liberation and wants to return home, back to Godhead, he should prepare himself for that purpose.

Our Kṛṣṇa consciousness movement is therefore the highest movement for the benediction of human society because this movement is teaching people how to go back home, back to Godhead. In *Bhagavad-gītā* (13.22) it is clearly stated that different forms of life are obtained by association with the three modes of material nature (*kāraṇaṁ guṇa-saṅgo 'sya sad-asad-yoni-janmasu*). According to one's association with the material qualities of goodness, passion and ignorance in this life, in one's next life one receives an appropriate body. Modern civilization does not know that because of varied association in material nature, the living entity, although eternal, is placed in different diseased conditions known as the many species of life. Modern civilization is unaware of the laws of nature.

prakṛteḥ kriyamāṇāni
guṇaiḥ karmāṇi sarvaśaḥ
ahaṅkāra-vimūḍhātmā
kartāham iti manyate

"The bewildered spirit soul, under the influence of the three modes of material nature, thinks himself the performer of activities that are in actuality carried out by nature." (Bg. 3.27) Every living entity is under the full control of the stringent laws of material nature, but rascals think themselves independent. Actually, however, they cannot be independent. This is foolishness. A foolish civilization is extremely risky, and therefore the Kṛṣṇa consciousness movement is trying to make people aware of their fully dependent condition under the stringent laws of nature and is trying to save them from being victimized by strong *māyā*, which is Kṛṣṇa's external energy. Behind the material laws is the supreme controller, Kṛṣṇa (*mayādhyakṣeṇa prakṛtiḥ sūyate sacarācaram*). Therefore if one surrenders unto Kṛṣṇa (*mām eva ye prapadyante māyām etāṁ taranti te*), one may immediately be freed from the control of external nature (*sa guṇān samatītyaitān brahma-bhūyāya kalpate*). This should be the aim of life.

TEXT 26

तत्रापि दम्पतीनां च सुखायान्यापनुत्तये ।
कर्माणि कुर्वतां दृष्ट्वा निवृत्तोऽस्मि विपर्ययम् ॥२६॥

tatrāpi dam-patīnāṁ ca
sukhāyānyāpanuttaye
karmāṇi kurvatāṁ dṛṣṭvā
nivṛtto 'smi viparyayam

tatra—there; *api*—also; *dam-patīnām*—of men and women united by marriage; *ca*—and; *sukhāya*—for the sake of pleasure, specifically the pleasure of sex life; *anya-apanuttaye*—for avoiding misery; *karmāṇi*—fruitive activities; *kurvatām*—always engaged in; *dṛṣṭvā*—by observing; *nivṛttaḥ asmi*—I have now ceased (from such activities); *viparyayam*—the opposite.

TRANSLATION

In this human form of life, a man and women unite for the sensual pleasure of sex, but by actual experience we have observed that none of them are happy. Therefore, seeing the contrary results, I have stopped taking part in materialistic activities.

PURPORT

As stated by Prahlāda Mahārāja, *yan maithunādi-gṛhamedhi-sukhaṁ hi tuccham.* Man and woman both seek sexual enjoyment, and when they are united by the ritualistic ceremony of marriage, they are happy for some time, but finally there is dissension, and thus there are so many cases of separation and divorce. Although every man and woman is actually eager to enjoy life through sexual unity, the result is disunity and distress. Marriage is recommended to give men and women a concession for restricted sex life, which is also recommended in *Bhagavad-gītā* by the Supreme Personality of Godhead. *Dharmāviruddho bhūteṣu kāmo 'smi:* sex life not against the principles of religion is Kṛṣṇa. Every living entity is always eager to enjoy sex life because materialistic life consists of eating, sleeping, sex and fear. In animal life, eating, sleeping, sexual enjoyment and fear cannot be regulated, but for human society the plan is that although men, like animals, must be allowed to eat, sleep, enjoy sex and take protection from fear, they must be regulated. The Vedic plan for eating recommends that one take *yajña-śiṣṭa*, or *prasāda*, food offered to Kṛṣṇa. *Yajña-śiṣṭāśinaḥ santo mucyante sarva-kilbiṣaiḥ:* "The devotees of the Lord are released from all kinds of sins because they eat food that is offered first for sacrifice." (Bg. 3.13) In material life, one commits sinful activities, especially in eating, and because of sinful activities one is condemned by nature's laws to accept another body, which is imposed as punishment. Sex and eating are essential, and therefore they are offered to human society under Vedic restrictions so that according to the Vedic injunctions people may eat, sleep, enjoy sex, be protected from fearful life and gradually be elevated and liberated from the punishment of material existence. Thus the Vedic injunctions for marriage offer a concession to human society, the idea being that a man and woman united in a ritualistic marriage ceremony should help one another advance in spiritual life. Unfortunately, especially in this age, men and women unite for unrestricted sexual enjoyment. Thus they are victimized, being obliged to take rebirth in the forms of animals to fulfill their animalistic propensities. The Vedic injunctions therefore warn, *nāyaṁ deho deha-bhājāṁ nṛloke kaṣṭān kāmān arhate viḍ-bhujāṁ ye.* One should not enjoy sex life like hogs, and eat everything, even to the limit of stool. A human being should eat *prasāda* offered to the Deity and should enjoy sex life according to the Vedic injunctions. He should engage himself in the business of Kṛṣṇa consciousness, he should save himself from the fearful condition of material existence, and he should sleep only to recover from fatigue due to working hard.

The learned *brāhmaṇa* said that since everything is misused by fruitive workers, he had retired from all fruitive activities.

TEXT 27

सुखमस्यात्मनो रूपं सर्वेहोपरतिस्तनुः ।
मनःसंस्पर्शजान् दृष्ट्वा भोगान्स्वप्स्यामि संविशन् ॥२७॥

sukham asyātmano rūpaṁ
sarvehoparatis tanuḥ

manaḥ-saṁsparśajān dṛṣṭvā
bhogān svapsyāmi saṁviśan

sukham—happiness; *asya*—of him; *ātmanaḥ*—of the living entity; *rūpam*—the natural position; *sarva*—all; *īha*—material activities; *uparatiḥ*—completely stopping; *tanuḥ*—the medium of its manifestation; *manaḥ-saṁsparśa-jān*—produced from demands for sense gratification; *dṛṣṭvā*—after seeing; *bhogān*—sense enjoyment; *svapsyāmi*—I am sitting silently, thinking deeply about these material activities; *saṁviśan*—entering into such activities.

TRANSLATION

The actual form of life for the living entities is one of spiritual happiness, which is real happiness. This happiness can be achieved only when one stops all materialistic activities. Material sense enjoyment is simply imagination. Therefore, considering this subject matter, I have ceased from all material activities and am lying down here.

PURPORT

The difference between the philosophy of the Māyāvādīs and that of the Vaiṣṇavas is explained herein. Both the Māyāvādīs and Vaiṣṇavas know that in materialistic activities there is no happiness. The Māyāvādī philosophers, therefore, adhering to the slogan *brahma satyaṁ jagan mithyā*, want to refrain from false, materialistic activities. They want to stop all activities and merge in the Supreme Brahman. According to the Vaiṣṇava philosophy, however, if one simply ceases from materialistic activity one cannot remain inactive for very long, and therefore everyone should engage himself in spiritual activities, which will solve the problem of suffering in this material world. It is said, therefore, that although the Māyāvādī philosophers strive to refrain from materialistic activities and merge in Brahman, and although they may actually merge in the Brahman existence, for want of activity they fall down again into materialistic activity (*āruhya kṛcchreṇa paraṁ padaṁ tataḥ patanty adhaḥ*). Thus the so-called renouncer, unable to remain in meditation upon Brahman, returns to materialistic activities by opening hospitals and schools and so on. Therefore, simply cultivating knowledge that materialistic activities cannot give one happiness, and that one should consequently cease from such activities, is insufficient. One should cease from materialistic activities and take up spiritual activities. Then the solution to the problem will be achieved. Spiritual activities are activities performed according to the order of Kṛṣṇa (*ānukūlyena kṛṣṇānuśīlanam*). If one does whatever Kṛṣṇa says, his activities are not material. For example, when Arjuna fought in response to the order of Kṛṣṇa, his activities were not material. Fighting for sense gratification is a materialistic activity, but fighting by the order of Kṛṣṇa is spiritual. By spiritual activities one becomes eligible to go back home, back to Godhead, and then enjoy blissful life eternally. Here, in the material world, everything is but a mental concoction that will never give us real happiness. The practical solution, therefore, is to cease from materialistic activities and engage in spiritual activities. *Yajñārthāt karmaṇo 'nyatra loko 'yaṁ karma-bandhanaḥ.* If one works for the sake of pleasing the Supreme Lord—Yajña, or Viṣṇu—one is in liberated life. If one fails to do so, however, he remains in a life of bondage.

TEXT 28

इत्येतदात्मनः स्वार्थं सन्तं विस्मृत्य वै पुमान् ।
विचित्रामसति द्वैते घोरामाप्नोति संसृतिम् ॥२८॥

ity etad ātmanaḥ svārthaṁ
santaṁ vismṛtya vai pumān
vicitrām asati dvaite
ghorām āpnoti saṁsṛtim

iti—in this way; *etat*—a person materially conditioned; *ātmanaḥ*—of his self; *sva-artham*—own interest; *santam*—existing within oneself; *vismṛtya*—forgetting; *vai*—indeed; *pumān*—the living entity; *vicitrām*—attractive false varieties; *asati*—in the material world; *dvaite*—other than the self; *ghorām*—very fearful (due to continuous acceptance of birth and death); *āpnoti*—one becomes entangled; *saṁsṛtim*—in material existence.

TRANSLATION

In this way the conditioned soul living within the body forgets his self-interest because he identifies himself with the body. Because the body is material, his natural tendency is to be attracted by the varieties of the material world. Thus the living entity suffers the miseries of material existence.

PURPORT

Everyone is trying to be happy because, as explained in the previous verse, *sukham asyātmano rūpaṁ sarvehoparatis tanuḥ:* when the living entity is in his original spiritual form, he is happy by nature. There is no question of miseries for the spiritual being. As Kṛṣṇa is always happy, the living entities, who are His parts and parcels, are also happy by nature, but because of being put within this material world and forgetting their eternal relationship with Kṛṣṇa, they have forgotten their real nature. Because every one of us is a part of Kṛṣṇa, we have a very affectionate relationship with Him, but because we have forgotten our identities and are considering the body to be the self, we are afflicted by all the troubles of birth, death, old age and disease. This misconception in materialistic life continues unless and until one comes to understand his relationship with Kṛṣṇa. The happiness sought by the conditioned soul is certainly only illusion, as explained in the next verse.

TEXT 29

जलं तदुद्भवैश्छन्नं हित्वाज्ञो जलकाम्यया ।
मृगतृष्णामुपाधावेत् तथान्यत्रार्थदृक् स्वतः ॥२९॥

jalaṁ tad-udbhavaiś channaṁ
hitvājño jala-kāmyayā
mṛgatṛṣṇām upādhāvet
tathānyatrārtha-dṛk svataḥ

jalam—water; *tat-udbhavaiḥ*—by grass grown from that water; *channam*—covered; *hitvā*—giving up; *ajñaḥ*—a foolish animal; *jala-kāmyayā*—desiring to drink water; *mṛgatṛṣṇām*—a mirage;

upādhāvet—runs after; *tathā*—similarly; *anyatra*—somewhere else; *artha-dṛk*—self-interested; *svataḥ*—in himself.

TRANSLATION

Just as a deer, because of ignorance, cannot see the water within a well covered by grass, but runs after water elsewhere, the living entity covered by the material body does not see the happiness within himself, but runs after happiness in the material world.

PURPORT

This is an accurate example depicting how the living entity, because of lack of knowledge, runs after happiness outside his own self. When one understands his real identity as a spiritual being, he can understand the supreme spiritual being, Kṛṣṇa, and the real happiness exchanged between Kṛṣṇa and one's self. It is very interesting to note how this verse points to the body's growth from the spirit soul. The modern materialistic scientist thinks that life grows from matter, but actually the fact is that matter grows from life. The life, or the spiritual soul, is compared herein to water, from which clumps of matter grow in the form of grass. One who is ignorant of scientific knowledge of the spirit soul does not look inside the body to find happiness in the soul; instead, he goes outside to search for happiness, just as a deer without knowledge of the water beneath the grass goes out to the desert to find water. The Kṛṣṇa consciousness movement is trying to remove the ignorance of misled human beings who are trying to find water outside the jurisdiction of life. *Raso vai saḥ. Raso 'ham apsu kaunteya.* The taste of water is Kṛṣṇa. To quench one's thirst, one must taste water by association with Kṛṣṇa. This is the Vedic injunction.

TEXT 30

देहादिभिर्दैवतन्त्रैरात्मनः सुखमीहतः ।
दुःखात्ययं चानीशस्य क्रिया मोघाः कृताः कृताः ॥३०॥

dehādibhir daiva-tantrair
ātmanaḥ sukham īhataḥ

duḥkhātyayaṁ cānīśasya
kriyā moghāḥ kṛtāḥ kṛtāḥ

deha-ādibhiḥ—with the body, mind, ego and intelligence; *daiva-tantraiḥ*—under the control of superior power; *ātmanaḥ*—of the self; *sukham*—happiness; *īhataḥ*—searching after; *duḥkha-atyayam*—diminution of miserable conditions; *ca*—also; *anīśasya*—of the living entity fully under the control of material nature; *kriyāḥ*—plans and activities; *moghāḥ kṛtāḥ kṛtāḥ*—become baffled again and again.

TRANSLATION

The living entity tries to achieve happiness and rid himself of the causes of distress, but because the various bodies of the living entities are under the full control of material nature, all his plans in different bodies, one after another, are ultimately baffled.

PURPORT

Because the materialist is in gross ignorance of how the laws of material nature act upon him as a result of his fruitive activity, he mistakenly plans to enjoy bodily comfort in the human form of life through so-called economic development, through pious activities for elevation to the higher planetary systems, and in many other ways, but factually he becomes a victim of the reactions of his fruitive activities. The Supreme Personality of Godhead is situated as the Supersoul within the cores of the hearts of all living entities. As the Lord says in *Bhagavad-gītā* (15.15):

sarvasya cāhaṁ hṛdi sanniviṣṭo
mattaḥ smṛtir jñānam apohanaṁ ca

"I am seated in everyone's heart, and from Me come remembrance, knowledge and forgetfulness." The desires and activities of the living being are observed by the Supersoul, who is the *upadraṣṭā*, the overseer, and who orders material nature to fulfill the various desires of the living being. As clearly stated in *Bhagavad-gītā* (18.61):

īśvaraḥ sarva-bhūtānāṁ
hṛd-deśe 'rjuna tiṣṭhati
bhrāmayan sarva-bhūtāni
yantrārūḍhāni māyayā

The Lord is situated in everyone's heart, and as one desires, the Lord gives one various types of bodies, which are like machines. Riding on such a machine, the living entity wanders throughout the universe, under the control of material nature and its modes. Thus the living being is not at all free to act, but is fully under the control of material nature, which is fully under the control of the Supreme Personality of Godhead.

As soon as a living entity is victimized by material desires to lord it over material nature, he is subjected to the control of material nature, which is supervised by the Supreme Soul. The result is that one again and again makes plans and is baffled, but as foolish as he is he cannot see the cause of his bafflement. This cause is distinctly stated in *Bhagavad-gītā:* because one has not surrendered to the Supreme Personality of Godhead, he must work under the control of material nature and its stringent laws (*daivī hy eṣā guṇamayī mama māyā duratyayā*). The only means of becoming free from this entanglement is to surrender to the Supreme Lord. In the human form of life, the living entity must accept this instruction from the Supreme Person, Kṛṣṇa: *sarva-dharmān parityajya mām ekaṁ śaraṇaṁ vraja.* "Do not plan to achieve happiness and drive away distress. You will never be successful. Simply surrender unto Me." Unfortunately, however, the living entity does not accept the Supreme Lord's clearly stated instructions from *Bhagavad-gītā*, and thus he becomes a perpetual captive of the laws of material nature.

Yajñārthāt karmaṇo 'nyatra loko 'yaṁ karma-bandhanaḥ: if one does not act for the satisfaction of Kṛṣṇa, who is known as Viṣṇu or Yajña, he must be entangled in the reactions of fruitive activities. These reactions are called *pāpa* and *puṇya*—sinful and pious. By pious activities one is elevated to the higher planetary systems, and by impious activities one is degraded to lower species of life, in which he is punished by the laws of nature. In the lower species of life there is an evolutionary process, and when the term of the living entity's imprisonment or punishment in the lower species is finished, he is again offered a human form and given a chance to decide for himself which way he should plan.

If he again misses the opportunity, he is again put into the cycle of birth and death, going sometimes higher and sometimes lower, turning on the *saṁsāra-cakra*, the wheel of material existence. As a wheel sometimes goes up and sometimes comes down, the stringent laws of material nature make the living entity in material existence sometimes happy and sometimes distressed. How he suffers in the cycle of happiness and distress is described in the next verse.

TEXT 31

आध्यात्मिकादिभिर्दुःखैरविमुक्तस्य कर्हिचित् ।
मर्त्यस्य कृच्छ्रोपनतैरर्थैः कामैः क्रियेत किम् ॥३१॥

ādhyātmikādibhir duḥkhair
avimuktasya karhicit
martyasya kṛcchropanatair
arthaiḥ kāmaiḥ kriyeta kim

ādhyātmika-ādibhiḥ—*adhyātmika, adhidaivika* and *adhibhautika; duḥkhaiḥ*—by the threefold miseries of material life; *avimuktasya*—of one who is not freed from such miserable conditions (or one who is subjected to birth, death, old age and disease); *karhicit*—sometimes; *martyasya*—of the living entity subjected to death; *kṛcchra-upanataiḥ*—things obtained because of severe miseries; *arthaiḥ*—even if some benefit is derived; *kāmaiḥ*—which can fulfill one's material desires; *kriyeta*—what do they do; *kim*—and what is the value of such happiness.

TRANSLATION

Materialistic activities are always mixed with three kinds of miserable conditions—adhyātmika, adhidaivika and adhibautika. Therefore, even if one achieves some success by performing such activities, what is the benefit of this success? One is still subjected to birth, death, old age, disease and the reactions of his fruitive activities.

PURPORT

According to the materialistic way of life, if a poor man, after laboring very, very hard, gets some material profit at the end of his life, he is considered a success, even though he again dies while suffering the threefold miseries—*adhyātmika, adhidaivika* and *adhibhautika.* No one can escape the threefold miseries of materialistic life, namely miseries pertaining to the body and mind, miseries pertaining to the difficulties imposed by society, community, nation and other living entities, and miseries inflicted upon us by natural disturbances from earthquakes, famines, droughts, floods, epidemics, and so on. If one works very hard, suffering the threefold miseries, and then is successful in getting some small benefit, what is the value of this benefit? Besides that, even if a *karmī* is successful in accumulating some material wealth, he still cannot enjoy it, for he must die in bereavement. I have even seen a dying man begging a medical attendant to increase his life by four years so that he could complete his material plans. Of course, the medical man was unsuccessful in expanding the life of the man, who therefore died in great bereavement. Everyone must die in this way, and after one's mental condition is taken into account by the laws of material nature, he is given another chance to fulfill his desires in a different body. Material plans for material happiness have no value, but under the spell of the illusory energy we consider them extremely valuable. There were many politicians, social reformers and philosophers who died very miserably, without deriving any practical value from their material plans. Therefore, a sane and sensible man never desires to work hard under the conditions of threefold miseries, only to die in disappointment.

TEXT 32

पश्यामि धनिनां क्लेशं लुब्धानामजितात्मनाम् ।
भयादलब्धनिद्राणां सर्वतोऽभिविशङ्किनाम् ॥३२॥

paśyāmi dhanināṁ kleśaṁ
lubdhānām ajitātmanām
bhayād alabdha-nidrāṇāṁ
sarvato 'bhiviśaṅkinām

paśyāmi—I can practically see; *dhaninām*—of persons who are very rich; *kleśam*—the miseries; *lubdhānām*—who are extremely greedy; *ajita-ātmanām*—who are victims of their senses; *bhayāt*—because of fear; *alabdha-nidrāṇām*—who are suffering from insomnia; *sarvataḥ*—from all sides; *abhiviśaṅkinām*—being particularly afraid.

TRANSLATION

The brāhmaṇa continued: I am actually seeing how a rich man, who is a victim of his senses, is very greedy to accumulate wealth, and therefore suffers from insomnia due to fear from all sides, despite his wealth and opulence.

PURPORT

Greedy capitalists accumulate wealth under so many miserable conditions, the result being that because they collect money by questionable means, their minds are always agitated. Thus they are unable to sleep at night, and they have to take pills for mental tranquility to invite sleep. And sometimes even the pills are a failure. Consequently the result of having accumulated money by so much labor is certainly not happiness, but only distress. What is the value of acquiring a comfortable position if one's mind is always disturbed? Narottama dāsa Ṭhākura has therefore sung:

saṁsāra-biṣānale, dibāniśi hiyā jvale,
juḍāite nā kainu upāya

"I am suffering from the poisonous effect of material enjoyment. Thus my heart is always burning and is almost on the verge of failure." The result of the greedy capitalist's unnecessary accumulation of wealth is that he must suffer from a blazing fire of anxiety and always be concerned with how to save his money and invest it properly to get more and more. Such a life is certainly not very happy, but because of the spell of the illusory energy, materialistic persons engage in such activities.

As far as our Kṛṣṇa consciousness movement is concerned, we are getting money naturally, by the grace of God, by selling our literature. This literature is not sold for our sense gratification; to spread the Kṛṣṇa consciousness movement we need so many things, and Kṛṣṇa is therefore supplying us the requisite money to advance this mission. The mission of Kṛṣṇa is to spread Kṛṣṇa consciousness all over the world, and for this purpose we naturally must have sufficient money. Therefore, according to the advice of Śrīla Rūpa Gosvāmī Prabhupāda, we should not give up attachment to money that can spread the Kṛṣṇa consciousness movement. Śrīla Rūpa Gosvāmī says in his *Bhakti-rasāmṛta-sindhu* (1.2.256):

prāpañcikatayā buddhyā
hari-sambandhi-vastunaḥ
mumukṣubhiḥ parityāgo
vairagyaṁ phalgu kathyate

"When persons eager to achieve liberation renounce things which are related to the Supreme Personality of Godhead, though they are material, this is called incomplete renunciation." Money that can help in spreading the Kṛṣṇa consciousness movement is not a part of the material world, and we should not give it up, thinking that it is material. Śrīla Rūpa Gosvāmī advises:

anāsaktasya viṣayān
yathārham upayuñjataḥ
nirbandhaḥ kṛṣṇa-sambandhe
yuktaṁ vairāgyam ucyate

"When one is not attached to anything, but at the same time accepts everything in relation to Kṛṣṇa, one is rightly situated above possessiveness." (*Bhakti-rasāmṛta-sindhu* 1.2.255) Money is undoubtedly coming in great quantities, but we should not be attached to this money for sense gratification; every cent should be spent for spreading the Kṛṣṇa consciousness movement, not for sense gratification. There is danger for a preacher when he receives great quantities of money, for as soon as he spends even a single cent of the collection for his personal sense gratification, he becomes a fallen victim. The preachers of the Kṛṣṇa consciousness movement should be extremely careful not to misuse the immense quantities of money needed to spread this movement. Let us not make this money the cause of our distress; it should be used for Kṛṣṇa, and that will cause our eternal happiness. Money is Lakṣmī, or the goddess of fortune, the companion of Nārāyaṇa. Lakṣmījī must always remain with Nārāyaṇa, and then there need be no fear of degradation.

TEXT 33

राजतश्चौरतः शत्रोः स्वजनात्पशुपक्षितः ।
अर्थिभ्यः कालतः स्वस्मान्नित्यं प्राणार्थवद्भयम् ॥३३॥

rājataś cauratah śatroḥ
sva-janāt paśu-pakṣitaḥ
arthibhyaḥ kālataḥ svasmān
nityaṁ prāṇārthavad bhayam

rājataḥ—from the government; *cauratah*—from thieves and rogues; *śatroḥ*—from enemies; *sva-janāt*—from relatives; *paśu-pakṣitaḥ*—from animals and birds; *arthibhyaḥ*—from beggars and persons seeking charity; *kālataḥ*—from the time factor; *svasmāt*—as well as from one's self; *nityam*—always; *prāṇa-artha-vat*—for one who has life or money; *bhayam*—fear.

TRANSLATION

Those who are considered materially powerful and rich are always full of anxieties because of governmental laws, thieves and rogues, enemies, family members, animals, birds, persons seeking charity, the inevitable time factor and even their own selves. Thus they are invariably afraid.

PURPORT

The word *svasmāt* means "from one's self." Because of attachment for money, the richest person is even afraid of himself. He fears that he may have locked his money in an unsafe manner or might have committed some mistake. Aside from the government and its income tax and aside from thieves, even a rich man's own relatives are always thinking of how to take advantage of him and take away his money. Sometimes these relatives are described as *sva-janaka-dasyu*, which means "rogues and thieves in the guise of relatives." Therefore, there is no need to accumulate wealth or unnecessarily endeavor for more and more money. The real business of life is to ask "Who am I?" and to understand one's self. One should understand the position of the living entity in this material world and understand how to return home, back to Godhead.

TEXT 34

शोकमोहभयक्रोधरागक्लैब्यश्रमादयः ।
यन्मूलाः स्युर्नृणां जह्यात् स्पृहां प्राणार्थयोर्बुधः ॥३४॥

śoka-moha-bhaya-krodha-
rāga-klaibya-śramādayaḥ
yan-mūlāḥ syur nṛṇāṁ jahyāt
spṛhāṁ prāṇārthayor budhaḥ

śoka—lamentation; *moha*—illusion; *bhaya*—fear; *krodha*—anger; *rāga*—attachment; *klaibya*—poverty; *śrama*—unnecessary labor; *ādayaḥ*—and so on; *yat-mūlāḥ*—the original cause of all these; *syuḥ*—become; *nṛṇām*—of human beings; *jahyāt*—should give up; *spṛhām*—the desire; *prāṇa*—for bodily strength or prestige; *arthayoḥ*—and accumulating money; *budhaḥ*—an intelligent person.

TRANSLATION

Those in human society who are intelligent should give up the original cause of lamentation, illusion, fear, anger, attachment, poverty and unnecessary labor. The original cause of all of these is the desire for unnecessary prestige and money.

PURPORT

Here is the difference between Vedic civilization and the modern demoniac civilization. Vedic civilization concerned itself with how to achieve self-realization, and for this purpose one was recommended to have a small income to maintain body and soul together. The society was divided into *brāhmaṇas, kṣatriyas, vaiśyas* and *śūdras*, and the members of this society would limit their endeavors to meeting their minimum demands. The *brāhmaṇas*, in particular, would have no material desires. Because the *kṣatriyas* had to rule the people, it was necessary for them to have money and prestige. But the *vaiśyas* were satisfied with agricultural produce and milk from the cow, and if by chance there were excess, trade was allowed. The *śūdras* were also happy, for they would get food and shelter from the three higher classes. In the demoniac civilization of the present day, however, there is no question of *brāhmaṇas* or *kṣatriyas;* there are only so-called workers and a flourishing mercantile class who have no goal in life.

According to Vedic civilization, the ultimate perfection of life is to take *sannyāsa,* but at the present moment people do not know why *sannyāsa* is accepted. Because of misunderstanding, they think that one accepts *sannyāsa* to escape social responsibilities. But one does not accept *sannyāsa* to escape from responsibility to society. Generally one accepts *sannyāsa* at the fourth stage of spiritual life. One begins as a *brahmacārī* then becomes a *gṛhastha,* a *vānaprastha* and finally a *sannyāsī* to take advantage of the duration of one's life by engaging oneself fully in self-realization. *Sannyāsa* does not mean begging from door to door to accumulate money for sense gratification. However, because in Kali-yuga people are more or less prone to sense gratification, immature *sannyāsa* is not recommended. Śrīla Rūpa Gosvāmī writes in his *Nectar of Instruction* (2):

atyāhāraḥ prayāsaś ca
prajalpo niyamāgrahaḥ
jana-saṅgaś ca laulyaṁ ca
ṣaḍbhir bhaktir vinaśyati

"One's devotional service is spoiled when he becomes too entangled in the following six activities: (1) eating more than necessary or collecting more funds than required; (2) overendeavoring for mundane things that are very difficult to obtain; (3) talking unnecessarily about mundane subject matters; (4) practicing the scriptural rules and regulations only for the sake of following them and not for the sake of spiritual advancement, or rejecting the rules and regulations of the scriptures and working independently or whimsically; (5) associating with worldly-minded persons who are not interested in Kṛṣṇa consciousness; and (6) being greedy for mundane achievements." A *sannyāsī* should have an institution meant to preach Kṛṣṇa consciousness; he need not accumulate money for himself. We recommend that as soon as money accumulates in our Kṛṣṇa consciousness movement, fifty per cent of it should be invested in printing books, and fifty per cent for expenditures, especially in establishing centers all over the world. The managers of the Kṛṣṇa consciousness movement should be extremely cautious in regard to this point. Otherwise money will be the cause of lamentation, illusion, fear, anger, material attachment, material poverty, and unnecessary hard work. When I was alone in Vṛndāvana, I never attempted to construct *maṭhās* or temples; rather, I was fully satisfied with the small amount of money I could gather by selling *Back to Godhead*, and thus I would provide for myself and also print the literature. When I went to foreign countries, I lived according to the same principle, but when Europeans and Americans began to give money profusely, I started temples and Deity worship. The same principle should still be followed. Whatever money is collected should be spent for Kṛṣṇa, and not a farthing for sense gratification. This is the *Bhāgavata* principle.

TEXT 35

मधुकारमहासर्पौ लोकेऽस्मिन्नो गुरूत्तमौ ।
वैराग्यं परितोषं च प्राप्ता यच्छिक्षया वयम् ॥३५॥

madhukāra-mahā-sarpau
loke 'smin no gurūttamau
vairāgyaṁ paritoṣaṁ ca
prāptā yac-chikṣayā vayam

madhukāra—bees that go from flower to flower to collect honey; *mahā-sarpau*—the big snake (the python, which does not move from one place to another); *loke*—in the world; *asmin*—this; *naḥ*—our; *guru*—spiritual masters; *uttamau*—first-class; *vairāgyam*—renunciation; *paritoṣam ca*—and satisfaction; *prāptāḥ*—obtained; *yat-śikṣayā*—by whose instruction; *vayam*—we.

TRANSLATION

The bee and the python are two excellent spiritual masters who give us exemplary instructions regarding how to be satisfied by collecting only a little and how to stay in one place and not move.

TEXT 36

विरागः सर्वकामेभ्यः शिक्षितो मे मधुव्रतात् ।
कृच्छ्राप्तं मधुवद् वित्तं हत्वाप्यन्यो हरेत्पतिम् ॥३६॥

virāgaḥ sarva-kāmebhyaḥ
śikṣito me madhu-vratāt
kṛcchrāptaṁ madhuvad vittaṁ
hatvāpy anyo haret patim

virāgaḥ—detachment; *sarva-kāmebhyaḥ*—from all material desires; *śikṣitaḥ*—has been taught; *me*—unto me; *madhu-vratāt*—from the bumblebee; *kṛcchra*—with great difficulties; *āptam*—acquired; *madhu-vat*—as good as honey ("money is honey"); *vittam*—money; *hatvā*—killing; *api*—even; *anyaḥ*—another; *haret*—takes away; *patim*—the owner.

TRANSLATION

From the bumblebee I have learned to be unattached to accumulating money, for although money is as good as honey, anyone can kill its owner and take it away.

PURPORT

The honey gathered in the comb is taken away by force. Therefore one who accumulates money should realize that he may be harassed by the government or by thieves or even killed by enemies. Especially in this age of Kali-yuga, it is said that instead of protecting the money of the citizens, the government itself will take away the money with the force of law. The learned *brāhmaṇa* had therefore decided that he should not accumulate any money. One should own as much as he immediately needs. There is no need to keep a big balance at hand, along with the fear that it may be plundered by the government or by thieves.

TEXT 37

अनीहः परितुष्टात्मा यदृच्छोपनतादहम् ।
नो चेच्छये बह्वहानि महाहिरिव सत्त्ववान् ॥३७॥

anīhaḥ parituṣṭātmā
yadṛcchopanatād aham

no cec chaye bahv-ahāni
mahāhir iva sattvavān

anīhaḥ—with no desire to possess more; *parituṣṭa*—very satisfied; *ātmā*—self; *yadṛcchā*—in its own way, without endeavor; *upanatāt*—by things brought in by possession; *aham*—I; *no*—not; *cet*—if so; *śaye*—I lie down; *bahu*—many; *ahāni*—days; *mahā-ahiḥ*—a python; *iva*—like; *sattva-vān*—enduring.

TRANSLATION

I do not endeavor to get anything, but am satisfied with whatever is achieved in its own way. If I do not get anything, I am patient and unagitated like a python and lie down in this way for many days.

PURPORT

One should learn detachment from the bumblebees, for they collect drops of honey here and there and keep it in their honeycomb, but then someone comes and by force takes all the honey away, leaving the bumblebees with nothing. Therefore one should learn from the bumblebee not to keep more money than one needs. Similarly, one should learn from the python to stay in one place for many, many days without food and then eat only if something comes in its own way. Thus the learned *brāhmaṇa* gave instructions gained from two creatures, namely the bumblebee and the python.

TEXT 38

क्वचिदल्पं क्वचिद् भूरि भुञ्जेऽन्नं स्वाद्वस्वादु वा ।
क्वचिद् भूरिगुणोपेतं गुणहीनमुत क्वचित् ।
श्रद्धयोपहृतं क्वापि कदाचिन्मानवर्जितम् ।
भुञ्जे भुक्त्वाथ कस्मिंश्चिद् दिवा नक्तं यदृच्छया ॥ ३८ ॥

kvacid alpaṁ kvacid bhūri
bhuñje 'nnaṁ svādv asvādu vā
kvacid bhūri guṇopetaṁ
guṇa-hīnam uta kvacit

śraddhayopahṛtaṁ kvāpi
kadācin māna-varjitam
bhuñje bhuktvātha kasmiṁś cid
divā naktaṁ yadṛcchayā

kvacit—sometimes; *alpam*—very little; *kvacit*—sometimes; *bhūri*—a great quantity; *bhuñje*—I eat; *annam*—food; *svādu*—palatable; *asvādu*—stale; *vā*—either; *kvacit*—sometimes; *bhūri*—great; *guṇa-upetam*—a nice flavor; *guṇa-hīnam*—without flavor; *uta*—whether; *kvacit*—sometimes; *śraddhayā*—respectfully; *upahṛtam*—brought by someone; *kvāpi*—sometimes; *kadācit*—sometimes; *māna-varjitam*—offered without respect; *bhuñje*—I eat; *bhuktvā*—after eating; *atha*—as such; *kasmin cit*—sometimes, in some place; *divā*—during the daytime; *naktam*—or at night; *yadṛcchayā*—as it is available.

TRANSLATION

Sometimes I eat a very small quantity and sometimes a great quantity. Sometimes the food is very palatable, and sometimes it is stale. Sometimes prasāda is offered with great respect, and sometimes food is given neglectfully. Sometimes I eat during the day and sometimes at night. Thus I eat what is easily available.

TEXT 39

क्षौमं दुकूलमजिनं चीरं वल्कलमेव वा ।
वसेऽन्यदपि सम्प्राप्तं दिष्टभुक् तुष्टधीरहम् ॥३९॥

kṣaumaṁ dukūlam ajinaṁ
cīraṁ valkalam eva vā
vase 'nyad api samprāptaṁ
diṣṭa-bhuk tuṣṭa-dhīr aham

kṣaumam—clothing made of linen; *dukūlam*—silk or cotton; *ajinam*—deerskin; *cīram*—loincloth; *valkalam*—bark; *eva*—as it is; *vā*—either; *vase*—I put on; *anyat*—something else; *api*—although;

samprāptam—as available; *diṣṭa-bhuk*—because of destiny; *tuṣṭa*—satisfied; *dhīḥ*—mind; *aham*—I am.

TRANSLATION

To cover my body I use whatever is available, whether it be linen, silk, cotton, bark or deerskin, according to my destiny, and I am fully satisfied and unagitated.

TEXT 40

क्वचिच्छये धरोपस्थे तृणपर्णाश्मभस्मसु ।
क्वचित् प्रासादपर्यङ्के कशिपौ वा परेच्छया ॥४०॥

kvacic chaye dharopasthe
tṛṇa-parṇāśma-bhasmasu
kvacit prāsāda-paryaṅke
kaśipau vā parecchayā

kvacit—sometimes; *śaye*—I lie down; *dhara-upasthe*—on the surface of the earth; *tṛṇa*—on grass; *parṇa*—leaves; *aśma*—stone; *bhasmasu*—or a pile of ashes; *kvacit*—sometimes; *prāsāda*—in palaces; *paryaṅke*—on a first-class bedstead; *kaśipau*—on a pillow; *vā*—either; *para*—of another; *icchayā*—by the wish.

TRANSLATION

Sometimes I lie on the surface of the earth, sometimes on leaves, grass or stone, sometimes on a pile of ashes, or sometimes, by the will of others, in a palace on a first-class bed with pillows.

PURPORT

The learned *brāhmaṇa's* description indicates different types of births, for one lies down according to one's body. Sometimes one takes birth as an animal and sometimes as a king. When he takes birth as an animal he must lie down on the ground, and when he takes birth as a king or a very rich man he is allowed to lie in first-class rooms in huge palaces decorated with beds and other furniture. Such facilities are not available, however, at the sweet will of the living entity; rather, they are available by the supreme will (*parecchayā*), or by the arrangement of *māyā*. As stated in *Bhagavad-gītā* (18.61):

īśvaraḥ sarva-bhūtānāṁ
hṛd-deśe 'rjuna tiṣṭhati
bhrāmayan sarva-bhūtāni
yantrārūḍhāni māyayā

"The Supreme Lord is situated in everyone's heart, O Arjuna, and is directing the wanderings of all living entities, who are seated as on a machine, made of the material energy." The living entity, according to his material desires, receives different types of bodies, which are nothing but machines offered by material nature according to the order of the Supreme Personality of Godhead. By the will of the Supreme, one must take different bodies with different means for lying down.

TEXT 41

क्वचित् स्नातोऽनुलिप्ताङ्गः सुवासाः स्रग्व्यलंकृतः ।
रथेभाश्वैश्चरे क्वापि दिग्वासा ग्रहवद् विभो ॥४१॥

kvacit snāto 'nuliptāṅgaḥ
suvāsāḥ sragvy alaṅkṛtaḥ
rathebhāśvaiś care kvāpi
dig-vāsā grahavad vibho

kvacit—sometimes; *snātaḥ*—bathing very nicely; *anulipta-aṅgaḥ*—with sandalwood pulp smeared all over the body; *su-vāsāḥ*—dressing with very nice garments; *sragvī*—decorated with garlands of flowers; *alaṅkṛtaḥ*—bedecked with various types of ornaments; *ratha*—on a chariot; *ibha*—on an elephant; *aśvaiḥ*—or on the back of a horse; *care*—I wander; *kvāpi*—sometimes; *dik-vāsāḥ*—completely naked; *graha-vat*—as if haunted by a ghost; *vibho*—O lord.

TRANSLATION

O my lord, sometimes I bathe myself very nicely, smear sandalwood pulp all over my body, put on a flower garland, and dress in

fine garments and ornaments. Then I travel like a king on the back of an elephant or on a chariot or horse. Sometimes, however, I travel naked, like a person haunted by a ghost.

TEXT 42

नाहं निन्दे न च स्तौमि स्वभावविषमं जनम् ।
एतेषां श्रेय आशासे उतैकात्म्यं महात्मनि ॥४२॥

nāhaṁ ninde na ca staumi
sva-bhāva-viṣamaṁ janam
eteṣāṁ śreya āśāse
utaikātmyaṁ mahātmani

na—not; *aham*—I; *ninde*—blaspheme; *na*—nor; *ca*—also; *staumi*—praise; *sva-bhāva*—whose nature; *viṣamam*—contradictory; *janam*—a living entity or human being; *eteṣām*—of all of them; *śreyaḥ*—the ultimate benefit; *āśāse*—I pray for; *uta*—indeed; *aikātmyam*—oneness; *mahā-ātmani*—in the Supersoul, the Parabrahman (Kṛṣṇa).

TRANSLATION

Different people are of different mentalities. Therefore it is not my business either to praise them or to blaspheme them. I only desire their welfare, hoping that they will agree to become one with the Supersoul, the Supreme Personality of Godhead, Kṛṣṇa.

PURPORT

As soon as one comes to the platform of *bhakti-yoga*, one understands fully the Supreme Personality of Godhead, Vāsudeva, is the goal of life (*vāsudevaḥ sarvam iti sa mahātmā sudurlabhaḥ*). This is the instruction of all the Vedic literature (*vedaiś ca sarvair aham eva vedyaḥ, sarva dharmān parityajya mām ekaṁ śaraṇaṁ vraja*). There is no use in praising someone for material qualifications or blaspheming him for material disqualifications. In the material world, good and bad have no meaning because if one is good he may be elevated to a higher planetary system and if one is bad he may be degraded to the lower planetary systems. People of different mentalities are sometimes elevated and sometimes degraded, but this is not the goal of life. Rather, the goal of life is to become free from elevation and degradation and take to Kṛṣṇa consciousness. Therefore a saintly person does not discriminate between that which is supposedly good and supposedly bad; rather, he desires for everyone to be happy in Kṛṣṇa consciousness, which is the ultimate goal of life.

TEXT 43

विकल्पं जुहुयाच्चित्तौ तां मनस्यर्थविभ्रमे ।
मनो वैकारिके हुत्वा तं मायायां जुहोत्यनु ॥४३॥

vikalpaṁ juhuyāc cittau
tāṁ manasy artha-vibhrame
mano vaikārike hutvā
taṁ māyāyāṁ juhoty anu

vikalpam—discrimination (between good and bad, one person and another, one nation and another, and all similar discrimination); *juhuyāt*—one should offer as oblations; *cittau*—in the fire of consciousness; *tām*—that consciousness; *manasi*—in the mind; *artha-vibhrame*—the root of all acceptance and rejection; *manaḥ*—that mind; *vaikārike*—in false ego, identification of oneself with matter; *hutvā*—offering as oblations; *tam*—this false ego; *māyāyām*—in the total material energy; *juhoti*—offers as oblations; *anu*—following this principle.

TRANSLATION

The mental concoction of discrimination between good and bad should be accepted as one unit and then invested in the mind, which should then be invested in the false ego. The false ego should be invested in the total material energy. This is the process of fighting false discrimination.

PURPORT

This verse describes how a *yogī* can become free from material affection. Because of material attraction, a *karmī* cannot see himself. *Jñānīs* can discriminate between matter and spirit, but the *yogīs*, the best of whom are the *bhakti-yogīs*, want to return home, back to Godhead. The *karmīs* are completely in illusion, the *jñānīs* are neither in illusion nor in positive knowledge, but the *yogīs*, especially the *bhakti-yogīs*, are completely on the spiritual platform. As confirmed in *Bhagavad-gītā* (14.26):

māṁ ca yo 'vyabhicāreṇa
bhakti-yogena sevate
sa guṇān samatītyaitān
brahma-bhūyāya kalpate

"One who engages in full devotional service, who does not fall down under any circumstance, at once transcends the modes of material nature and thus comes to the level of Brahman." Thus a devotee's position is secure. A devotee is at once elevated to the spiritual platform. Others, such as *jñānīs* and *haṭha-yogīs*, can only gradually ascend to the spiritual platform by nullifying their material discrimination on the platform of psychology and nullifying the false ego, by which one thinks, "I am this body, a product of matter." One must merge the false ego into the total material energy and merge the total material energy into the supreme energetic. This is the process of becoming free from material attraction.

TEXT 44

आत्मानुभूतौ तां मायां जुहुयात् सत्यदृङ् मुनिः ।
ततो निरीहो विरमेत् स्वानुभूत्यात्मनि स्थितः ॥४४॥

ātmānubhūtau tāṁ māyāṁ
juhuyāt satya-dṛṅ muniḥ
tato nirīho viramet
svānubhūty-ātmani sthitaḥ

ātma-anubhūtau—unto self-realization; *tām*—that; *māyām*—the false ego of material existence; *juhuyāt*—should offer as an oblation; *satya-dṛk*—one who has actually realized the ultimate truth; *muniḥ*—such a thoughtful person; *tataḥ*—because of this self-realization; *nirīhaḥ*—without material desires; *viramet*—one must completely retire from material activities; *sva-anubhūti-ātmani*—in self-realization; *sthitaḥ*—thus being situated.

TRANSLATION

A learned, thoughtful person must realize that material existence is illusion. This is possible only by self-realization. A self-realized person, who has actually seen the truth, should retire from all material activities, being situated in self-realization.

PURPORT

By an analytical study of the entire constitution of the body, one can surely come to the conclusion that the soul is different from all the body's material constituents, such as earth, water, fire and air. Thus the difference between the body and soul can be realized by a person who is thoughtful (*manīṣī* or *muni*), and after this realization of the individual spirit soul one can very easily understand the supreme spirit soul. If one thus realizes that the individual soul is subordinate to the supreme spirit soul, he achieves self-realization. As explained in the Thirteenth Chapter of *Bhagavad-gītā*, there are two souls within the body. The body is called *kṣetra*, and there are two *kṣetra-jñas*, or occupants of the body, namely the Supersoul (Paramātmā) and the individual soul. The Supersoul and the individual soul are like two birds sitting on the same tree (the material body). One bird, the individual, forgetful bird, is eating the fruit of the tree, not caring for the instructions of the other bird, which is only a witness to the activities of the first bird, who is his friend. When the forgetful bird comes to understand the supreme friend who is always with him and trying to give him guidance in different bodies, he takes shelter at the lotus feet of that supreme bird. As explained in the *yoga* process, *dhyānāvasthita-tad-gatena manasā paśyanti yaṁ yoginaḥ*. When one actually becomes a perfect *yogī*, by meditation he can see the supreme friend and surrender unto Him. This is the beginning of *bhakti-yoga*, or actual life in Kṛṣṇa consciousness.

TEXT 45

स्वात्मवृत्तं मयेत्थं ते सुगुप्तमपि वर्णितम् ।
व्यपेतं लोकशास्त्राभ्यां भवान् हि भगवत्परः ॥४५॥

svātma-vṛttaṁ mayetthaṁ te
suguptam api varṇitam

vyapetaṁ loka-śāstrābhyāṁ
bhavān hi bhagavat-paraḥ

sva-ātma-vṛttam—the information of the history of self-realization; *mayā*—by me; *ittham*—in this way; *te*—unto you; *su-guptam*—extremely confidential; *api*—although; *varṇitam*—explained; *vyapetam*—without; *loka-śāstrābhyām*—the opinion of the common man or common literatures; *bhavān*—your good self; *hi*—indeed; *bhagavat-paraḥ*—having fully realized the Personality of Godhead.

TRANSLATION

Prahlāda Mahārāja, you are certainly a self-realized soul and a devotee of the Supreme Lord. You do not care for public opinion or so-called scriptures. For this reason I have described to you without hesitation the history of my self-realization.

PURPORT

A person who is actually a devotee of Kṛṣṇa does not care about so-called public opinion and Vedic or philosophical literatures. Prahlāda Mahārāja, who is such a devotee, always defied the false instructions of his father and the so-called teachers who were appointed to teach him. Instead, he simply followed the instructions of Nārada Muni, his *guru*, and thus he always remained a stalwart devotee. This is the nature of an intelligent devotee. The *Śrīmad-Bhāgavatam* instructs, *yajñaiḥ saṅkīrtana-prāyair yajanti hi sumedhasaḥ*. One who is actually very intelligent must join the Kṛṣṇa consciousness movement, realizing his own self as an eternal servant of Kṛṣṇa, and thus practice constant chanting of the holy name of the Lord—Hare Kṛṣṇa, Hare Kṛṣṇa, Kṛṣṇa Kṛṣṇa, Hare Hare/ Hare Rāma, Hare Rāma, Rāma Rāma, Hare Hare.

TEXT 46

श्रीनारद उवाच

धर्मं पारमहंस्यं वै मुनेः श्रुत्वासुरेश्वरः ।
पूजयित्वा ततः प्रीत आमन्त्र्य प्रययौ गृहम् ॥४६॥

śrī-nārada uvāca
dharmaṁ pāramahaṁsyaṁ vai
muneḥ śrutvāsureśvaraḥ
pūjayitvā tataḥ prīta
āmantrya prayayau gṛham

śrī-nāradaḥ uvāca—Śrī Nārada Muni said; *dharmam*—the occupational duty; *pāramahaṁsyam*—of the *paramahaṁsas*, the most perfect human beings; *vai*—indeed; *muneḥ*—from the saintly person; *śrutvā*—thus hearing; *asura-īśvaraḥ*—the King of the *asuras*, Prahlāda Mahārāja; *pūjayitvā*—by worshiping the saintly person; *tataḥ*—thereafter; *prītaḥ*—being very pleased; *āmantrya*—taking permission; *prayayau*—left that place; *gṛham*—for his home.

TRANSLATION

Nārada Muni continued: After Prahlāda Mahārāja, the King of the demons, heard these instructions from the saint, he understood the occupational duties of a perfect person [paramahaṁsa]. Thus he duly worshiped the saint, took his permission and then left for his own home.

PURPORT

As quoted in *Caitanya-caritāmṛta* (*Madhya* 8.128), Śrī Caitanya Mahāprabhu said:

kibā vipra, kibā nyāsī, śūdra kene naya
yei kṛṣṇa-tattva-vettā sei 'guru' haya

A *guru*, or spiritual master, can be anyone who is well conversant with the science of Kṛṣṇa. Therefore although Prahlāda Mahārāja was a *gṛhastha* ruling over the demons, he was a *paramahaṁsa*, the best of human beings, and thus he is our *guru*. In the list of *gurus*, or authorities, Prahlāda Mahārāja's name is therefore mentioned:

svayambhūr nāradaḥ śambhuḥ
kumāraḥ kapilo manuḥ

prahlādo janako bhīṣmo
balir vaiyāsakir vayam
(*Bhāg.* 6.3.20)

The conclusion is that a *paramahaṁsa* is an exalted devotee (*bhagavat-priya*). Such a *paramahaṁsa* may be in any stage of life—*brahmacārī, gṛhastha, vānaprastha* or *sannyāsa*—and be equally liberated and exalted.

Thus end the Bhaktivedanta purports of the Seventh Canto, Thirteenth Chapter, of the Śrīmad-Bhāgavatam, *entitled "The Behavior of a Perfect Person."*

CHAPTER FOURTEEN

Ideal Family Life

This chapter describes the occupational duties of the householder according to the time, the country and the performer. When Yudhiṣṭhira Mahārāja became very much inquisitive about the occupational duties for the householder, Nārada Muni advised him that a *gṛhastha's* first duty is to be fully dependent on Vāsudeva, Kṛṣṇa, and to try to satisfy Him in all respects by executing one's prescribed devotional service. This devotional service will depend on the instructions of authorities and the association of devotees who are actually engaged in devotional service. The beginning of devotional service is *śravaṇam,* or hearing. One must hear from the mouths of realized souls. In this way the *gṛhastha's* attraction to his wife and children will gradually be reduced.

As for the maintenance of his family, a *gṛhastha,* while earning what he requires for his living, must be very conscientious and must not undergo extraordinary endeavor simply to accumulate money and unnecessarily increase in material comforts. Although a *gṛhastha* should externally be very active in earning his livelihood, he should internally be situated as a fully self-realized person, without attachment for material gains. His dealings with family members or friends should be performed simply to fulfill their purpose; one should not be extravagantly engaged in this way. Instructions from family members and society should be accepted superficially, but in essence the *gṛhastha* should be engaged in occupational duties advised by the spiritual master and *śāstra.* Specifically a *gṛhastha* should engage in agricultural activities to earn money. As stated in *Bhagavad-gītā* (18.44), *kṛṣi-go-rakṣya-vāṇijyam*—agriculture, cow protection and trade—are special duties of *gṛhasthas.* If by chance or by the grace of the Lord more money comes, it should be properly engaged for the Kṛṣṇa consciousness movement. One should not be eager to earn more money simply for sensual pleasure. A *gṛhastha* should always remember that one who is endeavoring to accumulate more money than necessary is to be considered a thief and is punishable by the laws of nature.

A *gṛhastha* should be very much affectionate toward lower animals, birds and bees, treating them exactly like his own children. A *gṛhastha* should not indulge in killing animals or birds for sense gratification. He should provide the necessities of life even to the dogs and the lowest creatures and should not exploit others for sense gratification. Factually, according to the instructions of *Śrīmad-Bhāgavatam*, every *gṛhastha* is a great communist who provides the means of living for everyone. Whatever a *gṛhastha* may possess he should equally distribute to all living entities, without discrimination. The best process is to distribute *prasāda.*

A *gṛhastha* should not be very much attached to his wife; he should engage even his own wife in serving a guest with all attention. Whatever money a *gṛhastha* accumulates by the grace of God he should spend in five activities, namely worshiping the Supreme Personality of Godhead, receiving Vaiṣṇavas and saintly persons, distributing *prasāda* to the general public and to all living entities, offering *prasāda* to his forefathers, and also offering *prasāda* to his own self. *Gṛhasthas* should always be ready to worship everyone as mentioned above. The *gṛhastha* should not eat anything not offered to the Supreme Personality of Godhead. As it is said in the *Bhagavad-gītā* (3.13), *yajña-śiṣṭāśinaḥ santo mucyante sarva-kilbiṣaiḥ:* "The devotees of the Lord are released from all kinds of sins because they eat food that is offered first for sacrifice." The *gṛhastha* should also visit the holy places of pilgrimage mentioned in the *Purāṇas.* In this way he should fully engage in worshiping the Supreme Personality of Godhead for the benefit of his family, his society, his country, and humanity at large.

TEXT 1

श्रीयुधिष्ठिर उवाच

गृहस्थ एतां पदवीं विधिना येन चाञ्जसा ।
यायाद् देवऋषे ब्रूहि मादृशो गृहमूढधीः ॥ १ ॥

śrī-yudhiṣṭhira uvāca
gṛhastha etāṁ padavīṁ
vidhinā yena cāñjasā
yāyād deva-ṛṣe brūhi
mādṛśo gṛha-mūḍha-dhīḥ

śrī-yudhiṣṭhiraḥ uvāca—Yudhiṣṭhira Mahārāja said; *gṛhasthaḥ*—a person living with his family; *etām*—this (the process mentioned in the previous chapter); *padavīm*—position of liberation; *vidhinā*—according to the instructions of Vedic scripture; *yena*—by which; *ca*—also; *añjasā*—easily; *yāyāt*—may get; *deva-ṛṣe*—O great sage among the demigods; *brūhi*—kindly explain; *mādṛśaḥ*—such as me; *gṛha-mūḍha-dhīḥ*—completely ignorant of the goal of life.

TRANSLATION

Mahārāja Yudhiṣṭhira inquired from Nārada Muni: O my lord, O great sage, kindly explain how we who are staying at home without knowledge of the goal of life may also easily attain liberation, according to the instructions of the Vedas.

PURPORT

In the previous chapters the great sage Nārada has explained how a *brahmacārī*, a *vānaprastha* and a *sannyāsī* should act. He first explained the dealings of a *brahmacārī*, *vānaprastha* and *sannyāsī* because these three *āśramas*, or statuses of life, are extremely important for fulfillment of the goal of life. One should note that in the *brahmacārī-āśrama*, *vānaprastha-āśrama* and *sannyāsa-āśrama* there is no scope for sex life, whereas sex is allowed in *gṛhastha* life under regulations. Nārada Muni, therefore, first described *brahmacarya*, *vānaprastha* and *sannyāsa* because he wanted to stress that sex is not at all necessary, although one who absolutely requires it is allowed to enter *gṛhastha* life, or household life, which is also regulated by the *śāstras* and *guru*. Yudhiṣṭhira Mahārāja could understand all this. Therefore, as a *gṛhastha*, he presented himself as *gṛha-mūḍha-dhīḥ*, one who is completely ignorant of the goal of life. A person who remains a householder in family life is certainly ignorant of life's goal; he is not very much advanced in intelligence. As soon as possible, one should give up his so-called comfortable life at home and prepare to undergo austerity, or *tapasya*. *Tapo divyaṁ putrakā*. According to the instructions given by Ṛṣabhadeva to His sons, we should not create a so-called comfortable situation, but must prepare to undergo austerity. This is how a human being should actually live to fulfill life's ultimate goal.

TEXT 2

श्रीनारद उवाच
गृहेष्ववस्थितो राजन्क्रियाः कुर्वन्यथोचिताः ।
वासुदेवार्पणं साक्षादुपासीत महामुनीन् ॥ २ ॥

śrī-nārada uvāca
gṛheṣv avasthito rājan
kriyāḥ kurvan yathocitāḥ
vāsudevārpaṇaṁ sākṣād
upāsīta mahā-munīn

śrī-nāradaḥ uvāca—Śrī Nārada Muni replied; *gṛheṣu*—at home; *avasthitaḥ*—staying (a householder generally stays home with his wife and children); *rājan*—O King; *kriyāḥ*—activities; *kurvan*—performing; *yathocitāḥ*—suitable (as instructed by the *guru* and *śāstra*); *vāsudeva*—unto Lord Vāsudeva; *arpaṇam*—dedicating; *sākṣāt*—directly; *upāsīta*—should worship; *mahā-munīn*—the great devotees.

TRANSLATION

Nārada Muni replied: My dear King, those who stay at home as householders must act to earn their livelihood, and instead of trying to enjoy the results of their work themselves, they should offer these results to Kṛṣṇa, Vāsudeva. How to satisfy Vāsudeva in this life can be perfectly understood through the association of great devotees of the Lord.

PURPORT

The format for *gṛhastha* life should be dedication to the Supreme Personality of Godhead. In *Bhagavad-gītā* (6.1) it is said:

anāśritaḥ karma-phalaṁ
kāryaṁ karma karoti yaḥ
sa sannyāsī ca yogī ca
na niragnir na cākriyaḥ

"One who is unattached to the fruits of his work and who works as he is obligated is in the renounced order of life, and he is the true mystic, not he who lights no fire and performs no work." Whether one acts as a *brahmacārī, gṛhastha, vānaprastha* or *sannyāsī*, he must act only for the satisfaction of the Supreme Personality of Godhead, Vāsudeva—Kṛṣṇa, the son of Vasudeva. This should be the principle for everyone's life. Nārada Muni has already described the principles of life for a *brahmacārī, vānaprastha* and *sannyāsī*, and now he is describing how a *gṛhastha* should live. The basic principle is to satisfy the Supreme Personality of Godhead.

The science of satisfying the Supreme Lord can be learned as described here: *sākṣād upāsīta mahā-munīn.* The word *mahā-munīn* refers to great saintly persons or devotees. Saintly persons are generally known as *munis*, or thoughtful philosophers concerned with transcendental subject matters, and *mahā-munīn* refers to those who have not only thoroughly studied the goal of life but who are actually engaged in satisfying the Supreme Personality of Godhead, Vāsudeva. These persons are known as devotees. Unless one associates with devotees, one cannot learn the science of *vāsudevārpaṇa*, or dedicating one's life to Vāsudeva, Kṛṣṇa, the Supreme Personality of Godhead.

In India the principles of this science were followed strictly. Even fifty years ago, I saw that in the villages of Bengal and the suburbs of Calcutta, people engaged in hearing *Śrīmad-Bhāgavatam* daily when all their activities ended, or at least in the evening before going to bed. Everyone would hear the *Bhāgavatam. Bhāgavata* classes were held in every village, and thus people had the advantage of hearing *Śrīmad-Bhāgavatam*, which describes everything about the aim of life—liberation or salvation. This will be clearly explained in the next verses.

TEXTS 3–4

शृण्वन्भगवतोऽभीक्ष्णमवतारकथामृतम् ।
श्रद्दधानो यथाकालमुपशान्तजनावृतः ॥ ३ ॥
सत्सङ्गाच्छनकैः सङ्गमात्मजायात्मजादिषु ।
विमुञ्चेन्मुच्यमानेषु स्वयं स्वप्नवदुत्थितः ॥ ४ ॥

śṛṇvan bhagavato 'bhīkṣṇam
avatāra-kathāmṛtam
śraddadhāno yathā-kālam
upaśānta-janāvṛtaḥ

sat-saṅgāc chanakaiḥ saṅgam
ātma-jāyātmajādiṣu
vimuñcen mucyamāneṣu
svayaṁ svapnavad utthitaḥ

śṛṇvan—hearing; *bhagavataḥ*—of the Lord; *abhīkṣṇam*—always; *avatāra*—of the incarnations; *kathā*—narrations; *amṛtam*—the nectar; *śraddadhānaḥ*—being very faithful in hearing about the Supreme Personality of Godhead; *yathā-kālam*—according to time (generally a *gṛhastha* can find time in the evening or in the afternoon); *upaśānta*—completely relieved of material activities; *jana*—by persons; *āvṛtaḥ*—being surrounded; *sat-saṅgāt*—from such good association; *śanakaiḥ*—gradually; *saṅgam*—association; *ātma*—in the body; *jāyā*—wife; *ātma-ja-ādiṣu*—as well as in children; *vimuñcet*—one should get free from the attachment for such association; *mucyamāneṣu*—being severed (from him); *svayam*—personally; *svapna-vat*—like a dream; *utthitaḥ*—awakened.

TRANSLATION

A gṛhastha must associate again and again with saintly persons, and with great respect he must hear the nectar of the activities of the Supreme Lord and His incarnations as these activities are described in Śrīmad-Bhāgavatam and other Purāṇas. Thus one should gradually become detached from affection for his wife and children, exactly like a man awakening from a dream.

PURPORT

The Kṛṣṇa consciousness movement has been established to give *gṛhasthas* all over the world an opportunity to hear *Śrīmad-Bhāgavatam* and *Bhagavad-gītā* specifically. The process, as described in many ways, is one of hearing and chanting (*śṛṇvatāṁ sva-kathāḥ kṛṣṇaḥ puṇya-śravaṇa-kīrtanaḥ*). Everyone, especially the *gṛhasthas*, who are *mūḍha-dhī*, ignorant about the goal of life, should be given opportunities to hear about Kṛṣṇa. Simply by hearing, by attending lectures in the different centers of the Kṛṣṇa consciousness movement, where topics of Kṛṣṇa from *Bhagavad-gītā* and *Śrīmad-Bhāgavatam* are discussed, they will be purified of their sinful inclination for constant indulgence in illicit sex, meat-eating, intoxication and gambling, which have all become prominent in modern days. Thus they can be raised to the status of light. *Puṇya-śravaṇa-kīrtanaḥ*. Simply by joining the *kīrtana*—Hare Kṛṣṇa, Hare Kṛṣṇa, Kṛṣṇa Kṛṣṇa, Hare Hare/ Hare Rāma, Hare Rāma, Rāma Rāma, Hare Hare—and by hearing about Kṛṣṇa from *Bhagavad-gītā*, one must be purified, especially if he also takes *prasāda*. This is all going on in the Kṛṣṇa consciousness movement.

Another specific description here is *śṛṇvan bhagavato 'bhīkṣṇam avatāra-kathāmṛtam*. It is not that because one has once finished *Bhagavad-gītā* he should not hear it again. The word *abhīkṣṇam* is very important. We should hear again and again. There is no question of stopping: even if one has read these topics many times, he should go on reading again and again because *bhagavat-kathā*, the words spoken by Kṛṣṇa and spoken by Kṛṣṇa's devotees about Kṛṣṇa, are *amṛtam*, nectar. The more one drinks this *amṛtam*, the more he advances in his eternal life.

The human form of life is meant for liberation, but unfortunately, due to the influence of Kali-yuga, every day the *gṛhasthas* are working hard like asses. Early in the morning they rise and travel even a hundred miles away to earn bread. Especially in the Western countries, I have seen that people awaken at five o'clock to go to offices and factories to earn their livelihood. People in Calcutta and Bombay also do this every day. They work very hard in the office or factory, and again they spend three or four hours in transportation returning home. Then they retire at ten o'clock and again rise early in the morning to go to their offices and factories. This kind of hard labor is described in the *śāstras* as the life of pigs and stool-eaters. *Nāyaṁ deho deha-bhājāṁ nṛloke kaṣṭān kāmān arhate viḍ-bhujāṁ ye:* "Of all living entities who have accepted material bodies in this world, one who has been awarded this human form should not work hard day and night simply for sense gratification, which is available even for dogs and hogs that eat stool." (*Bhāg.* 5.5.1) One must find some time for hearing *Śrīmad-Bhāgavatam* and *Bhagavad-gītā*. This is Vedic culture. One should work eight hours at the most to earn his livelihood, and either in the afternoon or in the evening a householder should associate with devotees to hear about the incarnations of

Kṛṣṇa and His activities and thus be gradually liberated from the clutches of *māyā*. However, instead of finding time to hear about Kṛṣṇa, the householders, after working hard in offices and factories, find time to go to a restaurant or a club where instead of hearing about Kṛṣṇa and His activities they are very much pleased to hear about the political activities of demons and nondevotees and to enjoy sex, wine, women and meat and in this way waste their time. This is not *gṛhastha* life, but demoniac life. The Kṛṣṇa consciousness movement, however, with its centers all over the world, gives such fallen and condemned persons an opportunity to hear about Kṛṣṇa.

In a dream we form a society of friendship and love, and when we awaken we see that it has ceased to exist. Similarly, one's gross society, family and love are also a dream, and this dream will be over as soon as one dies. Therefore, whether one is dreaming in a subtle way or a gross way, these dreams are all false and temporary. One's real business is to understand that one is soul (*ahaṁ brahmāsmi*) and that his activities should therefore be different. Then one can be happy.

brahma-bhūtaḥ prasannātmā
na śocati na kāṅkṣati
samaḥ sarveṣu bhūteṣu
mad-bhaktiṁ labhate parām

"One who is transcendentally situated at once realizes the Supreme Brahman and becomes fully joyful. He never laments nor desires to have anything; he is equally disposed toward all living entities. In that state he attains pure devotional service unto Me." (Bg. 18.54) One who is engaged in devotional service can very easily be liberated from the dream of materialistic life.

TEXT 5

यावदर्थमुपासीनो देहे गेहे च पण्डितः ।
विरक्तो रक्तवत् तत्र नृलोके नरतां न्यसेत् ॥ ५ ॥

yāvad-artham upāsīno
dehe gehe ca paṇḍitaḥ

virakto raktavat tatra
nṛ-loke naratāṁ nyaset

yāvat-artham—as much endeavor for one's livelihood as necessary; *upāsīnaḥ*—earning; *dehe*—in the body; *gehe*—in family matters; *ca*—also; *paṇḍitaḥ*—one who is learned; *viraktaḥ*—not at all attached; *rakta-vat*—as if very much attached; *tatra*—in this; *nṛ-loke*—human society; *naratām*—the human form of life; *nyaset*—one should depict.

TRANSLATION

While working to earn his livelihood as much as necessary to maintain body and soul together, one who is actually learned should live in human society unattached to family affairs, although externally appearing very much attached.

PURPORT

This is the picture of ideal family life. When Śrī Caitanya Mahāprabhu asked Rāmānanda Rāya about the goal of life, Rāmānanda Rāya described it in different ways, according to the recommendations of the revealed scriptures, and finally Śrī Rāmānanda Rāya explained that one may stay in his own position, whether as a *brāhmaṇa*, a *śūdra*, a *sannyāsī* or whatever, but one must try to inquire about life's goal (*athāto brahma-jijñāsā*). This is the proper utilization of the human form of life. When one misuses the gift of the human form by unnecessarily indulging in the animal propensities of eating, sleeping, mating and defending and does not try to get out of the clutches of *māyā*, which subjects one to repeated birth, death, old age and disease, one is again punished by being forced to descend to the lower species and undergo evolution according to the laws of nature. *Prakṛteḥ kriyamāṇāni guṇaiḥ karmāṇi sarvaśaḥ.* Being completely under the grip of material nature, the living entity must evolve again from the lower species to the higher species until he at last returns to human life and gets the chance to be freed from the material clutches. A wise man, however, learns from the *śāstras* and *guru* that we living entities are all eternal but are put into troublesome conditions because of associating with different modes under the laws of material nature. He therefore concludes that in the human form of life he should not endeavor for unnecessary necessities, but should live a very simple life, just maintaining body and soul together. Certainly one requires some means of livelihood, and according to one's *varṇa* and *āśrama* this means of livelihood is prescribed in the *śāstras.* One should be satisfied with this. Therefore, instead of hankering for more and more money, a sincere devotee of the Lord tries to invent some ways to earn his livelihood, and when he does so Kṛṣṇa helps him. Earning one's livelihood, therefore, is not a problem. The real problem is how to get free from the bondage of birth, death and old age. Attaining this freedom, and not inventing unnecessary necessities, is the basic principle of Vedic civilization. One should be satisfied with whatever means of life comes automatically. The modern materialistic civilization is just the opposite of the ideal civilization. Every day the so-called leaders of modern society invent something contributing to a cumbersome way of life that implicates people more and more in the cycle of birth, death, old age and disease.

TEXT 6

ज्ञातयः पितरौ पुत्रा भ्रातरः सुहृदोऽपरे ।
यद् वदन्ति यदिच्छन्ति चानुमोदेत निर्ममः ॥ ६ ॥

jñātayaḥ pitarau putrā
bhrātaraḥ suhṛdo 'pare
yad vadanti yad icchanti
cānumodeta nirmamaḥ

jñātayaḥ—relatives, family members; *pitarau*—the father and mother; *putrāḥ*—children; *bhrātaraḥ*—brothers; *suhṛdaḥ*—friends; *apare*—and others; *yat*—whatever; *vadanti*—they suggest (in regard to one's means of livelihood); *yat*—whatever; *icchanti*—they wish; *ca*—and; *anumodeta*—he should agree; *nirmamaḥ*—but without taking them seriously.

TRANSLATION

An intelligent man in human society should make his own program of activities very simple. If there are suggestions from his

friends, children, parents, brothers or anyone else, he should externally agree, saying, "Yes, that is all right," but internally he should be determined not to create a cumbersome life in which the purpose of life will not be fulfilled.

TEXT 7

दिव्यं भौमं चान्तरीक्षं वित्तमच्युतनिर्मितम् ।
तत् सर्वमुपयुञ्जान एतत् कुर्यात् स्वतो बुधः ।। ७ ।।

divyaṁ bhaumaṁ cāntarīkṣaṁ
vittam acyuta-nirmitam
tat sarvam upayuñjāna
etat kuryāt svato budhaḥ

divyam—easily obtained because of rainfall from the sky; *bhaumam*—obtained from the mines and the sea; *ca*—and; *āntarīkṣam*—obtained by chance; *vittam*—all property; *acyuta-nirmitam*—created by the Supreme Personality of Godhead; *tat*—those things; *sarvam*—all; *upayuñjāna*—utilizing (for all human society or all living beings); *etat*—this (maintaining body and soul together); *kuryāt*—one must do; *svataḥ*—obtained of itself, without extra endeavor; *budhaḥ*—the intelligent person.

TRANSLATION

The natural products created by the Supreme Personality of Godhead should be utilized to maintain the bodies and souls of all living entities. The necessities of life are of three types: those produced from the sky [from rainfall], from the earth [from the mines, the seas or the fields], and from the atmosphere [that which is obtained suddenly and unexpectedly].

PURPORT

We living entities in different forms are all children of the Supreme Personality of Godhead, as confirmed by the Lord in *Bhagavad-gītā* (14.4):

sarva-yoniṣu kaunteya
mūrtayaḥ sambhavanti yāḥ
tāsāṁ brahma mahad-yonir
ahaṁ bīja-pradaḥ pitā

"It should be understood that all species of life, O son of Kuntī, are made possible by birth in this material nature, and that I am the seed-giving father." The Supreme Lord, Kṛṣṇa, is the father of all living entities in different species and forms. One who is intelligent can see that all living entities in the 8,400,000 bodily forms are part of the Supreme Personality of Godhead and are His sons. Everything within the material and spiritual worlds is the property of the Supreme Lord (*īśāvāsyam idaṁ sarvam*), and therefore everything has a relationship with Him. Śrīla Rūpa Gosvāmī says in this regard:

prāpañcikatayā buddhyā
hari-sambandhi-vastunaḥ
mumukṣubhiḥ parityāgo
vairāgyaṁ phalgu kathyate

"One who rejects anything without knowledge of its relationship to Kṛṣṇa is incomplete in his renunciation." (*Bhakti-rasāmṛta-sindhu* 1.2.256) Although Māyāvādī philosophers say that the material creation is false, actually it is not false; it is factual, but the idea that everything belongs to human society is false. Everything belongs to the Supreme Personality of Godhead, for everything is created by Him. All living entities, being the Lord's sons, His eternal parts and parcels, have the right to use their father's property by nature's arrangement. As stated in the *Upaniṣads, tena tyaktena bhuñjīthā mā gṛdhaḥ kasya svid dhanam.* Everyone should be satisfied with the things allotted him by the Supreme Personality of Godhead; no one should encroach upon another's rights or property.

In *Bhagavad-gītā* it is said:

annād bhavanti bhūtāni
parjanyād anna-sambhavaḥ
yajñād bhavati parjanyo
yajñaḥ karma-samudbhavaḥ

"All living bodies subsist on food grains, which are produced from rains. Rains are produced by performance of *yajña* [sacrifice], and *yajña* is born of prescribed duties." (Bg. 3.14) When food grains are sufficiently produced, both animals and human beings can be nourished without difficulty for their maintenance. This is nature's arrangement. *Prakṛteḥ kriyamāṇāni guṇaiḥ karmāṇi sarvaśaḥ.* Everyone is acting under the influence of material nature, and only fools think they can improve upon what God has created. The householders are specifically responsible for seeing that the laws of the Supreme Personality of Godhead are maintained, without fighting between men, communities, societies or nations. Human society should properly utilize the gifts of God, especially the food grains that grow because of rain falling from the sky. As stated in *Bhagavad-gītā, yajñād bhavati parjanyaḥ.* So that rainfall will be regulated, humanity should perform *yajñas,* sacrifices. *Yajñas* were previously performed with offerings of oblations of ghee and food grains, but in this age, of course, this is no longer possible, for the production of ghee and food grains has diminished because of the sinful life of human society. However, people should take to Kṛṣṇa consciousness and chant the Hare Kṛṣṇa *mantra,* as recommended in the *śāstras* (*yajñaiḥ saṅkīrtana-prāyair yajanti hi sumedhasaḥ*). If people throughout the world take to the Kṛṣṇa consciousness movement and chant the easy sound vibration of the transcendental name and fame of the Supreme Personality of Godhead, there will be no scarcity of rainfall; consequently food grains, fruits and flowers will be properly produced, and all the necessities of life will be easily obtained. *Gṛhasthas,* or householders, should take the responsibility for organizing such natural production. It is therefore said, *tasyaiva hetoḥ prayateta kovidaḥ.* An intelligent person should try to spread Kṛṣṇa consciousness through the chanting of the holy name of the Lord, and all the necessities of life will automatically follow.

TEXT 8

यावद् भ्रियेत जठरं तावत् स्वत्वं हि देहिनाम् ।
अधिकं योऽभिमन्येत स स्तेनो दण्डमर्हति ॥ ८ ॥

yāvad bhriyeta jaṭharaṁ
tāvat svatvaṁ hi dehinām

adhikaṁ yo 'bhimanyeta
sa steno daṇḍam arhati

yāvat—as much as; *bhriyeta*—may be filled; *jaṭharam*—the stomach; *tāvat*—that much; *svatvam*—proprietorship; *hi*—indeed; *dehinām*—of the living entities; *adhikam*—more than that; *yaḥ*—anyone who; *abhimanyeta*—may accept; *saḥ*—he; *stenaḥ*—a thief; *daṇḍam*—punishment; *arhati*—deserves.

TRANSLATION

One may claim proprietorship to as much wealth as required to maintain body and soul together, but one who desires proprietorship over more than that must be considered a thief, and he deserves to be punished by the laws of nature.

PURPORT

By God's favor we sometimes get large quantities of food grains or suddenly receive some contribution or unexpected profit in business. In this way we may get more money than needed. So, how should that be spent? There is no need to accumulate money in the bank merely to increase one's bank balance. Such a mentality is described in *Bhagavad-gītā* (16.13) as asuric, demoniac.

idam adya mayā labdham
imaṁ prāpsye manoratham
idam astīdam api me
bhaviṣyati punar dhanam

"The demoniac person thinks, 'So much wealth do I have today, and I will gain more according to my schemes. So much is mine now, and it will increase in the future, more and more.'" The *asura* is concerned with how much wealth he has in the bank today and how it will increase tomorrow, but unrestricted accumulation of wealth is not permitted either by the *śāstra* or, in the modern age, by the government. Actually, if one has more than one requires for his necessities, the extra money should be spent for Kṛṣṇa. According to the Vedic civilization. it should all be given to the Kṛṣṇa consciousness movement, as ordered by the Lord Himself in *Bhagavad-gītā* (9.27):

yat karoṣi yad aśnāsi
yaj juhoṣi dadāsi yat
yat tapasyasi kaunteya
tat kuruṣva mad-arpaṇam

"O son of Kuntī, all that you do, all that you eat, all that you offer and give away, as well as all austerities that you may perform, should be done as an offering unto Me." *Gṛhasthas* should spend extra money only for the Kṛṣṇa consciousness movement.

The *gṛhasthas* should give contributions for constructing temples of the Supreme Lord and for preaching of *Śrīmad Bhagavad-gītā*, or Kṛṣṇa consciousness, all over the world. *Śṛṇvan bhagavato 'bhīkṣṇam avatāra-kathāmṛtam.* In the *śāstras*—the *Purāṇas* and other Vedic literatures—there are so many narrations describing the transcendental activities of the Supreme Personality of Godhead, and everyone should hear them again and again. For example, even if we read the entire *Bhagavad-gītā* every day, all eighteen chapters, in each reading we shall find a new explanation. That is the nature of transcendental literature. The Kṛṣṇa consciousness movement therefore affords one an opportunity to spend his extra earnings for the benefit of all human society by expanding Kṛṣṇa consciousness. In India especially we see hundreds and thousands of temples that were constructed by the wealthy men of society who did not want to be called thieves and be punished.

This verse is very important. As stated here, one who accumulates more money than needed is a thief, and by the laws of nature he will be punished. One who acquires more money than necessary becomes desirous of enjoying material comforts more and more. Materialists are inventing so many artificial necessities, and those who have money, being allured by such artificial necessities, try to accumulate money to possess more and more. This is the idea of modern economic development. Everyone is engaged in earning money, and the money is kept in the bank, which then offers money to the public. In this cycle of activities, everyone is engaged in getting more and more money, and therefore the ideal goal of human life is being lost. Concisely, it may be said that everyone is a thief and is liable to be punished. Punishment by the laws of nature takes place in the cycle of birth and death. No one dies fully satisfied by the fulfillment of material desires, for that is not possible. Therefore at the time of one's death one is very sorry, being unable to fulfill his desires. By the laws of nature one is then offered another body to fulfill his unsatisfied desires, and upon taking birth again, accepting another material body, one voluntarily accepts the threefold miseries of life.

TEXT 9

मृगोष्ट्रखरमर्काखुसरीसृप्खगमक्षिकाः ।
आत्मनः पुत्रवत् पश्येत्तैरेषामन्तरं कियत् ॥ ९ ॥

mṛgoṣṭra-khara-markākhu-
sarīsṛp khaga-makṣikāḥ
ātmanaḥ putravat paśyet
tair eṣām antaraṁ kiyat

mṛga—deer; *uṣṭra*—camels; *khara*—asses; *marka*—monkeys; *ākhu*—mice; *sarīsṛp*—snakes; *khaga*—birds; *makṣikāḥ*—flies; *ātmanaḥ*—of one's self; *putra-vat*—like the sons; *paśyet*—one should see; *taiḥ*—with those sons; *eṣām*—of these animals; *antaram*—difference; *kiyat*—how little.

TRANSLATION

One should treat animals such as deer, camels, asses, monkeys, mice, snakes, birds and flies exactly like one's own son. How little difference there actually is between children and these innocent animals.

PURPORT

One who is in Kṛṣṇa consciousness understands that there is no difference between the animals and the innocent children in one's home. Even in ordinary life, it is our practical experience that a household dog or cat is regarded on the same level as one's children, without any envy. Like children, the unintelligent animals are also sons of the Supreme

Personality of Godhead, and therefore a Kṛṣṇa conscious person, even though a householder, should not discriminate between children and poor animals. Unfortunately, modern society has devised many means for killing animals in different forms of life. For example, in the agricultural fields there may be many mice, flies and other creatures that disturb production, and sometimes they are killed by pesticides. In this verse, however, such killing is forbidden. Every living entity should be nourished by the food given by the Supreme Personality of Godhead. Human society should not consider itself the only enjoyer of all the properties of God; rather, men should understand that all the other animals also have a claim to God's property. In this verse even the snake is mentioned, indicating that a householder should not be envious even of a snake. If everyone is fully satisfied by eating food that is a gift from the Lord, why should there be envy between one living being and another? In modern days people are very much inclined toward communistic ideas of society, but we do not think that there can be any better communistic idea than that which is explained in this verse of *Śrīmad-Bhāgavatam*. Even in the communistic countries the poor animals are killed without consideration, although they also should have the right to take their allotted food with which to live.

TEXT 10

त्रिवर्गं नातिकृच्छ्रेण भजेत गृहमेध्यपि ।
यथादेशं यथाकालं यावद्दैवोपपादितम् ॥१०॥

tri-vargaṁ nātikṛcchreṇa
bhajeta gṛha-medhy api
yathā-deśaṁ yathā-kālaṁ
yāvad-daivopapāditam

tri-vargam—three principles, namely religiosity, economic development and sense gratification; *na*—not; *ati-kṛcchreṇa*—by very severe endeavor; *bhajeta*—should execute; *gṛha-medhī*—a person interested only in family life; *api*—although; *yathā-deśam*—according to the place; *yathā-kālam*—according to the time; *yāvat*—as much as; *daiva*—by the grace of the Lord; *upapāditam*—obtained.

TRANSLATION

Even if one is a householder rather than a brahmacārī, a sannyāsī or a vānaprastha, one should not endeavor very hard for religiosity, economic development or satisfaction of the senses. Even in householder life, one should be satisfied to maintain body and soul together with whatever is available with minimum endeavor, according to place and time, by the grace of the Lord. One should not engage oneself in ugra-karma.

PURPORT

In human life there are four principles to be fulfilled—*dharma, artha, kāma* and *mokṣa* (religion, economic development, sense gratification, and liberation). First one should be religious, observing various rules and regulations, and then one must earn some money for maintenance of his family and the satisfaction of his senses. The most important ceremony for sense gratification is marriage because sexual intercourse is one of the principal necessities of the material body. *Yan maithunādi-gṛhamedhi-sukhaṁ hi tuccham.* Although sexual intercourse is not a very exalted requisite in life, both animals and men require some sense gratification because of material propensities. One should be satisfied with married life and not expend energy for extra sense gratification or sex life.

As for economic development, the responsibility for this should be entrusted mainly to the *vaiśyas* and *gṛhasthas.* Human society should be divided into *varṇas* and *āśramas—brāhmaṇa, kṣatriya, vaiśya, śūdra, brahmacarya, gṛhastha, vānaprastha* and *sannyāsa.* Economic development is necessary for *gṛhasthas. Brāhmaṇa gṛhasthas* should be satisfied with a life of *adhyayana, adhyāpana, yajana* and *yājana*—being learned scholars, teaching others to be scholars, learning how to worship the Supreme Personality of Godhead, Viṣṇu, and also teaching others how to worship Lord Viṣṇu, or even the demigods. A *brāhmaṇa* should do this without remuneration, but he is allowed to accept charity from a person whom he teaches how to be a human being. As for the *kṣatriyas,* they are supposed to be the kings of the land, and the land should be distributed to the *vaiśyas* for agricultural activities, cow protection and trade. *Śūdras* must work; sometimes they should engage in occupational duties as cloth manufacturers, weavers, blacksmiths, goldsmiths, brass-smiths, and so on, or else they should engage in hard labor to produce food grains.

These are the different occupational duties by which men should earn their livelihood, and in this way human society should be simple. At the present moment, however, everyone is engaged in technological advancement, which is described in *Bhagavad-gītā* as *ugra-karma*—extremely severe endeavor. This *ugra-karma* is the cause of agitation within the human mind. Men are engaging in many sinful activities and becoming degraded by opening slaughterhouses, breweries and cigarette factories, as well as nightclubs and other establishments for sense enjoyment. In this way they are spoiling their lives. In all of these activities, of course, householders are involved, and therefore it is advised here, with the use of the word *api*, that even though one is a householder, one should not engage himself in severe hardships. One's means of livelihood should be extremely simple. As for those who are not *gṛhasthas*—the *brahmacārīs*, *vānaprasthas* and *sannyāsīs*—they don't have to do anything but strive for advancement in spiritual life. This means that three fourths of the entire population should stop sense gratification and simply be engaged in the advancement of Kṛṣṇa consciousness. Only one fourth of the population should be *gṛhastha*, and that should be according to laws of restricted sense gratification. The *gṛhasthas*, *vānaprasthas*, *brahmacārīs* and *sannyāsīs* should endeavor together with their total energy to become Kṛṣṇa conscious. This type of civilization is called *daiva-varṇāśrama*. One of the objectives of the Kṛṣṇa consciousness movement is to establish this *daiva-varṇāśrama*, but not to encourage so-called *varṇāśrama* without scientifically organized endeavor by human society.

TEXT 11

आश्वाघान्तेऽवसायिभ्यः कामान्संविभजेद् यथा ।
अप्येकामात्मनो दारां नृणां स्वत्वग्रहो यतः ॥११॥

āśvāghānte 'vasāyibhyaḥ
kāmān saṁvibhajed yathā
apy ekām ātmano dārāṁ
nṛṇāṁ svatva-graho yataḥ

ā—even up to; *śva*—the dog; *agha*—sinful animals or living entities; *ante avasāyibhyaḥ*—unto the *caṇḍālas*, the lowest of men (dog-eaters and hog-eaters); *kāmān*—the necessities of life; *saṁvibhajet*—should divide; *yathā*—as much as (deserved); *api*—even; *ekām*—one; *ātmanaḥ*—own; *dārām*—the wife; *nṛṇām*—of the people in general; *svatva-grahaḥ*—the wife is accepted as being identical with one's self; *yataḥ*—because of which.

TRANSLATION

Dogs, fallen persons and untouchables, including caṇḍālas [dog-eaters], should all be maintained with their proper necessities, which should be contributed by the householders. Even one's wife at home, with whom one is most intimately attached, should be offered for the reception of guests and people in general.

PURPORT

Although in modern society the dog is accepted as part of one's household paraphernalia, in the Vedic system of household life the dog is untouchable; as mentioned here, a dog may be maintained with proper food, but it cannot be allowed to enter one's house, what to speak of the bedroom. Outcastes or untouchable *caṇḍālas* should also be provided with the necessities for life. The word used in this connection is *yathā*, which means "as much as deserved." The outcastes should not be given money with which to indulge in more than they need, for otherwise they will misuse it. At the present moment, for example, low-class men are generally paid quite amply, but instead of using their money to cultivate knowledge and advance in life, such low-class men use their extra money for wine-drinking and similar sinful activities. As mentioned in *Bhagavad-gītā* (4.13), *cātur-varṇyaṁ mayā sṛṣṭaṁ guṇa-karma-vibhāgaśaḥ:* there must be four divisions of human society according to the work and qualities of men. Men with the lowest qualities cannot do any work that requires higher intelligence. However, although such a division of men must exist according to their quality and work, it is suggested herewith that everyone must have the necessities of life. The communists of the present day are in favor of supplying the necessities of life to everyone, but they consider only the human beings and not the lower animals. The *Bhāgavatam's* principles are so broad, however, that it recommends that the necessities of life be supplied to everyone, man or animal, regardless of good or bad qualities.

The idea of giving even one's wife to the service of the public is that one's intimate relationship with his wife, or one's excessive attachment for his wife, by which one thinks his wife to be his better half or to be identical with himself, must gradually be given up. As formerly suggested, the idea of ownership, even of one's family, must be abandoned. The dream of material life is the cause of bondage in the cycle of birth and death, and therefore one should give up this dream. Consequently, in the human form of life one's attachment for his wife should be given up, as suggested herein.

TEXT 12

जह्याद् यदर्थे स्वान् प्राणान्हन्याद् वा पितरं गुरुम् ।
तस्यां स्वत्वं स्त्रियां जह्याद् यस्तेन ह्यजितो जितः ॥१२॥

jahyād yad-arthe svān prāṇān
hanyād vā pitaraṁ gurum
tasyāṁ svatvaṁ striyāṁ jahyād
yas tena hy ajito jitaḥ

jahyāt—one may give up; *yat-arthe*—for whom; *svān*—one's own; *prāṇān*—life; *hanyāt*—one may kill; *vā*—or; *pitaram*—the father; *gurum*—the teacher or spiritual master; *tasyām*—unto her; *svatvam*—ownership; *striyām*—unto the wife; *jahyāt*—one must give up; *yaḥ*—one who (the Supreme Personality of Godhead); *tena*—by him; *hi*—indeed; *ajitaḥ*—cannot be conquered; *jitaḥ*—conquered.

TRANSLATION

One so seriously considers one's wife to be his own that he sometimes kills himself for her or kills others, including even his parents or his spiritual master or teacher. Therefore if one can give up his attachment to such a wife, he conquers the Supreme Personality of Godhead, who is never conquered by anyone.

PURPORT

Every husband is too much attached to his wife. Therefore, to give up one's connection with his wife is extremely difficult, but if one can somehow or other give it up for the service of the Supreme Personality of Godhead, then the Lord Himself, although not able to be conquered by anyone, comes very much under the control of the devotee. And if the Lord is pleased with a devotee, what is there that is unobtainable? Why should one not give up his affection for his wife and children and take shelter of the Supreme Personality of Godhead? Where is the loss of anything material? Householder life means attachment for one's wife, whereas *sannyāsa* means detachment from one's wife and attachment to Kṛṣṇa.

TEXT 13

क्रिमिविड्भस्मनिष्ठान्तं क्वेदं तुच्छं कलेवरम् ।
क्व तदीयरतिर्भार्या क्वायमात्मा नभश्छदिः ॥१३॥

kṛmi-viḍ-bhasma-niṣṭhāntaṁ
kvedaṁ tucchaṁ kalevaram
kva tadīya-ratir bhāryā
kvāyam ātmā nabhaś-chadiḥ

kṛmi—insects, germs; *viṭ*—stool; *bhasma*—ashes; *niṣṭha*—attachment; *antam*—at the end; *kva*—what is; *idam*—this (body); *tuccham*—very insignificant; *kalevaram*—material tabernacle; *kva*—what is that; *tadīya-ratiḥ*—attraction for that body; *bhāryā*—wife; *kva ayam*—what is the value of this body; *ātmā*—the Supreme Soul; *nabhaḥ-chadiḥ*—all-pervading like the sky.

TRANSLATION

Through proper deliberation, one should give up attraction to his wife's body because that body will ultimately be transformed into small insects, stool or ashes. What is the value of this insignificant body? How much greater is the Supreme Being, who is all-pervading like the sky?

PURPORT

Here also, the same point is stressed: one should give up attachment for his wife—or, in other words, for sex life. If one is intelligent, he can think of his wife's body as nothing but a lump of matter that will ultimately be transformed into small insects, stool or ashes. In different societies there are different ways of dealing with the human body at the time of the funeral ceremony. In some societies the body is given to the vultures to be eaten, and therefore the body ultimately turns to vulture stool. Sometimes the body is merely abandoned, and in that case the body is consumed by small insects. In some societies the body is immediately burned after death, and thus it becomes ashes. In any case, if one intelligently considers the constitution of the body and the soul beyond it, what is the value of the body? *Antavanta ime dehā nityasyoktāḥ śarīriṇaḥ:* the body may perish at any moment, but the soul is eternal. If one gives up attachment for the body and increases his attachment for the spirit soul, his life is successful. It is merely a matter of deliberation.

TEXT 14

सिद्धैर्यज्ञावशिष्टार्थैः कल्पयेद् वृत्तिमात्मनः ।
शेषे स्वत्वं त्यजन्प्राज्ञः पदवीं महतामियात् ॥१४॥

siddhair yajñāvaśiṣṭārthaiḥ
kalpayed vṛttim ātmanaḥ
śeṣe svatvaṁ tyajan prājñaḥ
padavīṁ mahatām iyāt

siddhaiḥ—things obtained by the grace of the Lord; *yajñā-avaśiṣṭa-arthaiḥ*—things obtained after a sacrifice is offered to the Lord or after the recommended *pañca-sūnā yajña* is performed; *kalpayet*—one should consider; *vṛttim*—the means of livelihood; *ātmanaḥ*—for the self; *śeṣe*—at the end; *svatvam*—so-called proprietorship over one's wife, children, home, business and so on; *tyajan*—giving up; *prājñaḥ*—those who are wise; *padavīm*—the position; *mahatām*—of the great personalities who are fully satisfied in spiritual consciousness; *iyāt*—should achieve.

TRANSLATION

An intelligent person should be satisfied with eating prasāda [food offered to the Lord] or with performing the five different

kinds of yajña [pañca-sūnā]. By such activities, one can give up attachment for the body and so-called proprietorship with reference to the body. When one is able to do this, he is firmly fixed in the position of a mahātmā.

PURPORT

Nature already has an arrangement to feed us. By the order of the Supreme Personality of Godhead, there is an arrangement for eatables for every living entity within the 8,400,000 forms of life. *Eko bahūnāṁ yo vidadhāti kāmān.* Every living entity has to eat something, and in fact the necessities for his life have already been provided by the Supreme Personality of Godhead. The Lord has provided food for both the elephant and the ant. All living beings are living at the cost of the Supreme Lord, and therefore one who is intelligent should not work very hard for material comforts. Rather, one should save his energy for advancing in Kṛṣṇa consciousness. All created things in the sky, in the air, on land and in the sea belong to the Supreme Personality of Godhead, and every living being is provided with food. Therefore one should not be very much anxious about economic development and unnecessarily waste time and energy with the risk of falling down in the cycle of birth and death.

TEXT 15

देवानृषीन् नृभूतानि पितॄनात्मानमन्वहम् ।
स्ववृत्त्यागतवित्तेन यजेत पुरुषं पृथक् ॥१५॥

devān ṛṣīn nṛ-bhūtāni
pitṝn ātmānam anvaham
sva-vṛttyāgata-vittena
yajeta puruṣaṁ pṛthak

devān—unto the demigods; *ṛṣīn*—unto the great sages; *nṛ*—unto human society; *bhūtāni*—unto the living entities in general; *pitṝn*—unto the forefathers; *ātmānam*—one's self or the Supreme Self; *anvaham*—daily; *sva-vṛttyā*—by one's means of livelihood; *āgata-vittena*—money that automatically comes; *yajeta*—one should worship; *puruṣam*—the person situated in everyone's heart; *pṛthak*—separately.

TRANSLATION

Every day, one should worship the Supreme Being who is situated in everyone's heart, and on this basis one should separately worship the demigods, the saintly persons, ordinary human beings and living entities, one's forefathers and one's self. In this way one is able to worship the Supreme Being in the core of everyone's heart.

TEXT 16

यर्ह्यात्मनोऽधिकाराद्याः सर्वाः स्युर्यज्ञसम्पदः ।
वैतानिकेन विधिना अग्निहोत्रादिना यजेत् ॥१६॥

yarhy ātmano 'dhikārādyāḥ
sarvāḥ syur yajña-sampadaḥ
vaitānikena vidhinā
agni-hotrādinā yajet

yarhi—when; *ātmanaḥ*—of one's self; *adhikāra-ādyāḥ*—things possessed by him under full control; *sarvāḥ*—everything; *syuḥ*—becomes; *yajña-sampadaḥ*—paraphernalia for performing *yajña,* or the means for pleasing the Supreme Personality of Godhead; *vaitānikena*—with authorized books that direct the performance of *yajña; vidhinā*—according to regulative principles; *agni-hotra-ādinā*—by offering sacrifices to the fire, etc.; *yajet*—one should worship the Supreme Personality of Godhead.

TRANSLATION

When one is enriched with wealth and knowledge which are under his full control and by means of which he can perform yajña or please the Supreme Personality of Godhead, one must perform sacrifices, offering oblations to the fire according to the directions of the śāstras. In this way one should worship the Supreme Personality of Godhead.

PURPORT

If a *gṛhastha,* or householder, is sufficiently educated in Vedic knowledge and has become sufficiently rich to offer worship to please the Supreme Personality of Godhead, he must perform *yajñas* as directed by the authorized scriptures. *Bhagavad-gītā* (3.9) clearly says, *yajñārthāt karmaṇo 'nyatra loko 'yaṁ karma-bandhanaḥ:* everyone may be engaged in his occupational duties, but the result of these duties should be offered for sacrifice to satisfy the Supreme Lord. If one is fortunate enough to possess transcendental knowledge as well as the money with which to perform sacrifices, one must do it according to the directions given in the *śāstras*. It is said in *Śrīmad-Bhāgavatam* (12.3.52):

kṛte yad dhyāyato viṣṇuṁ
tretāyāṁ yajato makhaiḥ
dvāpare paricaryāyāṁ
kalau tad dhari-kīrtanāt

The entire Vedic civilization aims at satisfying the Supreme Personality of Godhead. This was possible in Satya-yuga by meditation upon the Supreme Lord within the core of one's heart and in Tretā-yuga by the performance of costly *yajñas*. The same goal could be achieved in Dvāpara-yuga by worship of the Lord in the temple, and in this age of Kali one can achieve the same goal by performing *saṅkīrtana-yajña*. Therefore one who has education and wealth must use them to satisfy the Supreme Personality of Godhead by helping the *saṅkīrtana* movement that has already begun—the Hare Kṛṣṇa movement, or Kṛṣṇa consciousness movement. All educated and wealthy persons must join this movement, since money and education are meant for service to the Supreme Personality of Godhead. If money and education are not engaged in the service of the Lord, these valuable assets must be engaged in the service of *māyā*. The education of so-called scientists, philosophers and poets is now engaged in the service of *māyā*, and the wealth of the rich is also engaged in *māyā's* service. The service of *māyā*, however, creates a chaotic condition in the world. Therefore the wealthy man and the educated man should sacrifice their knowledge and opulence by dedicating them for the satisfaction of the Supreme Lord and joining this *saṅkīrtana* movement (*yajñaiḥ saṅkīrtana-prāyair yajanti hi sumedhasaḥ*).

TEXT 17

न ह्यग्निमुखतोऽयं वै भगवान्सर्वयज्ञभुक् ।
इज्येत हविषा राजन्यथा विप्रमुखे हुतैः ॥१७॥

na hy agni-mukhato 'yaṁ vai
bhagavān sarva-yajña-bhuk
ijyeta haviṣā rājan
yathā vipra-mukhe hutaiḥ

na—not; *hi*—indeed; *agni*—fire; *mukhataḥ*—from the mouth or the flames; *ayam*—this; *vai*—certainly; *bhagavān*—Lord Śrī Kṛṣṇa; *sarva-yajña-bhuk*—the enjoyer of the results of all kinds of sacrifices; *ijyeta*—is worshiped; *haviṣā*—by offering of clarified butter; *rājan*—O King; *yathā*—as much as; *vipra-mukhe*—through the mouth of a *brāhmaṇa; hutaiḥ*—by offering him first-class food.

TRANSLATION

The Supreme Personality of Godhead, Śrī Kṛṣṇa, is the enjoyer of sacrificial offerings. Yet although His Lordship eats the oblations offered in the fire, my dear King, He is still more satisfied when nice food made of grains and ghee is offered to Him through the mouths of qualified brāhmaṇas.

PURPORT

As stated in *Bhagavad-gītā* (3.9), *yajñārthāt karmaṇo 'nyatra loko 'yaṁ karma-bandhanaḥ:* all fruitive activities should be performed for sacrifice, which should be directed toward pleasing Kṛṣṇa. As stated elsewhere in *Bhagavad-gītā* (5.29), *bhoktāraṁ yajña-tapasāṁ sarva-loka-maheśvaram:* He is the Supreme Lord and enjoyer of everything. However, although sacrifice may be offered to please Kṛṣṇa, He is more pleased when grains and ghee, instead of being offered in the fire, are prepared as *prasāda* and distributed, first to the *brāhmaṇas* and then to others. This system pleases Kṛṣṇa more than anything else. Furthermore, at the present time there is very little chance to offer sacrifices by pouring oblations of food grains and ghee into the fire. Especially in India, there is practically no ghee; for everything that should be done with ghee, people use a certain type of oil preparation. Oil, however, is never recommended for offering in a sacrificial fire. In Kali-yuga, the available quantity of food grains and ghee is gradually diminishing, and people are embarrassed that they cannot produce sufficient ghee and food grains.

Under the circumstances, the *śāstras* enjoin, *yajñaiḥ saṅkīrtana-prāyair yajanti hi sumedhasaḥ:* in this age, those who are intellectual offer *yajña*, or perform sacrifices, through the *saṅkīrtana* movement. Everyone should join the *saṅkīrtana* movement, offering to the fire of this movement the oblations of his knowledge and riches. In our *saṅkīrtana* movement, or Hare Kṛṣṇa movement, we offer sumptuous *prasāda* to the Deity and later distribute the same *prasāda* to the *brāhmaṇas*, the Vaiṣṇavas and then to the people in general. Kṛṣṇa's *prasāda* is offered to the *brāhmaṇas* and Vaiṣṇavas, and the *prasāda* of the *brāhmaṇas* and Vaiṣṇavas is offered to the general populace. This kind of sacrifice—chanting of the Hare Kṛṣṇa *mantra* and distribution of *prasāda*—is the most perfect and bona fide way of offering sacrifice for the pleasure of Yajña, or Viṣṇu.

TEXT 18

तस्माद् ब्राह्मणदेवेषु मर्त्यादिषु यथार्हतः ।
तैस्तैः कामैर्यजस्वैनं क्षेत्रज्ञं ब्राह्मणाननु ॥१८॥

tasmād brāhmaṇa-deveṣu
martyādiṣu yathārhataḥ
tais taiḥ kāmair yajasvainaṁ
kṣetra-jñaṁ brāhmaṇān anu

tasmāt—therefore; *brāhmaṇa-deveṣu*—through the *brāhmaṇas* and the demigods; *martya-ādiṣu*—through ordinary human beings and other living entities; *yathā-arhataḥ*—according to your ability; *taiḥ taiḥ*—with all those; *kāmaiḥ*—various objects of enjoyment such as sumptuous food, flower garlands, sandalwood paste, etc.; *yajasva*—you should worship; *enam*—this; *kṣetra-jñam*—Supreme Lord situated in the hearts of all beings; *brāhmaṇān*—the *brāhmaṇas; anu*—after.

TRANSLATION

Therefore, my dear King, first offer prasāda unto the brāhmaṇas and the demigods, and after sumptuously feeding them you may distribute prasāda to other living entities according to your ability.

In this way you will be able to worship all living entities—or, in other words, the supreme living entity within every living entity.

PURPORT

To distribute *prasāda* to all living entities, the process is that we must first offer *prasāda* to the *brāhmaṇas* and the Vaiṣṇavas, for the demigods are represented by the *brāhmaṇas.* In this way the Supreme Personality of Godhead, who is situated in everyone's heart, will be worshiped. This is the Vedic system of offering *prasāda.* Whenever there is a ceremony for distribution of *prasāda,* the *prasāda* is offered first to the *brāhmaṇas,* then to the children and old men, then to the women, and then to animals like dogs and other domestic animals. When it is said that Nārāyaṇa, the Supreme Being, is situated in everyone's heart, this does not mean that everyone has become Nārāyaṇa or that a particular poor man has become Nārāyaṇa. Such a conclusion is rejected herein.

TEXT 19

कुर्यादपरपक्षीयं मासि प्रौष्ठपदे द्विजः ।
श्राद्धं पित्रोर्यथावित्तं तद्बन्धूनां च वित्तवान् ॥१९॥

kuryād apara-pakṣīyaṁ
māsi prauṣṭha-pade dvijaḥ
śrāddhaṁ pitror yathā-vittaṁ
tad-bandhūnāṁ ca vittavān

kuryāt—one should perform; *apara-pakṣīyam*—during the fortnight of the dark moon; *māsi*—in the month of Āśvina (October–November); *prauṣṭha-pade*—in the month of Bhādra (August–September); *dvijaḥ*—twiceborn; *śrāddham*—oblations; *pitroḥ*—unto the forefathers; *yathā-vittam*—according to one's means of income; *tat-bandhūnām ca*—as well as relatives of forefathers; *vitta-vān*—one who is sufficiently rich.

TRANSLATION

A brāhmaṇa who is sufficiently rich must offer oblations to the forefathers during the dark-moon fortnight in the latter part of the month of Bhādra. Similarly, he should offer oblations to the

relatives of the forefathers during the mahālayā ceremonies in the month of Āśvina.*

TEXTS 20–23

अयने विषुवे कुर्याद् व्यतीपाते दिनक्षये ।
चन्द्रादित्योपरागे च द्वादश्यां श्रवणेषु च ॥२०॥
तृतीयायां शुक्लपक्षे नवम्यामथ कार्तिके ।
चतसृष्वप्यष्टकासु हेमन्ते शिशिरे तथा ॥२१॥
माघे च सितसप्तम्यां मघाराकासमागमे ।
राकया चानुमत्या च मासर्क्षाणि युतान्यपि ॥२२॥
द्वादश्यामनुराधा स्याच्छ्रवणस्तिस्र उत्तराः ।
तिसृष्वेकादशी वासु जन्मर्क्षश्रोणयोगयुक् ॥२३॥

ayane viṣuve kuryād
vyatīpāte dina-kṣaye
candrādityoparāge ca
dvādaśyāṁ śravaṇeṣu ca

tṛtīyāyāṁ śukla-pakṣe
navamyām atha kārtike
catasṛṣv apy aṣṭakāsu
hemante śiśire tathā

māghe ca sita-saptamyāṁ
maghā-rākā-samāgame
rākayā cānumatyā ca
māsarkṣāṇi yutāny api

dvādaśyām anurādhā syāc
chravaṇas tisra uttarāḥ
tisṛṣv ekādaśī vāsu
janmarkṣa-śroṇa-yoga-yuk

---

*The mahālayā festivals are observed on the fifteenth day of the dark fortnight of the month of Āśvina and mark the last day of the Vedic lunar year.

ayane—on the day when the sun begins to move north, or Makara-saṅkrānti, and on the day when the sun begins to move south, or Karkaṭa-saṅkrānti; *viṣuve*—on the Meṣa-saṅkrānti and on the Tulā-saṅkrānti; *kuryāt*—one should perform; *vyatīpāte*—in the *yoga* named Vyatīpāta; *dina-kṣaye*—on that day in which three *tithis* are combined; *candra-āditya-uparāge*—at the time of the eclipse of either the moon or the sun; *ca*—and also; *dvādaśyām śravaṇeṣu*—on the twelfth lunar day and in the *nakṣatra* named Śravaṇa; *ca*—and; *tṛtīyāyām*—on the Akṣaya-tṛtīyā day; *śukla-pakṣe*—in the bright fortnight of the month; *navamyām*—on the ninth lunar day; *atha*—also; *kārtike*—in the month of Kārtika (October–November); *catasṛṣu*—on the four; *api*—also; *aṣṭakāsu*—on the Aṣṭakās; *hemante*—before the winter season; *śiśire*—in the winter season; *tathā*—and also; *māghe*—in the month of Māgha (January–February); *ca*—and; *sita-saptamyām*—on the seventh lunar day of the bright fortnight; *maghā-rākā-samāgame*—in the conjunction of Maghā-*nakṣatra* and the full-moon day; *rākayā*—with a day of the completely full moon; *ca*—and; *anumatyā*—with a full-moon day when the moon is slightly less than completely full; *ca*—and; *māsa-ṛkṣāṇi*—the *nakṣatras* that are the sources of the names of the various months; *yutāni*—are conjoined; *api*—also; *dvādaśyām*—on the twelfth lunar day; *anurādhā*—the *nakṣatra* named Anurādhā; *syāt*—may occur; *śravaṇaḥ*—the *nakṣatra* named Śravaṇa; *tisraḥ*—the three (*nakṣatras*); *uttarāḥ*—the *nakṣatras* named Uttarā (Uttara-phalgunī, Uttarāṣāḍhā and Uttara-bhādrapadā); *tisṛṣu*—on three; *ekādaśī*—the eleventh lunar day; *vā*—or; *āsu*—on these; *janma-ṛkṣa*—of one's own *janma-nakṣatra*, or birth star; *śroṇa*—of Śravaṇa-*nakṣatra; yoga*—by a conjunction; *yuk*—having.

TRANSLATION

One should perform the śrāddha ceremony on the Makara-saṅkrānti [the day when the sun begins to move north] or on the Karkaṭa-saṅkrānti [the day when the sun begins to move south]. One should also perform this ceremony on the Meṣa-saṅkrānti day and the Tulā-saṅkrānti day, in the yoga named Vyatīpāta, on that day in which three lunar tithis are conjoined, during an eclipse of either the moon or the sun, on the twelfth lunar day, and in the Śravaṇa-nakṣatra. One should perform this ceremony on the Akṣaya-tṛtīyā day, on the ninth lunar day of the bright fortnight of

the month of Kārtika, on the four aṣṭakās in the winter season and cool season, on the seventh lunar day of the bright fortnight of the month of Māgha, during the conjunction of Maghā-nakṣatra and the full-moon day, and on the days when the moon is completely full, or not quite completely full, when these days are conjoined with the nakṣatras from which the names of certain months are derived. One should also perform the śrāddha ceremony on the twelfth lunar day when it is in conjunction with any of the nakṣatras named Anurādhā, Śravaṇa, Uttara-phalgunī, Uttarāṣāḍhā or Uttara-bhādrapadā. Again, one should perform this ceremony when the eleventh lunar day is in conjunction with either Uttara-phalgunī, Uttarāṣāḍhā or Uttara-bhādrapadā. Finally, one should perform this ceremony on days conjoined with one's own birth star [janma-nakṣatra] or with Śravaṇa-nakṣatra.

PURPORT

The word *ayana* means "path" or "going." The six months when the sun moves toward the north are called *uttarāyaṇa*, or the northern path, and the six months when it moves south are called *dakṣiṇāyana*, or the southern path. These are mentioned in *Bhagavad-gītā* (8.24–25). The first day when the sun begins to move north and enter the zodiacal sign of Capricorn is called Makara-saṅkrānti, and the first day when the sun begins to move south and enter the sign of Cancer is called Karkaṭa-saṅkrānti. On these two days of the year, one should perform the *śrāddha* ceremony.

Viṣuva, or Viṣuva-saṅkrānti, means Meṣa-saṅkrānti, or the day on which the sun enters the sign Aries. Tulā-saṅkrānti is the day on which the sun enters the sign Libra. Both of these days occur only once within a year. The word *yoga* refers to a certain relationship between the sun and moon as they move in the sky. There are twenty-seven different degrees of *yoga*, of which the seventeenth is called Vyatīpāta. On the day when this occurs, one should perform the *śrāddha* ceremony. A *tithi*, or lunar day, consists of the distance between the longitude of the sun and that of the moon. Sometimes a *tithi* is less than twenty-four hours. When it starts after sunrise on a certain day and ends before the sunrise of the following day, the previous *tithi* and the following *tithi* both "touch" the twenty-four-hour day between the sunrises. This is called *tryaha-sparśa*, or a day touched by some portion of three *tithis*.

Śrīla Jīva Gosvāmī has given quotations from many *śāstras* stating that the *śrāddha* ceremony of oblations to the forefathers should not be performed on Ekādaśī *tithi*. When the *tithi* of the death anniversary falls on the Ekādaśī day, the *śrāddha* ceremony should be held not on Ekādaśī but on the next day, or *dvādaśī*. In the *Brahma-vaivarta Purāṇa* it is said:

ye kurvanti mahīpāla
śrāddhaṁ caikādaśī-dine
trayas te narakaṁ yānti
dātā bhoktā ca prerakaḥ

If one performs the *śrāddha* ceremony of oblations to the forefathers on the Ekādaśī *tithi*, then the performer, the forefathers for whom the *śrāddha* is observed, and the *purohita*, or the family priest who encourages the ceremony, all go to hell.

TEXT 24

त एते श्रेयसः काला नृणां श्रेयोविवर्धनाः ।
कुर्यात् सर्वात्मनैतेषु श्रेयोऽमोघं तदायुषः ॥२४॥

ta ete śreyasaḥ kālā
nṛṇāṁ śreyo-vivardhanāḥ
kuryāt sarvātmanaiteṣu
śreyo 'moghaṁ tad-āyuṣaḥ

te—therefore; *ete*—all these (descriptions of astronomical calculations); *śreyasaḥ*—of auspiciousness; *kālāḥ*—times; *nṛṇām*—for human beings; *śreyaḥ*—auspiciousness; *vivardhanāḥ*—increase; *kuryāt*—one should perform; *sarva-ātmanā*—by other activities (not only the *śrāddha* ceremony); *eteṣu*—in these (seasons); *śreyaḥ*—(causing) auspiciousness; *amogham*—and success; *tat*—of a human being; *āyuṣaḥ*—of the duration of life.

TRANSLATION

All of these seasonal times are considered extremely auspicious for humanity. At such times, one should perform all auspicious activities, for by such activities a human being attains success in his short duration of life.

PURPORT

When one comes to the human form of life through natural evolution, one must then take the responsibility for further progress. As stated in *Bhagavad-gītā* (9.25), *yānti deva-vratā devān:* one who worships the demigods can be promoted to their planets. *Yānti mad-yājino 'pi mām:* and if one practices devotional service to the Lord, he goes back home, back to Godhead. In the human form of life, therefore, one is meant to act auspiciously in order to return home, back to Godhead. Devotional service, however, does not depend on material conditions. *Ahaituky apratihatā.* Of course, for those who are engaged in fruitive activities on the material platform, the times and seasons mentioned above are extremely congenial.

TEXT 25

एषु स्नानं जपो होमो व्रतं देवद्विजार्चनम् ।
पितृदेवनृभूतेभ्यो यद्द दत्तं तद्ध्यनश्वरम् ॥२५॥

eṣu snānaṁ japo homo
vrataṁ deva-dvijārcanam
pitṛ-deva-nṛ-bhūtebhyo
yad dattaṁ tad dhy anaśvaram

eṣu—in all these (seasonal times); *snānam*—bathing in the Ganges, Yamunā or any other sacred places; *japaḥ*—chanting; *homaḥ*—performing fire sacrifices; *vratam*—executing vows; *deva*—the Supreme Lord; *dvija-arcanam*—worshiping the *brāhmaṇas* or Vaiṣṇavas; *pitṛ*—unto the forefathers; *deva*—demigods; *nṛ*—human beings in general; *bhūtebhyaḥ*—and all other living entities; *yat*—whatever; *dattam*—offered; *tat*—that; *hi*—indeed; *anaśvaram*—permanently beneficial.

TRANSLATION

During these periods of seasonal change, if one bathes in the Ganges, in the Yamunā or in another sacred place, if one chants, offers fire sacrifices or executes vows, or if one worships the Supreme Lord, the brāhmaṇas, the forefathers, the demigods and the living entities in general, whatever he gives in charity yields a permanently beneficial result.

TEXT 26

संस्कारकालो जायाया अपत्यस्यात्मनस्तथा ।
प्रेतसंस्था मृताहश्च कर्मण्यभ्युदये नृप ॥२६॥

saṁskāra-kālo jāyāyā
apatyasyātmanas tathā
preta-saṁsthā mṛtāhaś ca
karmaṇy abhyudaye nṛpa

saṁskāra-kālaḥ—at the proper time indicated for Vedic reformatory performances; *jāyāyāḥ*—for the wife; *apatyasya*—for the children; *ātmanaḥ*—and one's own self; *tathā*—as well as; *preta-saṁsthā*—funeral ceremonies; *mṛta-ahaḥ*—annual death ceremonies; *ca*—and; *karmaṇi*—of fruitive activity; *abhyudaye*—for furtherance; *nṛpa*—O King.

TRANSLATION

O King Yudhiṣṭhira, at the time prescribed for reformatory ritualistic ceremonies for one's self, one's wife or one's children, or during funeral ceremonies and annual death ceremonies, one must perform the auspicious ceremonies mentioned above in order to flourish in fruitive activities.

PURPORT

The *Vedas* recommend many ritualistic ceremonies to be performed with one's wife, on the birthdays of one's children, or during funeral ceremonies, and there are also personal reformatory methods like initiation. These must be observed according to time and circumstances and the directions of the *śāstra. Bhagavad-gītā* strongly recommends, *jñātvā śāstra-vidhānoktam:* everything must be performed as indicated in the *śāstras.* For Kali-yuga, the *śāstras* enjoin that *saṅkīrtana-yajña* be performed always: *kīrtanīyaḥ sadā hariḥ.* All the ritualistic ceremonies recommended in the *śāstras* must be preceded and followed by *saṅkīrtana.* This is the recommendation of Śrīla Jīva Gosvāmī.

TEXTS 27–28

अथ देशान्प्रवक्ष्यामि धर्मादिश्रेयआवहान् ।
स वै पुण्यतमो देशः सत्पात्रं यत्र लभ्यते ॥२७॥
बिम्बं भगवतो यत्र सर्वमेतच्चराचरम् ।
यत्र ह ब्राह्मणकुलं तपोविद्यादयान्वितम् ॥२८॥

atha deśān pravakṣyāmi
dharmādi-śreya-āvahān
sa vai puṇyatamo deśaḥ
sat-pātraṁ yatra labhyate

bimbaṁ bhagavato yatra
sarvam etac carācaram
yatra ha brāhmaṇa-kulaṁ
tapo-vidyā-dayānvitam

atha—thereafter; *deśān*—places; *pravakṣyāmi*—I shall describe; *dharma-ādi*—religious performances, etc.; *śreya*—auspiciousness; *āvahān*—which can bring; *saḥ*—that; *vai*—indeed; *puṇya-tamaḥ*—the most sacred; *deśaḥ*—place; *sat-pātram*—a Vaiṣṇava; *yatra*—wherein; *labhyate*—is available; *bimbam*—the Deity (in the temple); *bhagavataḥ*—of the Supreme Personality of Godhead (who is the support); *yatra*—where; *sarvam etat*—of this entire cosmic manifestation; *cara-acaram*—with all the moving and nonmoving living entities; *yatra*—wherein; *ha*—indeed; *brāhmaṇa-kulam*—association with *brāhmaṇas; tapaḥ*—austerities; *vidyā*—education; *dayā*—mercy; *anvitam*—endowed with.

TRANSLATION

Nārada Muni continued: Now I shall describe the places where religious performances may be well executed. Any place where a Vaiṣṇava is available is an excellent place for all auspicious activities. The Supreme Personality of Godhead is the support of this entire cosmic manifestation, with all its moving and nonmoving living entities, and the temple where the Deity of the Lord is installed is a most sacred place. Furthermore, places where learned brāhmaṇas observe Vedic principles by means of austerity, education and mercy are also most auspicious and sacred.

PURPORT

In this verse it is indicated that a Vaiṣṇava temple where the Supreme Personality of Godhead, Kṛṣṇa, is worshiped, and where Vaiṣṇavas are engaged in the service of the Lord, is the best sacred place for performing any religious ceremonies. At the present day, especially in big, big cities, people live in small apartments and are not able to establish a Deity or temple. Under the circumstances, therefore, the centers and temples being established by the expanding Kṛṣṇa consciousness movement are the best sacred places for performing religious ceremonies. Although people in general are no longer interested in religious ceremonies or Deity worship, the Kṛṣṇa consciousness movement gives everyone the chance to advance in spiritual life by becoming Kṛṣṇa conscious.

TEXT 29

यत्र यत्र हरेरर्चा स देशः श्रेयसां पदम् ।
यत्र गङ्गादयो नद्यः पुराणेषु च विश्रुताः ॥२९॥

yatra yatra harer arcā
sa deśaḥ śreyasāṁ padam
yatra gaṅgādayo nadyaḥ
purāṇeṣu ca viśrutāḥ

yatra yatra—wherever; *hareḥ*—of the Supreme Personality of Godhead, Kṛṣṇa; *arcā*—the Deity is worshiped; *saḥ*—that; *deśaḥ*—place, country or neighborhood; *śreyasām*—of all auspiciousness; *padam*—the place; *yatra*—wherever; *gaṅgā-ādayaḥ*—like the Ganges, Yamunā, Narmadā and Kāverī; *nadyaḥ*—sacred rivers; *purāṇeṣu*—in the *Purāṇas* (supplementary Vedic literature); *ca*—also; *viśrutāḥ*—are celebrated.

TRANSLATION

Auspicious indeed are the places where there is a temple of the Supreme Personality of Godhead, Kṛṣṇa, in which He is duly worshiped, and also the places where there flow the celebrated sacred rivers mentioned in the Purāṇas, the supplementary Vedic literatures. Anything spiritual done there is certainly very effective.

PURPORT

There are many atheists who oppose the worship of the Deity of the Supreme Personality of Godhead in the temple. In this verse, however, it is authoritatively stated that any place where the Deity is worshiped is transcendental; it does not belong to the material world. It is also said that the forest is in the mode of goodness, and therefore those who want to cultivate spiritual life are advised to go to the forest (*vanaṁ gato yad dharim āśrayeta*). But one should not go to the forest simply to live like a monkey. Monkeys and other ferocious animals also live in the forest, but a person who goes to the forest for spiritual culture must accept the lotus feet of the Supreme Personality of Godhead as shelter (*vanaṁ gato yad dharim āśrayeta*). One should not be satisfied simply to go to the forest; one must take shelter of the lotus feet of the Supreme Personality of Godhead. In this age, therefore, since it is impossible to go to the forest for spiritual culture, one is recommended to live in the temple community as a devotee, regularly worship the Deity, follow the regulative principles and thus make the place like Vaikuṇṭha. The forest may be in goodness, the cities and villages in passion, and the brothels, hotels and restaurants in ignorance, but when one lives in the temple community he lives in Vaikuṇṭha. Therefore it is said here, *śreyasāṁ padam:* it is the best, most auspicious place.

In many places throughout the world we are constructing communities to give shelter to devotees and worship the Deity in the temple. The Deity cannot be worshiped except by devotees. Temple worshipers who fail to give importance to the devotees are third class. They are *kaniṣṭha-adhikārīs* in the lower stage of spiritual life. As it is said in *Śrīmad-Bhāgavatam* (11.2.47):

arcāyām eva haraye
pūjāṁ yaḥ śraddhayehate
na tad-bhakteṣu cānyeṣu
sa bhaktaḥ prākṛtaḥ smṛtaḥ

"A person who is very faithfully engaged in the worship of the Deity in the temple but does not know how to behave toward devotees or people in general is called a *prākṛta-bhakta*, or *kaniṣṭha-adhikārī.*" Therefore, in the temple there must be the Deity of the Lord, and the Lord should be worshiped by the devotees. This combination of the devotees and the Deity creates a first-class transcendental place.

Aside from this, if a *gṛhastha* devotee worships the *śālagrāma-śilā*, or the form of the Deity at home, his home also becomes a very great place. It was therefore customary for members of the three higher classes—namely the *brāhmaṇas*, *kṣatriyas* and *vaiśyas*—to worship the *śālagrāma-śilā*, or a small Deity of Rādhā-Kṛṣṇa or Sītā-Rāma in each and every home. This made everything auspicious. But now they have given up the Deity worship. Men have become modernized and are consequently indulging in all sorts of sinful activities, and therefore they are extremely unhappy.

According to Vedic civilization, therefore, the holy places of pilgrimage are considered most sacred, and still there are hundreds and thousands of holy places like Jagannātha Purī, Vṛndāvana, Hardwar, Rāmeśvara, Prayāga and Mathurā. India is the place for worshiping or for cultivating spiritual life. The Kṛṣṇa consciousness movement invites everyone from all over the world, without discrimination as to caste or creed, to come to its centers and cultivate spiritual life perfectly.

TEXTS 30–33

सरांसि पुष्करादीनि क्षेत्राण्यर्हाश्रितान्युत ।
कुरुक्षेत्रं गयशिरः प्रयागः पुलहाश्रमः ॥३०॥

नैमिषं फाल्गुनं सेतुः प्रभासोऽथ कुशस्थली ।
वाराणसी मधुपुरी पम्पा बिन्दुसरस्तथा ॥३१॥
नारायणाश्रमो नन्दा सीतारामाश्रमादयः ।
सर्वे कुलाचला राजन्महेन्द्रमलयादयः ॥३२॥
एते पुण्यतमा देशा हरेरर्चाश्रिताश्च ये ।
एतान्देशान् निषेवेत श्रेयस्कामो ह्यभीक्ष्णशः ।
धर्मो ह्यत्रेहितः पुंसां सहस्राधिफलोदयः ॥३३॥

sarāṁsi puṣkarādīni
kṣetrāṇy arhāśritāny uta
kurukṣetraṁ gaya-śiraḥ
prayāgaḥ pulahāśramaḥ

naimiṣaṁ phālgunaṁ setuḥ
prabhāso 'tha kuśa-sthalī
vārāṇasī madhu-purī
pampā bindu-saras tathā

nārāyaṇāśramo nandā
sītā-rāmāśramādayaḥ
sarve kulācalā rājan
mahendra-malayādayaḥ

ete puṇyatamā deśā
harer arcāśritāś ca ye
etān deśān niṣeveta
śreyas-kāmo hy abhīkṣṇaśaḥ
dharmo hy atrehitaḥ puṁsāṁ
sahasrādhi-phalodayaḥ

sarāṁsi—lakes; *puṣkara-ādīni*—such as Puṣkara; *kṣetrāṇi*—sacred places (like Kurukṣetra, Gayākṣetra and Jagannātha Purī); *arha*—for worshipable, saintly persons; *āśritāni*—places of shelter; *uta*—celebrated; *kurukṣetram*—a particular sacred place (*dharma-kṣetra*); *gaya-śiraḥ*—the place known as Gayā, where Gayāsura took shelter of the lotus feet of Lord Viṣṇu; *prayāgaḥ*—Allahabad, at the confluence of the two sacred rivers Ganges and Yamunā; *pulaha-āśramaḥ*—the residence of Pulaha Muni; *naimiṣam*—the place known as Naimiṣāraṇya (near Lucknow); *phālgunam*—the place where the Phālgu River flows; *setuḥ*—Setubandha, where Lord Rāmacandra constructed a bridge between India and Laṅkā; *prabhāsaḥ*—Prabhāsakṣetra; *atha*—as well as; *kuśa-sthalī*—Dvāravatī, or Dvārakā; *vārāṇasī*—Benares; *madhupurī*—Mathurā; *pampā*—a place where there is a lake called Pampā; *bindu-saraḥ*—the place where Bindu-sarovara is situated; *tathā*—there; *nārāyaṇa-āśramaḥ*—known as Badarikāśrama; *nandā*—the place where the Nandā River flows; *sītā-rāma*—of Lord Rāmacandra and mother Sītā; *āśrama-ādayaḥ*—places of shelter like Citrakūṭa; *sarve*—all (such places); *kulācalāḥ*—hilly tracts of land; *rājan*—O King; *mahendra*—known as Mahendra; *malaya-ādayaḥ*—and others, like Malayācala; *ete*—all of them; *puṇya-tamāḥ*—extremely sacred; *deśāḥ*—places; *hareḥ*—of the Supreme Personality of Godhead; *arca-āśritāḥ*—places where the Deity of Rādhā-Kṛṣṇa is worshiped (such as big American cities like New York, Los Angeles and San Francisco, and European cities like London and Paris, or wherever there are centers of Kṛṣṇa consciousness); *ca*—as well as; *ye*—those which; *etān deśān*—all these countries; *niṣeveta*—should worship or visit; *śreyaḥ-kāmaḥ*—one who desires auspiciousness; *hi*—indeed; *abhīkṣṇaśaḥ*—again and again; *dharmaḥ*—religious activities; *hi*—from which; *atra*—in these places; *īhitaḥ*—performed; *puṁsām*—of the persons; *sahasra-adhi*—more than a thousand times; *phala-udayaḥ*—effective.

TRANSLATION

The sacred lakes like Puṣkara and places where saintly persons live, like Kurukṣetra, Gayā, Prayāga, Pulahāśrama, Naimiṣāraṇya, the banks of the Phālgu River, Setubandha, Prabhāsa, Dvārakā, Vārāṇasī, Mathurā, Pampā, Bindu-sarovara, Badarikāśrama [Nārāyaṇāśrama], the places where the Nandā River flows, the places where Lord Rāmacandra and mother Sītā took shelter, such as Citrakūṭa, and also the hilly tracts of land known as Mahendra and Malaya—all of these are to be considered most pious and sacred. Similarly, places outside India where there are centers of the Kṛṣṇa consciousness movement and where Rādhā-Kṛṣṇa

Deities are worshiped must all be visited and worshiped by those who want to be spiritually advanced. One who intends to advance in spiritual life may visit all these places and perform ritualistic ceremonies to get results a thousand times better than the results of the same activities performed in any other place.

PURPORT

In these verses and in verse twenty-nine, stress is given to one point: *harer arcāśritāś ca ye* or *harer arcā.* In other words, any place where the Deity of the Supreme Personality of Godhead is worshiped by devotees is most significant. The Kṛṣṇa consciousness movement is giving the population of the entire world a chance to take advantage of Kṛṣṇa consciousness through the ISKCON centers, where one may perform Deity worship and chant the Hare Kṛṣṇa *mahā-mantra* and in this way obtain results with effectiveness increased a thousand times. This constitutes the best welfare activity for human society. This was Śrī Caitanya Mahāprabhu's mission as it was predicted by Him in the *Caitanya-bhāgavata* (*Antya* 4.126):

pṛthivīte āche yata nagarādi-grāma
sarvatra pracāra haibe mora nāma

Śrī Caitanya Mahāprabhu wanted the Hare Kṛṣṇa movement, with installed Deities, to spread to every village and town in the world, so that everyone in the world might take advantage of this movement and become all-auspicious in spiritual life. Without spiritual life, nothing is auspicious. *Moghāśā mogha-karmāṇo mogha-jñānā vicetasaḥ* (Bg. 9.12). No one can become successful in fruitive activities or speculative knowledge without being Kṛṣṇa conscious. As recommended in the *śāstras,* everyone should be very eagerly interested in taking part in the Kṛṣṇa consciousness movement and understanding the value of spiritual life.

TEXT 34

पात्रं त्वत्र निरुक्तं वै कविभिः पात्रवित्तमैः ।
हरिरेवैक उर्वीश यन्मयं वै चराचरम् ॥३४॥

pātraṁ tv atra niruktaṁ vai
kavibhiḥ pātra-vittamaiḥ
harir evaika urvīśa
yan-mayaṁ vai carācaram

pātram—the true person to whom charity must be given; *tu*—but; *atra*—in the world; *niruktam*—decided; *vai*—indeed; *kavibhiḥ*—by learned scholars; *pātra-vittamaiḥ*—who are expert in finding the actual person to whom charity must be given; *hariḥ*—the Supreme Personality of Godhead; *eva*—indeed; *ekaḥ*—only one; *urvī-īśa*—O King of the earth; *yat-mayam*—in whom everything is resting; *vai*—from whom everything is coming; *cara-acaram*—all that is moving or nonmoving within this universe.

TRANSLATION

O King of the earth, it has been decided by expert, learned scholars that only the Supreme Personality of Godhead, Kṛṣṇa, in whom all that is moving or nonmoving within this universe is resting and from whom everything is coming, is the best person to whom everything must be given.

PURPORT

Whenever we perform some religious act in terms of *dharma, artha, kāma* and *mokṣa,* we must perform it according to the time, place and person (*kāla, deśa, pātra*). Nārada Muni has already described the *deśa* (place) and *kāla* (time). The *kāla* has been described in verses twenty through twenty-four, beginning with the words *ayane viṣuve kuryād vyatīpāte dina-kṣaye.* And the places for giving charity or performing ritualistic ceremonies have been described in verses thirty through thirty-three, beginning with *sarāṁsi puṣkarādīni kṣetrāṇy arhāśritāny uta.* Now, to whom everything must be given is decided in this verse. *Harir evaika urvīśa yan-mayaṁ vai carācaram.* The Supreme Personality of Godhead, Kṛṣṇa, is the root of everything, and therefore He is the best *pātra,* or person, to whom everything must be given. In *Bhagavad-gītā* (5.29) it is said:

bhoktāraṁ yajña-tapasāṁ
sarva-loka-maheśvaram

suhṛdaṁ sarva-bhūtānāṁ
jñātvā māṁ śāntim ṛcchati

If one wants to enjoy real peace and prosperity, he should give everything to Kṛṣṇa, who is the real enjoyer, real friend and real proprietor. It is therefore said:

yathā taror mūla-niṣecanena
tṛpyanti tat-skandha-bhujopaśākhāḥ
prāṇopahārāc ca yathendriyāṇāṁ
tathaiva sarvārhaṇam acyutejyā
(*Bhāg.* 4.31.14)

By worshiping or satisfying Acyuta, the Supreme Personality of Godhead, Kṛṣṇa, one can satisfy everyone, just as one can water the branches, leaves and flowers of a tree simply by watering its root or as one satisfies all the senses of the body by giving food to the stomach. Therefore, a devotee simply offers everything to the Supreme Personality of Godhead to receive the best results of charity, religious performances, sense gratification and even liberation (*dharma, artha, kāma, mokṣa*).

TEXT 35

देवर्ष्यर्हत्सु वै सत्सु तत्र ब्रह्मात्मजादिषु ।
राजन्यदग्रपूजायां मतः पात्रतयाच्युतः ॥३५॥

devarṣy-arhatsu vai satsu
tatra brahmātmajādiṣu
rājan yad agra-pūjāyāṁ
mataḥ pātratayācyutaḥ

deva-ṛṣi—among the demigods and great saintly persons, including Nārada Muni; *arhatsu*—the most venerable and worshipable personalities; *vai*—indeed; *satsu*—the great devotees; *tatra*—there (at the Rājasūya-yajña); *brahma-ātma-jādiṣu*—and the sons of Lord Brahmā (such as Sanaka, Sanandana, Sanat and Sanātana); *rājan*—O King; *yat*—

from whom; *agra-pūjāyām*—the first to be worshiped; *mataḥ*—decision; *pātratayā*—selected as the best person to preside over the Rājasūya-yajña; *acyutaḥ*—Kṛṣṇa.

TRANSLATION

O King Yudhiṣṭhira, the demigods, many great sages and saints including even the four sons of Lord Brahmā, and I myself were present at your Rājasūya sacrificial ceremony, but when there was a question of who should be the first person worshiped, everyone decided upon Lord Kṛṣṇa, the Supreme Person.

PURPORT

This is a reference to the Rājasūya sacrifice performed by Mahārāja Yudhiṣṭhira. In that meeting there was a great turmoil over selecting the best person to be worshiped first. Everyone decided to worship Śrī Kṛṣṇa. The only protest came from Śiśupāla, and because of his vehement opposition he was killed by the Supreme Personality of Godhead.

TEXT 36

जीवराशिभिराकीर्ण अण्डकोशाङ्घ्रिपो महान् ।
तन्मूलत्वादच्युतेज्या सर्वजीवात्मतर्पणम् ॥३६॥

jīva-rāśibhir ākīrṇa
aṇḍa-kośāṅghripo mahān
tan-mūlatvād acyutejyā
sarva-jīvātma-tarpaṇam

jīva-rāśibhiḥ—by millions and millions of living entities; *ākīrṇaḥ*—filled up or spread over; *aṇḍa-kośa*—the whole universe; *aṅghripaḥ*—like a tree; *mahān*—very, very great; *tat-mūlatvāt*—because of being the root of this tree; *acyuta-ijyā*—worship of the Supreme Personality of Godhead; *sarva*—of all; *jīva-ātma*—living entities; *tarpaṇam*—satisfaction.

TRANSLATION

The entire universe, which is full of living entities, is like a tree whose root is the Supreme Personality of Godhead, Acyuta

[Kṛṣṇa]. Therefore simply by worshiping Lord Kṛṣṇa one can worship all living entities.

PURPORT

In *Bhagavad-gītā* (10.8) the Lord says:

ahaṁ sarvasya prabhavo
mattaḥ sarvaṁ pravartate
iti matvā bhajante māṁ
budhā bhāva-samanvitāḥ

"I am the source of all spiritual and material worlds. Everything emanates from Me. The wise who perfectly know this engage in My devotional service and worship Me with all their hearts." People are very much anxious to give service to other living entities, especially to the poor, but although they have manufactured many ways to give such help, actually they are expert in killing the poor living entities. This sort of service or mercy is not recommended in the Vedic wisdom. As stated in a previous verse, it has been decided (*niruktam*) by expert saintly persons that Kṛṣṇa is the root of everything and that worshiping Kṛṣṇa is worshiping everyone, just as supplying water to the root of a tree means satisfying all of its branches and twigs.

Another point is that this universe is full of living entities from top to bottom, on every planet (*jīva-rāśibhir ākīrṇaḥ*). Modern scientists and so-called scholars think that there are no living entities on planets other than this one. Recently they have said that they have gone to the moon but did not find any living entities there. But *Śrīmad-Bhāgavatam* and the other Vedic literatures do not agree with this foolish conception. There are living entities everywhere, not only one or two but *jīva-rāśibhiḥ*—many millions of living entities. Even on the sun there are living entities, although it is a firey planet. The chief living entity on the sun is called Vivasvān (*imaṁ vivasvate yogaṁ proktavān aham avyayam*). All the different planets are filled with different types of living entities according to different living conditions. To suggest that only this planet is filled with living entities and that others are vacant is foolish. This betrays a lack of real knowledge.

TEXT 37

पुराण्यनेन सृष्टानि नृतिर्यगृषिदेवताः ।
शेते जीवेन रूपेण पुरेषु पुरुषो ह्यसौ ॥३७॥

purāṇy anena sṛṣṭāni
nṛ-tiryag-ṛṣi-devatāḥ
śete jīvena rūpeṇa
pureṣu puruṣo hy asau

purāṇi—residential places or bodies; *anena*—by Him (the Supreme Personality of Godhead); *sṛṣṭāni*—among those creations; *nṛ*—man; *tiryak*—other than human beings (animals, birds, etc); *ṛṣi*—saintly persons; *devatāḥ*—and demigods; *śete*—lies down; *jīvena*—with the living entities; *rūpeṇa*—in the form of Paramātmā; *pureṣu*—within these residential places or bodies; *puruṣaḥ*—the Supreme Lord; *hi*—indeed; *asau*—He (the Personality of Godhead).

TRANSLATION

The Supreme Personality of Godhead has created many residential places like the bodies of human beings, animals, birds, saints and demigods. In all of these innumerable bodily forms, the Lord resides with the living being as Paramātmā. Thus He is known as the puruṣāvatāra.

PURPORT

In *Bhagavad-gītā* (18.61) it is said:

īśvaraḥ sarva-bhūtānāṁ
hṛd-deśe 'rjuna tiṣṭhati
bhrāmayan sarva-bhūtāni
yantrārūḍhāni māyayā

"The Supreme Lord is situated in everyone's heart, O Arjuna, and is directing the wanderings of all living entities, who are seated as on a machine, made of the material energy." The living entity, who is part and parcel of the Supreme Personality of Godhead, exists on the mercy of the Lord, who is always with him in any form of body. The living entity desires a particular type of material enjoyment, and thus the Lord supplies him with a body, which is like a machine. Just to keep him alive in that body, the Lord remains with him as the *puruṣa* (Kṣīrodakaśāyī Viṣṇu). This is also confirmed in *Brahma-saṁhitā* (5.35):

eko 'py asau racayituṁ jagad-aṇḍa-koṭiṁ
yac-chaktir asti jagad-aṇḍa-cayā yad-antaḥ
aṇḍāntara-stha-paramāṇu-cayāntara-sthaṁ
govindam ādi-puruṣaṁ tam ahaṁ bhajāmi

"I worship the Personality of Godhead, Govinda, who enters the existence of every universe and every atom by one of His plenary portions and thus manifests His infinite energy throughout the material creation." The living entity, being part and parcel of the Lord, is known as *jīva*. The Supreme Lord *puruṣa* remains with the *jīva* to enable him to enjoy material facilities.

TEXT 38

तेष्वेव भगवान्राजंस्तारतम्येन वर्तते ।
तस्मात् पात्रं हि पुरुषो यावानात्मा यथेयते ॥३८॥

teṣv eva bhagavān rājaṁs
tāratamyena vartate
tasmāt pātraṁ hi puruṣo
yāvān ātmā yatheyate

teṣu—among the different types of bodies (demigod, human, animal, bird, etc.); *eva*—indeed; *bhagavān*—the Supreme Personality of Godhead in His Paramātmā feature; *rājan*—O King; *tāratamyena*—comparatively, more or less; *vartate*—is situated; *tasmāt*—therefore; *pātram*—the Supreme Person; *hi*—indeed; *puruṣaḥ*—Paramātmā; *yāvān*—as far as; *ātmā*—the degree of understanding; *yathā*—development of austerity and penance; *īyate*—is manifest.

TRANSLATION

O King Yudhiṣṭhira, the Supersoul in every body gives intelligence to the individual soul according to his capacity for under-

standing. Therefore the Supersoul is the chief within the body. The Supersoul is manifested to the individual soul according to the individual's comparative development of knowledge, austerity, penance and so on.

PURPORT

In *Bhagavad-gītā* (15.15) it is said, *mattaḥ smṛtir jñānam apohanaṁ ca:* the Supreme Personality of Godhead in His localized aspect gives intelligence to the individual soul as far as he is able to grasp it. Therefore we find the individual soul in different high and low positions. A living entity with the body of a bird or beast cannot take instructions from the Supreme Soul as adequately as an advanced human being. Thus there are gradations of bodily forms. In human society, the perfect *brāhmaṇa* is supposed to be the most advanced in spiritual consciousness, and further advanced than the *brāhmaṇa* is the Vaiṣṇava. Therefore the best persons are the Vaiṣṇavas and Viṣṇu. When charity is to be given, one should take instruction from *Bhagavad-gītā* (17.20):

dātavyam iti yad dānaṁ
dīyate 'nupakāriṇe
deśe kāle ca pātre ca
tad dānaṁ sāttvikaṁ smṛtam

"That gift which is given out of duty, at the proper time and place, to a worthy person, and without expectation of return, is considered to be charity in the mode of goodness." One should give charity to the *brāhmaṇas* and Vaiṣṇavas, for thus the Supreme Personality of Godhead will be worshiped. In this connection, Śrīla Madhvācārya comments:

brahmādi-sthāvarānteṣu
na viśeṣo hareḥ kvacit
vyakti-mātra-viśeṣeṇa
tāratamyaṁ vadanti ca

Beginning from Brahmā down to the ant, everyone is conducted by the Supersoul (*īśvaraḥ sarva-bhūtānāṁ hṛd-deśe 'rjuna tiṣṭhati*). But because of a particular person's advancement in spiritual consciousness, he is considered to be important. Therefore, the *brāhmaṇa* Vaiṣṇava is important, and, above all, the Supersoul, the Personality of Godhead, is the most important personality.

TEXT 39

दृष्ट्वा तेषां मिथो नृणामवज्ञानात्मतां नृप ।
त्रेतादिषु हरेरर्चा क्रियायै कविभिः कृता ॥३९॥

dṛṣṭvā teṣāṁ mitho nṛṇām
avajñānātmatāṁ nṛpa
tretādiṣu harer arcā
kriyāyai kavibhiḥ kṛtā

dṛṣṭvā—after practically seeing; *teṣām*—among the *brāhmaṇas* and Vaiṣṇavas; *mithaḥ*—mutually; *nṛṇām*—of human society; *avajñāna-ātmatām*—the mutually disrespectful behavior; *nṛpa*—O King; *tretā-ādiṣu*—beginning from Tretā-yuga; *hareḥ*—of the Supreme Personality of Godhead; *arcā*—the Deity worship (in the temple); *kriyāyai*—for the purpose of introducing the method of worship; *kavibhiḥ*—by learned persons; *kṛtā*—has been done.

TRANSLATION

My dear King, when great sages and saintly persons saw mutually disrespectful dealings at the beginning of Tretā-yuga, Deity worship in the temple was introduced with all paraphernalia.

PURPORT

As it is said in *Śrīmad-Bhāgavatam* (12.3.52):

kṛte yad dhyāyato viṣṇuṁ
tretāyāṁ yajato makhaiḥ
dvāpare paricaryāyāṁ
kalau tad dhari-kīrtanāt

"Whatever result one obtained in Satya-yuga by meditating on Viṣṇu, in Tretā-yuga by performing sacrifices and in Dvāpara-yuga by serving the

Lord's lotus feet one can also obtain in Kali-yuga simply by chanting the Hare Kṛṣṇa *mahā-mantra*." In Satya-yuga, every person was spiritually advanced, and there was no envy between great personalities. Gradually, however, because of material contamination with the advance of the ages, disrespectful dealings appeared even among *brāhmaṇas* and Vaiṣṇavas. Actually, an advanced Vaiṣṇava is to be respected more than Viṣṇu. As stated in the *Padma Purāṇa, ārādhanānāṁ sarveṣāṁ viṣṇor ārādhanaṁ param:* of all kinds of worship, worship of Lord Viṣṇu is the best. *Tasmāt parataraṁ devi tadīyānāṁ samarcanam:* and recommended more than worship of Viṣṇu is worship of the Vaiṣṇava.

Formerly, all activities were performed in connection with Viṣṇu, but after Satya-yuga there were symptoms of disrespectful dealings among Vaiṣṇavas. Śrīla Bhaktivinoda Ṭhākura has said that a Vaiṣṇava is he who has helped others become Vaiṣṇavas. An example of one who has converted many others into Vaiṣṇavas is Nārada Muni. A powerful Vaiṣṇava who has converted others into Vaiṣṇavas is to be worshiped, but because of material contamination, sometimes such an exalted Vaiṣṇava is disrespected by other, minor Vaiṣṇavas. When great saintly persons saw this contamination, they introduced worship of the Deity in the temple. This began in Tretā-yuga and was especially prominent in Dvāpara-yuga (*dvāpare paricaryāyāṁ*). But in Kali-yuga, worship of the Deity is being neglected. Therefore chanting of the Hare Kṛṣṇa *mantra* is more powerful than Deity worship. Śrī Caitanya Mahāprabhu set a practical example in that He did not establish any temples or Deities, but He profusely introduced the *saṅkīrtana* movement. Therefore Kṛṣṇa consciousness preachers should give more stress to the *saṅkīrtana* movement, especially by distributing transcendental literature more and more. This helps the *saṅkīrtana* movement. Whenever there is a possibility to worship the Deity, we may establish many centers, but generally we should give more stress to the distribution of transcendental literature, for this will be more effective in converting people to Kṛṣṇa consciousness.

It is said in *Śrīmad-Bhāgavatam* (11.2.47):

arcāyām eva haraye
pūjāṁ yaḥ śraddhayehate

na tad-bhakteṣu cānyeṣu
sa bhaktaḥ prākṛtaḥ smṛtaḥ

"A person who is very faithfully engaged in the worship of the Deity in the temple but does not know how to behave toward devotees or people in general is called a *prākṛta-bhakta*, or *kaniṣṭha-adhikārī*." A *prākṛta* devotee, or neophyte devotee, is still on the material platform. He certainly engages in worshiping the Deity, but he cannot appreciate the activities of a pure devotee. It has actually been seen that even an authorized devotee who is engaged in the service of the Lord by preaching the mission of Kṛṣṇa consciousness is sometimes criticized by neophyte devotees. Such neophytes are described by Viśvanātha Cakravartī Ṭhākura: *sarva-prāṇi-sammānanāsamarthānām avajñā spardhādimatāṁ tu bhagavat-pratimaiva pātram ity āha.* For those who cannot properly appreciate the activities of authorized devotees, Deity worship is the only way for spiritual advancement. In the *Caitanya-caritāmṛta* (*Antya* 7.11) it is clearly said, *kṛṣṇa-śakti vinā nahe tāra pravartana:* without being authorized by Kṛṣṇa, one cannot preach the holy name of the Lord throughout the entire world. Nevertheless, a devotee who does so is criticized by neophyte devotees, *kaniṣṭha-adhikārīs* , who are on the lower stages of devotional service. For them, Deity worship is strongly recommended.

TEXT 40

ततोऽर्चायां हरिं केचित् संश्रद्धाय सपर्यया ।
उपासत उपास्तापि नार्थदा पुरुषद्विषाम् ॥४०॥

tato 'rcāyāṁ hariṁ kecit
saṁśraddhāya saparyayā
upāsata upāstāpi
nārthadā puruṣa-dviṣām

tataḥ—thereafter; *arcāyām*—the Deity; *harim*—who is the Supreme Personality of Godhead (the form of the Lord being identical with the Lord); *kecit*—someone; *saṁśraddhāya*—with great faith; *saparyayā*—and with the required paraphernalia; *upāsate*—worships; *upāstā api*—

although worshiping the Deity (with faith and regularity); *na*—not; *artha-dā*—beneficial; *puruṣa-dviṣām*—for those who are envious of Lord Viṣṇu and His devotees.

TRANSLATION

Sometimes a neophyte devotee offers all the paraphernalia for worshiping the Lord, and he factually worships the Lord as the Deity, but because he is envious of the authorized devotees of Lord Viṣṇu, the Lord is never satisfied with his devotional service.

PURPORT

Deity worship is especially meant for purifying the neophyte devotees. Actually, however, preaching is more important. In *Bhagavad-gītā* (18.69) it is said, *na ca tasmān manuṣyeṣu kaścin me priya-kṛttamaḥ:* if one wants to be recognized by the Supreme Personality of Godhead, he must preach the glories of the Lord. One who worships the Deity must therefore be extremely respectful to preachers; otherwise simply worshiping the Deity will keep one in the lower stage of devotion.

TEXT 41

पुरुषेष्वपि राजेन्द्र सुपात्रं ब्राह्मणं विदुः ।
तपसा विद्यया तुष्ट्या धत्ते वेदं हरेस्तनुम् ॥४१॥

puruṣeṣv api rājendra
supātraṁ brāhmaṇaṁ viduḥ
tapasā vidyayā tuṣṭyā
dhatte vedaṁ hares tanum

puruṣeṣu—among persons; *api*—indeed; *rāja-indra*—O best of kings; *su-pātram*—the best person; *brāhmaṇam*—the qualified *brāhmaṇa; viduḥ*—one should know; *tapasā*—due to austerity; *vidyayā*—education; *tuṣṭyā*—and satisfaction; *dhatte*—he assumes; *vedam*—the transcendental knowledge known as *Veda; hareḥ*—of the Supreme Personality of Godhead; *tanum*—body, or representation.

TRANSLATION

My dear King, of all persons a qualified brāhmaṇa must be accepted as the best within this material world because such a brāhmaṇa, by practicing austerity, Vedic studies and satisfaction, becomes the counterpart body of the Supreme Personality of Godhead.

PURPORT

From the *Vedas* we learn that the Personality of Godhead is the Supreme Person. Every living entity is an individual person, and the Supreme Personality of Godhead, Kṛṣṇa, is the Supreme Person. A *brāhmaṇa* who is well versed in Vedic knowledge and fully conversant with transcendental matters becomes a representative of the Supreme Personality of Godhead, and therefore one should worship such a *brāhmaṇa* or Vaiṣṇava. A Vaiṣṇava is superior to a *brāhmaṇa* because whereas a *brāhmaṇa* knows that he is Brahman, not matter, a Vaiṣṇava knows that he is not only Brahman but also an eternal servant of the Supreme Brahman. Therefore, worship of a Vaiṣṇava is superior to worship of the Deity in the temple. Viśvanātha Cakravartī Ṭhākura says, *sākṣād dharitvena samasta-śāstraiḥ:* in all the scriptures the spiritual master, who is the best of the *brāhmaṇas*, the best of the Vaiṣṇavas, is considered to be as good as the Supreme Personality of Godhead. This does not mean, however, that the Vaiṣṇava thinks himself God, for this is blasphemous. Although a *brāhmaṇa* or Vaiṣṇava is worshiped as being as good as the Supreme Personality of Godhead, such a devotee always remains a faithful servant of the Lord and never tries to enjoy the prestige that might accrue to him from being the Supreme Lord's representative.

TEXT 42

नन्वस्य ब्राह्मणा राजन्कृष्णस्य जगदात्मनः ।
पुनन्तः पादरजसा त्रिलोकीं दैवतं महत् ॥४२॥

nanv asya brāhmaṇā rājan
kṛṣṇasya jagad-ātmanaḥ
punantaḥ pāda-rajasā
tri-lokīṁ daivataṁ mahat

nanu—but; *asya*—by Him; *brāhmaṇāḥ*—the qualified *brāhmaṇas; rājan*—O King; *kṛṣṇasya*—by Lord Kṛṣṇa, the Supreme Personality of Godhead; *jagat-ātmanaḥ*—who is the life and soul of the whole creation; *punantaḥ*—sanctifying; *pāda-rajasā*—by the dust of their lotus feet; *tri-lokīm*—the three worlds; *daivatam*—worshipable; *mahat*—most exalted.

TRANSLATION

My dear King Yudhiṣṭhira, the brāhmaṇas, especially those engaged in preaching the glories of the Lord throughout the entire world, are recognized and worshiped by the Supreme Personality of Godhead, who is the heart and soul of all creation. The brāhmaṇas, by their preaching, sanctify the three worlds with the dust of their lotus feet, and thus they are worshipable even for Kṛṣṇa.

PURPORT

As admitted by Lord Kṛṣṇa in *Bhagavad-gītā* (18.69), *na ca tasmān manuṣyeṣu kaścin me priya-kṛttamaḥ.* The *brāhmaṇas* preach the cult of Kṛṣṇa consciousness all around the world, and therefore, although they worship Kṛṣṇa, the Supreme Personality of Godhead, the Lord also recognizes them as worshipable. The relationship is reciprocal. The *brāhmaṇas* want to worship Kṛṣṇa, and similarly Kṛṣṇa wants to worship the *brāhmaṇas.* In conclusion, therefore, *brāhmaṇas* and Vaiṣṇavas who are engaged in preaching the glories of the Lord must be worshiped by religionists, philosophers and people in general. At the Rājasūya-yajña of Mahārāja Yudhiṣṭhira, many hundreds and thousands of *brāhmaṇas* were present, yet Kṛṣṇa was selected to be worshiped first. Therefore, Kṛṣṇa is always the Supreme Person, but by His causeless mercy He recognizes the *brāhmaṇas* as dearmost to Him.

Thus end the Bhaktivedanta purports of the Seventh Canto, Fourteenth Chapter, of the Śrīmad-Bhāgavatam, *entitled "Ideal Family Life."*

CHAPTER FIFTEEN

Instructions for Civilized Human Beings

The summary of the Fifteenth Chapter is as follows. In the previous chapter, Śrī Nārada Muni proved the importance of the *brāhmaṇa* in society. Now, in this chapter, he will show the differences between different grades of *brāhmaṇas.* Among the *brāhmaṇas,* some are householders and are mostly attached to fruitive activities or the betterment of social conditions. Above them, however, are *brāhmaṇas* who are very much attracted by austerities and penances and who retire from family life. They are known as *vānaprasthas.* Other *brāhmaṇas* are very much interested in studying the *Vedas* and explaining the purport of the *Vedas* to others. Such *brāhmaṇas* are called *brahmacārīs.* And still other *brāhmaṇas* are interested in different types of *yoga,* especially *bhakti-yoga* and *jñāna-yoga.* Such *brāhmaṇas* are mostly *sannyāsīs,* members of the renounced order of life.

As far as householders are concerned, they engage in different types of scriptural activities, especially in offering oblations to their forefathers and giving as charity to other *brāhmaṇas* the paraphernalia engaged in such sacrifices. Generally the charity is given to *sannyāsīs, brāhmaṇas* in the renounced order of life. If such a *sannyāsī* is not available, the charity is given to *brāhmaṇa* householders engaged in fruitive activities.

One should not make very elaborate arrangements to perform the *śrāddha* ceremony of offering oblations to one's forefathers. The best process for the *śrāddha* ceremony is to distribute *bhāgavata-prasāda* (remnants of food that has first been offered to Kṛṣṇa) to all of one's forefathers and relatives. This makes a first-class *śrāddha* ceremony. In the *śrāddha* ceremony there is no need to offer meat or eat meat. Unnecessary killing of animals must be avoided. Those who are in the lower grades of society prefer to perform sacrifices by killing animals, but one who is advanced in knowledge must avoid such unnecessary violence.

Brāhmaṇas should execute their regulative duties in worshiping Lord Viṣṇu. Those who are advanced in knowledge of religious principles must avoid five kinds of irreligion, known as *vidharma*, *para-dharma*, *dharmābhāsa*, *upadharma* and *chala-dharma*. One must act according to the religious principles that suit his constitutional position; it is not that everyone must adhere to the same type of religion. A general principle is that a poor man should not unnecessarily endeavor for economic development. One who refrains from such endeavors but who engages in devotional service is most auspicious.

One who is not satisfied with the mind must fall to degradation. One must conquer lusty desires, anger, greed, fear, lamentation, illusion, fright, unnecessary talks on material subjects, violence, the four miseries of material existence, and the three material qualities. That is the objective of human life. One who has no faith in the spiritual master, who is identical with Śrī Kṛṣṇa, cannot get any benefit from reading *śāstra*. One should never consider the spiritual master an ordinary human being, even though the members of the spiritual master's family may think of him as such. Meditation and other processes of austerity are useful only if they help in advancement toward Kṛṣṇa consciousness; otherwise, they are simply a waste of time and labor. For those who are not devotees, such meditation and austerity cause falldown.

Every householder should be very careful because even though a householder may try to conquer the senses, he becomes a victim to the association of relatives and falls down. Thus a *gṛhastha* must become a *vānaprastha* or *sannyāsī*, live in a secluded place, and be satisfied with food gotten by begging from door to door. He must chant the *oṁkāra mantra* or Hare Kṛṣṇa *mantra*, and in this way he will perceive transcendental bliss within himself. After taking *sannyāsa*, however, if one returns to *gṛhastha* life, he is called a *vāntāśī*, which means "one who eats his own vomit." Such a person is shameless. A householder should not give up the ritualistic ceremonies, and a *sannyāsī* should not live in society. If a *sannyāsī* is agitated by the senses, he is a cheater influenced by the modes of passion and ignorance. When one assumes a role in goodness by starting philanthropic and altruistic activities, such activities become impediments on the path of devotional service.

The best process for advancing in devotional service is to abide by the orders of the spiritual master, for only by his direction can one conquer the senses. Unless one is completely Kṛṣṇa conscious, there is a chance of falling down. Of course, in performing ritualistic ceremonies and other fruitive activities there are also many dangers at every moment. Fruitive activities have been divided into twelve portions. Because of performing fruitive activities, which are called the path of *dharma*, one has to accept the cycle of birth and death, but when one takes the path of *mokṣa*, or liberation, which is described in *Bhagavad-gītā* as *arcanā-mārga*, one can get relief from the cycle of birth and death. The *Vedas* describe these two paths as *pitṛ-yāna* and *deva-yāna*. Those who follow the paths of *pitṛ-yāna* and *deva-yāna* are never bewildered, even while in the material body. A monistic philosopher who gradually develops control of the senses understands that the objective of all the different *āśramas*, the statuses of life, is salvation. One must live and act according to *śāstras*.

If one who is performing the Vedic ritualistic ceremonies becomes a devotee, even if he is a *gṛhastha*, he can receive the causeless mercy of Kṛṣṇa. The objective of a devotee is to return home, back to Godhead. Such a devotee, even though not performing ritualistic ceremonies, advances in spiritual consciousness by the supreme will of the Personality of Godhead. One may actually become successful in spiritual consciousness by the mercy of devotees, or one may fall from spiritual consciousness by being disrespectful to devotees. In this regard, Nārada Muni narrated the history of how he had fallen from the Gandharva kingdom, how he was born in a *śūdra* family, and how by serving exalted *brāhmaṇas* he become the son of Lord Brahmā and was reinstated in his transcendental position. After narrating all these stories, Nārada Muni praised the mercy received from the Lord by the Pāṇḍavas. Mahārāja Yudhiṣṭhira, after hearing from Nārada, become ecstatic in love of Kṛṣṇa, and then Nārada Muni left that place and returned to his own place. Thus Śukadeva Gosvāmī, having described various descendants of the daughters of Dakṣa, ends the Seventh Canto of *Śrīmad-Bhāgavatam*.

TEXT 1

श्रीनारद उवाच
कर्मनिष्ठा द्विजाः केचित् तपोनिष्ठा नृपापरे ।
स्वाध्यायेऽन्ये प्रवचने केचन ज्ञानयोगयोः ॥ १ ॥

śrī-nārada uvāca
karma-niṣṭhā dvijāḥ kecit
tapo-niṣṭhā nṛpāpare

svādhyāye 'nye pravacane
kecana jñāna-yogayoḥ

śrī-nāradaḥ uvāca—Nārada Muni said; *karma-niṣṭhāḥ*—attached to ritualistic ceremonies (according to one's social status as a *brāhmaṇa, kṣatriya, vaiśya* or *śūdra*); *dvi-jāḥ*—the twiceborn (especially the *brāhmaṇas*); *kecit*—some; *tapaḥ-niṣṭhāḥ*—very much attached to austerities and penances; *nṛpa*—O King; *apare*—others; *svādhyāye*—in studying Vedic literature; *anye*—others; *pravacane*—delivering speeches on Vedic literature; *kecana*—some; *jñāna-yogayoḥ*—in culturing knowledge and practicing *bhakti-yoga.*

TRANSLATION

Nārada Muni continued: My dear King, some brāhmaṇas are very much attached to fruitive activities, some are attached to austerities and penances, and still others study the Vedic literature, whereas some, although very few, cultivate knowledge and practice different yogas, especially bhakti-yoga.

TEXT 2

ज्ञाननिष्ठाय देयानि कव्यान्यानन्त्यमिच्छता ।
दैवे च तदभावे स्यादितरेभ्यो यथार्हतः ॥ २ ॥

jñāna-niṣṭhāya deyāni
kavyāny ānantyam icchatā
daive ca tad-abhāve syād
itarebhyo yathārhataḥ

jñāna-niṣṭhāya—to the impersonalist or the transcendentalist desiring to merge into the Supreme; *deyāni*—to be given in charity; *kavyāni*—ingredients offered to the forefathers as oblations; *ānantyam*—liberation from material bondage; *icchatā*—by a person desiring; *daive*—the ingredients to be offered to the demigods; *ca*—also; *tat-abhāve*—in the absence of such advanced transcendentalists; *syāt*—it should be done; *itarebhyaḥ*—to others (namely, those addicted to fruitive activities); *yathā-arhataḥ*—comparatively or with discrimination.

TRANSLATION

A person desiring liberation for his forefathers or himself should give charity to a brāhmaṇa who adheres to impersonal monism [jñāna-niṣṭhā]. In the absence of such an advanced brāhmaṇa, charity may be given to a brāhmaṇa addicted to fruitive activities [karma-kāṇḍa].

PURPORT

There are two processes by which to get free from material bondage. One involves *jñāna-kāṇḍa* and *karma-kāṇḍa*, and the other involves *upāsanā-kāṇḍa*. Vaiṣṇavas never want to merge into the existence of the Supreme; rather, they want to be everlastingly servants of the Lord to render loving service unto Him. In this verse the words *ānantyam icchatā* refer to persons who desire to achieve liberation from material bondage and merge into the existence of the Lord. Devotees, however, whose objective is to associate personally with the Lord, have no desire to accept the activities of *karma-kāṇḍa* or *jñāna-kāṇḍa*, for pure devotional service is above both *karma-kāṇḍa* and *jñāna-kāṇḍa*. *Anyābhilāṣitā-śūnyaṁ jñāna-karmādy-anāvṛtam.* In pure devotional service there is not even a pinch of *jñāna* or *karma*. Consequently, when Vaiṣṇavas distribute charity, they do not need to find a *brāhmaṇa* performing the activities of *jñāna-kāṇḍa* or *karma-kāṇḍa*. The best example in this regard is provided by Advaita Gosvāmī, who, after performing the *śrāddha* ceremony for his father, offered charity to Haridāsa Ṭhākura, although it was known to everyone that Haridāsa Ṭhākura was born in a Mohammedan family, not a *brāhmaṇa* family, and was not interested in the activities of *jñāna-kāṇḍa* or *karma-kāṇḍa*.

Charity, therefore, should be given to the first-class transcendentalist, the devotee, because the *śāstras* recommend:

muktānām api siddhānāṁ
nārāyaṇa-parāyaṇaḥ
sudurlabhaḥ praśāntātmā
koṭiṣv api mahā-mune

"O great sage, among many millions who are liberated and perfect in knowledge of liberation, one may be a devotee of Lord Nārāyaṇa, or

Kṛṣṇa. Such devotees, who are fully peaceful, are extremely rare." (*Bhāg.* 6.14.5) A Vaiṣṇava is in a higher position than a *jñānī*, and therefore Advaita Ācārya selected Haridāsa Ṭhākura to be the person to accept His charity. The Supreme Lord also says:

na me 'bhaktaś catur-vedī
mad-bhaktaḥ śva-pacaḥ priyaḥ
tasmai deyaṁ tato grāhyaṁ
sa ca pūjyo yathā hy aham

"Even though a person is a very learned scholar of the Sanskrit Vedic literatures, he is not accepted as My devotee unless he is pure in devotional service. However, even though a person is born in a family of dog-eaters, he is very dear to Me if he is a pure devotee who has no motive to enjoy fruitive activity or mental speculation. Indeed, all respect should be given to him, and whatever he offers should be accepted. Such devotees are as worshipable as I am." (*Hari-bhakti-vilāsa* 10.127) Therefore, even if not born in a *brāhmaṇa* family, a devotee, because of his devotion to the Lord, is above all kinds of *brāhmaṇas*, whether they be *karma-kāṇḍīs* or *jñāna-kāṇḍīs.*

In this regard, it may be mentioned that *brāhmaṇas* in Vṛndāvana who are *karma-kāṇḍīs* and *jñāna-kāṇḍīs* sometimes decline to accept invitations to our temple because our temple is known as the *aṅgarejī* temple, or "Anglican temple." But in accordance with the evidence given in the *śāstra* and the example set by Advaita Ācārya, we give *prasāda* to devotees regardless of whether they come from India, Europe or America. It is the conclusion of the *śāstra* that instead of feeding many *jñāna-kāṇḍī* or *karma-kāṇḍī brāhmaṇas*, it is better to feed a pure Vaiṣṇava, regardless of where he comes from. This is also confirmed in *Bhagavad-gītā* (9.30):

api cet sudurācāro
bhajate mām ananya-bhāk
sādhur eva sa mantavyaḥ
samyag vyavasito hi saḥ

"Even if one commits the most abominable actions, if he is engaged in devotional service he is to be considered saintly because he is properly situated." Thus it doesn't matter whether a devotee comes from a *brāhmaṇa* family or non-*brāhmaṇa* family; if he is fully devoted to Kṛṣṇa, he is a *sādhu*.

TEXT 3

द्वौ दैवे पितृकार्ये त्रीनेकैकमुभयत्र वा ।
भोजयेत् सुसमृद्धोऽपि श्राद्धे कुर्यान्न विस्तरम् ॥ ३ ॥

dvau daive pitṛ-kārye trīn
ekaikam ubhayatra vā
bhojayet susamṛddho 'pi
śrāddhe kuryān na vistaram

dvau—two; *daive*—during the period when oblations are offered to the demigods; *pitṛ-kārye*—in the *śrāddha* ceremony, in which oblations are offered to the forefathers; *trīn*—three; *eka*—one; *ekam*—one; *ubhayatra*—for both occasions; *vā*—either; *bhojayet*—one should feed; *su-samṛddhaḥ api*—even though one is very rich; *śrāddhe*—when offering oblations to the forefathers; *kuryāt*—one should do; *na*—not; *vistaram*—very expensive arrangements.

TRANSLATION

During the period for offering oblations to the demigods, one should invite only two brāhmaṇas, and while offering oblations to the forefathers, one may invite three brāhmaṇas. Or, in either case, only one brāhmaṇa will suffice. Even though one is very opulent, he should not endeavor to invite more brāhmaṇas or make various expensive arrangements on those occasions.

PURPORT

As we have already mentioned, Śrīla Advaita Ācārya, during the generally observed ceremony to offer oblations to the forefathers, invited only Haridāsa Ṭhākura. Thus He followed this principle: *na me 'bhaktaś catur-vedī mad-bhaktaḥ śva-pacaḥ priyaḥ*. The Lord says, "It is not necessary that one become very expert in Vedic knowledge before he can become My *bhakta*, or devotee. Even if one is born in a family of dog-eaters, he can become My devotee and be very dear to Me, in spite of having taken birth in such a family. Therefore, offerings should be given to My devotee, and whatever My devotee has offered Me should be accepted." Following this principle, one should invite a first-class *brāhmaṇa* or Vaiṣṇava—a realized soul—and feed him while observing the *śrāddha* ceremony to offer oblations to one's forefathers.

TEXT 4

देशकालोचितश्रद्धाद्रव्यपात्रार्हणानि च ।
सम्यग् भवन्ति नैतानि विस्तरात् स्वजनार्पणात् ॥४॥

deśa-kālocita-śraddhā-
dravya-pātrārhaṇāni ca
samyag bhavanti naitāni
vistarāt sva-janārpaṇāt

deśa—place; *kāla*—time; *ucita*—proper; *śraddhā*—respect; *dravya*—ingredients; *pātra*—a suitable person; *arhaṇāni*—paraphernalia for worship; *ca*—and; *samyak*—proper; *bhavanti*—are; *na*—not; *etāni*—all these; *vistarāt*—due to expansion; *sva-jana-arpaṇāt*—or due to inviting relatives.

TRANSLATION

If one arranges to feed many brāhmaṇas or relatives during the śrāddha ceremony, there will be discrepancies in the time, place, respectability and ingredients, the person to be worshiped, and the method of offering worship.

PURPORT

Nārada Muni has prohibited unnecessarily gorgeous arrangements to feed relatives or *brāhmaṇas* during the *śrāddha* ceremony. Those who are materially opulent spend lavishly during this ceremony. Indians spend especially lavishly on three occasions—at the birth of a child, at marriage and while observing the *śrāddha* ceremony—but the *śāstras* prohibit the excessive expenditures involved in inviting many *brāhmaṇas* and relatives, especially during the *śrāddha* ceremony.

TEXT 5

देशे काले च सम्प्राप्ते मुन्यन्नं हरिदैवतम् ।
श्रद्धया विधिवत् पात्रे न्यस्तं कामधुगक्षयम् ॥ ५ ॥

deśe kāle ca samprāpte
muny-annaṁ hari-daivatam
śraddhayā vidhivat pātre
nyastaṁ kāmadhug akṣayam

deśe—in a proper place, namely a holy place of pilgrimage; *kāle*—at an auspicious time; *ca*—also; *samprāpte*—when available; *muni-annam*—foodstuffs prepared with ghee and suitable to be eaten by great saintly persons; *hari-daivatam*—unto the Supreme Personality of Godhead, Hari; *śraddhayā*—with love and affection; *vidhi-vat*—according to the directions of the spiritual master and the *śāstras; pātre*—unto the suitable person; *nyastam*—if it is so offered; *kāmadhuk*—becomes a source of prosperity; *akṣayam*—everlasting.

TRANSLATION

When one gets the opportunity of a suitable auspicious time and place, one should, with love, offer food prepared with ghee to the Deity of the Supreme Personality of Godhead and then offer the prasāda to a suitable person—a Vaiṣṇava or brāhmaṇa. This will be the cause of everlasting prosperity.

TEXT 6

देवर्षिपितृभूतेभ्य आत्मने स्वजनाय च ।
अन्नं संविभजन्पश्येत् सर्वं तत् पुरुषात्मकम् ॥ ६ ॥

devarṣi-pitṛ-bhūtebhya
ātmane sva-janāya ca
annaṁ saṁvibhajan paśyet
sarvaṁ tat puruṣātmakam

deva—unto the demigods; *ṛṣi*—saintly persons; *pitṛ*—forefathers; *bhūtebhyaḥ*—the living entities in general; *ātmane*—relatives; *sva-*

janāya—family members and friends; *ca*—and; *annam*—foodstuff (*prasāda*); *saṁvibhajan*—offering; *paśyet*—one should see; *sarvam*—all; *tat*—them; *puruṣa-ātmakam*—related to the Supreme Personality of Godhead.

TRANSLATION

One should offer prasāda to the demigods, the saintly persons, one's forefathers, the people in general, one's family members, one's relatives and one's friends, seeing them all as devotees of the Supreme Personality of Godhead.

PURPORT

As mentioned above, it is recommended that everyone distribute *prasāda*, considering every living being a part and parcel of the Supreme Lord. Even in feeding the poor, one should distribute *prasāda*. In Kali-yuga there is a scarcity of food almost every year, and thus philanthropists spend lavishly to feed the poor. For this they invent the term *daridra-nārāyaṇa-sevā*. This is prohibited. One should distribute sumptuous *prasāda*, considering everyone a part of the Supreme Lord, but one should not juggle words to make a poor man Nārāyaṇa. Everyone is related to the Supreme Lord, but one should not mistakenly think that because one is related to the Supreme Personality of Godhead, he has become the Supreme Personality of Godhead, Nārāyaṇa. Such a Māyāvāda philosophy is extremely dangerous, especially for a devotee. Śrī Caitanya Mahāprabhu has therefore strictly forbidden us to associate with Māyāvādī philosophers. *Māyāvādi-bhāṣya śunile haya sarva-nāśa:* if one associates with the Māyāvāda philosophy, his devotional life is doomed.

TEXT 7

न दद्यादामिषं श्राद्धे न चाद्याद् धर्मतत्त्ववित् ।
मुन्यन्नैः स्यात्परा प्रीतिर्यथा न पशुहिंसया ॥ ७ ॥

na dadyād āmiṣaṁ śrāddhe
na cādyād dharma-tattvavit
muny-annaiḥ syāt parā prītir
yathā na paśu-hiṁsayā

na—never; *dadyāt*—should offer; *āmiṣam*—meat, fish, eggs and so on; *śrāddhe*—in the performance of the *śrāddha* ceremony; *na*—nor; *ca*—also; *adyāt*—one should eat personally; *dharma-tattva-vit*—one who is actually learned in regard to religious activities; *muni-annaiḥ*—by preparations made with ghee for saintly persons; *syāt*—should be; *parā*—first-class; *prītiḥ*—satisfaction; *yathā*—for the forefathers and the Supreme Personality of Godhead; *na*—not; *paśu-hiṁsayā*—by killing animals unnecessarily.

TRANSLATION

A person fully aware of religious principles should never offer anything like meat, eggs or fish in the śrāddha ceremony, and even if one is a kṣatriya, he himself should not eat such things. When suitable food prepared with ghee is offered to saintly persons, the function is pleasing to the forefathers and the Supreme Lord, who are never pleased when animals are killed in the name of sacrifice.

TEXT 8

नैतादृशः परो धर्मो नृणां सद्धर्ममिच्छताम् ।
न्यासो दण्डस्य भूतेषु मनोवाक्कायजस्य यः ॥ ८ ॥

naitādṛśaḥ paro dharmo
nṛṇāṁ sad-dharmam icchatām
nyāso daṇḍasya bhūteṣu
mano-vāk-kāyajasya yaḥ

na—never; *etādṛśaḥ*—like this; *paraḥ*—a supreme or superior; *dharmaḥ*—religion; *nṛṇām*—of persons; *sat-dharmam*—superior religion; *icchatām*—being desirous of; *nyāsaḥ*—giving up; *daṇḍasya*—causing trouble because of envy; *bhūteṣu*—unto the living entities; *manaḥ*—in terms of the mind; *vāk*—words; *kāya-jasya*—and body; *yaḥ*—which.

TRANSLATION

Persons who want to advance in superior religion are advised to give up all envy of other living entities, whether in relationship to the body, words or mind. There is no religion superior to this.

TEXT 9

**एके कर्ममयान् यज्ञान् ज्ञानिनो यज्ञवित्तमाः ।
आत्मसंयमनेऽनीहा जुह्वति ज्ञानदीपिते ॥ ९ ॥**

eke karmamayān yajñān
jñānino yajña-vittamāḥ
ātma-saṁyamane 'nīhā
juhvati jñāna-dīpite

eke—some; *karma-mayān*—resulting in a reaction (such as the killing of animals); *yajñān*—sacrifices; *jñāninaḥ*—persons advanced in knowledge; *yajña-vit-tamāḥ*—who know perfectly well the purpose of sacrifice; *ātma-saṁyamane*—by self-control; *anīhāḥ*—who are without material desires; *juhvati*—execute sacrifice; *jñāna-dīpite*—enlightened in perfect knowledge.

TRANSLATION

Because of an awakening of spiritual knowledge, those who are intelligent in regard to sacrifice, who are actually aware of religious principles and who are free from material desires, control the self in the fire of spiritual knowledge, or knowledge of the Absolute Truth. They may give up the process of ritualistic ceremonies.

PURPORT

People are generally very much interested in *karma-kāṇḍa* ritualistic ceremonies for elevation to the higher planetary systems, but when one awakens his spiritual knowledge, he becomes uninterested in such elevation and engages himself fully in *jñāna-yajña* to find the objective of life. The objective of life is to stop completely the miseries of birth and death and to return home, back to Godhead. When one cultivates knowledge for this purpose, he is considered to be on a higher platform than one who is engaged in *karma-yajña*, or fruitive activities.

TEXT 10

**द्रव्ययज्ञैर्यक्ष्यमाणं दृष्ट्वा भूतानि बिभ्यति ।
एष माकरुणो हन्यादतज्ज्ञो ह्यसुतृप् ध्रुवम् ॥१०॥**

dravya-yajñair yakṣyamāṇaṁ
dṛṣṭvā bhūtāni bibhyati
eṣa mākaruṇo hanyād
ataj-jño hy asu-tṛp dhruvam

dravya-yajñaiḥ—with animals and other eatable things; *yakṣyamāṇam*—the person engaged in such sacrifices; *dṛṣṭvā*—by seeing; *bhūtāni*—the living entities (animals); *bibhyati*—become afraid; *eṣaḥ*—this person (the performer of sacrifice); *mā*—us; *akaruṇaḥ*—who is inhumane and merciless; *hanyāt*—will kill; *a-tat-jñaḥ*—most ignorant; *hi*—indeed; *asu-tṛp*—who is most satisfied by killing others; *dhruvam*—certainly.

TRANSLATION

Upon seeing the person engaged in performing the sacrifice, animals meant to be sacrificed are extremely afraid, thinking, "This merciless performer of sacrifices, being ignorant of the purpose of sacrifice and being most satisfied by killing others, will surely kill us."

PURPORT

Animal sacrifice in the name of religion is current practically all over the world in every established religion. It is said that Lord Jesus Christ, when twelve years old, was shocked to see the Jews sacrificing birds and animals in the synagogues and that he therefore rejected the Jewish system of religion and started the religious system of Christianity, adhering to the Old Testament commandment "Thou shalt not kill." At the present day, however, not only are animals killed in the name of sacrifice, but the killing of animals has increased enormously because of the increasing number of slaughterhouses. Slaughtering animals, either for religion or for food, is most abominable and is condemned herein. Unless one is merciless, one cannot sacrifice animals, either in the name of religion or for food.

TEXT 11

तस्माद् दैवोपपन्नेन मुन्यन्नेनापि धर्मवित् ।
सन्तुष्टोऽहरहः कुर्यान्नित्यनैमित्तिकीः क्रियाः॥११॥

tasmād daivopapannena
muny-annenāpi dharmavit
santuṣṭo 'har ahaḥ kuryān
nitya-naimittikīḥ kriyāḥ

tasmāt—therefore; *daiva-upapannena*—obtainable very easily by the grace of the Lord; *muni-annena*—with food (prepared in ghee and offered to the Supreme Lord); *api*—indeed; *dharma-vit*—one who is actually advanced in religious principles; *santuṣṭaḥ*—very happily; *ahaḥ ahaḥ*—day after day; *kuryāt*—one should perform; *nitya-naimittikīḥ*—regular and occasional; *kriyāḥ*—duties.

TRANSLATION

Therefore, day by day, one who is actually aware of religious principles and is not heinously envious of poor animals should happily perform daily sacrifices and those for certain occasions with whatever food is available easily by the grace of the Lord.

PURPORT

The word *dharmavit,* meaning "one who knows the actual purpose of religion," is very significant. As explained in *Bhagavad-gītā* (18.66), *sarva-dharmān parityajya mām ekaṁ śaraṇaṁ vraja:* becoming Kṛṣṇa conscious is the topmost stage in understanding of religious principles. One who reaches this stage performs the *arcanā* process in devotional service. Anyone, whether a *gṛhastha* or a *sannyāsī,* can keep small Deities of the Lord suitably packed or, if possible, installed, and thus worship the Deities of Rādhā-Kṛṣṇa, Sītā-Rāma, Lakṣmī-Nārāyaṇa, Lord Jagannātha or Śrī Caitanya Mahāprabhu by offering food prepared in ghee and then offering the sanctified *prasāda* to the forefathers, demigods and other living entities as a matter of routine daily work. All the centers of our Kṛṣṇa consciousness movement have Deity worship programs very nicely going on in which food is offered to the Deity and distributed to the first-class *brāhmaṇas* and Vaiṣṇavas and even to the people in general. This performance of sacrifice brings complete satisfaction. The members of the Kṛṣṇa consciousness movement engage daily in such transcendental activities. Thus in our Kṛṣṇa consciousness movement there is no question at all of killing animals.

TEXT 12

विधर्मः परधर्मश्च आभास उपमा छलः ।
अधर्मशाखाः पञ्चेमा धर्मज्ञोऽधर्मवत् त्यजेत् ॥१२॥

vidharmaḥ para-dharmaś ca
ābhāsa upamā chalaḥ
adharma-śākhāḥ pañcemā
dharma-jño 'dharmavat tyajet

vidharmaḥ—irreligion; *para-dharmaḥ*—religious principles practiced by others; *ca*—and; *ābhāsaḥ*—pretentious religious principles; *upamā*—principles that appear religious but are not; *chalaḥ*—a cheating religion; *adharma-śākhāḥ*—which are different branches of irreligion; *pañca*—five; *imāḥ*—these; *dharma-jñaḥ*—one who is aware of religious principles; *adharma-vat*—accepting them as irreligious; *tyajet*—should give up.

TRANSLATION

There are five branches of irreligion, appropriately known as irreligion [vidharma], religious principles for which one is unfit [para-dharma], pretentious religion [ābhāsa], analogical religion [upadharma] and cheating religion [chala-dharma]. One who is aware of real religious life must abandon these five as irreligious.

PURPORT

Any religious principles opposed to the principle of surrendering to the lotus feet of the Supreme Personality of Godhead, Kṛṣṇa, are to be considered religious principles of irregularity or cheating, and one who is actually interested in religion must give them up. One should simply follow the instructions of Kṛṣṇa and surrender unto Him. To do this, of course, one needs very good intelligence, which may be awakened after many, many births through good association with devotees and the practice of Kṛṣṇa consciousness. Everything but the principle of religion recommended by Kṛṣṇa—*sarva-dharmān parityajya mām ekaṁ śaraṇaṁ vraja*—should be given up as irreligion.

TEXT 13

धर्मबाधो विधर्मः स्यात् परधर्मोऽन्यचोदितः ।
उपधर्मस्तु पाखण्डो दम्भो वा शब्दभिच्छलः ॥१३॥

dharma-bādho vidharmaḥ syāt
para-dharmo 'nya-coditaḥ
upadharmas tu pākhaṇḍo
dambho vā śabda-bhic chalaḥ

dharma-bādhaḥ—obstructs the execution of one's own religious principles; *vidharmaḥ*—against the principles of religion; *syāt*—should be; *para-dharmaḥ*—imitating religious systems for which one is unfit; *anya-coditaḥ*—which is introduced by someone else; *upadharmaḥ*—concocted religious principles; *tu*—indeed; *pākhaṇḍaḥ*—by one who is against the principles of *Vedas*, standard scriptures; *dambhaḥ*—who is falsely proud; *vā*—or; *śabda-bhit*—by word jugglery; *chalaḥ*—a cheating religious system.

TRANSLATION

Religious principles that obstruct one from following his own religion are called vidharma. Religious principles introduced by others are called para-dharma. A new type of religion created by one who is falsely proud and who opposes the principles of the Vedas is called upadharma. And interpretation by one's jugglery of words is called chala-dharma.

PURPORT

To create a new type of *dharma* has become fashionable in this age. So-called *svāmīs* and *yogīs* support that one may follow any type of religious system, according to one's own choice, because all systems are ultimately the same. In *Śrīmad-Bhāgavatam*, however, such fashionable ideas are called *vidharma* because they go against one's own religious system. The real religious system is described by the Supreme Personality of Godhead: *sarva-dharmān parityajya mām ekaṁ śaraṇaṁ vraja.* The real religious system is that of surrender to the lotus feet of the Lord. In the Sixth Canto of *Śrīmad-Bhāgavatam*, in connection with

Ajāmila's deliverance, Yamarāja says, *dharmaṁ tu sākṣād bhagavat-praṇītam:* real religion is that which is given by the Supreme Personality of Godhead, just as real law is that which is given by the government. No one can manufacture actual law at home, nor can one manufacture actual religion. Elsewhere it is said, *sa vai puṁsāṁ paro dharmo yato bhaktir adhokṣaje:* the real religious system is that which leads one to become a devotee of the Supreme Lord. Therefore, anything opposed to this religious system of progressive Kṛṣṇa consciousness is called *vidharma, para-dharma, upadharma* or *chala-dharma.* Misinterpretation of *Bhagavad-gītā* is *chala-dharma.* When Kṛṣṇa directly says something and some rascal interprets it to mean something different, this is *chala-dharma*—a religious system of cheating—or *śabda-bhit,* a jugglery of words. One should be extremely careful to avoid these various types of cheating systems of religion.

TEXT 14

यस्त्विच्छया कृतः पुम्भिराभासो ह्याश्रमात् पृथक् ।
स्वभावविहितो धर्मः कस्य नेष्टः प्रशान्तये ॥१४॥

yas tv icchayā kṛtaḥ pumbhir
ābhāso hy āśramāt pṛthak
sva-bhāva-vihito dharmaḥ
kasya neṣṭaḥ praśāntaye

yaḥ—that which; *tu*—indeed; *icchayā*—whimsically; *kṛtaḥ*—conducted; *pumbhiḥ*—by persons; *ābhāsaḥ*—dim reflection; *hi*—indeed; *āśramāt*—from one's own order of life; *pṛthak*—different; *sva-bhāva*—according to one's own nature; *vihitaḥ*—regulated; *dharmaḥ*—religious principle; *kasya*—in what respect; *na*—not; *iṣṭaḥ*—capable; *praśāntaye*—for relieving all kinds of distress.

TRANSLATION

A pretentious religious system manufactured by one who willfully neglects the prescribed duties of his order of life is called ābhāsa [a dim reflection or false similarity]. But if one performs the prescribed duties for his particular āśrama or varṇa, why are they not sufficient to mitigate all material distresses?

PURPORT

It is indicated here that everyone should strictly follow the principles of *varṇa* and *āśrama* as given in the *śāstra*. In the *Viṣṇu Purāṇa* (3.8.9) it is said:

varṇāśramācāravatā
puruṣeṇa paraḥ pumān
viṣṇur ārādhyate panthā
nānyat tat-toṣa-kāraṇam

One should focus upon the destination for progress, which is to become Kṛṣṇa conscious. This is the aim and end of all *varṇas* and *āśramas*. However, if Viṣṇu is not worshiped, the followers of the *varṇāśrama* institution manufacture some concocted God. Thus it has now become fashionable for any rascal or fool to be elected God, and there are many missionaries who have concocted their own gods, giving up their relationship with the real God. In *Bhagavad-gītā* it is clearly said that one who worships the demigods has lost his intelligence. Nonetheless we find that even an illiterate person who has lost all intelligence is elected God, and although he has a temple, it has meat-eating *sannyāsīs*, and many polluted activities go on there. This type of religious system, which misguides its poor followers, is strictly forbidden. Such pretentious religions should be stopped altogether.

The original system is that a *brāhmaṇa* should actually become a *brāhmaṇa;* he should not only take birth in a *brāhmaṇa* family, but must also be qualified. Also, even if one is not born in a *brāhmaṇa* family but has brahminical qualifications, he must be considered a *brāhmaṇa*. By strictly following this system, one can be happy without extra endeavor. *Sva-bhāva-vihito dharmaḥ kasya neṣṭaḥ praśāntaye.* The real aim of life is to mitigate distress, and one can do this very easily by following the principles of *śāstra*.

TEXT 15

धर्मार्थमपि नेहेत यात्रार्थं वाधनो धनम् ।
अनीहानीहमानस्य महाहेरिव वृत्तिदा ॥१५॥

dharmārtham api neheta
yātrārthaṁ vādhano dhanam
anīhānīhamānasya
mahāher iva vṛttidā

dharma-artham—in religion or economic development; *api*—indeed; *na*—not; *īheta*—should try to obtain; *yātrā-artham*—just to maintain the body and soul together; *vā*—either; *adhanaḥ*—one who has no wealth; *dhanam*—money; *anīhā*—the desirelessness; *anīhamānasya*—of a person who does not endeavor even to earn his livelihood; *mahā-aheḥ*—the great serpent known as the python; *iva*—like; *vṛtti-dā*—which obtains its livelihood without endeavor.

TRANSLATION

Even if a man is poor, he should not endeavor to improve his economic condition just to maintain his body and soul together or to become a famous religionist. Just as a great python, although lying in one place, not endeavoring for its livelihood, gets the food it needs to maintain body and soul, one who is desireless also obtains his livelihood without endeavor.

PURPORT

Human life is simply meant for developing Kṛṣṇa consciousness. One need not even try to earn a livelihood to maintain body and soul together. This is illustrated here by the example of the great python, which lies in one place, never going here and there to earn a livelihood to maintain itself, and yet is maintained by the grace of the Lord. As advised by Nārada Muni (*Bhāg.* 1.5.18), *tasyaiva hetoḥ prayateta kovidaḥ:* one should simply endeavor to increase his Kṛṣṇa consciousness. One should not desire to do anything else, even to earn his livelihood. There are many, many examples of this attitude. Mādhavendra Purī, for instance, would never go to anyone to ask for food. Śukadeva Gosvāmī has also said, *kasmād bhajanti kavayo dhana-durmadāndhān.* Why should one approach a person who is blind with wealth? Rather, one should depend on Kṛṣṇa, and He will give everything. All the members of our Kṛṣṇa consciousness movement, whether they be *gṛhasthas* or *sannyāsīs,* should try to spread the Kṛṣṇa consciousness movement with determination, and Kṛṣṇa will supply all necessities. The process of *ājagara-vṛtti*, the means of livelihood of a python, is very much appreciated in this regard. Even though one may be very poor, he should simply try to advance in Kṛṣṇa consciousness and not endeavor to earn his livelihood.

TEXT 16

सन्तुष्टस्य निरीहस्य स्वात्मारामस्य यत् सुखम् ।
कुतस्तत् कामलोभेन धावतोऽर्थेहया दिशः ॥१६॥

santuṣṭasya nirīhasya
svātmārāmasya yat sukham
kutas tat kāma-lobhena
dhāvato 'rthehayā diśaḥ

santuṣṭasya—of one who is fully satisfied in Kṛṣṇa consciousness; *nirīhasya*—who does not endeavor for his livelihood; *sva*—own; *ātma-ārāmasya*—who is self-satisfied; *yat*—that; *sukham*—happiness; *kutaḥ*—where; *tat*—such happiness; *kāma-lobhena*—impelled by lust and greed; *dhāvataḥ*—of one who is wandering here and there; *artha-īhayā*—with a desire for accumulating wealth; *diśaḥ*—in all directions.

TRANSLATION

One who is content and satisfied and who links his activities with the Supreme Personality of Godhead residing in everyone's heart enjoys transcendental happiness without endeavoring for his livelihood. Where is such happiness for a materialistic man who is impelled by lust and greed and who therefore wanders in all directions with a desire to accumulate wealth?

TEXT 17

सदा सन्तुष्टमनसः सर्वाः शिवमया दिशः ।
शर्कराकण्टकादिभ्यो यथोपानत्पदः शिवम् ॥१७॥

sadā santuṣṭa-manasaḥ
sarvāḥ śivamayā diśaḥ
śarkarā-kaṇṭakādibhyo
yathopānat-padaḥ śivam

sadā—always; *santuṣṭa-manasaḥ*—for a person who is self-satisfied; *sarvāḥ*—everything; *śiva-mayāḥ*—auspicious; *diśaḥ*—in all directions; *śarkarā*—from pebbles; *kaṇṭaka-ādibhyaḥ*—and thorns, etc.; *yathā*—as; *upānat-padaḥ*—for a person who has suitable shoes; *śivam*—there is no danger (auspicious).

TRANSLATION

For a person who has suitable shoes on his feet, there is no danger even when he walks on pebbles and thorns. For him, everything is auspicious. Similarly, for one who is always self-satisfied there is no distress; indeed, he feels happiness everywhere.

TEXT 18

सन्तुष्टः केन वा राजन्न वर्तेतापि वारिणा ।
औपस्थ्यजैह्व्यकार्पण्याद् गृहपालायते जनः ॥१८॥

santuṣṭaḥ kena vā rājan
na vartetāpi vāriṇā
aupasthya-jaihvya-kārpaṇyād
gṛha-pālāyate janaḥ

santuṣṭaḥ—a person who is always self-satisfied; *kena*—why; *vā*—or; *rājan*—O King; *na*—not; *varteta*—should live (happily); *api*—even; *vāriṇā*—by drinking water; *aupasthya*—due to the genitals; *jaihvya*—and the tongue; *kārpaṇyāt*—because of a wretched or miserly condition; *gṛha-pālāyate*—he becomes exactly like a household dog; *janaḥ*—such a person.

TRANSLATION

My dear King, a self-satisfied person can be happy even with only drinking water. However, one who is driven by the senses, especially by the tongue and genitals, must accept the position of a household dog to satisfy his senses.

PURPORT

According to the *śāstras*, a *brāhmaṇa*, or a cultured person in Kṛṣṇa consciousness, will not enter anyone's service to maintain body and soul together, and especially not for satisfaction of the senses. A true *brāhmaṇa* is always satisfied. Even if he has nothing to eat, he can drink a little water and be satisfied. This is only a matter of practice. Unfortunately, however, no one is educated in how to be satisfied in self-realization. As explained above, a devotee is always satisfied because he feels the presence of the Supersoul within his heart and thinks of Him twenty-four hours a day. That is real satisfaction. A devotee is never driven by the dictations of the tongue and genitals, and thus he is never victimized by the laws of material nature.

TEXT 19

असन्तुष्टस्य विप्रस्य तेजो विद्या तपो यशः ।
स्रवन्तीन्द्रियलौल्येन ज्ञानं चैवावकीर्यते ॥१९॥

asantuṣṭasya viprasya
tejo vidyā tapo yaśaḥ
sravantīndriya-laulyena
jñānaṁ caivāvakīryate

asantuṣṭasya—of one who is not self-satisfied; *viprasya*—of such a *brāhmaṇa; tejaḥ*—strength; *vidyā*—education; *tapaḥ*—austerity; *yaśaḥ*—fame; *sravanti*—dwindle; *indriya*—of the senses; *laulyena*—because of greed; *jñānam*—knowledge; *ca*—and; *eva*—certainly; *avakīryate*—gradually vanishes.

TRANSLATION

Because of greed for the sake of the senses, the spiritual strength, education, austerity and reputation of a devotee or brāhmaṇa who is not self-satisfied dwindle, and his knowledge gradually vanishes.

TEXT 20

कामस्यान्तं हि क्षुत्तृड्भ्यां क्रोधस्यैतत्फलोदयात् ।
जनो याति न लोभस्य जित्वा भुक्त्वा दिशो भुवः ॥२०॥

kāmasyāntaṁ hi kṣut-tṛḍbhyāṁ
krodhasyaitat phalodayāt
jano yāti na lobhasya
jitvā bhuktvā diśo bhuvaḥ

kāmasya—of the desire for sense gratification or the urgent needs of the body; *antam*—end; *hi*—indeed; *kṣut-tṛḍbhyām*—by one who is very hungry or thirsty; *krodhasya*—of anger; *etat*—this; *phala-udayāt*—by venting chastisement and its reaction; *janaḥ*—a person; *yāti*—crosses over; *na*—not; *lobhasya*—greed; *jitvā*—conquering; *bhuktvā*—enjoying; *diśaḥ*—all directions; *bhuvaḥ*—of the globe.

TRANSLATION

The strong bodily desires and needs of a person disturbed by hunger and thirst are certainly satisfied when he eats. Similarly, if one becomes very angry, that anger is satisfied by chastisement and its reaction. But as for greed, even if a greedy person has conquered all the directions of the world or has enjoyed everything in the world, still he will not be satisfied.

PURPORT

In *Bhagavad-gītā* (3.37) it is stated that lust, anger and greed are the causes of the conditioned soul's bondage in this material world. *Kāma eṣa krodha eṣa rajo-guṇa-samudbhavaḥ.* When strong lusty desires for sense gratification are unfulfilled, one becomes angry. This anger can be satisfied when one chastises his enemy, but when there is an increase in *lobha,* or greed, which is the greatest enemy caused by *rajo-guṇa,* the mode of passion, how can one advance in Kṛṣṇa consciousness?

If one is very greedy to enhance his Kṛṣṇa consciousness, this is a great boon. *Tatra laulyam ekalaṁ mūlam.* This is the best path available.

TEXT 21

पण्डिता बहवो राजन्बहुज्ञाः संशयच्छिदः ।
सदसस्पतयोऽप्येके असन्तोषात् पतन्त्यधः ॥२१॥

paṇḍitā bahavo rājan
bahu-jñāḥ saṁśaya-cchidaḥ

sadasas patayo 'py eke
asantoṣāt patanty adhaḥ

paṇḍitāḥ—very learned scholars; *bahavaḥ*—many; *rājan*—O King (Yudhiṣṭhira); *bahu-jñāḥ*—persons with varied experience; *saṁśaya-cchidaḥ*—expert in legal advice; *sadasaḥ patayaḥ*—persons eligible to become presidents of learned assemblies; *api*—even; *eke*—by one disqualification; *asantoṣāt*—simply by dissatisfaction or greed; *patanti*—fall down; *adhaḥ*—into hellish conditions of life.

TRANSLATION

O King Yudhiṣṭhira, many persons with varied experience, many legal advisers, many learned scholars and many persons eligible to become presidents of learned assemblies fall down into hellish life because of not being satisfied with their positions.

PURPORT

For spiritual advancement, one should be materially satisfied, for if one is not materially satisfied, his greed for material development will result in the frustration of his spiritual advancement. There are two things that nullify all good qualities. One is poverty. *Daridra-doṣo guṇa-rāśi-nāśī.* If one is poverty-stricken, all his good qualities become null and void. Similarly, if one becomes too greedy, his good qualifications are lost. Therefore the adjustment is that one should not be poverty-stricken, but one must try to be fully satisfied with the bare necessities of life and not be greedy. For a devotee to be satisfied with the bare necessities is therefore the best advice for spiritual advancement. Learned authorities in devotional life consequently advise that one not endeavor to increase the number of temples and *maṭhas.* Such activities can be undertaken only by devotees experienced in propagating the Kṛṣṇa consciousness movement. All the *ācāryas* in South India, especially Śrī Rāmānujācārya, constructed many big temples, and in North India all the Gosvāmīs of Vṛndāvana constructed large temples. Śrīla Bhaktisiddhānta Sarasvatī Ṭhākura also constructed large centers, known as Gauḍīya Maṭhas. Therefore temple construction is not bad, provided proper care is taken for the propagation of Kṛṣṇa consciousness. Even if such endeavors are considered greedy, the greed is to satisfy Kṛṣṇa, and therefore these are spiritual activities.

TEXT 22

असङ्कल्पाज्जयेत् कामं क्रोधं कामविवर्जनात् ।
अर्थानर्थेक्षया लोभं भयं तत्त्वावमर्शनात् ॥२२॥

asaṅkalpāj jayet kāmaṁ
krodhaṁ kāma-vivarjanāt
arthānartheksayā lobhaṁ
bhayaṁ tattvāvamarśanāt

asaṅkalpāt—by determination; *jayet*—one should conquer; *kāmam*—lusty desire; *krodham*—anger; *kāma-vivarjanāt*—by giving up the objective of sense desire; *artha*—accumulation of wealth; *anartha*—a cause of trouble; *īkṣayā*—by considering; *lobham*—greed; *bhayam*—fear; *tattva*—the truth; *avamarśanāt*—by considering.

TRANSLATION

By making plans with determination, one should give up lusty desires for sense gratification. Similarly, by giving up envy one should conquer anger, by discussing the disadvantages of accumulating wealth one should give up greed, and by discussing the truth one should give up fear.

PURPORT

Śrīla Viśvanātha Cakravartī Ṭhākura has suggested how one can conquer lusty desires for sense gratification. One cannot give up thinking of women, for thinking in this way is natural; even while walking on the street, one will see so many women. However, if one is determined not to live with a woman, even while seeing a woman he will not become lusty. If one is determined not to have sex, he can automatically conquer lusty desires. The example given in this regard is that even if one is hungry, if on a particular day he is determined to observe fasting, he can naturally conquer the disturbances of hunger and thirst. If one is determined not to be envious of anyone, he can naturally conquer anger. Similarly, one can give up the desire to accumulate wealth simply by considering how difficult it is to protect the money in one's possession. If one keeps a large amount of cash with him, he is always anxious about keeping it properly. Thus if one discusses the disadvantages of accumulating wealth, he can naturally give up business without difficulty.

TEXT 23

आन्वीक्षिक्या शोकमोहौ दम्भं महदुपासया ।
योगान्तरायान् मौनेन हिंसां कामाद्यनीहया ॥२३॥

ānvīkṣikyā śoka-mohau
dambhaṁ mahad-upāsayā
yogāntarāyān maunena
hiṁsāṁ kāmādy-anīhayā

ānvīkṣikyā—by deliberation upon material and spiritual subject matters; *śoka*—lamentation; *mohau*—and illusion; *dambham*—false pride; *mahat*—a Vaiṣṇava; *upāsayā*—by serving; *yoga-antarāyān*—obstacles on the path of *yoga; maunena*—by silence; *hiṁsām*—envy; *kāma-ādi*—for sense gratification; *anīhayā*—without endeavor.

TRANSLATION

By discussing spiritual knowledge one can conquer lamentation and illusion, by serving a great devotee one can become prideless, by keeping silent one can avoid obstacles on the path of mystic yoga, and simply by stopping sense gratification one can conquer envy.

PURPORT

If one's son has died, one may certainly be affected by lamentation and illusion and cry for the dead son, but one may overcome lamentation and illusion by considering the verses of *Bhagavad-gītā.*

jātasya hi dhruvo mṛtyur
dhruvaṁ janma mṛtasya ca

As the soul transmigrates, one who has taken birth must give up the present body, and then he must certainly accept another body. This should be no cause for lamentation. Therefore Lord Kṛṣṇa says, *dhīras tatra na muhyati:* one who is *dhīra*, or sober, who is learned in philosophy and established in knowledge, cannot be unhappy over the transmigration of the soul.

TEXT 24

कृपया भूतजं दुःखं दैवं जह्यात् समाधिना ।
आत्मजं योगवीर्येण निद्रां सत्त्वनिषेवया ॥२४॥

kṛpayā bhūtajaṁ duḥkhaṁ
daivaṁ jahyāt samādhinā
ātmajaṁ yoga-vīryeṇa
nidrāṁ sattva-niṣevayā

kṛpayā—by being merciful to all other living entities; *bhūta-jam*—because of other living entities; *duḥkham*—suffering; *daivam*—sufferings imposed by providence; *jahyāt*—one should give up; *samādhinā*—by trance or meditation; *ātma-jam*—sufferings due to the body and mind; *yoga-vīryeṇa*—by practicing *haṭha-yoga, prāṇāyāma* and so forth; *nidrām*—sleeping; *sattva-niṣevayā*—by developing brahminical qualifications or the mode of goodness.

TRANSLATION

By good behavior and freedom from envy one should counteract sufferings due to other living entities, by meditation in trance one should counteract sufferings due to providence, and by practicing haṭha-yoga, prāṇāyāma and so forth one should counteract sufferings due to the body and mind. Similarly, by developing the mode of goodness, especially in regard to eating, one should conquer sleep.

PURPORT

By practice, one should avoid eating in such a way that other living entities will be disturbed and suffer. Since I suffer when pinched or killed by others, I should not attempt to pinch or kill any other living entity. People do not know that because of killing innocent animals they themselves will have to suffer severe reactions from material nature. Any country where people indulge in unnecessary killing of animals will have to suffer from wars and pestilence imposed by material nature. Comparing one's own suffering to the suffering of others, therefore, one should be kind to all living entities. One cannot avoid the sufferings inflicted by providence, and therefore when suffering comes one should fully absorb oneself in chanting the Hare Kṛṣṇa *mantra.* One can avoid sufferings from the body and mind by practicing mystic *haṭha-yoga.*

TEXT 25

रजस्तमश्च सत्त्वेन सत्त्वं चोपशमेन च ।
एतत् सर्वं गुरौ भक्त्या पुरुषो ह्यञ्जसा जयेत् ॥२५॥

rajas tamaś ca sattvena
sattvaṁ copaśamena ca
etat sarvaṁ gurau bhaktyā
puruṣo hy añjasā jayet

rajaḥ tamaḥ—the modes of passion and ignorance; *ca*—and; *sattvena*—by developing the mode of goodness; *sattvam*—the mode of goodness; *ca*—also; *upaśamena*—by giving up attachment; *ca*—and; *etat*—these; *sarvam*—all; *gurau*—unto the spiritual master; *bhaktyā*—by rendering service in devotion; *puruṣaḥ*—a person; *hi*—indeed; *añjasā*—easily; *jayet*—can conquer.

TRANSLATION

One must conquer the modes of passion and ignorance by developing the mode of goodness, and then one must become detached from the mode of goodness by promoting oneself to the platform of śuddha-sattva. All this can be automatically done if one engages in the service of the spiritual master with faith and devotion. In this way one can conquer the influence of the modes of nature.

PURPORT

Just by treating the root cause of an ailment, one can conquer all bodily pains and sufferings. Similarly, if one is devoted and faithful to the spiritual master, he can conquer the influence of *sattva-guṇa, rajo-guṇa* and *tamo-guṇa* very easily. *Yogīs* and *jñānīs* practice in many ways to conquer the senses, but the *bhakta* immediately attains the mercy of the Supreme Personality of Godhead through the mercy of the spiritual master. *Yasya prasādād bhagavat-prasādo.* If the spiritual master is favorably inclined, one naturally receives the mercy of the Supreme Lord, and by the mercy of the Supreme Lord one immediately becomes transcendental, conquering all the influences of *sattva-guṇa, rajo-guṇa* and *tamo-guṇa* within this material world. This is confirmed in *Bhagavad-gītā* (*sa guṇān samatītyaitān brahma-bhūyāya kalpate*). If one is a pure devotee acting under the directions of the *guru*, one easily gets the mercy of the Supreme Lord and thus becomes immediately situated on the transcendental platform. This is explained in the next verse.

TEXT 26

यस्य साक्षाद् भगवति ज्ञानदीपप्रदे गुरौ ।
मर्त्यासद्धीः श्रुतं तस्य सर्वं कुञ्जरशौचवत् ॥२६॥

yasya sākṣād bhagavati
jñāna-dīpa-prade gurau
martyāsad-dhīḥ śrutaṁ tasya
sarvaṁ kuñjara-śaucavat

yasya—one who; *sākṣāt*—directly; *bhagavati*—the Supreme Personality of Godhead; *jñāna-dīpa-prade*—who enlightens with the torch of knowledge; *gurau*—unto the spiritual master; *martya-asat-dhīḥ*—considers the spiritual master to be like an ordinary human being and maintains such an unfavorable attitude; *śrutam*—Vedic knowledge; *tasya*—for him; *sarvam*—everything; *kuñjara-śauca-vat*—like the bath of an elephant in a lake.

TRANSLATION

The spiritual master should be considered to be directly the Supreme Lord because he gives transcendental knowledge for

enlightenment. Consequently, for one who maintains the material conception that the spiritual master is an ordinary human being, everything is frustrated. His enlightenment and his Vedic studies and knowledge are like the bathing of an elephant.

PURPORT

It is recommended that one honor the spiritual master as being on an equal status with the Supreme Personality of Godhead. *Sākṣād dharitvena samasta-śāstraiḥ.* This is enjoined in every scripture. *Ācāryaṁ māṁ vijānīyāt.* One should consider the *ācārya* to be as good as the Supreme Personality of Godhead. In spite of all these instructions, if one considers the spiritual master an ordinary human being, one is doomed. His study of the *Vedas* and his austerities and penances for enlightenment are all useless, like the bathing of an elephant. An elephant bathes in a lake quite thoroughly, but as soon as it comes on the shore it takes some dust from the ground and strews it over its body. Thus there is no meaning to the elephant's bath. One may argue by saying that since the spiritual master's relatives and the men of his neighborhood consider him an ordinary human being, what is the fault on the part of the disciple who considers the spiritual master an ordinary human being? This will be answered in the next verse, but the injunction is that the spiritual master should never be considered an ordinary man. One should strictly adhere to the instructions of the spiritual master, for if he is pleased, certainly the Supreme Personality of Godhead is pleased. *Yasya prasādād bhagavat-prasādo yasyāprasādān na gatiḥ kuto 'pi.*

TEXT 27

एष वै भगवान्साक्षात् प्रधानपुरुषेश्वरः ।
योगेश्वरैर्विमृग्याङ्घ्रिर्लोको यं मन्यते नरम् ॥२७॥

eṣa vai bhagavān sākṣāt
pradhāna-puruṣeśvaraḥ
yogeśvarair vimṛgyāṅghrir
loko yaṁ manyate naram

eṣaḥ—this; *vai*—indeed; *bhagavān*—Supreme Personality of Godhead; *sākṣāt*—directly; *pradhāna*—the chief cause of the material nature; *puruṣa*—of all living entities or of the *puruṣāvatāra*, Lord Viṣṇu; *īśvaraḥ*—the supreme controller; *yoga-īśvaraiḥ*—by great saintly persons, *yogīs; vimṛgya-aṅghriḥ*—Lord Kṛṣṇa's lotus feet, which are sought; *lokaḥ*—people in general; *yam*—Him; *manyate*—consider; *naram*—a human being.

TRANSLATION

The Supreme Personality of Godhead, Lord Kṛṣṇa, is the master of all other living entities and of the material nature. His lotus feet are sought and worshiped by great saintly persons like Vyāsa. Nonetheless, there are fools who consider Lord Kṛṣṇa an ordinary human being.

PURPORT

The example of Lord Kṛṣṇa's being the Supreme Personality of Godhead is appropriate in regard to understanding the spiritual master. The spiritual master is called *sevaka-bhagavān*, the servitor Personality of Godhead, and Kṛṣṇa is called *sevya-bhagavān*, the Supreme Personality of Godhead who is to be worshiped. The spiritual master is the worshiper God, whereas the Supreme Personality of Godhead, Kṛṣṇa, is the worshipable God. This is the difference between the spiritual master and the Supreme Personality of Godhead.

Another point: *Bhagavad-gītā*, which constitutes the instructions of the Supreme Personality of Godhead, is presented by the spiritual master as it is, without deviation. Therefore the Absolute Truth is present in the spiritual master. As clearly stated in Text 26, *jñāna-dīpa-prade*. The Supreme Personality of Godhead gives real knowledge to the entire world, and the spiritual master, as the representative of the Supreme Godhead, carries the message throughout the world. Therefore, on the absolute platform, there is no difference between the spiritual master and the Supreme Personality of Godhead. If someone considers the Supreme Personality—Kṛṣṇa or Lord Rāmacandra—to be an ordinary human being, this does not mean that the Lord becomes an ordinary human being. Similarly, if the family members of the spiritual master, who is the bona fide representative of the Supreme Personality of Godhead, consider the spiritual master an ordinary human being, this does not mean that he becomes an ordinary human being. The spiritual master is as good as the Supreme Personality of Godhead, and therefore one who is very serious about spiritual advancement must regard the spiritual master in this way. Even a slight deviation from this understanding can create disaster in the disciple's Vedic studies and austerities.

TEXT 28

षड्वर्गसंयमैकान्ताः सर्वा नियमचोदनाः ।
तदन्ता यदि नो योगानावहेयुः श्रमावहाः ॥२८॥

ṣaḍ-varga-saṁyamaikāntāḥ
sarvā niyama-codanāḥ
tad-antā yadi no yogān
āvaheyuḥ śramāvahāḥ

ṣaṭ-varga—the six elements, namely the five working senses and the mind; *saṁyama-ekāntāḥ*—the ultimate aim of subjugating; *sarvāḥ*—all such activities; *niyama-codanāḥ*—the regulative principles further meant for controlling the senses and mind; *tat-antāḥ*—the ultimate goal of such activities; *yadi*—if; *no*—not; *yogān*—the positive link with the Supreme; *āvaheyuḥ*—did lead to; *śrama-āvahāḥ*—a waste of time and labor.

TRANSLATION

Ritualistic ceremonies, regulative principles, austerities and the practice of yoga are all meant to control the senses and mind, but even after one is able to control the senses and mind, if he does not come to the point of meditation upon the Supreme Lord, all such activities are simply labor in frustration.

PURPORT

One may argue that one may achieve the ultimate goal of life—realization of the Supersoul—by practicing the *yoga* system and ritualistic performances according to the Vedic principles, even without staunch devotion to the spiritual master. The actual fact, however, is that by practicing *yoga* one must come to the platform of meditating upon the Supreme Personality of Godhead. As stated in the scriptures, *dhyānāvasthita-tad-gatena manasā paśyanti yaṁ yoginaḥ:* a person in meditation achieves the perfection of *yoga* practice when he can see the Supreme Personality of Godhead. By various practices, one may come to the point of controlling the senses, but simply controlling the senses does not bring one to a substantial conclusion. However, by staunch faith in the spiritual master and the Supreme Personality of Godhead, one not only controls the senses but also realizes the Supreme Lord.

yasya deve parā bhaktir
yathā deve tathā gurau
tasyaite kathitā hy arthāḥ
prakāśante mahātmanaḥ

"Only unto those great souls who have implicit faith in both the Lord and the spiritual master are all the imports of the Vedic knowledge automatically revealed." (*Śvetāśvatara Upaniṣad* 6.23) It is further stated, *tuṣyeyaṁ sarva-bhūtātmā guru-śuśrūṣayā* and *taranty añjo bhavārṇavam.* Simply by rendering service to the spiritual master, one crosses the ocean of nescience and returns home, back to Godhead. Thus he gradually sees the Supreme Lord face to face and enjoys life in association with the Lord. The ultimate goal of *yoga* is to come in contact with the Supreme Personality of Godhead. Unless this point is achieved, one's so-called *yoga* practice is simply labor without any benefit.

TEXT 29

यथा वार्तादयो ह्यर्था योगस्यार्थं न बिभ्रति ।
अनर्थाय भवेयुः स्म पूर्तमिष्टं तथासतः ॥२९॥

yathā vārtādayo hy arthā
yogasyārthaṁ na bibhrati
anarthāya bhaveyuḥ sma
pūrtam iṣṭaṁ tathāsataḥ

yathā—as; *vārtā-ādayaḥ*—activities like occupational or professional duties; *hi*—certainly; *arthāḥ*—income (from such occupational duties); *yogasya*—of mystic power for self-realization; *artham*—benefit; *na*—

not; *bibhrati*—help; *anarthāya*—without value (binding one to repeated birth and death); *bhaveyuḥ*—they are; *sma*—at all times; *pūrtam iṣṭam*—ritualistic Vedic ceremonies; *tathā*—similarly; *asataḥ*—of a materialistic nondevotee.

TRANSLATION

As professional activities or business profits cannot help one in spiritual advancement but are a source of material entanglement, the Vedic ritualistic ceremonies cannot help anyone who is not a devotee of the Supreme Personality of Godhead.

PURPORT

If one becomes very rich through his professional activities, through trade or through agriculture, this does not mean that he is spiritually advanced. To be spiritually advanced is different from being materially rich. Although the purpose of life is to become spiritually rich, unfortunate men, misguided as they are, are always engaged in trying to become materially rich. Such material engagements, however, do not help one in the actual fulfillment of the human mission. On the contrary, material engagements lead one to be attracted to many unnecessary necessities, which are accompanied by the risk that one may be born in a degraded condition. As confirmed in *Bhagavad-gītā* (14.18):

ūrdhvaṁ gacchanti sattva-sthā
madhye tiṣṭhanti rājasāḥ
jaghanya-guṇa-vṛtti-sthā
adho gacchanti tāmasāḥ

"Those situated in the mode of goodness gradually go upward to the higher planets; those in the mode of passion live on the earthly planets; and those in the mode of ignorance go down to the hellish worlds." Especially in this Kali-yuga, material advancement means degradation and attraction to many unwanted necessities that create a low mentality. Therefore, *jaghanya-guṇa-vṛtti-sthā:* since people are contaminated by the lower qualities, they will lead their next lives either as animals or in other degraded forms of life. Making a show of religion without Kṛṣṇa consciousness may make one popular in the estimation of unintelligent men, but factually such a materialistic display of spiritual advancement does not help one at all; it will not prevent one from missing the goal of life.

TEXT 30

यश्चित्तविजये यत्तः स्यान्निःसङ्गोऽपरिग्रहः ।
एको विविक्तशरणो भिक्षुर्भैक्ष्यमिताशनः ॥३०॥

yaś citta-vijaye yattaḥ
syān niḥsaṅgo 'parigrahaḥ
eko vivikta-śaraṇo
bhikṣur bhaikṣya-mitāśanaḥ

yaḥ—one who; *citta-vijaye*—conquering the mind; *yattaḥ*—is engaged; *syāt*—must be; *niḥsaṅgaḥ*—without contaminated association; *aparigrahaḥ*—without being dependent (on the family); *ekaḥ*—alone; *vivikta-śaraṇaḥ*—taking shelter of a solitary place; *bhikṣuḥ*—a renounced person; *bhaikṣya*—by begging alms just to maintain the body; *mita-aśanaḥ*—frugal in eating.

TRANSLATION

One who desires to conquer the mind must leave the company of his family and live in a solitary place, free from contaminated association. To maintain the body and soul together, he should beg as much as he needs for the bare necessities of life.

PURPORT

This is the process for conquering the agitation of the mind. One is recommended to take leave of his family and live alone, maintaining body and soul together by begging alms and eating only as much as needed to keep himself alive. Without such a process, one cannot conquer lusty desires. *Sannyāsa* means accepting a life of begging, which makes one automatically very humble and meek and free from lusty desires. In this regard, the following verse appears in the *Smṛti* literature:

dvandvāhatasya gārhasthyaṁ
dhyāna-bhaṅgādi-kāraṇam

lakṣayitvā gṛhī spaṣṭaṁ
sannyased avicārayan

In this world of duality, family life is the cause that spoils one's spiritual life or meditation. Specifically understanding this fact, one should accept the order of *sannyāsa* without hesitation.

TEXT 31

देशे शुचौ समे राजन्संस्थाप्यासनमात्मनः ।
स्थिरं सुखं समं तस्मिन्नासीतर्ज्वङ्ग ओमिति ॥३१॥

deśe śucau same rājan
saṁsthāpyāsanam ātmanaḥ
sthiraṁ sukhaṁ samaṁ tasminn
āsītarjv-aṅga om iti

deśe—in a place; *śucau*—very sacred; *same*—level; *rājan*—O King; *saṁsthāpya*—placing; *āsanam*—on the seat; *ātmanaḥ*—one's self; *sthiram*—very steady; *sukham*—comfortably; *samam*—equipoised; *tasmin*—on that sitting place; *āsīta*—one should sit down; *ṛju-aṅgaḥ*—the body perpendicularly straight; *oṁ*—The Vedic *mantra praṇava; iti*—in this way.

TRANSLATION

My dear King, in a sacred and holy place of pilgrimage one should select a place in which to perform yoga. The place must be level and not too high or low. There one should sit very comfortably, being steady and equipoised, keeping his body straight, and thus begin chanting the Vedic praṇava.

PURPORT

Generally the chanting of *oṁ* is recommended because in the beginning one cannot understand the Personality of Godhead. As stated in *Śrīmad-Bhāgavatam* (1.2.11):

vadanti tat tattva-vidas
tattvaṁ yaj jñānam advayam

brahmeti paramātmeti
bhagavān iti śabdyate

"Learned transcendentalists who know the Absolute Truth call this nondual substance Brahman, Paramātmā or Bhagavān." Unless one is fully convinced of the Supreme Personality of Godhead, one has the tendency to become an impersonalist *yogī* searching for the Supreme Lord within the core of his heart (*dhyānāvasthita-tad-gatena manasā paśyanti yaṁ yoginaḥ*). Here the chanting of *oṁkāra* is recommended because in the beginning of transcendental realization, instead of chanting the Hare Kṛṣṇa *mahā-mantra*, one may chant *oṁkāra* (*praṇava*). There is no difference between the Hare Kṛṣṇa *mahā-mantra* and *oṁkāra* because both of them are sound representations of the Supreme Personality of Godhead. *Praṇavaḥ sarva-vedeṣu.* In all Vedic literatures, the sound vibration *oṁkāra* is the beginning. *Oṁ namo bhagavate vāsudevāya.* The difference between chanting *oṁkāra* and chanting the Hare Kṛṣṇa *mantra* is that the Hare Kṛṣṇa *mantra* may be chanted without consideration of the place or the sitting arrangements recommended in *Bhagavad-gītā* (6.11):

śucau deśe pratiṣṭhāpya
sthiram āsanam ātmanaḥ
nāty-ucchritaṁ nātinīcaṁ
cailājina-kuśottaram

"To practice *yoga*, one should go to a secluded place and should lay *kuśa* grass on the ground and then cover it with a deerskin and a soft cloth. The seat should neither be too high nor too low and should be situated in a sacred place." The Hare Kṛṣṇa *mantra* may be chanted by anyone, without consideration of the place or how one sits. Śrī Caitanya Mahāprabhu has openly declared, *niyamitaḥ smaraṇe na kālaḥ.* In chanting the Hare Kṛṣṇa *mahā-mantra* there are no particular injunctions regarding one's sitting place. The injunction *niyamitaḥ smaraṇe na kālaḥ* includes *deśa*, *kāla* and *pātra*—place, time and the individual. Therefore anyone may chant the Hare Kṛṣṇa *mantra*, without consideration of the time and place. Especially in this age, Kali-yuga, it is very difficult to find a suitable place according to the recommendations of *Bhagavad-gītā.* The Hare Kṛṣṇa *mahā-mantra*, however, may be chanted at any place and any time, and this will bring results very quickly. Yet even while chanting the Hare Kṛṣṇa *mantra* one may observe regulative principles. Thus while sitting and chanting one may keep his body straight, and this will help one in the chanting process; otherwise one may feel sleepy.

TEXTS 32–33

प्राणापानौ सन्निरुन्ध्यात् पूरकुम्भकरेचकैः ।
यावन्मनस्त्यजेत् कामान् स्वनासाग्रनिरीक्षणः ॥३२॥
यतो यतो निःसरति मनः कामहतं भ्रमत् ।
ततस्तत उपाहृत्य हृदि रुन्ध्याच्छनैर्बुधः ॥३३॥

prāṇāpānau sannirundhyāt
pūra-kumbhaka-recakaiḥ
yāvan manas tyajet kāmān
sva-nāsāgra-nirīkṣaṇaḥ

yato yato niḥsarati
manaḥ kāma-hataṁ bhramat
tatas tata upāhṛtya
hṛdi rundhyāc chanair budhaḥ

prāṇa—incoming breath; *apānau*—outgoing breath; *sannirundhyāt*—should stop; *pūra-kumbhaka-recakaiḥ*—by inhaling, exhaling and holding, which are technically known as *pūraka, kumbhaka* and *recaka; yāvat*—so long; *manaḥ*—the mind; *tyajet*—should give up; *kāmān*—all material desires; *sva*—one's own; *nāsa-agra*—the tip of the nose; *nirīkṣaṇaḥ*—looking at; *yataḥ yataḥ*—from whatever and wherever; *niḥsarati*—withdraws; *manaḥ*—the mind; *kāma-hatam*—being defeated by lusty desires; *bhramat*—wandering; *tataḥ tataḥ*—from here and there; *upāhṛtya*—after bringing it back; *hṛdi*—within the core of the heart; *rundhyāt*—should arrest (the mind); *śanaiḥ*—gradually, by practice; *budhaḥ*—a learned *yogī.*

TRANSLATION

While continuously staring at the tip of the nose, a learned yogī practices the breathing exercises through the technical means

known as pūraka, kumbhaka and recaka—controlling inhalation and exhalation and then stopping them both. In this way the yogī restricts his mind from material attachments and gives up all mental desires. As soon as the mind, being defeated by lusty desires, drifts toward feelings of sense gratification, the yogī should immediately bring it back and arrest it within the core of his heart.

PURPORT

The practice of *yoga* is concisely explained herein. When this practice of *yoga* is perfect, one sees the Supersoul, the Paramātmā feature of the Supreme Personality of Godhead, within the core of one's heart. However, in *Bhagavad-gītā* (6.47) the Supreme Lord says:

yoginām api sarveṣām
mad-gatenāntarātmanā
śraddhāvān bhajate yo māṁ
sa me yuktatamo mataḥ

"Of all *yogīs*, he who always abides in Me with great faith, worshiping Me in transcendental loving service, is most intimately united with Me in *yoga* and is the highest of all." A devotee can immediately become a perfect *yogī* because he practices keeping Kṛṣṇa constantly within the core of his heart. This is another way to practice *yoga* easily. The Lord says:

man-manā bhava mad-bhakto
mad-yājī māṁ namaskuru

"Always think of Me and become My devotee. Worship Me and offer your homage unto Me." (Bg. 18.65) If one practices devotional service by always keeping Kṛṣṇa within the core of his heart (*man-manāḥ*), he immediately becomes a first-class *yogī.* Furthermore, keeping Kṛṣṇa within the mind is not a difficult task for the devotee. For an ordinary man in the bodily concept of life, the practice of *yoga* may be helpful, but one who immediately takes to devotional service can immediately become a perfect *yogī* without difficulty.

TEXT 34

एवमभ्यस्यतश्चित्तं कालेनाल्पीयसा यतेः ।
अनिशं तस्य निर्वाणं यात्यनिन्धनवह्निवत् ॥३४॥

evam abhyasyataś cittaṁ
kālenālpīyasā yateḥ
aniśaṁ tasya nirvāṇaṁ
yāty anindhana-vahnivat

evam—in this way; *abhyasyataḥ*—of the person practicing this *yoga* system; *cittam*—the heart; *kālena*—in due course of time; *alpīyasā*—very shortly; *yateḥ*—of the person practicing *yoga; aniśam*—without cessation; *tasya*—of him; *nirvāṇam*—purification from all material contamination; *yāti*—reaches; *anindhana*—without flame or smoke; *vahnivat*—like a fire.

TRANSLATION

When the yogī regularly practices in this way, in a short time his heart becomes fixed and free from disturbance, like a fire without flames or smoke.

PURPORT

Nirvāṇa means the cessation of all material desires. Sometimes desirelessness is understood to imply an end to the workings of the mind, but this is not possible. The living entity has senses, and if the senses stopped working, the living entity would no longer be a living entity; he would be exactly like stone or wood. This is not possible. Because he is living, he is *nitya* and *cetana*—eternally sentient. For those who are not very advanced, the practice of *yoga* is recommended in order to stop the mind from being agitated by material desires, but if one fixes his mind on the lotus feet of Kṛṣṇa, his mind naturally becomes peaceful very soon. This peace is described in *Bhagavad-gītā* (5.29):

bhoktāraṁ yajña-tapasāṁ
sarva-loka-maheśvaram
suhṛdaṁ sarva-bhūtānāṁ
jñātvā māṁ śāntim ṛcchati

If one can understand Kṛṣṇa as the supreme enjoyer, the supreme proprietor of everything, and the supreme friend of everyone, one is established in peace and is free from material agitation. However, for one who cannot understand the Supreme Personality of Godhead, the practice of *yoga* is recommended.

TEXT 35

कामादिभिरनाविद्धं प्रशान्ताखिलवृत्ति यत् ।
चित्तं ब्रह्मसुखस्पृष्टं नैवोत्तिष्ठेत कर्हिचित् ॥३५॥

kāmādibhir anāviddhaṁ
praśāntākhila-vṛtti yat
cittaṁ brahma-sukha-spṛṣṭaṁ
naivottiṣṭheta karhicit

kāma-ādibhiḥ—by various lusty desires; *anāviddham*—unaffected; *praśānta*—calm and peaceful; *akhila-vṛtti*—in every respect, or in all activities; *yat*—that which; *cittam*—consciousness; *brahma-sukha-spṛṣṭam*—being situated on the transcendental platform in eternal bliss; *na*—not; *eva*—indeed; *uttiṣṭheta*—can come out; *karhicit*—at any time.

TRANSLATION

When one's consciousness is uncontaminated by material lusty desires, it becomes calm and peaceful in all activities, for one is situated in eternal blissful life. Once situated on that platform, one does not return to materialistic activities.

PURPORT

Brahma-sukha-spṛṣṭam is also described in *Bhagavad-gītā* (18.54):

brahma-bhūtaḥ prasannātmā
na śocati na kāṅkṣati
samaḥ sarveṣu bhūteṣu
mad-bhaktiṁ labhate parām

"One who is transcendentally situated at once realizes the Supreme Brahman and becomes fully joyful. He never laments nor desires to have anything; he is equally disposed toward every living entity. In this situation, he begins transcendental activities, or devotional service to the Lord." Generally, once elevated to the transcendental platform of *brahma-sukha*, transcendental bliss, one never comes down. But if one does not engage in devotional service, there is a chance of his returning to the material platform. *Āruhya kṛcchreṇa paraṁ padaṁ tataḥ patanty adho 'nādṛta-yuṣmad-aṅghrayaḥ:* one may rise to the platform of *brahma-sukha*, transcendental bliss, but even from that platform one may fall down to the material platform if he does not engage himself in devotional service.

TEXT 36

यः प्रव्रज्य गृहात् पूर्वं त्रिवर्गावपनात् पुनः ।
यदि सेवेत तान्भिक्षुः स वै वान्ताश्यपत्रपः ॥३६॥

yaḥ pravrajya gṛhāt pūrvaṁ
tri-vargāvapanāt punaḥ
yadi seveta tān bhikṣuḥ
sa vai vāntāśy apatrapaḥ

yaḥ—one who; *pravrajya*—being finished for good and leaving for the forest (being situated in transcendental bliss); *gṛhāt*—from home; *pūrvam*—at first; *tri-varga*—the three principles of religion, economic development and sense gratification; *āvapanāt*—from the field in which they are sown; *punaḥ*—again; *yadi*—if; *seveta*—should accept; *tān*—materialistic activities; *bhikṣuḥ*—a person who has accepted the *sannyāsa* order; *saḥ*—that person; *vai*—indeed; *vānta-āśī*—one who eats his own vomit; *apatrapaḥ*—without shame.

TRANSLATION

One who accepts the sannyāsa order gives up the three principles of materialistic activities in which one indulges in the field of household life—namely religion, economic development and sense gratification. One who first accepts sannyāsa but then returns

to such materialistic activities is to be called a vāntāśī, or one who eats his own vomit. He is indeed a shameless person.

PURPORT

Materialistic activities are regulated by the institution of *varṇāśrama-dharma.* Without *varṇāśrama-dharma,* materialistic activities constitute animal life. Yet even in human life, while observing the principles of *varṇa* and *āśrama—brāhmaṇa, kṣatriya, vaiśya, śūdra, brahmacarya, gṛhastha, vānaprastha* and *sannyāsa*—one must ultimately accept *sannyāsa,* the renounced order, for only by the renounced order can one be situated in *brahma-sukha,* or transcendental bliss. In *brahma-sukha* one is no longer attracted by lusty desires. Indeed, when one is no longer disturbed, especially by lusty desires for sexual indulgence, he is fit to become a *sannyāsī.* Otherwise, one should not accept the *sannyāsa* order. If one accepts *sannyāsa* at an immature stage, there is every possibility of his being attracted by women and lusty desires and thus again becoming a so-called *gṛhastha* or a victim of women. Such a person is most shameless, and he is called *vāntāśī,* or one who eats that which he has already vomited. He certainly leads a condemned life. In our Kṛṣṇa consciousness movement it is advised, therefore, that the *sannyāsīs* and *brahmacārīs* keep strictly aloof from the association of women so that there will be no chance of their falling down again as victims of lusty desires.

TEXT 37

यैः स्वदेहः स्मृतो नात्मा मर्त्यो विट्कृमिभस्मवत् ।
त एनमात्मसात्कृत्वा श्लाघयन्ति ह्यसत्तमाः ॥३७॥

yaiḥ sva-dehaḥ smṛto 'nātmā
martyo viṭ-kṛmi-bhasmavat
ta enam ātmasāt kṛtvā
ślāghayanti hy asattamāḥ

yaiḥ—by *sannyāsīs* who; *sva-dehaḥ*—own body; *smṛtaḥ*—consider; *anātmā*—different from the soul; *martyaḥ*—subjected to death; *viṭ*—becoming stool; *kṛmi*—worms; *bhasma-vat*—or ashes; *te*—such persons; *enam*—this body; *ātmasāt kṛtvā*—again identifying with the self; *ślāghayanti*—glorify as very important; *hi*—indeed; *asat-tamāḥ*—the greatest rascals.

TRANSLATION

Sannyāsīs who first consider that the body is subject to death, when it will be transformed into stool, worms or ashes, but who again give importance to the body and glorify it as the self, are to be considered the greatest rascals.

PURPORT

A *sannyāsī* is one who has clearly understood, through advancement in knowledge, that Brahman—he, the person himself—is the soul, not the body. One who has this understanding may take *sannyāsa*, for he is situated in the "*ahaṁ brahmāsmi*" position. *Brahma-bhūtaḥ prasannātmā na śocati na kāṅkṣati.* Such a person, who no longer laments or hankers to maintain his body and who can accept all living entities as spirit souls, can then enter the devotional service of the Lord. If one does not enter the devotional service of the Lord but artificially considers himself Brahman or Nārāyaṇa, not perfectly understanding that the soul and body are different, one certainly falls down (*patanty adhaḥ*). Such a person again gives importance to the body. There are many *sannyāsīs* in India who stress the importance of the body. Some of them give special importance to the body of the poor man, accepting him as *daridra-nārāyaṇa*, as if Nārāyaṇa had a material body. Many other *sannyāsīs* stress the importance of the social position of the body as a *brāhmaṇa, kṣatriya, vaiśya* or *śūdra*. Such *sannyāsīs* are considered the greatest rascals (*asattamāḥ*). They are shameless because they have not yet understood the difference between the body and the soul and instead have accepted the body of a *brāhmaṇa* to be a *brāhmaṇa*. Brahmanism (*brāhmaṇya*) consists of the knowledge of Brahman. But actually the body of a *brāhmaṇa* is not Brahman. Similarly, the body is neither rich nor poor. If the body of a poor man were *daridra-nārāyaṇa*, this would mean that the body of a rich man, on the contrary, must be *dhanī-nārāyaṇa*. Therefore *sannyāsīs* who do not know the meaning of Nārāyaṇa, those who regard the body as Brahman or as Nārāyaṇa, are described here as *asattamāḥ*, the most abominable rascals. Following the bodily concept of life, such *sannyāsīs* make various programs to serve the body. They conduct farcical missions consisting of so-called religious activities meant to mislead all of human society. These *sannyāsīs* have been described herein as *apatrapaḥ* and *asattamāḥ*—shameless and fallen from spiritual life.

TEXTS 38–39

गृहस्थस्य क्रियात्यागो व्रतत्यागो वटोरपि ।
तपस्विनो ग्रामसेवा भिक्षोरिन्द्रियलोलता ॥३८॥
आश्रमापसदा ह्येते खल्वाश्रमविडम्बनाः ।
देवमायाविमूढांस्तानुपेक्षेतानुकम्पया ॥३९॥

gṛhasthasya kriyā-tyāgo
vrata-tyāgo vaṭor api
tapasvino grāma-sevā
bhikṣor indriya-lolatā

āśramāpasadā hy ete
khalv āśrama-viḍambanāḥ
deva-māyā-vimūḍhāṁs tān
upekṣetānukampayā

gṛhasthasya—for a person situated in householder life; *kriyā-tyāgaḥ*—to give up the duty of a householder; *vrata-tyāgaḥ*—to give up vows and austerity; *vaṭoḥ*—for a *brahmacārī; api*—also; *tapasvinaḥ*—for a *vānaprastha*, one who has adopted a life of austerities; *grāma-sevā*—to live in a village and serve the people therein; *bhikṣoḥ*—for a *sannyāsī* who lived by begging alms; *indriya-lolatā*—addicted to sense enjoyment; *āśrama*—of the spiritual orders of life; *apasadāḥ*—the most abominable; *hi*—indeed; *ete*—all these; *khalu*—indeed; *āśrama-viḍambanāḥ*—imitating and therefore cheating the different spiritual orders; *deva-māyā-vimūḍhān*—who are bewildered by the external energy of the Supreme Lord; *tān*—them; *upekṣeta*—one should reject and not accept as genuine; *anukampayā*—or by compassion (teach them real life).

TRANSLATION

It is abominable for a person living in the gṛhastha-āśrama to give up the regulative principles, for a brahmacārī not to follow the brahmacārī vows while living under the care of the guru, for a vānaprastha to live in the village and engage in so-called social activities, or for a sannyāsī to be addicted to sense gratification. One who acts in this way is to be considered the lowest renegade. Such a pretender is bewildered by the external energy of the Supreme Personality of Godhead, and one should either reject him from any position, or taking compassion upon him, teach him, if possible, to resume his original position.

PURPORT

We have repeatedly stressed that human culture does not begin unless one takes to the principles of *varṇāśrama-dharma.* Although *gṛhastha* life is a concession for the enjoyment of sex, one cannot enjoy sex without following the rules and regulations of householder life. Furthermore, as already instructed, a *brahmacārī* must live under the care of the *guru: brahmacārī guru-kule vasan dānto guror hitam.* If a *brahmacārī* does not live under the care of the *guru,* if a *vānaprastha* engages in ordinary activities, or if a *sannyāsī* is greedy and eats meat, eggs and all kinds of nonsense for the satisfaction of his tongue, he is a cheater and should immediately be rejected as unimportant. Such persons should be shown compassion, and if one has sufficient strength one should teach them to stop them from following the wrong path in life. Otherwise one should reject them and pay them no attention.

TEXT 40

आत्मानं चेद् विजानीयात् परं ज्ञानधुताशयः ।
किमिच्छन्कस्य वा हेतोर्देहं पुष्णाति लम्पटः ॥४०॥

ātmānaṁ ced vijānīyāt
paraṁ jñāna-dhutāśayaḥ
kim icchan kasya vā hetor
dehaṁ puṣṇāti lampaṭaḥ

ātmānam—the soul and the Supersoul; *cet*—if; *vijānīyāt*—can understand; *param*—who are transcendental, beyond this material world; *jñāna*—by knowledge; *dhuta-āśayaḥ*—one who has cleansed his consciousness; *kim*—what; *icchan*—desiring material comforts; *kasya*—for whom; *vā*—or; *hetoḥ*—for what reason; *deham*—the material body; *puṣṇāti*—he maintains; *lampaṭaḥ*—being unlawfully addicted to sense gratification.

TRANSLATION

The human form of body is meant for understanding the self and the Supreme Self, the Supreme Personality of Godhead, both of whom are transcendentally situated. If both of them can be understood when one is purified by advanced knowledge, for what reason and for whom does a foolish, greedy person maintain the body for sense gratification?

PURPORT

Of course, everyone in this material world is interested in maintaining the body for sense gratification, but by cultivating knowledge one should gradually understand that the body is not the self. Both the soul and the Supersoul are transcendental to the material world. This is to be understood in the human form of life, especially when one takes *sannyāsa.* A *sannyāsī*, one who has understood the self, should be engaged in elevating the self and associating with the Superself. Our Kṛṣṇa consciousness movement is meant for elevating the living being for promotion back home, back to Godhead. Seeking such elevation is one's duty in the human form of life. Unless one performs this duty, why should one maintain the body? Especially if a *sannyāsī* not only maintains the body by ordinary means but does everything to maintain the body, including even eating meat and other abominable things, he must be a *lampaṭaḥ*, a greedy person simply engaged in sense gratification. A *sannyāsī* must specifically remove himself from the urges of the tongue, belly and genitals, which disturb one as long as one is not fully aware that the body is separate from the soul.

TEXT 41

आहुः शरीरं रथमिन्द्रियाणि
हयानभीषून् मन इन्द्रियेशम् ।

वर्त्मानि मात्रा धिषणां च सूतं
सत्त्वं बृहद् बन्धुरमीशसृष्टम् ॥४१॥

āhuḥ śarīraṁ ratham indriyāṇi
hayān abhīṣūn mana indriyeśam
vartmāni mātrā dhiṣaṇāṁ ca sūtaṁ
sattvaṁ bṛhad bandhuram īśa-sṛṣṭam

āhuḥ—it is said; *śarīram*—the body; *ratham*—the chariot; *indriyāṇi*—the senses; *hayān*—the horses; *abhīṣūn*—the reins; *manaḥ*—the mind; *indriya*—of the senses; *īśam*—the master; *vartmāni*—the destinations; *mātrāḥ*—the sense objects; *dhiṣaṇām*—the intelligence; *ca*—and; *sūtam*—the chariot driver; *sattvam*—consciousness; *bṛhat*—great; *bandhuram*—bondage; *īśa*—by the Supreme Personality of Godhead; *sṛṣṭam*—created.

TRANSLATION

Transcendentalists who are advanced in knowledge compare the body, which is made by the order of the Supreme Personality of Godhead, to a chariot. The senses are like the horses; the mind, the master of the senses, is like the reins; the objects of the senses are the destinations; intelligence is the chariot driver; and consciousness, which spreads throughout the body, is the cause of bondage in this material world.

PURPORT

For a bewildered person in the materialistic way of life, the body, the mind and the senses, which are engaged in sense gratification, are the cause of bondage to repeated birth, death, old age and disease. But for one who is advanced in spiritual knowledge, the same body, senses and mind are the cause of liberation. This is confirmed in the *Kaṭha Upaniṣad* (1.3.3–4,9) as follows:

ātmānaṁ rathinaṁ viddhi
śarīraṁ ratham eva ca
buddhiṁ tu sārathiṁ viddhi
manaḥ pragraham eva ca

indriyāṇi hayān āhur
viṣayāṁs teṣu gocarān

so 'dhvanaḥ pāram āpnoti
tad viṣṇoḥ paramaṁ padam

The soul is the occupant of the chariot of the body, of which the driver is the intelligence. The mind is the determination to reach the destination, the senses are the horses, and the sense objects are also included in that activity. Thus one can reach the destination, Viṣṇu, who is *paramaṁ padam*, the supreme goal of life. In conditioned life the consciousness in the body is the cause of bondage, but the same consciousness, when transformed into Kṛṣṇa consciousness, becomes the cause for one's returning home, back to Godhead.

The human body, therefore, may be used in two ways—for going to the darkest regions of ignorance or for going forward, back home, back to Godhead. To go back to Godhead, the path is *mahat-sevā*, to accept the self-realized spiritual master. *Mahat-sevāṁ dvāram āhur vimukteḥ.* For liberation, one should accept the direction of authorized devotees who can actually endow one with perfect knowledge. On the other hand, *tamo-dvāraṁ yoṣitāṁ saṅgi-saṅgam:* if one wants to go to the darkest regions of material existence, one may continue to associate with persons who are attached to women (*yoṣitāṁ saṅgi-saṅgam*). The word *yoṣit* means "woman." Persons who are too materialistic are attached to women.

It is said, therefore, *ātmānaṁ rathinaṁ viddhi śarīraṁ ratham eva ca.* The body is just like a chariot or car in which one may go anywhere. One may drive well, or else one may drive whimsically, in which case it is quite possible that he may have an accident and fall into a ditch. In other words, if one takes directions from the experienced spiritual master one can go back home, back to Godhead; otherwise, one may return to the cycle of birth and death. Therefore Kṛṣṇa personally advises:

aśraddadhānāḥ puruṣā
dharmasyāsya parantapa
aprāpya māṁ nivartante
mṛtyu-saṁsāra-vartmani

"Those who are not faithful on the path of devotional service cannot attain Me, O conqueror of foes, but return to birth and death in this material world." (Bg. 9.3) The Supreme Personality of Godhead, Kṛṣṇa, personally gives instructions on how one can return home, back to Godhead, but if one does not care to listen to His instructions, the result will be that one will never go back to Godhead, but will continue life in this miserable condition of repeated birth and death in material existence (*mṛtyu-saṁsāra-vartmani*).

The advice of experienced transcendentalists, therefore, is that the body be fully engaged for achieving the ultimate goal of life (*svārtha-gatim*). The real interest or goal of life is to return home, back to Godhead. To enable one to fulfill this purpose, there are so many Vedic literatures, including *Vedānta-sūtra*, the *Upaniṣads*, *Bhagavad-gītā*, *Mahābhārata* and the *Rāmāyaṇa*. One should take lessons from these Vedic literatures and learn how to practice *nivṛtti-mārga*. Then one's life will be perfect. The body is important as long as it has consciousness. Without consciousness, the body is merely a lump of matter. Therefore, to return home, back to Godhead, one must change his consciousness from material consciousness to Kṛṣṇa consciousness. One's consciousness is the cause of material bondage, but if this consciousness is purified by *bhakti-yoga*, one can then understand the falsity of his *upādhi*, his designations as Indian, American, Hindu, Muslim, Christian and so on. *Sarvopādhi-vinirmuktaṁ tat-paratvena nirmalam.* One must forget these designations and use this consciousness only for the service of Kṛṣṇa. Therefore if one takes advantage of the Kṛṣṇa consciousness movement, his life is certainly successful.

TEXT 42

अक्षं दशप्राणमधर्मधर्मौ
चक्रेऽभिमानं रथिनं च जीवम् ।
धनुर्हि तस्य प्रणवं पठन्ति
शरं तु जीवं परमेव लक्ष्यम् ॥४२॥

akṣaṁ daśa-prāṇam adharma-dharmau
cakre 'bhimānaṁ rathinaṁ ca jīvam

dhanur hi tasya praṇavaṁ paṭhanti
śaraṁ tu jīvaṁ param eva lakṣyam

akṣam—the spokes (on the chariot wheel); *daśa*—ten; *prāṇam*—the ten kinds of air flowing within the body; *adharma*—irreligion; *dharmau*—religion (two sides of the wheel, up and down); *cakre*—in the wheel; *abhimānam*—false identification; *rathinam*—the charioteer or master of the body; *ca*—also; *jīvam*—the living entity; *dhanuḥ*—the bow; *hi*—indeed; *tasya*—his; *praṇavam*—the Vedic *mantra oṁkāra; paṭhanti*—it is said; *śaram*—an arrow; *tu*—but; *jīvam*—the living entity; *param*—the Supreme Lord; *eva*—indeed; *lakṣyam*—the target.

TRANSLATION

The ten kinds of air acting within the body are compared to the spokes of the chariot's wheels, and the top and bottom of the wheel itself are called religion and irreligion. The living entity in the bodily concept of life is the owner of the chariot. The Vedic mantra praṇava is the bow, the pure living entity himself is the arrow, and the target is the Supreme Being.

PURPORT

Ten kinds of life air always flow within the material body. They are called *prāṇa, apāna, samāna, vyāna, udāna, nāga, kūrma, kṛkala, devadatta* and *dhanañjaya.* They are compared here to the spokes of the chariot's wheels. The life air is the energy for all of a living being's activities, which are sometimes religious and sometimes irreligious. Thus religion and irreligion are said to be the upper and lower portions of the chariot's wheels. When the living entity decides to go back home, back to Godhead, his target is Lord Viṣṇu, the Supreme Personality of Godhead. In the conditioned state of life, one does not understand that the goal of life is the Supreme Lord. *Na te viduḥ svārtha-gatiṁ hi viṣṇuṁ durāśayā ye bahir-artha-māninaḥ.* The living entity tries to be happy within this material world, not understanding the target of his life. When he is purified, however, he gives up his bodily conception of life and his false identity as belonging to a certain community, a certain nation, a certain society, a certain family and so on (*sarvopādhi-vinirmuktaṁ tat-*

paratvena nirmalam). Then he takes the arrow of his purified life, and with the help of the bow—the transcendental chanting of *praṇava*, or the Hare Kṛṣṇa *mantra*—he throws himself toward the Supreme Personality of Godhead.

Śrīla Viśvanātha Cakravartī Ṭhākura has commented that because the words "bow" and "arrow" are used in this verse, one might argue that the Supreme Personality of Godhead and the living entity have become enemies. However, although the Supreme Personality of Godhead may become the so-called enemy of the living being, this is His chivalrous pleasure. For example, the Lord fought with Bhīṣma, and when Bhīṣma pierced the Lord's body on the Battlefield of Kurukṣetra, this was a kind of humor or relationship, of which there are twelve. When the conditioned soul tries to reach the Lord by hurling an arrow at Him, the Lord takes pleasure, and the living entity gains the profit of going back home, back to Godhead. Another example given in this regard is that Arjuna, as a result of piercing the *ādhāra-mīna*, or the fish within the *cakra*, achieved the valuable gain of Draupadī. Similarly, if with the arrow of chanting the holy name of the Lord one pierces Lord Viṣṇu's lotus feet, by dint of performing this heroic activity of devotional service one receives the benefit of returning home, back to Godhead.

TEXTS 43–44

रागो द्वेषश्च लोभश्च शोकमोहौ भयं मदः ।
मानोऽवमानोऽसूया च माया हिंसा च मत्सरः ॥४३॥
रजः प्रमादः क्षुन्निद्रा शत्रवस्त्वेवमादयः ।
रजस्तमःप्रकृतयः सत्त्वप्रकृतयः क्वचित् ॥४४॥

rāgo dveṣaś ca lobhaś ca
śoka-mohau bhayaṁ madaḥ
māno 'vamāno 'sūyā ca
māyā hiṁsā ca matsaraḥ

rajaḥ pramādaḥ kṣun-nidrā
śatravas tv evam ādayaḥ
rajas-tamaḥ-prakṛtayaḥ
sattva-prakṛtayaḥ kvacit

rāgaḥ—attachment; *dveṣaḥ*—hostility; *ca*—also; *lobhaḥ*—greed; *ca*—also; *śoka*—lamentation; *mohau*—illusion; *bhayam*—fear; *madaḥ*—madness; *mānaḥ*—false prestige; *avamānaḥ*—insult; *asūyā*—finding fault with others; *ca*—also; *māyā*—deception; *hiṁsā*—envy; *ca*—also; *matsaraḥ*—intolerance; *rajaḥ*—passion; *pramādaḥ*—bewilderment; *kṣut*—hunger; *nidrā*—sleep; *śatravaḥ*—enemies; *tu*—indeed; *evam ādayaḥ*—even other such conceptions of life; *rajaḥ-tamaḥ*—because of the conception of passion and ignorance; *prakṛtayaḥ*—causes; *sattva*—because of the conception of goodness; *prakṛtayaḥ*—causes; *kvacit*—sometimes.

TRANSLATION

In the conditioned stage, one's conceptions of life are sometimes polluted by passion and ignorance, which are exhibited by attachment, hostility, greed, lamentation, illusion, fear, madness, false prestige, insults, fault-finding, deception, envy, intolerance, passion, bewilderment, hunger and sleep. All of these are enemies. Sometimes one's conceptions are also polluted by goodness.

PURPORT

The actual aim of life is to go back home, back to Godhead, but there are many hindrances created by the three modes of material nature—sometimes by a combination of *rajo-guṇa* and *tamo-guṇa*, the modes of passion and ignorance, and sometimes by the mode of goodness. In the material world, even if one is a philanthropist, a nationalist and a good man according to materialistic estimations, these conceptions of life form a hindrance to spiritual advancement. How much more of a hindrance, then, are hostility, greed, illusion, lamentation and too much attachment to material enjoyment? To progress toward the target of Viṣṇu, which is our real self-interest, one must become very powerful in conquering these various hindrances or enemies. In other words, one should not be attached to being a good man or a bad man in this material world.

In this material world, so-called goodness and badness are the same because they consist of the three modes of material nature. One must transcend this material nature. Even the Vedic ritualistic ceremonies consist of the three modes of material nature. Therefore Kṛṣṇa advised Arjuna:

traiguṇya-viṣayā vedā
nistraiguṇyo bhavārjuna
nirdvandvo nitya-sattva-stho
niryoga-kṣema ātmavān

"The *Vedas* mainly deal with the subject of the three modes of material nature. Rise above these modes, O Arjuna. Be transcendental to all of them. Be free from all dualities and from all anxieties for gain and safety, and be established in the self." (Bg. 2.45) Elsewhere in *Bhagavad-gītā* the Lord says, *ūrdhvaṁ gacchanti sattva-sthāḥ:* if one becomes a very good person—in other words, if one is in the mode of goodness—he may be elevated to the higher planetary systems. Similarly, if one is infected by *rajo-guṇa* and *tamo-guṇa*, he may remain in this world or go down to the animal kingdom. But all of these situations are hindrances on the path of spiritual salvation. Śrī Caitanya Mahāprabhu therefore says:

brahmāṇḍa bhramite kona bhāgyavān jīva
guru-kṛṣṇa-prasāde pāya bhakti-latā-bīja

If one is fortunate enough to transcend all this so-called goodness and badness and come to the platform of devotional service by the mercy of Kṛṣṇa and the *guru*, his life becomes successful. In this regard, one must be very bold so that he can conquer these enemies of Kṛṣṇa consciousness. Not caring for the good and bad of this material world, one must boldly propagate Kṛṣṇa consciousness.

TEXT 45

यावन्नृकायरथमात्मवशोपकल्पं
धत्ते गरिष्ठचरणार्चनया निशातम् ।
ज्ञानासिमच्युतबलो दधदस्तशत्रुः
स्वानन्दतुष्ट उपशान्त इदं विजह्यात् ॥४५॥

yāvan nṛ-kāya-ratham ātma-vaśopakalpaṁ
dhatte gariṣṭha-caraṇārcanayā niśātam

jñānāsim acyuta-balo dadhad asta-śatruḥ
svānanda-tuṣṭa upaśānta idaṁ vijahyāt

yāvat—as long as; *nṛ-kāya*—this human form of body; *ratham*—considered to be a chariot; *ātma-vaśa*—dependent upon one's own control; *upakalpam*—in which there are many other subordinate parts; *dhatte*—one possesses; *gariṣṭha-caraṇa*—the lotus feet of the superiors (namely the spiritual master and his predecessors); *arcanayā*—by serving; *niśātam*—sharpened; *jñāna-asim*—the sword or weapon of knowledge; *acyuta-balaḥ*—by the transcendental strength of Kṛṣṇa; *dadhat*—holding; *asta-śatruḥ*—until the enemy is defeated; *sva-ānanda-tuṣṭaḥ*—being fully self-satisfied by transcendental bliss; *upaśāntaḥ*—the consciousness being cleansed of all material contamination; *idam*—this body; *vijahyāt*—one should give up.

TRANSLATION

As long as one has to accept a material body, with its different parts and paraphernalia, which are not fully under one's control, one must have the lotus feet of his superiors, namely his spiritual master and the spiritual master's predecessors. By their mercy, one can sharpen the sword of knowledge, and with the power of the Supreme Personality of Godhead's mercy one must then conquer the enemies mentioned above. In this way, the devotee should be able to merge into his own transcendental bliss, and then he may give up his body and resume his spiritual identity.

PURPORT

In *Bhagavad-gītā* (4.9) the Lord says:

janma karma ca me divyam
evaṁ yo vetti tattvataḥ
tyaktvā dehaṁ punar janma
naiti mām eti so 'rjuna

"One who knows the transcendental nature of My appearance and activities does not, upon leaving the body, take his birth again in this material world, but attains My eternal abode, O Arjuna." This is the highest perfection of life, and the human body is meant for this purpose. It is said in *Śrīmad-Bhāgavatam* (11.20.17):

nṛ-deham ādyaṁ sulabhaṁ sudurlabhaṁ
plavaṁ sukalpaṁ guru-karṇadhāram
mayānukūlena nabhasvateritaṁ
pumān bhavābdhiṁ na taret sa ātma-hā

This human form of body is a most valuable boat, and the spiritual master is the captain, *guru-karṇadhāram,* to guide the boat in plying across the ocean of nescience. The instruction of Kṛṣṇa is a favorable breeze. One must use all these facilities to cross over the ocean of nescience. Since the spiritual master is the captain, one must serve the spiritual master very sincerely so that by his mercy one will be able to get the mercy of the Supreme Lord.

A significant word here is *acyuta-balaḥ.* The spiritual master is certainly very merciful to his disciples, and consequently by satisfying him a devotee gets strength from the Supreme Personality of Godhead. Śrī Caitanya Mahāprabhu therefore says, *guru-kṛṣṇa-prasāde pāya bhakti-latā-bīja:* one must first please the spiritual master, and then one automatically pleases Kṛṣṇa and gets the strength with which to cross the ocean of nescience. If one seriously desires to return home, back to Godhead, one must therefore become strong enough by pleasing the spiritual master, for thus one gets the weapon with which to conquer the enemy, and one also gets the grace of Kṛṣṇa. Simply getting the weapon of *jñāna* is insufficient. One must sharpen the weapon by serving the spiritual master and adhering to his instructions. Then the candidate will get the mercy of the Supreme Personality of Godhead. In general warfare one must take help from his chariot and horses in order to conquer his enemy, and after conquering his enemies he may give up the chariot and its paraphernalia. Similarly, as long as one has a human body, one should fully use it to obtain the highest perfection of life, namely going back home, back to Godhead.

The perfection of knowledge is certainly to become transcendentally situated (*brahma-bhūta*). As the Lord says in *Bhagavad-gītā* (18.54):

brahma-bhūtaḥ prasannātmā
na śocati na kāṅkṣati
samaḥ sarveṣu bhūteṣu
mad-bhaktiṁ labhate parām

"One who is transcendentally situated at once realizes the Supreme Brahman and becomes fully joyful. He never laments nor desires to have anything; he is equally disposed toward all living entities. In that state he attains pure devotional service." Simply by cultivating knowledge as the impersonalists do, one cannot get out of the clutches of *māyā*. One must attain the platform of *bhakti.*

bhaktyā mām abhijānāti
yāvān yaś cāsmi tattvataḥ
tato māṁ tattvato jñātvā
viśate tad-anantaram

"One can understand the Supreme Personality as He is only by devotional service. And when one is in full consciousness of the Supreme Lord by such devotion, he can enter into the kingdom of God." (Bg. 18.55) Unless one has attained the stage of devotional service and the mercy of the spiritual master and Kṛṣṇa, there is a possibility that one may fall down and again accept a material body. Therefore Kṛṣṇa stresses in *Bhagavad-gītā* (4.9):

janma karma ca me divyam
evaṁ yo vetti tattvataḥ
tyaktvā dehaṁ punar janma
naiti mām eti so 'rjuna

"One who knows the transcendental nature of My appearance and activities does not, upon leaving the body, take his birth again in this material world, but attains My eternal abode, O Arjuna."

The word *tattvataḥ,* meaning "in reality," is very important. *Tato māṁ tattvato jñātvā.* Unless one understands Kṛṣṇa in truth by the mercy of the spiritual master, one is not free to give up his material body. As it is said, *āruhya kṛcchreṇa paraṁ padaṁ tataḥ patanty adho 'nādṛta-yuṣmad-aṅghrayaḥ:* if one neglects to serve the lotus feet of Kṛṣṇa, one cannot become free from the material clutches simply by knowledge. Even if one attains the stage of *brahma-padam,* merging in Brahman, without *bhakti* he is prone to fall down. One must be very careful in regard to the danger of falling down again into material bondage. The only insurance is to come to the stage of *bhakti,* from which one is sure not to fall. Then one is free from the activities of the material world. In summary, as stated by Śrī Caitanya Mahāprabhu, one must get in touch with a bona fide spiritual master coming in the *paramparā* of Kṛṣṇa consciousness, for by his mercy and instructions one is able to get strength from Kṛṣṇa. Thus one engages in devotional service and attains the ultimate goal of life, the lotus feet of Viṣṇu.

Significant in this verse are the words *jñānāsim acyuta-balaḥ. Jñānāsim,* the sword of knowledge, is given by Kṛṣṇa, and when one serves the *guru* and Kṛṣṇa in order to hold the sword of Kṛṣṇa's instructions, Balarāma gives one strength. Balarāma is Nityānanda. *Vrajendra-nandana yei, śacī-suta haila sei, balarāma ha-ila nitāi.* This *bala*—Balarāma—comes with Śrī Caitanya Mahāprabhu, and both of Them are so merciful that in this age of Kali one may very easily take shelter of Their lotus feet. They come especially to deliver the fallen souls of this age. *Pāpī tāpī yata chila, hari-nāme uddhārila.* Their weapon is *saṅkīrtana, hari-nāma.* Thus one should accept the sword of knowledge from Kṛṣṇa and be strong with the mercy of Balarāma. We are therefore worshiping Kṛṣṇa-Balarāma in Vṛndāvana. In the *Muṇḍaka Upaniṣad* (3.2.4) it is said:

nāyam ātmā bala-hīnena labhyo
na ca pramādāt tapaso vāpy aliṅgāt
etair upāyair yatate yas tu vidvāṁs
tasyaiṣa ātmā viśate brahma-dhāma

One cannot attain the goal of life without the mercy of Balarāma. Śrī Narottama dāsa Ṭhākura therefore says, *nitāiyera karuṇā habe, vraje rādhā-kṛṣṇa pābe:* when one receives the mercy of Balarāma, Nityānanda, one can attain the lotus feet of Rādhā and Kṛṣṇa very easily.

se sambandha nāhi yāra, bṛthā janma gela tāra,
vidyā-kule hi karibe tāra

If one has no connection with Nitāi, Balarāma, then even though one is a very learned scholar or *jñānī* or has taken birth in a very respectable family, these assets will not help him. We must therefore conquer the enemies of Kṛṣṇa consciousness with the strength received from Balarāma.

TEXT 46

नोचेत् प्रमत्तमसदिन्द्रियवाजिसूता
नीत्वोत्पथं विषयदस्युषु निक्षिपन्ति ।
ते दस्यवः सहयसूतममुं तमोऽन्धे
संसारकूप उरुमृत्युभये क्षिपन्ति ॥४६॥

nocet pramattam asad-indriya-vāji-sūtā
nītvotpathaṁ viṣaya-dasyuṣu nikṣipanti
te dasyavaḥ sahaya-sūtam amuṁ tamo 'ndhe
saṁsāra-kūpa uru-mṛtyu-bhaye kṣipanti

nocet—if we do not follow the instructions of Acyuta, Kṛṣṇa, and do not take shelter of Balarāma; *pramattam*—careless, inattentive; *asat*—which are always prone to material consciousness; *indriya*—the senses; *vāji*—acting as the horses; *sūtāḥ*—the chariot driver (intelligence); *nītvā*—bringing; *utpatham*—to the roadway of material desire; *viṣaya*—the sense objects; *dasyuṣu*—in the hands of the plunderers; *nikṣipanti*—throw; *te*—those; *dasyavaḥ*—plunderers; *sa*—with; *haya-sūtam*—the horses and chariot driver; *amum*—all of them; *tamaḥ*—dark; *andhe*—blind; *saṁsāra-kūpe*—into the well of material existence; *uru*—great; *mṛtyu-bhaye*—fear of death; *kṣipanti*—throw.

TRANSLATION

Otherwise, if one does not take shelter of Acyuta and Baladeva, then the senses, acting as the horses, and the intelligence, acting as the driver, both being prone to material contamination, inattentively bring the body, which acts as the chariot, to the path of sense gratification. When one is thus attracted again by the rogues of viṣaya—eating, sleeping and mating—the horses and chariot

driver are thrown into the blinding dark well of material existence, and one is again put into a dangerous and extremely fearful situation of repeated birth and death.

PURPORT

Without the protection of Gaura-Nitāi—Kṛṣṇa and Balarāma—one cannot get out of the dark well of ignorance in material existence. This is indicated here by the word *nocet*, which means that one will always remain in the dark well of material existence. The living entity must get strength from Nitāi-Gaura, or Kṛṣṇa-Balarāma. Without the mercy of Nitāi-Gaura, there is no way to come out of this dark well of ignorance. As stated in the *Caitanya-caritāmṛta* (*Ādi* 1.2):

vande śrī-kṛṣṇa-caitanya-
nityānandau sahoditau
gauḍodaye puṣpavantau
citrau śandau tamo-nudau

"I offer my respectful obeisances unto Śrī Kṛṣṇa Caitanya and Lord Nityānanda, who are like the sun and moon. They have arisen simultaneously on the horizon of Gauḍa to dissipate the darkness of ignorance and thus wonderfully bestow benediction upon all." This material world is a dark well of ignorance. The fallen soul in this dark well must take shelter of the lotus feet of Gaura-Nitāi, for thus he can easily emerge from material existence. Without Their strength, simply attempting to get out of the clutches of matter by speculative knowledge will be insufficient.

TEXT 47

प्रवृत्तं च निवृत्तं च द्विविधं कर्म वैदिकम् ।
आवर्तते प्रवृत्तेन निवृत्तेनाश्नुतेऽमृतम् ॥४७॥

pravṛttaṁ ca nivṛttaṁ ca
dvi-vidhaṁ karma vaidikam
āvartate pravṛttena
nivṛttenāśnute 'mṛtam

pravṛttam—inclination for material enjoyment; *ca*—and; *nivṛttam*—cessation of material enjoyment; *ca*—and; *dvi-vidham*—these two varieties; *karma*—of activities; *vaidikam*—recommended in the *Vedas;* *āvartate*—one travels up and down through the cycle of *saṁsāra;* *pravṛttena*—by an inclination for enjoying material activities; *nivṛttena*—but by ceasing such activities; *aśnute*—one enjoys; *amṛtam*—eternal life.

TRANSLATION

According to the Vedas, there are two kinds of activities—pravṛtti and nivṛtti. Pravṛtti activities involve raising oneself from a lower to a higher condition of materialistic life, whereas nivṛtti means the cessation of material desire. Through pravṛtti activities one suffers from material entanglement, but by nivṛtti activities one is purified and becomes fit to enjoy eternal, blissful life.

PURPORT

As confirmed in *Bhagavad-gītā* (16.7), *pravṛttiṁ ca nivṛttiṁ ca janā na vidur āsurāḥ:* the *asuras,* nondevotees, cannot distinguish between *pravṛtti* and *nivṛtti.* Whatever they like they do. Such persons think themselves independent of the strong material nature, and therefore they are irresponsible and do not care to act piously. Indeed, they do not distinguish between pious and impious activity. *Bhakti,* of course, does not depend on pious or impious activity. As stated in *Śrīmad-Bhāgavatam* (1.2.6):

sa vai puṁsāṁ paro dharmo
yato bhaktir adhokṣaje
ahaituky apratihatā
yayātmā suprasīdati

"The supreme occupation [*dharma*] for all humanity is that by which men can attain to loving devotional service unto the transcendent Lord. Such devotional service must be unmotivated and uninterrupted in order to completely satisfy the self." Nonetheless, those who act piously have a better chance to become devotees. As Kṛṣṇa says in *Bhagavad-gītā* (7.16), *catur-vidhā bhajante māṁ janāḥ sukṛtino 'rjuna:* "O Arjuna, four kinds of pious men render devotional service unto Me." One who takes to devotional service, even with some material motive, is considered pious, and because he has come to Kṛṣṇa, he will gradually come to the stage of *bhakti.* Then, like Dhruva Mahārāja, he will refuse to accept any material benediction from the Lord (*svāmin kṛtārtho 'smi varaṁ na yāce*). Therefore, even if one is materially inclined, one may take to the shelter of the lotus feet of Kṛṣṇa and Balarāma, or Gaura and Nitāi, so that he will very soon be purified of all material desires (*kṣipraṁ bhavati dharmātmā śaśvac chāntiṁ nigacchati*). As soon as one is freed from inclinations toward pious and impious activities, he becomes a perfect candidate for returning home, back to Godhead.

TEXTS 48–49

हिंस्रं द्रव्यमयं काम्यमग्निहोत्राद्यशान्तिदम् ।
दर्शश्च पूर्णमासश्च चातुर्मास्यं पशुः सुतः ॥४८॥
एतदिष्टं प्रवृत्ताख्यं हुतं प्रहुतमेव च ।
पूर्तं सुरालयारामकूपाजीव्यादिलक्षणम् ॥४९॥

hiṁsraṁ dravyamayaṁ kāmyam
agni-hotrādy-aśāntidam
darśaś ca pūrṇamāsaś ca
cāturmāsyaṁ paśuḥ sutaḥ

etad iṣṭaṁ pravṛttākhyaṁ
hutaṁ prahutam eva ca
pūrtaṁ surālayārāma-
kūpājīvyādi-lakṣaṇam

hiṁsram—a system of killing and sacrificing animals; *dravya-mayam*—requiring much paraphernalia; *kāmyam*—full of unlimited material desires; *agni-hotra-ādi*—ritualistic ceremonies such as the *agni-hotra-yajña; aśānti-dam*—causing anxieties; *darśaḥ*—the *darśa* ritualistic ceremony; *ca*—and; *pūrṇamāsaḥ*—the *pūrṇamāsa* ritualistic ceremony; *ca*—also; *cāturmāsyam*—observing four months of regulative principles; *paśuḥ*—the ceremony of sacrificing animals or *paśu-yajña; sutaḥ*—the *soma-yajña; etat*—of all this; *iṣṭam*—the goal;

pravṛtta-ākhyam—known as material attachment; *hutam*—Vaiśvadeva, an incarnation of the Supreme Personality of Godhead; *prahutam*—a ceremony called Baliharaṇa; *eva*—indeed; *ca*—also; *pūrtam*—for the benefit of the public; *sura-ālaya*—constructing temples for demigods; *ārāma*—resting houses and gardens; *kūpa*—digging wells; *ājīvya-ādi*—activities like distributing food and water; *lakṣaṇam*—symptoms.

TRANSLATION

The ritualistic ceremonies and sacrifices known as agni-hotra-yajña, darśa-yajña, pūrṇamāsa-yajña, cāturmāsya-yajña, paśu-yajña and soma-yajña are all symptomized by the killing of animals and the burning of many valuables, especially food grains, all for the fulfillment of material desires and the creation of anxiety. Performing such sacrifices, worshiping Vaiśvadeva, and performing the ceremony of Baliharaṇa, which all supposedly constitute the goal of life, as well as constructing temples for demigods, building resting houses and gardens, digging wells for the distribution of water, establishing booths for the distribution of food, and performing activities for public welfare—these are all symptomized by attachment to material desires.

TEXTS 50–51

द्रव्यसूक्ष्मविपाकश्च धूमो रात्रिरपक्षयः ।
अयनं दक्षिणं सोमो दर्श ओषधिवीरुधः ॥५०॥
अन्नं रेत इति क्ष्मेश पितृयानं पुनर्भवः ।
एकैकश्येनानुपूर्वं भूत्वा भूत्वेह जायते ॥५१॥

dravya-sūkṣma-vipākaś ca
dhūmo rātrir apakṣayaḥ
ayanaṁ dakṣiṇaṁ somo
darśa oṣadhi-vīrudhaḥ

annaṁ reta iti kṣmeśa
pitṛ-yānaṁ punar-bhavaḥ
ekaikaśyenānupūrvaṁ
bhūtvā bhūtveha jāyate

dravya-sūkṣma-vipākaḥ—the paraphernalia offered as oblations in the fire, such as food grains mixed with ghee; *ca*—and; *dhūmaḥ*—turned to smoke, or the demigod in charge of smoke; *rātriḥ*—the demigod in charge of night; *apakṣayaḥ*—in the dark fortnight of the moon; *ayanam*—the demigod in charge of the passing of the sun; *dakṣiṇam*—in the southern zone; *somaḥ*—the moon; *darśaḥ*—returning; *oṣadhi*—plant life (on the surface of the earth); *vīrudhaḥ*—vegetation in general (the birth of lamentation); *annam*—food grains; *retaḥ*—semen; *iti*—in this way; *kṣma-īśa*—O King Yudhiṣṭhira, lord of the earth; *pitṛ-yānam*—the way of taking birth from the father's semen; *punaḥ-bhavaḥ*—again and again; *eka-ekaśyena*—one after another; *anupūrvam*—successively, according to the gradation; *bhūtvā*—taking birth; *bhūtvā*—again taking birth; *iha*—in this material world; *jāyate*—one exists in the materialistic way of life.

TRANSLATION

My dear King Yudhiṣṭhira, when oblations of ghee and food grains like barley and sesame are offered in sacrifice, they turn into celestial smoke, which carries one to successively higher planetary systems like the kingdoms of Dhumā, Rātri, Kṛṣṇapakṣa, Dakṣiṇam and ultimately the moon. Then, however, the performers of sacrifice descend again to earth to become herbs, creepers, vegetables and food grains. These are eaten by different living entities and turned to semen, which is injected into female bodies. Thus one takes birth again and again.

PURPORT

This is explained in *Bhagavad-gītā* (9.21):

te taṁ bhuktvā svarga-lokaṁ viśālaṁ
kṣīṇe puṇye martya-lokaṁ viśanti
evaṁ trayī-dharmam anuprapannā
gatāgataṁ kāma-kāmā labhante

"When those who follow the *pravṛtti-mārga* have enjoyed heavenly sense pleasure, they return to this mortal planet again. Thus, through the Vedic principles, they achieve only flickering happiness." Following the *pravṛtti-mārga*, the living entity who desires to be promoted to the higher planetary systems performs sacrifices regularly, and how he goes up and comes down again is described here in *Śrīmad-Bhāgavatam*, as well as in *Bhagavad-gītā*. It is also said, *traiguṇya-viṣayā vedāḥ:* "The *Vedas* deal mainly with the three modes of material nature." The *Vedas*, especially three *Vedas*, namely *Sāma*, *Yajur* and *Ṛk*, vividly describe this process of ascending to the higher planets and returning. But Kṛṣṇa advises Arjuna, *traiguṇya-viṣayā vedā nistraiguṇyo bhavārjuna:* one has to transcend these three modes of material nature, and then one will be released from the cycle of birth and death. Otherwise, although one may be promoted to a higher planetary system such as Candraloka, one must again come down (*kṣīṇe puṇye martya-lokaṁ viśanti*). After one's enjoyment due to pious activities is finished, one must return to this planet in rainfall and first take birth as a plant or creeper, which is eaten by various animals, including human beings, and turned to semen. This semen is injected into the female body, and thus the living entity takes birth. Those who return to earth in this way take birth especially in higher families like those of *brāhmaṇas*.

It may be remarked in this connection that even the modern so-called scientists who are going to the moon are not able to stay there, but are returning to their laboratories. Therefore, whether one goes to the moon by modern mechanical arrangements or by performing pious activities, one must return to earth. That is clearly stated in this verse and explained in *Bhagavad-gītā*. Even if one goes to the higher planetary systems (*yānti deva-vratā devān*), one's place there is not secure; one must return to *martya-loka*. *Ābrahma-bhuvanāl lokāḥ punar āvartino 'rjuna:* aside from the moon, even if one goes to Brahmaloka, one must return. *Yaṁ prāpya na nivartante tad dhāma paramaṁ mama:* but if one goes back home, back to Godhead, he need not return to this material world.

TEXT 52

निषेकादिश्मशानान्तैः संस्कारैः संस्कृतो द्विजः ।
इन्द्रियेषु क्रियायज्ञान् ज्ञानदीपेषु जुह्वति ॥५२॥

niṣekādi-śmaśānāntaiḥ
saṁskāraiḥ saṁskṛto dvijaḥ

indriyeṣu kriyā-yajñān
jñāna-dīpeṣu juhvati

niṣeka-ādi—the beginning of life (the purificatory process of *garbhādhāna*, performed when the father begets a child by discharging semen into the womb of the mother); *śmaśāna-antaiḥ*—and at death, when the body is put into a crematorium and burnt to ashes; *saṁskāraiḥ*—by such purificatory processes; *saṁskṛtaḥ*—purified; *dvi-jaḥ*—a twiceborn *brāhmaṇa; indriyeṣu*—into the senses; *kriyā-yajñān*—activities and sacrifices (which elevate one to a higher planetary system); *jñāna-dīpeṣu*—by enlightenment in real knowledge; *juhvati*—offers.

TRANSLATION

A twiceborn brāhmaṇa [dvija] gains his life by the grace of his parents through the process of purification known as garbhādhāna. There are also other processes of purification, until the end of life, when the funeral ceremony [antyeṣṭi-kriyā] is performed. Thus in due course a qualified brāhmaṇa becomes uninterested in materialistic activities and sacrifices, but he offers the sensual sacrifices, in full knowledge, into the working senses, which are illuminated by the fire of knowledge.

PURPORT

Those interested in materialistic activities remain in the cycle of birth and death. *Pravṛtti-mārga*, or the inclination to stay in the material world to enjoy varieties of sense gratification, has been explained in the previous verse. Now, in this verse, it is explained that one who has perfect brahminical knowledge rejects the process of elevation to higher planets and accepts *nivṛtti-mārga;* in other words, he prepares himself to go back home, back to Godhead. Those who are not *brāhmaṇas* but atheists do not know what is *pravṛtti-mārga* or *nivṛtti-mārga;* they simply want to obtain pleasure at any cost. Our Kṛṣṇa consciousness movement is therefore training devotees to give up the *pravṛtti-mārga* and accept the *nivṛtti-mārga* in order to return home, back to Godhead. This is a little difficult to understand, but it is very easy if one takes to Kṛṣṇa consciousness seriously and tries to understand Kṛṣṇa. A Kṛṣṇa conscious person can understand that performing *yajña* according to the *karma-kāṇḍa* system is a useless waste of time and that merely giving up the *karma-kāṇḍa* and accepting the process of speculation is also unfruitful. Therefore Narottama dāsa Ṭhākura has sung in his *Prema-bhakti-candrikā:*

karma-kāṇḍa, jñāna-kāṇḍa, kevala viṣera bhāṇḍa
'amṛta' baliyā yebā khāya
nānā yoni sadā phire, kadarya bhakṣaṇa kare,
tāra janma adhaḥ-pāte yāya

A life of *karma-kāṇḍa* or *jñāna-kāṇḍa* is like a poison pot, and one who takes to such a life is doomed. In the *karma-kāṇḍa* system, one is destined to accept birth and death again and again. Similarly, with *jñāna-kāṇḍa* one falls down again to this material world. Only worship of the Supreme Person offers one the safety of going back home, back to Godhead.

TEXT 53

इन्द्रियाणि मनस्यूर्मौ वाचि वैकारिकं मनः ।
वाचं वर्णसमाम्नाये तमोङ्कारे स्वरे न्यसेत् ।
ओङ्कारं बिन्दौ नादे तं तं तु प्राणे महत्यमुम् ॥५३॥

indriyāṇi manasy ūrmau
vāci vaikārikaṁ manaḥ
vācaṁ varṇa-samāmnāye
tam oṁkāre svare nyaset
oṁkāraṁ bindau nāde taṁ
taṁ tu prāṇe mahaty amum

indriyāṇi—the senses (acting and knowledge-gathering); *manasi*—in the mind; *ūrmau*—in the waves of acceptance and rejection; *vāci*—in the words; *vaikārikam*—infected by changes; *manaḥ*—the mind; *vācam*—the words; *varṇa-samāmnāye*—in the aggregate of all alphabets; *tam*—that (aggregate of all alphabets); *oṁkāre*—in the concise form of *oṁkāra; svare*—in the vibration; *nyaset*—one should give up; *oṁkāram*—the concise sound vibration; *bindau*—in the point of *oṁkāra; nāde*—in the sound vibration; *tam*—that; *tam*—that (sound vibration); *tu*—indeed; *prāṇe*—in the life air; *mahati*—unto the Supreme; *amum*—the living entity.

TRANSLATION

The mind is always agitated by waves of acceptance and rejection. Therefore all the activities of the senses should be offered into the mind, which should be offered into one's words. Then one's words should be offered into the aggregate of all alphabets, which should be offered into the concise form oṁkāra. Oṁkāra should be offered into the point bindu, bindu into the vibration of sound, and that vibration into the life air. Then the living entity, who is all that remains, should be placed in Brahman, the Supreme. This is the process of sacrifice.

PURPORT

The mind is always agitated by acceptance and rejection, which are compared to mental waves that are constantly tossing. The living entity is floating in the waves of material existence because of his forgetfulness. Śrīla Bhaktivinoda Ṭhākura has therefore sung in his *Gītāvalī: miche māyāra vaśe, yāccha bhese', khāccha hābuḍubu, bhāi.* "My dear mind, under the influence of *māyā* you are being carried away by the waves of rejection and acceptance. Simply take shelter of Kṛṣṇa." *Jīva kṛṣṇa-dāsa, ei viśvāsa, karle ta' āra duḥkha nāi:* if we simply regard the lotus feet of Kṛṣṇa as our ultimate shelter, we shall be saved from all these waves of *māyā*, which are variously exhibited as mental and sensual activities and the agitation of rejection and acceptance. Kṛṣṇa instructs in *Bhagavad-gītā* (18.66):

sarva-dharmān parityajya
mām ekaṁ śaraṇaṁ vraja
ahaṁ tvāṁ sarva-pāpebhyo
mokṣayiṣyāmi mā śucaḥ

"Abandon all varieties of religion and just surrender unto Me. I shall deliver you from all sinful reaction. Do not fear." Therefore if we simply place ourselves at the lotus feet of Kṛṣṇa by taking to Kṛṣṇa consciousness and keeping always in touch with Him by chanting the Hare Kṛṣṇa *mantra,* we need not take much trouble in arranging to return to the spiritual world. By the mercy of Śrī Caitanya Mahāprabhu, this is very easy.

harer nāma harer nāma
harer nāmaiva kevalam
kalau nāsty eva nāsty eva
nāsty eva gatir anyathā

TEXT 54

अग्निः सूर्यो दिवा प्राह्णः शुक्लो राकोत्तरं स्वराट् ।
विश्वोऽथ तैजसः प्राज्ञस्तुर्य आत्मा समन्वयात् ॥५४॥

agniḥ sūryo divā prāhṇaḥ
śuklo rākottaraṁ sva-rāṭ
viśvo 'tha taijasaḥ prājñas
turya ātmā samanvayāt

agniḥ—fire; *sūryaḥ*—sun; *divā*—day; *prāhṇaḥ*—the end of the day; *śuklaḥ*—the bright fortnight of the moon; *rāka*—the full moon at the end of the *śukla-pakṣa; uttaram*—the period when the sun passes to the north; *sva-rāṭ*—the Supreme Brahman or Lord Brahmā; *viśvaḥ*—gross designation; *atha*—Brahmaloka, the ultimate in material enjoyment; *taijasaḥ*—subtle designation; *prājñaḥ*—the witness in the causal designation; *turyaḥ*—transcendental; *ātmā*—the soul; *samanvayāt*—as a natural consequence.

TRANSLATION

On his path of ascent, the progressive living entity enters the different worlds of fire, the sun, the day, the end of the day, the bright fortnight, the full moon, and the passing of the sun in the north, along with their presiding demigods. When he enters Brahmaloka, he enjoys life for many millions of years, and finally

his material designation comes to an end. He then comes to a subtle designation, from which he attains the causal designation, witnessing all previous states. Upon the annihilation of this causal state, he attains his pure state, in which he identifies with the Supersoul. In this way the living entity becomes transcendental.

TEXT 55

देवयानमिदं प्राहुर्भूत्वा भूत्वानुपूर्वशः ।
आत्मयाज्युपशान्तात्मा ह्यात्मस्थो न निवर्तते ॥५५॥

deva-yānam idaṁ prāhur
bhūtvā bhūtvānupūrvaśaḥ
ātma-yājy upaśāntātmā
hy ātma-stho na nivartate

deva-yānam—the process of elevation known as *deva-yāna; idam*—on this (path); *prāhuḥ*—it is said; *bhūtvā bhūtvā*—having repeated birth; *anupūrvaśaḥ*—consecutively; *ātma-yājī*—one who is eager for self-realization; *upaśānta-ātmā*—completely free from all material desires; *hi*—indeed; *ātma-sthaḥ*—situated in his own self; *na*—not; *nivartate*—does return.

TRANSLATION

This gradual process of elevation for self-realization is meant for those who are truly aware of the Absolute Truth. After repeated birth on this path, which is known as deva-yāna, one attains these consecutive stages. One who is completely free from all material desires, being situated in the self, need not traverse the path of repeated birth and death.

TEXT 56

य एते पितृदेवानामयने वेदनिर्मिते ।
शास्त्रेण चक्षुषा वेद जनस्थोऽपि न मुह्यति ॥५६॥

ya ete pitṛ-devānām
ayane veda-nirmite

śāstreṇa cakṣuṣā veda
jana-stho 'pi na muhyati

yaḥ—one who; *ete*—on this path (as recommended above); *pitṛ-devānām*—known as *pitṛ-yāna* and *deva-yāna; ayane*—on this path; *veda-nirmite*—recommended in the *Vedas; śāstreṇa*—by regular study of the scriptures; *cakṣuṣā*—by enlightened eyes; *veda*—is fully aware; *jana-sthaḥ*—a person situated in a material body; *api*—even though; *na*—never; *muhyati*—is bewildered.

TRANSLATION

Even though situated in a material body, one who is fully aware of the paths known as pitṛ-yāna and deva-yāna, and who thus opens his eyes in terms of Vedic knowledge, is never bewildered in this material world.

PURPORT

Ācāryavān puruṣo veda: one who is guided by the bona fide spiritual master knows everything as stated in the *Vedas*, which set forth the standard of infallible knowledge. As recommended in *Bhagavad-gītā, ācāryopāsanam:* one must approach the *ācārya* for real knowledge. *Tad-vijñānārthaṁ sa gurum evābhigacchet:* one must approach the *ācārya*, for then one will receive perfect knowledge. When guided by the spiritual master, one attains the ultimate goal of life.

TEXT 57

आदावन्ते जनानां सद् बहिरन्तः परावरम् ।
ज्ञानं ज्ञेयं वचो वाच्यं तमो ज्योतिस्त्वयं स्वयम् ॥५७॥

ādāv ante janānāṁ sad
bahir antaḥ parāvaram
jñānaṁ jñeyaṁ vaco vācyaṁ
tamo jyotis tv ayaṁ svayam

ādau—in the beginning; *ante*—at the end; *janānām*—of all living entities; *sat*—always existing; *bahiḥ*—externally; *antaḥ*—internally; *para*—transcendental; *avaram*—material; *jñānam*—knowledge;

jñeyam—the objective; *vacaḥ*—expression; *vācyam*—the ultimate object; *tamaḥ*—darkness; *jyotiḥ*—light; *tu*—indeed; *ayam*—this one (the Supreme Lord); *svayam*—Himself.

TRANSLATION

He who exists internally and externally, at the beginning and end of everything and of all living beings, as that which is enjoyable and as the enjoyer of everything, superior and inferior, is the Supreme Truth. He always exists as knowledge and the object of knowledge, as expression and the object of understanding, as darkness and as light. Thus He, the Supreme Lord, is everything.

PURPORT

Here the Vedic aphorism *sarvaṁ khalv idaṁ brahma* is explained. It is also explained in the *catuḥ-ślokī Bhāgavatam. Aham evāsam evāgre.* The Supreme Lord existed in the beginning, He exists after the creation and maintains everything, and after destruction everything merges in Him, as stated in *Bhagavad-gītā* (*prakṛtiṁ yānti māmikām*). Thus the Supreme Lord is actually everything. In the conditioned state, we are bewildered in our understanding, but in the perfect stage of liberation we can understand that Kṛṣṇa is the cause of everything.

īśvaraḥ paramaḥ kṛṣṇaḥ
sac-cid-ānanda-vigrahaḥ
anādir ādir govindaḥ
sarva-kāraṇa-kāraṇam

"Kṛṣṇa, who is known as Govinda, is the supreme controller. He has an eternal, blissful, spiritual body. He is the origin of all. He has no other origin, for He is the prime cause of all causes." (Bs. 5.1) This is the perfection of knowledge.

TEXT 58

आबाधितोऽपि ह्याभासो यथा वस्तुतया स्मृतः ।
दुर्घटत्वादैन्द्रियकं तद्वदर्थविकल्पितम् ॥५८॥

ābādhito 'pi hy ābhāso
yathā vastutayā smṛtaḥ
durghaṭatvād aindriyakaṁ
tadvad artha-vikalpitam

ābādhitaḥ—rejected; *api*—although; *hi*—certainly; *ābhāsaḥ*—a reflection; *yathā*—as; *vastutayā*—a form of reality; *smṛtaḥ*—accepted; *durghaṭatvāt*—because of being very difficult to prove the reality; *aindriyakam*—knowledge derived from the senses; *tadvat*—similarly; *artha*—reality; *vikalpitam*—speculated or doubtful.

TRANSLATION

Although one may consider the reflection of the sun from a mirror to be false, it has its factual existence. Accordingly, to prove by speculative knowledge that there is no reality would be extremely difficult.

PURPORT

The impersonalists try to prove that the varieties in the vision of the empiric philosopher are false. The impersonalist philosophy, *vivarta-vāda,* generally cites the acceptance of a rope to be a snake as an example of this fact. According to this example, the varieties within our vision are false, just as a rope seen to be a snake is false. The Vaiṣṇavas say, however, that although the idea that the rope is a snake is false, the snake is not false; one has experience of a snake in reality, and therefore he knows that although the representation of the rope as a snake is false or illusory, there is a snake in reality. Similarly, this world, which is full of varieties, is not false; it is a reflection of the reality in the Vaikuṇṭha world, the spiritual world.

The reflection of the sun from a mirror is nothing but light within darkness. Thus although it is not exactly sunlight, without the sunlight the reflection would be impossible. Similarly, the varieties of this world would be impossible unless there were a real prototype in the spiritual world. The Māyāvādī philosopher cannot understand this, but a real philosopher must be convinced that light is not possible at all without a background of sunlight. Thus the jugglery of words used by the

Māyāvādī philosopher to prove that this material world is false may amaze inexperienced children, but a man with full knowledge knows perfectly well that there cannot be any existence without Kṛṣṇa. Therefore a Vaiṣṇava insists on the platform of somehow or other accepting Kṛṣṇa (*tasmāt kenāpy upāyena manaḥ kṛṣṇe niveśayet*).

When we raise our unmixed faith to the lotus feet of Kṛṣṇa, everything is revealed. Kṛṣṇa also says in *Bhagavad-gītā* (7.1):

mayy āsakta-manāḥ pārtha
yogaṁ yuñjan mad-āśrayaḥ
asaṁśayaṁ samagraṁ māṁ
yathā jñāsyasi tac chṛṇu

"Now hear, O son of Pṛthā [Arjuna], how by practicing *yoga* in full consciousness of Me, with mind attached to Me, you can know Me in full, free from doubt." Simply by raising one's staunch faith in Kṛṣṇa and His instructions, one can understand reality without a doubt (*asaṁśayaṁ samagraṁ mām*). One can understand how Kṛṣṇa's material and spiritual energies are working and how He is present everywhere although everything is not Him. This philosophy of *acintya-bhedābheda*, inconceivable oneness and difference, is the perfect philosophy enunciated by the Vaiṣṇavas. Everything is an emanation from Kṛṣṇa, but it is not that everything must therefore be worshiped. Speculative knowledge cannot give us reality as it is, but will continue to be nefariously imperfect. So-called scientists try to prove that there is no God and that everything is happening because of the laws of nature, but this is imperfect knowledge because nothing can work unless directed by the Supreme Personality of Godhead. This is explained in *Bhagavad-gītā* (9.10) by the Lord Himself:

mayādhyakṣeṇa prakṛtiḥ
sūyate sacarācaram
hetunānena kaunteya
jagad viparivartate

"This material nature is working under My direction, O son of Kuntī, and it is producing all moving and unmoving beings. By its rule this manifestation is created and annihilated again and again." In this regard, Śrīla Madhvācārya gives this note: *durghaṭatvād arthatvena parameśvareṇaiva kalpitam.* The background of everything is the Supreme Personality of Godhead, Vāsudeva. *Vāsudevaḥ sarvam iti sa mahātmā sudurlabhaḥ.* This can be understood by a *mahātmā* who is perfect in knowledge. Such a *mahātmā* is rarely seen.

TEXT 59

क्षित्यादीनामिहार्थानां छाया न कतमापि हि ।
न संघातो विकारोऽपि न पृथङ् नान्वितो मृषा ॥५९॥

kṣity-ādīnām ihārthānāṁ
chāyā na katamāpi hi
na saṅghāto vikāro 'pi
na pṛthaṅ nānvito mṛṣā

kṣiti-ādīnām—of the five elements, beginning with the earth; *iha*—in this world; *arthānām*—of those five elements; *chāyā*—shadow; *na*—neither; *katamā*—which of them; *api*—indeed; *hi*—certainly; *na*—nor; *saṅghātaḥ*—combination; *vikāraḥ*—transformation; *api*—although; *na pṛthak*—nor separated; *na anvitaḥ*—nor inherent in; *mṛṣā*—all these theories are without substance.

TRANSLATION

In this world there are five elements—namely earth, water, fire, air and ether—but the body is not a reflection of them, nor a combination or transformation of them. Because the body and its ingredients are neither distinct nor amalgamated, all such theories are insubstantial.

PURPORT

A forest is certainly a transformation of the earth, but one tree does not depend on another tree; if one is cut down, this does not mean that the others are cut down. Therefore, the forest is neither a combination nor a transformation of the trees. The best explanation is given by Kṛṣṇa Himself:

mayā tatam idaṁ sarvaṁ
jagad avyakta-mūrtinā
mat-sthāni sarva-bhūtāni
na cāhaṁ teṣv avasthitaḥ

"By Me, in My unmanifested form, this entire universe is pervaded. All beings are in Me, but I am not in them." (Bg. 9.4) Everything is an expansion of Kṛṣṇa's energy. As it is said, *parāsya śaktir vividhaiva śrūyate:* the Lord has multi-energies, which are expressed in different ways. The energies are existing, and the Supreme Personality of Godhead also exists simultaneously; because everything is His energy, He is simultaneously one with everything and different from everything. Thus our speculative theories that *ātmā,* the living force, is a combination of matter, that matter is a transformation of the soul, or that the body is part of the soul are all insubstantial.

Since all the Lord's energies are simultaneously existing, one must understand the Supreme Personality of Godhead. But although He is everything, He is not present in everything. The Lord must be worshiped in His original form as Kṛṣṇa. He can also present Himself in any one of His various expanded energies. When we worship the Deity of the Lord in the temple, the Deity appears to be stone or wood. Now, because the Supreme Lord does not have a material body, He is not stone or wood, yet stone and wood are not different from Him. Thus by worshiping stone or wood we get no result, but when the stone and wood are represented in the Lord's original form, by worshiping the Deity we get the desired result. This is supported by Śrī Caitanya Mahāprabhu's philosophy, *acintya-bhedābheda,* which explains how the Lord can present Himself everywhere and anywhere in a form of His energy to accept service from the devotee.

TEXT 60

धातवोऽवयवित्वाच्च तन्मात्रावयवैर्विना ।
न स्युर्ह्यसत्यवयविन्यसन्नवयवोऽन्ततः ॥६०॥

dhātavo 'vayavitvāc ca
tan-mātrāvayavair vinā

na syur hy asaty avayaviny
asann avayavo 'ntataḥ

dhātavaḥ—the five elements; *avayavitvāt*—being the cause of the bodily conception; *ca*—and; *tat-mātra*—the sense objects (sound, taste, touch, etc.); *avayavaiḥ*—the subtle parts; *vinā*—without; *na*—not; *syuḥ*—can exist; *hi*—indeed; *asati*—unreal; *avayavini*—in the formation of the body; *asan*—not existing; *avayavaḥ*—the part of the body; *antataḥ*—at the end.

TRANSLATION

Because the body is formed of the five elements, it cannot exist without the subtle sense objects. Therefore, since the body is false, the sense objects are also naturally false or temporary.

TEXT 61

स्यात् सादृश्यभ्रमस्तावद् विकल्पे सति वस्तुनः ।
जाग्रत्स्वापौ यथा स्वप्ने तथा विधिनिषेधता ॥६१॥

syāt sādṛśya-bhramas tāvad
vikalpe sati vastunaḥ
jāgrat-svāpau yathā svapne
tathā vidhi-niṣedhatā

syāt—it so becomes; *sādṛśya*—similarity; *bhramaḥ*—mistake; *tāvat*—as long as; *vikalpe*—in separation; *sati*—the part; *vastunaḥ*—from the substance; *jāgrat*—waking; *svāpau*—sleeping; *yathā*—as; *svapne*—in a dream; *tathā*—similarly; *vidhi-niṣedhatā*—the regulative principles, consisting of injunctions and prohibitions.

TRANSLATION

When a substance and its parts are separated, the acceptance of similarity between one and the other is called illusion. While dreaming, one creates a separation between the existences called wakefulness and sleep. It is in such a state of mind that the

regulative principles of the scriptures, consisting of injunctions and prohibitions, are recommended.

PURPORT

In material existence there are many regulative principles and formalities. If material existence is temporary or false, this does not mean that the spiritual world, although similar, is also false. That one's material body is false or temporary does not mean that the body of the Supreme Lord is also false or temporary. The spiritual world is real, and the material world is similar to it. For example, in the desert we sometimes find a mirage, but although the water in a mirage is false, this does not mean that there is no water in reality; water exists, but not in the desert. Similarly, nothing real is in this material world, but reality is in the spiritual world. The Lord's form and His abode—Goloka Vṛndāvana in the Vaikuṇṭha planets—are eternal realities.

From *Bhagavad-gītā* we understand that there is another *prakṛti*, or nature, which is real. This is explained by the Lord Himself in the Eighth Chapter of *Bhagavad-gītā* (8.19–21):

bhūta-grāmaḥ sa evāyaṁ
bhūtvā bhūtvā pralīyate
rātry-āgame 'vaśaḥ pārtha
prabhavaty ahar-āgame

paras tasmāt tu bhāvo 'nyo
'vyakto 'vyaktāt sanātanaḥ
yaḥ sa sarveṣu bhūteṣu
naśyatsu na vinaśyati

avyakto 'kṣara ity uktas
tam āhuḥ paramāṁ gatim
yaṁ prāpya na nivartante
tad dhāma paramaṁ mama

"Again and again the day of Brahmā comes, and all living beings are active; and again the night falls, O Pārtha, and they are helplessly dissolved. Yet there is another nature, which is eternal and is transcendental to this manifested and unmanifested matter. It is supreme and is never annihilated. When all in this world is annihilated, that part remains as it is. That supreme abode is called unmanifested and infallible, and it is the supreme destination. When one goes there, he never comes back. That is My supreme abode." The material world is a reflection of the spiritual world. The material world is temporary or false, but the spiritual world is an eternal reality.

TEXT 62

भावाद्वैतं क्रियाद्वैतं द्रव्याद्वैतं तथात्मनः ।
वर्तयन्स्वानुभूत्येह त्रीन्स्वप्नान्धुनुते मुनिः ॥६२॥

bhāvādvaitaṁ kriyādvaitaṁ
dravyādvaitaṁ tathātmanaḥ
vartayan svānubhūtyeha
trīn svapnān dhunute muniḥ

bhāva-advaitam—oneness in one's conception of life; *kriyā-advaitam*—oneness in activities; *dravya-advaitam*—oneness in different paraphernalia; *tathā*—as well as; *ātmanaḥ*—of the soul; *vartayan*—considering; *sva*—one's own; *anubhūtyā*—according to realization; *iha*—in this material world; *trīn*—the three; *svapnān*—living conditions (wakefulness, dreaming and sleep); *dhunute*—gives up; *muniḥ*—the philosopher or speculator.

TRANSLATION

After considering the oneness of existence, activity and paraphernalia and after realizing the self to be different from all actions and reactions, the mental speculator [muni], according to his own realization, gives up the three states of wakefulness, dreaming and sleep.

PURPORT

The three words *bhāvādvaita*, *kriyādvaita* and *dravyādvaita* are explained in the following verses. However, one has to give up all the nonduality of philosophical life in the material world and come to the actual life of reality in the spiritual world in order to attain perfection.

TEXT 63

कार्यकारणवस्त्वैक्यदर्शनं पटतन्तुवत् ।
अवस्तुत्वाद् विकल्पस्य भावाद्वैतं तदुच्यते ॥६३॥

kārya-kāraṇa-vastv-aikya-
darśanaṁ paṭa-tantuvat
avastutvād vikalpasya
bhāvādvaitaṁ tad ucyate

kārya—the result or effect; *kāraṇa*—the cause; *vastu*—substance; *aikya*—oneness; *darśanam*—observation; *paṭa*—the cloth; *tantu*—the thread; *vat*—like; *avastutvāt*—because of being ultimately unreality; *vikalpasya*—of differentiation; *bhāva-advaitam*—the conception of oneness; *tat ucyate*—that is called.

TRANSLATION

When one understands that result and cause are one and that duality is ultimately unreal, like the idea that the threads of a cloth are different from the cloth itself, one reaches the conception of oneness called bhāvādvaita.

TEXT 64

यद् ब्रह्मणि परे साक्षात् सर्वकर्मसमर्पणम् ।
मनोवाक्तनुभिः पार्थ क्रियाद्वैतं तदुच्यते ॥६४॥

yad brahmaṇi pare sākṣāt
sarva-karma-samarpaṇam
mano-vāk-tanubhiḥ pārtha
kriyādvaitaṁ tad ucyate

yat—that which; *brahmaṇi*—in the Supreme Brahman; *pare*—transcendental; *sākṣāt*—directly; *sarva*—of all; *karma*—activities; *samarpaṇam*—dedication; *manaḥ*—by the mind; *vāk*—the words; *tanubhiḥ*—and the body; *pārtha*—O Mahārāja Yudhiṣṭhira; *kriyā-advaitam*—oneness in activities; *tat ucyate*—it is called.

TRANSLATION

My dear Yudhiṣṭhira [Pārtha], when all the activities one performs with his mind, words and body are dedicated directly to the service of the Supreme Personality of Godhead, one reaches oneness of activities, called kriyādvaita.

PURPORT

The Kṛṣṇa consciousness movement is teaching people how to come to the stage of dedicating everything to the service of the Supreme Personality of Godhead. Kṛṣṇa says in *Bhagavad-gītā* (9.27):

yat karoṣi yad aśnāsi
yaj juhoṣi dadāsi yat
yat tapasyasi kaunteya
tat kuruṣva mad-arpaṇam

"O son of Kuntī, all that you do, all that you eat, all that you offer and give away, as well as all austerities that you may perform, should be done as an offering unto Me." If whatever we do, whatever we eat, whatever we think and whatever we plan is for the advancement of the Kṛṣṇa consciousness movement, this is oneness. There is no difference between chanting for Kṛṣṇa consciousness and working for Kṛṣṇa consciousness. On the transcendental platform, they are one. But we must be guided by the spiritual master about this oneness; we should not manufacture our own oneness.

TEXT 65

आत्मजायासुतादीनामन्येषां सर्वदेहिनाम् ।
यत् स्वार्थकामयोरैक्यं द्रव्याद्वैतं तदुच्यते ।।६५।।

ātma-jāyā-sutādīnām
anyeṣāṁ sarva-dehinām
yat svārtha-kāmayor aikyaṁ
dravyādvaitaṁ tad ucyate

ātma—of one's self; *jāyā*—wife; *suta-ādīnām*—and children; *anyeṣām*—of one's relatives, etc.; *sarva-dehinām*—of all other living entities; *yat*—whatever; *sva-artha-kāmayoḥ*—of one's ultimate goal and benefit; *aikyam*—oneness; *dravya-advaitam*—oneness of interest; *tat ucyate*—it is called.

TRANSLATION

When the ultimate goal and interest of one's self, one's wife, one's children, one's relatives and all other embodied living beings is one, this is called dravyādvaita, or oneness of interest.

PURPORT

The actual interest of all living entities—indeed, the goal of life—is to return home, back to Godhead. This is the interest of one's own self, one's wife, one's children, one's disciples and one's friends, relatives, countrymen and all humanity. The Kṛṣṇa consciousness movement can give directions for management by which everyone can partake in Kṛṣṇa conscious activities and reach the ultimate goal, which is known as *svārtha-gatim*. This objective of everyone's interest is Viṣṇu, but because people do not know this (*na te viduḥ svārtha-gatiṁ hi viṣṇum*), they are making various plans by which to fulfill so many concocted interests in life. The Kṛṣṇa consciousness movement is trying to bring everyone to the highest interest. The process may be differently named, but if the aim is one, people should follow it to achieve the ultimate goal in life. Unfortunately, people are thinking of different interests, and blind leaders are misleading them. Everyone is trying to reach the goal of complete happiness materially; because people do not know what complete happiness is, they are materially diverted toward different interests.

TEXT 66

यद् यस्य वानिषिद्धं स्याद् येन यत्र यतो नृप ।
स तेनेहेत कार्याणि नरो नान्यैरनापदि ॥६६॥

yad yasya vāniṣiddhaṁ syād
yena yatra yato nṛpa
sa teneheta kāryāṇi
naro nānyair anāpadi

yat—whatever; *yasya*—of a man; *vā*—either; *aniṣiddham*—not forbidden; *syāt*—it is so; *yena*—by which means; *yatra*—in place and time; *yataḥ*—from which; *nṛpa*—O King; *saḥ*—such a person; *tena*—by such a process; *īheta*—should perform; *kāryāṇi*—prescribed activities; *naraḥ*—a person; *na*—not; *anyaiḥ*—by other ways; *anāpadi*—in the absence of danger.

TRANSLATION

In normal conditions, in the absence of danger, O King Yudhiṣṭhira, a man should perform his prescribed activities according to his status of life with the things, endeavors, process and living place that are not forbidden for him, and not by any other means.

PURPORT

This instruction is given for men in all statuses of life. Generally society is divided into *brāhmaṇas, kṣatriyas, vaiśyas, śūdras, brahmacārīs, vānaprasthas, sannyāsīs* and *gṛhasthas*. Everyone must act according to his position and try to please the Supreme Personality of Godhead, for that will make one's life successful. This was instructed in Naimiṣāraṇya:

ataḥ pumbhir dvija-śreṣṭhā
varṇāśrama-vibhāgaśaḥ
svanuṣṭhitasya dharmasya
saṁsiddhir hari-toṣaṇam

"O best among the twiceborn, it is therefore concluded that the highest perfection one can achieve, by discharging his prescribed duties [*dharma*] according to caste divisions and order of life, is to please the Lord Hari." (*Bhāg.* 1.2.13) Everyone should act according to his occupational duties just to please the Supreme Personality of Godhead. Then everyone will be happy.

TEXT 67

एतैरन्यैश्च वेदोक्तैर्वर्तमानः स्वकर्मभिः ।
गृहेऽप्यस्य गतिं यायाद् राजंस्तद्भक्तिभाङ् नरः ॥६७॥

etair anyaiś ca vedoktair
vartamānaḥ sva-karmabhiḥ
gṛhe 'py asya gatiṁ yāyād
rājaṁs tad-bhakti-bhāṅ naraḥ

etaiḥ—by these ways; *anayiḥ*—by other ways; *ca*—and; *veda-uktaiḥ*—as directed in the Vedic literatures; *vartamānaḥ*—abiding; *sva-karmabhiḥ*—by one's occupational duties; *gṛhe api*—even at home; *asya*—of Lord Kṛṣṇa; *gatim*—destination; *yāyāt*—can reach; *rājan*—O King; *tat-bhakti-bhāk*—who renders devotional service unto the Supreme Personality of Godhead; *naraḥ*—any person.

TRANSLATION

O King, one should perform his occupational duties according to these instructions, as well as other instructions given in the Vedic literature, just to remain a devotee of Lord Kṛṣṇa. Thus, even while at home, one will be able to reach the destination.

PURPORT

The ultimate goal of life is Viṣṇu, Kṛṣṇa. Therefore, either by Vedic regulative principles or by materialistic activities, if one tries to reach the destination of Kṛṣṇa, that is the perfection of life. Kṛṣṇa should be the target; everyone should try to reach Kṛṣṇa, from any position of life.

Kṛṣṇa accepts service from anyone. The Lord says in *Bhagavad-gītā* (9.32):

māṁ hi pārtha vyapāśritya
ye 'pi syuḥ pāpa-yonayaḥ
striyo vaiśyās tathā śūdrās
te 'pi yānti parāṁ gatim

"O son of Pṛthā, those who take shelter in Me, though they be of lower birth—women, *vaiśyas* [merchants], as well as *śūdras* [workers]—can approach the supreme destination." It does not matter what one's position is; if one aims at reaching Kṛṣṇa by performing his occupational duty under the direction of the spiritual master, his life is successful. It is not that only *sannyāsīs*, *vānaprasthas* and *brahmacārīs* can reach

Kṛṣṇa. A *gṛhastha*, a householder, can also reach Kṛṣṇa, provided he becomes a pure devotee without material desires. An example of this is cited in the next verse.

TEXT 68

यथा हि यूयं नृपदेव दुस्त्यजा-
दापद्गणादुत्तरतात्मनः प्रभोः ।
यत्पादपङ्केरुहसेवया भवा-
नहारषीन्निर्जितदिग्गजः क्रतून् ॥६८॥

yathā hi yūyaṁ nṛpa-deva dustyajād
āpad-gaṇād uttaratātmanaḥ prabhoḥ
yat-pāda-paṅkeruha-sevayā bhavān
ahāraṣīn nirjita-dig-gajaḥ kratūn

yathā—as; *hi*—indeed; *yūyam*—all of you (Pāṇḍavas); *nṛpa-deva*—O lord of the kings, human beings and demigods; *dustyajāt*—insurmountable; *āpat*—dangerous conditions; *gaṇāt*—from all; *uttarata*—escaped; *ātmanaḥ*—own; *prabhoḥ*—of the Lord; *yat-pāda-paṅkeruha*—whose lotus feet; *sevayā*—by serving; *bhavān*—yourself; *ahāraṣīt*—performed; *nirjita*—defeating; *dik-gajaḥ*—the most powerful enemies, who were like elephants; *kratūn*—ritualistic ceremonies.

TRANSLATION

O King Yudhiṣṭhira, because of your service to the Supreme Lord, all of you Pāṇḍavas defeated the greatest dangers posed by numerous kings and demigods. By serving the lotus feet of Kṛṣṇa, you conquered great enemies, who were like elephants, and thus you collected ingredients for sacrifice. By His grace, may you be delivered from material involvement.

PURPORT

Placing himself as an ordinary householder, Mahārāja Yudhiṣṭhira inquired from Nārada Muni how a *gṛha-mūḍha-dhī*, a person who is entangled in household life and who thus continues to remain a fool, can be delivered. Nārada Muni encouraged Mahārāja Yudhiṣṭhira by saying, "You are already on the safe side because you, along with your entire family, have become a pure devotee of Kṛṣṇa." By Kṛṣṇa's grace, the Pāṇḍavas conquered in the Battle of Kurukṣetra and were saved from many dangers posed not only by kings but sometimes even by the demigods. Thus they are a practical example of how to live in security and safety by the grace of Kṛṣṇa. Everyone should follow the example of the Pāṇḍavas, who showed how to be saved by the grace of Kṛṣṇa. Our Kṛṣṇa consciousness movement is intended to teach how everyone can live peacefully in this material world and at the end of life return home, back to Godhead. In the material world there are always dangers at every step (*padaṁ padaṁ yad vipadāṁ na teṣām*). Nonetheless, if one takes shelter of Kṛṣṇa without hesitation and keeps under the shelter of Kṛṣṇa, he can easily cross the ocean of nescience. *Samāśritā ye pada-pallava-plavaṁ mahat-padaṁ puṇya-yaśo murāreḥ.* To the devotee, this great ocean of nescience becomes like a puddle of water in the hoofprint of a cow. A pure devotee, without embarrassing himself by trying for elevation in so many ways, stays in the safest position as a servant of Kṛṣṇa, and thus his life is eternally safe without a doubt.

TEXT 69

अहं पुराभवं कश्चिद् गन्धर्व उपबर्हणः ।
नाम्नातीते महाकल्पे गन्धर्वाणां सुसम्मतः ॥६९॥

ahaṁ purābhavaṁ kaścid
gandharva upabarhaṇaḥ
nāmnātīte mahā-kalpe
gandharvāṇāṁ susammataḥ

aham—I myself; *purā*—formerly; *abhavam*—existed as; *kaścit gandharvaḥ*—one of the denizens of Gandharvaloka; *upabarhaṇaḥ*—Upabarhaṇa; *nāmnā*—by the name; *atīte*—long, long ago; *mahā-kalpe*—in a life of Brahmā, which is known as a *mahā-kalpa;* *gandharvāṇām*—among the Gandharvas; *su-sammataḥ*—a very respectable person.

TRANSLATION

Long, long ago, in another mahā-kalpa [millennium of Brahmā], I existed as the Gandharva known as Upabarhaṇa. I was very respected by the other Gandharvas.

PURPORT

Śrīla Nārada Muni is giving a practical example from his past life. Formerly, during the previous lifetime of Lord Brahmā, Nārada Muni was one of the denizens of Gandharvaloka, but unfortunately, as will be explained, he fell from his exalted position in Gandharvaloka, where the inhabitants are extremely beautiful and expert in singing, to become a *śūdra.* Nonetheless, because of his association with devotees, he became more fortunate than he was in Gandharvaloka. Even though cursed by the *prajāpatis* to become a *śūdra,* in his next life he became the son of Lord Brahmā.

The word *mahā-kalpe* is described by Śrīla Madhvācārya as *atīta-brahma-kalpe.* Brahmā dies at the end of a life of many millions of years. The day of Brahmā is described in *Bhagavad-gītā* (8.17):

sahasra-yuga-paryantam
ahar yad brahmaṇo viduḥ
rātriṁ yuga-sahasrāntāṁ
te 'ho-rātra-vido janāḥ

"By human calculation, a thousand ages taken together is the duration of Brahmā's one day. And such also is the duration of his night." Bhagavān Śrī Kṛṣṇa can remember incidents from millions of years ago. Similarly, His pure devotee like Nārada Muni can also remember incidents from a past life millions and millions of years ago.

TEXT 70

रूपपेशलमाधुर्यसौगन्ध्यप्रियदर्शनः ।
स्त्रीणां प्रियतमो नित्यं मत्तः स्वपुरलम्पटः ॥७०॥

rūpa-peśala-mādhurya-
saugandhya-priya-darśanaḥ

strīṇāṁ priyatamo nityaṁ
mattaḥ sva-pura-lampaṭaḥ

rūpa—beauty; *peśala*—formation of the body; *mādhurya*—attractiveness; *saugandhya*—very fragrant, being decorated with various flower garlands and sandalwood pulp; *priya-darśanaḥ*—very beautiful to see; *strīṇām*—of the women; *priya-tamaḥ*—naturally attracted; *nityam*—daily; *mattaḥ*—proud like a madman; *sva-pura*—in his own city; *lampaṭaḥ*—very much attached to women because of lusty desires.

TRANSLATION

I had a beautiful face and a pleasing, attractive bodily structure. Decorated with flower garlands and sandalwood pulp, I was most pleasing to the women of my city. Thus I was bewildered, always feeling lusty desires.

PURPORT

From the description of the beauty of Nārada Muni when he was one of the denizens of Gandharvaloka, it appears that everyone on that planet is extremely beautiful and pleasing and always decorated with flowers and sandalwood. Upabarhaṇa was Nārada Muni's name previously. Upabarhaṇa was specifically expert in decorating himself to attract the attention of women, and thus he became a playboy, as described in the next verse. To be a playboy in this life is unfortunate because too much attraction to women will lead one to fall into the association of *śūdras*, who can easily take advantage of mingling with women without restriction. In this present age of Kali, when people are *mandāḥ sumanda-matayaḥ*—very bad because of a *śūdra* mentality—such free mingling is prominent. Among the higher classes—*brāhmaṇa, kṣatriya* and *vaiśya*—there is no chance for men to mingle with women freely, but in the *śūdra* community such mingling is open. Because there is no cultural education in this age of Kali, everyone is spiritually untrained, and everyone is therefore to be considered *śūdra* (*aśuddhāḥ śūdra-kalpā hi brāhmaṇāḥ kali-sambhavāḥ*). When all the people become *śūdras*, certainly they are very bad (*mandāḥ sumanda-matayaḥ*). Thus they manufacture their own way of life, with the result that they gradually become unfortunate (*manda-bhāgyāḥ*), and furthermore they are always disturbed by various circumstances.

TEXT 71

एकदा देवसत्रे तु गन्धर्वाप्सरसां गणाः ।
उपहूता विश्वसृग्भिर्हरिगाथोपगायने ॥७१॥

ekadā deva-satre tu
gandharvāpsarasāṁ gaṇāḥ
upahūtā viśva-sṛgbhir
hari-gāthopagāyane

ekadā—once upon a time; *deva-satre*—in an assembly of the demigods; *tu*—indeed; *gandharva*—of the inhabitants of Gandharvaloka; *apsarasām*—and the inhabitants of Apsaroloka; *gaṇāḥ*—all; *upahūtāḥ*—were invited; *viśva-sṛgbhiḥ*—by the great demigods known as the *prajāpatis; hari-gātha-upagāyane*—on an occasion of *kīrtana* for glorifying the Supreme Lord.

TRANSLATION

Once there was a saṅkīrtana festival to glorify the Supreme Lord in an assembly of the demigods, and the Gandharvas and Apsarās were invited by the prajāpatis to take part in it.

PURPORT

Saṅkīrtana means chanting of the holy name of the Lord. The Hare Kṛṣṇa movement is not a new movement as people sometimes mistakenly think. The Hare Kṛṣṇa movement is present in every millennium of Lord Brahmā's life, and the holy name is chanted in all the higher planetary systems, including Brahmaloka and Candraloka, not to speak of Gandharvaloka and Apsaroloka. The *saṅkīrtana* movement that was started in this world five hundred years ago by Śrī Caitanya Mahāprabhu is therefore not a new movement. Sometimes, because of our bad luck, this movement is stopped, but Śrī Caitanya Mahāprabhu and His servants again start the movement for the benefit of the entire word or, indeed, the entire universe.

TEXT 72

अहं च गायंस्तद्विद्वान् स्त्रीभिः परिवृतो गतः ।
ज्ञात्वा विश्वसृजस्तन्मे हेलनं शेपुरोजसा ।
याहि त्वं शूद्रतामाशु नष्टश्रीः कृतहेलनः ॥७२॥

ahaṁ ca gāyaṁs tad-vidvān
strībhiḥ parivṛto gataḥ
jñātvā viśva-sṛjas tan me
helanaṁ śepur ojasā
yāhi tvaṁ śūdratām āśu
naṣṭa-śrīḥ kṛta-helanaḥ

aham—I myself; *ca*—and; *gāyan*—singing the glories of other demigods rather than those of the Lord; *tat-vidvān*—knowing very well the art of singing; *strībhiḥ*—by women; *parivṛtaḥ*—being surrounded; *gataḥ*—went there; *jñātvā*—knowing well; *viśva-sṛjaḥ*—the *prajāpatis*, to whom the management of universal affairs was entrusted; *tat*—the attitude of my singing; *me*—my; *helanam*—negligence; *śepuḥ*—cursed; *ojasā*—with great force; *yāhi*—become; *tvam*—you; *śūdratām*—a *śūdra; āśu*—immediately; *naṣṭa*—devoid of; *śrīḥ*—beauty; *kṛta-helanaḥ*—because of transgressing the etiquette.

TRANSLATION

Nārada Muni continued: Being invited to that festival, I also joined, and, surrounded by women, I began musically singing the glories of the demigods. Because of this, the prajāpatis, the great demigods in charge of the affairs of the universe, forcefully cursed me with these words: "Because you have committed an offense, may you immediately become a śūdra, devoid of beauty."

PURPORT

As far as *kīrtana* is concerned, the *śāstras* say, *śravaṇaṁ kīrtanaṁ viṣṇoḥ:* one should chant the glories of the Supreme Lord and the holy name of the Supreme Lord. This is clearly stated. *Śravaṇaṁ kīrtanaṁ viṣṇoḥ:* one should chant about and glorify Lord Viṣṇu, not any demigod. Unfortunately, there are foolish persons who invent some process of *kīrtana* on the basis of a demigod's name. This is an offense. *Kīrtana* means glorifying the Supreme Lord, not any demigod. Sometimes people invent Kālī-*kīrtana* or Śiva-*kīrtana*, and even big *sannyāsīs* in the Māyāvāda school say that one may chant any name and still get the same result. But here we find that millions and millions of years ago, when Nārada Muni was a Gandharva, he neglected the order to glorify the Lord, and being mad in the association of women, he began to chant otherwise. Thus he was cursed to become a *śūdra.* His first offense was that he went to join the *saṅkīrtana* party in the company of lusty women, and another offense was that he considered ordinary songs, like cinema songs and other such songs, to be equal to *saṅkīrtana.* For this offense he was punished with becoming a *śūdra.*

TEXT 73

तावद्दास्यामहं जज्ञे तत्रापि ब्रह्मवादिनाम् ।
शुश्रूषयानुषङ्गेण प्राप्तोऽहं ब्रह्मपुत्रताम् ॥७३॥

tāvad dāsyām ahaṁ jajñe
tatrāpi brahma-vādinām
śuśrūṣayānuṣaṅgeṇa
prāpto 'haṁ brahma-putratām

tāvat—since being cursed; *dāsyām*—in the womb of a maidservant; *aham*—I; *jajñe*—took birth; *tatrāpi*—although (being a *śūdra*); *brahma-vādinām*—unto persons well conversant with the Vedic knowledge; *śuśrūṣayā*—by rendering service; *anuṣaṅgeṇa*—simultaneously; *prāptaḥ*—obtained; *aham*—I; *brahma-putratām*—a birth as the son of Lord Brahmā (in this life).

TRANSLATION

Although I took birth as a śūdra from the womb of a maidservant, I engaged in the service of Vaiṣṇavas who were well-versed in Vedic knowledge. Consequently, in this life I got the opportunity to take birth as the son of Lord Brahmā.

PURPORT

The Supreme Personality of Godhead says in *Bhagavad-gītā* (9.32):

māṁ hi pārtha vyapāśritya
ye 'pi syuḥ pāpa-yonayaḥ
striyo vaiśyās tathā śūdrās
te 'pi yānti parāṁ gatiṁ

"O son of Pṛthā, those who take shelter in Me, though they be of lower birth—women, *vaiśyas* [merchants], as well as *śūdras* [workers]—can approach the supreme destination." It doesn't matter whether a person is born as a *śūdra*, a woman or a *vaiśya;* if he associates with devotees repeatedly or always (*sādhu-saṅgena*), he can be elevated to the highest perfection. Nārada Muni is explaining this in relation to his own life. The *saṅkīrtana* movement is important, for regardless of whether one is a *śūdra, vaiśya, mleccha, yavana* or whatever, if one associates with a pure devotee, follows his instructions and serves the pure devotee, his life is successful. This is *bhakti. Ānukūlyena kṛṣṇānuśīlanam. Bhakti* consists of serving Kṛṣṇa and His devotees very favorably. *Anyābhilāṣitā-śūnyam.* If one has no desire other than to serve Kṛṣṇa and His devotee, then his life is successful. This is explained by Nārada Muni through this practical example from his own life.

TEXT 74

धर्मस्ते गृहमेधीयो वर्णितः पापनाशनः ।
गृहस्थो येन पदवीमञ्जसा न्यासिनामियात् ॥७४॥

dharmas te gṛha-medhīyo
varṇitaḥ pāpa-nāśanaḥ
gṛhastho yena padavīm
añjasā nyāsinām iyāt

dharmaḥ—that religious process; *te*—to you; *gṛha-medhīyaḥ*—although attached to household life; *varṇitaḥ*—explained (by me); *pāpa-nāśanaḥ*—the destruction of sinful reactions; *gṛhasthaḥ*—a person in household life; *yena*—by which; *padavīm*—the position; *añjasā*—very easily; *nyāsinām*—of those in the renounced order of life; *iyāt*—can obtain.

TRANSLATION

The process of chanting the holy name of the Lord is so powerful that by this chanting even householders [gṛhasthas] can very easily gain the ultimate result achieved by persons in the renounced order. Mahārāja Yudhiṣṭhira, I have now explained to you that process of religion.

PURPORT

This is a confirmation of the Kṛṣṇa consciousness movement. Anyone who takes part in this movement, regardless of what he is, can gain the topmost result achieved by a perfect *sannyāsī*, namely *brahma-jñāna* (spiritual knowledge). Even more important, he can advance in devotional service. Mahārāja Yudhiṣṭhira thought that because he was a *gṛhastha* there was no hope of his being liberated, and therefore he asked Nārada Muni how he could get out of material entanglement. But Nārada Muni, citing a practical example from his own life, established that by associating with devotees and chanting the Hare Kṛṣṇa *mantra*, any man in any condition of life can achieve the highest perfection without a doubt.

TEXT 75

यूयं नृलोके बत भूरिभागा
लोकं पुनाना मुनयोऽभियन्ति ।
येषां गृहानावसतीति साक्षाद्
गूढं परं ब्रह्म मनुष्यलिङ्गम् ॥७५॥

yūyaṁ nṛ-loke bata bhūri-bhāgā
lokaṁ punānā munayo 'bhiyanti
yeṣāṁ gṛhān āvasatīti sākṣād
gūḍhaṁ paraṁ brahma manuṣya-liṅgam

yūyam—all of you Pāṇḍavas; *nṛ-loke*—in this material world; *bata*—indeed; *bhūri-bhāgāḥ*—extremely fortunate; *lokam*—all the planets of the universe; *punānāḥ*—who can purify; *munayaḥ*—great saintly persons; *abhiyanti*—come to visit (just like ordinary persons); *yeṣām*—of whom; *gṛhān*—the house of the Pāṇḍavas; *āvasati*—resides; *iti*—thus; *sākṣāt*—directly; *gūḍham*—very confidential; *param*—transcendental; *brahma*—the Parabrahman, Kṛṣṇa; *manuṣya-liṅgam*—as if an ordinary human being.

TRANSLATION

My dear Mahārāja Yudhiṣṭhira, you Pāṇḍavas are so very fortunate in this world that many, many great saints, who can purify all the planets of the universe, come to your house just like ordinary visitors. Furthermore, the Supreme Personality of Godhead, Kṛṣṇa, is living confidentially with you in your house, just like your brother.

PURPORT

Here is a statement exalting a Vaiṣṇava. In human society, a *brāhmaṇa* is the most respected person. A *brāhmaṇa* is one who can understand Brahman, the impersonal Brahman, but hardly ever can one understand the Supreme Personality of Godhead, who is described by Arjuna in *Bhagavad-gītā* as *paraṁ brahma.* A *brāhmaṇa* may be extremely fortunate in having achieved *brahma-jñāna,* but the Pāṇḍavas were so exalted that the Parabrahman, the Supreme Personality of Godhead, was living in their house like an ordinary human being. The word *bhūri-bhāgāḥ* indicates that the Pāṇḍavas were in a still higher position than *brahmacārīs* and *brāhmaṇas.* In the following verses, Nārada Muni repeatedly glorifies the position of the Pāṇḍavas.

TEXT 76

स वा अयं ब्रह्म महद्विमृग्य
कैवल्यनिर्वाणसुखानुभूतिः ।
प्रियः सुहृद् वः खलु मातुलेय
आत्मार्हणीयो विधिकृद् गुरुश्च ॥७६॥

sa vā ayaṁ brahma mahad-vimṛgya-
kaivalya-nirvāṇa-sukhānubhūtiḥ
priyaḥ suhṛd vaḥ khalu mātuleya
ātmārhaṇīyo vidhi-kṛd guruś ca

saḥ—that Supreme Personality of Godhead; *vā*—either; *ayam*—Kṛṣṇa; *brahma*—the Supreme Brahman; *mahat-vimṛgya*—sought by great, great saintly persons (devotees of Kṛṣṇa); *kaivalya-nirvāṇa-sukha*—of liberation and transcendental bliss; *anubhūtiḥ*—for the realization; *priyaḥ*—very dear; *suhṛt*—the well-wisher; *vaḥ*—of all of you Pāṇḍavas; *khalu*—famous as; *mātuleyaḥ*—the son of your maternal uncle; *ātmā*—heart and soul; *arhaṇīyaḥ*—the most worshipable person; *vidhi-kṛt*—giving direction; *guruḥ*—your spiritual master; *ca*—and.

TRANSLATION

How wonderful it is that the Supreme Personality of Godhead, the Parabrahman, Kṛṣṇa, who is sought by great, great sages for the sake of liberation and transcendental bliss, is acting as your best well-wisher, your friend, your cousin, your heart and soul, your worshipable director, and your spiritual master.

PURPORT

Kṛṣṇa can become the director and spiritual master of anyone who is serious about getting the mercy of Kṛṣṇa. The Lord sends the spiritual master to train a devotee, and when the devotee is advanced, the Lord acts as the spiritual master within his heart.

teṣāṁ satata-yuktānāṁ
bhajatāṁ prīti-pūrvakam
dadāmi buddhi-yogaṁ taṁ
yena māṁ upayānti te

"To those who are constantly devoted and worhip Me with love, I give the understanding by which they can come to Me." Kṛṣṇa does not become the direct spiritual master unless one is fully trained by His representative spiritual master. Therefore, as we have already discussed, the Lord's representative spiritual master should not be considered an ordinary human being. The representative spiritual master never gives any false knowledge to his disciple, but only perfect knowledge. Thus he is the representative of Kṛṣṇa. Kṛṣṇa helps as the *guru*, or spiritual master, from within and from without. From without He helps the devotee as His representative, and from within He talks personally with the pure devotee and gives him instructions by which he may return home, back to Godhead.

TEXT 77

न यस्य साक्षाद्भवपद्मजादिभी
रूपं धिया वस्तुतयोपवर्णितम् ।
मौनेन भक्त्योपशमेन पूजितः
प्रसीदतामेष स सात्वतां पतिः ॥७७॥

na yasya sākṣād bhava-padmajādibhī
rūpaṁ dhiyā vastutayopavarṇitam
maunena bhaktyopaśamena pūjitaḥ
prasīdatām eṣa sa sātvatāṁ patiḥ

na—not; *yasya*—of whom (Lord Śrī Kṛṣṇa); *sākṣāt*—directly; *bhava*—by Lord Śiva; *padma-ja-ādibhiḥ*—Lord Brahmā and others; *rūpam*—the form; *dhiyā*—by meditation; *vastutayā*—factually; *upavarṇitam*—could be explained; *maunena*—by silence; *bhaktyā*—by devotional service; *upaśamena*—by finishing all material activities; *pūjitaḥ*—one who is so worshiped; *prasīdatām*—may be pleased with us; *eṣaḥ*—this; *saḥ*—the same Personality of Godhead; *sātvatām*—of the devotees; *patiḥ*—who is the maintainer, master and guide.

TRANSLATION

Present here now is the same Supreme Personality of Godhead whose true form cannot be understood even by such great personalities as Lord Brahmā and Lord Śiva. He is realized by devotees because of their unflinching surrender. May that same Personality of Godhead, who is the maintainer of His devotees and who is worshiped by silence, by devotional service and by cessation of material activities, be pleased with us.

PURPORT

Lord Kṛṣṇa is not properly understood even by such exalted personalities as Lord Śiva and Lord Brahmā, what to speak of ordinary men, but by His causeless mercy He bestows the benediction of devotion upon His devotees, who can thus understand Kṛṣṇa as He is. *Bhaktyā mām abhijānāti yāvān yaś cāsmi tattvataḥ.* No one within this universe can understand Kṛṣṇa in truth, but if one engages in devotional service one can understand Him perfectly well. This is also confirmed by the Lord in the Seventh Chapter of *Bhagavad-gītā* (7.1):

mayy āsakta-manāḥ pārtha
yogaṁ yuñjan mad-āśrayaḥ
asaṁśayaṁ samagraṁ māṁ
yathā jñāsyasi tac chṛṇu

"Now, hear, O son of Pṛthā [Arjuna], how by practicing *yoga* in full consciousness of Me, with mind attached to Me, you can know Me in full, free from doubt." Lord Kṛṣṇa Himself teaches how one can understand Him perfectly well, without a doubt. Not only the Pāṇḍavas but everyone who sincerely accepts the instructions of Kṛṣṇa can understand the Supreme Personality of Godhead as He is. After instructing Yudhiṣṭhira Mahārāja, Nārada Muni prays for the Lord's blessings that He be pleased with everyone and that everyone become perfect in God consciousness and return home, back to Godhead.

TEXT 78

श्रीशुक उवाच
इति देवर्षिणा प्रोक्तं निशम्य भरतर्षभः ।
पूजयामास सुप्रीतः कृष्णं च प्रेमविह्वलः ॥७८॥

śrī-śuka uvāca
iti devarṣiṇā proktaṁ
niśamya bharatarṣabhaḥ
pūjayām āsa suprītaḥ
kṛṣṇaṁ ca prema-vihvalaḥ

śrī-śukaḥ uvāca—Śrī Śukadeva Gosvāmī said; *iti*—thus; *deva-ṛṣinā*—by the great saint (Nārada Muni); *proktam*—described; *niśamya*—hearing; *bharata-ṛṣabhaḥ*—the best of the descendants in Bharata Mahārāja's dynasty, namely Mahārāja Yudhiṣṭhira; *pūjayām āsa*—

worshiped; *su-prītaḥ*—being extremely pleased; *kṛṣṇam*—unto Lord Kṛṣṇa; *ca*—also; *prema-vihvalaḥ*—in the ecstasy of love of Kṛṣṇa.

TRANSLATION

Śrī Śukadeva Gosvāmī said: Mahārāja Yudhiṣṭhira, the best member of the Bharata dynasty, thus learned everything from the descriptions of Nārada Muni. After hearing these instructions, he felt great pleasure from within his heart, and in great ecstasy, love and affection, he worshiped Lord Kṛṣṇa.

PURPORT

It is natural that when someone belonging to one's family circle is understood to be very great, one becomes ecstatic in love, thinking, "Oh, such a great personality is our relative!" When Śrī Kṛṣṇa, who was already known to the Pāṇḍavas, was further described by Nārada Muni to be the Supreme Personality of Godhead, naturally the Pāṇḍavas were amazed, thinking, "The Supreme Personality of Godhead is with us as our cousin!" Certainly their ecstasy was extraordinary.

TEXT 79

कृष्णपार्थावुपामन्त्र्य पूजितः प्रययौ मुनिः ।
श्रुत्वा कृष्णं परं ब्रह्म पार्थः परमविस्मितः ॥७९॥

kṛṣṇa-pārthāv upāmantrya
pūjitaḥ prayayau muniḥ
śrutvā kṛṣṇaṁ paraṁ brahma
pārthaḥ parama-vismitaḥ

kṛṣṇa—Lord Kṛṣṇa; *pārthau*—and Mahārāja Yudhiṣṭhira; *upāmantrya*—bidding farewell; *pūjitaḥ*—being worshiped by them; *prayayau*—left (that place); *muniḥ*—Nārada Muni; *śrutvā*—after hearing; *kṛṣṇam*—about Kṛṣṇa; *param brahma*—as the Supreme Personality of Godhead; *pārthaḥ*—Mahārāja Yudhiṣṭhira; *parama-vismitaḥ*—became most amazed.

TRANSLATION

Nārada Muni, being worshiped by Kṛṣṇa and Mahārāja Yudhiṣṭhira, bade them farewell and went away. Yudhiṣṭhira Mahārāja, having heard that Kṛṣṇa, his cousin, is the Supreme Personality of Godhead, was struck with wonder.

PURPORT

After hearing the conversation between Nārada and Yudhiṣṭhira, if one still has any doubts about Kṛṣṇa's being the Supreme Personality of Godhead, one should immediately give them up. *Asaṁśayaṁ samagram.* Without any doubt and without any defect, one should understand Kṛṣṇa to be the Supreme Personality of Godhead and thus surrender at His lotus feet. Ordinary persons do not do this, even after hearing all the *Vedas*, but if one is fortunate, although it may be even after many, many births, he comes to this conclusion (*bahūnāṁ janmanām ante jñānavān māṁ prapadyate*).

TEXT 80

इति दाक्षायणीनां ते पृथग्वंशाः प्रकीर्तिताः ।
देवासुरमनुष्याद्या लोका यत्र चराचराः ॥८०॥

iti dākṣāyaṇīnāṁ te
pṛthag vaṁśāḥ prakīrtitāḥ
devāsura-manuṣyādyā
lokā yatra carācarāḥ

iti—thus; *dākṣāyaṇīnām*—of the daughters of Mahārāja Dakṣa, like Aditi and Diti; *te*—to you; *pṛthak*—separately; *vaṁśāḥ*—the dynasties; *prakīrtitāḥ*—described (by me); *deva*—the demigods; *asura*—demons; *manuṣya*—and human beings; *ādyāḥ*—and so on; *lokāḥ*—all the planets within the universe; *yatra*—wherein; *cara-acarāḥ*—moving and nonmoving living entities.

TRANSLATION

On all the planets within this universe, the varieties of living entities, moving and nonmoving, including the demigods, demons and human beings, were all generated from the daughters of

Mahārāja Dakṣa. I have now described them and their different dynasties.

Thus end the Bhaktivedanta purports of the Seventh Canto, Fifteenth Chapter, of the Śrīmad-Bhāgavatam, *entitled "Instructions for Civilized Human Beings."*

—Completed on the night of Vaiśākhī Śukla Ekādaśī, the tenth of May, 1976, in the temple of the Pañcatattva, New Navadvīpa (Honolulu), by the mercy of *śrī-kṛṣṇa-caitanya prabhu nityānanda śrī-advaita gadādhara śrīvāsādi-gaura-bhakta-vṛnda.* Thus we may happily chant Hare Kṛṣṇa, Hare Kṛṣṇa, Kṛṣṇa Kṛṣṇa, Hare Hare/ Hare Rāma, Hare Rāma, Rāma Rāma, Hare Hare.

END OF THE SEVENTH CANTO

Appendixes

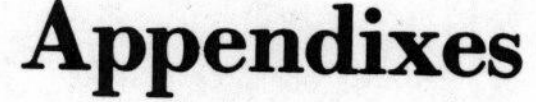

The Author

His Divine Grace A. C. Bhaktivedanta Swami Prabhupāda appeared in this world in 1896 in Calcutta, India. He first met his spiritual master, Śrīla Bhaktisiddhānta Sarasvatī Gosvāmī, in Calcutta in 1922. Bhaktisiddhānta Sarasvatī, a prominent devotional scholar and the founder of sixty-four Gauḍīya Maṭhas (Vedic institutes), liked this educated young man and convinced him to dedicate his life to teaching Vedic knowledge. Śrīla Prabhupāda became his student, and eleven years later (1933) at Allahabad he became his formally initiated disciple.

At their first meeting, in 1922, Śrīla Bhaktisiddhānta Sarasvatī Ṭhākura requested Śrīla Prabhupāda to broadcast Vedic knowledge through the English language. In the years that followed, Śrīla Prabhupāda wrote a commentary on the *Bhagavad-gītā,* assisted the Gauḍīya Maṭha in its work and, in 1944, without assistance, started an English fortnightly magazine, edited it, typed the manuscripts and checked the galley proofs. He even distributed the individual copies freely and struggled to maintain the publication. Once begun, the magazine never stopped; it is now being continued by his disciples in the West.

Recognizing Śrīla Prabhupāda's philosophical learning and devotion, the Gauḍīya Vaiṣṇava Society honored him in 1947 with the title "Bhaktivedanta." In 1950, at the age of fifty-four, Śrīla Prabhupāda retired from married life, and four years later he adopted the *vānaprastha* (retired) order to devote more time to his studies and writing. Śrīla Prabhupāda traveled to the holy city of Vṛndāvana, where he lived in very humble circumstances in the historic medieval temple of Rādhā-Dāmodara. There he engaged for several years in deep study and writing. He accepted the renounced order of life (*sannyāsa*) in 1959. At Rādhā-Dāmodara, Śrīla Prabhupāda began work on his life's masterpiece: a multivolume translation and commentary on the eighteen thousand verse *Śrīmad-Bhāgavatam* (*Bhāgavata Purāṇa*). He also wrote *Easy Journey to Other Planets.*

After publishing three volumes of *Bhāgavatam,* Śrīla Prabhupāda came to the United States, in 1965, to fulfill the mission of his spiritual master. Since that time, His Divine Grace has written over forty volumes of authoritative translations, commentaries and summary studies of the philosophical and religious classics of India.

In 1965, when he first arrived by freighter in New York City, Śrīla Prabhupāda was practically penniless. It was after almost a year of great difficulty that he established the International Society for Krishna Consciousness in July of 1966. Under his careful guidance, the Society has grown within a decade to a worldwide confederation of almost one hundred *āśramas*, schools, temples, institutes and farm communities.

In 1968, Śrīla Prabhupāda created New Vṛndāvana, an experimental Vedic community in the hills of West Virginia. Inspired by the success of New Vṛndāvana, now a thriving farm community of more than one thousand acres, his students have since founded several similar communities in the United States and abroad.

In 1972, His Divine Grace introduced the Vedic system of primary and secondary education in the West by founding the Gurukula school in Dallas, Texas. The school began with 3 children in 1972, and by the beginning of 1975 the enrollment had grown to 150.

Śrīla Prabhupāda has also inspired the construction of a large international center at Śrīdhāma Māyāpur in West Bengal, India, which is also the site for a planned Institute of Vedic Studies. A similar project is the magnificent Kṛṣṇa-Balarāma Temple and International Guest House in Vṛndāvana, India. These are centers where Westerners can live to gain firsthand experience of Vedic culture.

Śrīla Prabhupāda's most significant contribution, however, is his books. Highly respected by the academic community for their authoritativeness, depth and clarity, they are used as standard textbooks in numerous college courses. His writings have been translated into eleven languages. The Bhaktivedanta Book Trust, established in 1972 exclusively to publish the works of His Divine Grace, has thus become the world's largest publisher of books in the field of Indian religion and philosophy. Its latest project is the publishing of Śrīla Prabhupāda's most recent work: a seventeen-volume translation and commentary—completed by Śrīla Prabhupāda in only eighteen months—on the Bengali religious classic *Śrī Caitanya-caritāmṛta*.

In the past ten years, in spite of his advanced age, Śrīla Prabhupāda has circled the globe twelve times on lecture tours that have taken him to six continents. In spite of such a vigorous schedule, Śrīla Prabhupāda continues to write prolifically. His writings constitute a veritable library of Vedic philosophy, religion, literature and culture.

References

The purports of *Śrīmad-Bhāgavatam* are all confirmed by standard Vedic authorities. The following authentic scriptures are specifically cited in this volume:

Bhagavad-gītā, 10–11, 27, 29, 42, 46, 49, 52, 55, 66, 68, 73, 89–90, 109, 110, 111, 112, 117, 117–118, 131, 134, 135, 139, 140, 142–143, 146, 149–150, 150–151, 151, 152, 153, 157, 158, 164, 165, 170, 172, 174, 180, 181–182, 184, 185, 187, 191, 193, 200–201, 208, 217, 220, 223, 228, 231, 233, 234, 235–236, 243–244, 248, 249–250, 250–251, 251, 255, 255–256, 258, 262, 265, 266, 268, 268–269, 270, 272–273, 275, 278, 281, 286, 288, 291

Bhakti-rasāmṛta-sindhu, 29–30, 108, 122, 150

Brahma-saṁhitā, 50, 72, 186, 266

Brahma-vaivarta Purāṇa, 171

Caitanya-bhāgavata, 180

Caitanya-caritāmṛta, 137, 190, 254

Gītāvalī, 91, 262

Hari-bhakti-vilāsa, 200

Kaṭha Upaniṣad, 242–243

Manu-saṁhitā, 37

Muṇḍaka Upaniṣad, 252

Padma Purāṇa, 189

Prema-bhakti-candrikā, 261

Smṛti-śāstras, 229–230

Śrīmad-Bhāgavatam, 16, 29, 34, 107, 136, 137–138, 145, 164, 177, 182, 188–189, 189–190, 199–200, 210–211, 213, 230–231, 250, 255, 266, 277

Śvetāśvatara Upaniṣad, 227

Upaniṣads, 150

Viṣṇu Purāṇa, 212

Yājñavalkya-smṛti, 29

Glossary

A

Ācārya—a spiritual master who teaches by example.

Ājagara-vṛtti—the life pattern of a python.

Antyajas—one of the seven mixed castes lower than *śūdra.*

Ārati—a ceremony for greeting the Lord with offerings of food, lamps, fans, flowers and incense.

Arcanā—the devotional process of Deity worship.

Artha—economic development.

Āśrama—the four spiritual orders of life: celibate student, householder, retired life and renounced life.

Aṣṭakā—the eighth day after the full moon.

Asuras—atheistic demons.

Avatāra—a descent of the Supreme Lord.

B

Bābājī—one who dwells alone in one place, performing severe austerities and penance.

Bahūdaka—the second stage of the *sannyāsa* order, in which one begs from door to door.

Bhagavad-gītā—the basic directions for spiritual life spoken by the Lord Himself.

Bhakta—a devotee.

Bhakti-yoga—linking with the Supreme Lord by devotional service.

Brahma-bandhu—one who has taken birth in a *brāhmaṇa* family but lacks brahminical qualifications.

Brahmacarya—celibate student life; the first order of Vedic spiritual life.

Brahma-jijñāsā—inquiry into the Absolute Truth.

Brahman—the Absolute Truth; especially the impersonal aspect of the Absolute.

Brāhmaṇa—one wise in the *Vedas,* who can guide society; the first Vedic social order.

C

Caṇḍāla—lowborn person accustomed to filthy habits such as dog-eating.

D

Daṇḍa—a staff carried by those in the renounced orders of life.

Daśa-vidhā-saṁskāra—ten Vedic rituals performed for the purification of children from the time of conception to early childhood.

Dharma—eternal occupational duty; religious principles.

E

Ekādaśī—a special fast day for increased remembrance of Kṛṣṇa, which comes on the eleventh day of both the waxing and waning moon.

G

Ghee—clarified butter.

Goloka (Kṛṣṇaloka)—the highest spiritual planet, containing Kṛṣṇa's personal abodes Dvārakā, Mathurā and Vṛndāvana.

Gopīs—Kṛṣṇa's cowherd girl friends; His most confidential servitors.

Gosvāmī—(*go*—senses; *svāmī*—controller), title of one in the *sannyāsa* order.

Gṛhastha—regulated householder life; the second order of Vedic spiritual life.

Guru—a spiritual master.

Guru-kula—the school of Vedic learning; boys begin at the age of five and live as celibate students, guided by a spiritual master.

H

Hare Kṛṣṇa mantra—*See: Mahā-mantra*

J

Jīva-tattva—the living entities, atomic parts of the Lord.

Jñāna-kāṇḍa—the *Upaniṣad* portion of the *Vedas* containing knowledge of Brahman, spirit.

K

Kali-yuga (Age of Kali)—the present age, which is characterized by quarrel. It is last in the cycle of four, and began five thousand years ago.

Kāma—lust.

Kamaṇḍalu—water pot carried by *sannyāsīs.*

Karatālas—hand cymbals used in *kīrtana.*

Karma—fruitive action, for which there is always reaction, good or bad.

Karma-kāṇḍa—section of the *Vedas* prescribing fruitive activities for elevation to a higher material position.

Karmī—a person satisfied with working hard for flickering sense gratification.

Kīrtana—chanting the glories of the Supreme Lord.

Kṛṣṇaloka—*See:* Goloka

Kṣatriyas—a warrior or administrator; the second Vedic social order.

Kuṭīcaka—the first stage of the *sannyāsa* order; the *kuṭīcaka* lives in a hut nearby his village and his family brings him food.

M

Mahā-mantra—the great chanting for deliverance:

Hare Kṛṣṇa, Hare Kṛṣṇa, Kṛṣṇa Kṛṣṇa, Hare Hare
Hare Rāma, Hare Rāma, Rāma Rāma, Hare Hare

Mahātmā—a self-realized soul.

Mantra—a sound vibration that can deliver the mind from illusion.

Maṭhas—monasteries.

Mathurā—Lord Kṛṣṇa's abode, surrounding Vṛndāvana, where He took birth and later returned to after performing His Vṛndāvana pastimes.

Māyā—(mā—not; *yā*—this), illusion; forgetfulness of one's relationship with Kṛṣṇa.

Māyāvādīs—impersonal philosophers who say that the Lord cannot have a transcendental body.

Mlecchas—meat-eaters.

Mokṣa—liberation into the spiritual effulgence surrounding the Lord.

Mṛdaṅga—a clay drum used for congregational chanting.

P

Pāñcarātrikī-vidhi—rules and regulations as found in the 108 Pañcarātra saṁhitās.

Paramahaṁsa—the highest stage of the *sannyāsa* order; a topmost devotee of the Lord.

Paramparā—the chain of spiritual masters in disciplic succession.

Parivrājakācārya—the third stage of the *sannyāsa* order; the *parivrājakācārya* constantly travels throughout the world, preaching the glories of the Lord.

Pradhāna—the total material energy in its unmanifest state.

Prāṇāyāma—control of the breathing process; performed in *aṣṭāṅga yoga.*

Prasāda—food spiritualized by being offered to the Lord.

Purāṇas—Vedic supplementary histories in relation to the Supreme Lord and His devotees.

S

Sac-cid-ānanda-vigraha—the Lord's transcendental form, which is eternal, full of knowledge and bliss.

Śālagrāma-śilā—the Supreme Lord in the form of a black stone, worshiped by *brāhmaṇas.*

Saṅkīrtana—public chanting of the names of God, the approved *yoga* process for this age.

Sannyāsa—renounced life; the fourth order of Vedic spiritual life.

Śāstras—revealed scriptures.

Smṛti—supplementary explanations of the *Vedas.*

Śrāddha—ceremony performed to release one's forefathers from hellish conditions of life.

Śravaṇaṁ kīrtanaṁ viṣṇoḥ—the devotional processes of hearing and chanting about Lord Viṣṇu.

Śruti—the original *Veda,* given to Brahmā by the Lord.

Śūdra—a laborer; the fourth of the Vedic social orders.

Svāmī—one who controls his mind and senses; title of one in the renounced order of life.

T

Tapasya—austerity; accepting some voluntary inconvenience for a higher purpose.

Tilaka—auspicious clay marks that sanctify a devotee's body as a temple of the Lord.

U

Upāsanā-kāṇḍa—section of the *Vedas* prescribing worship of demigods for fruitive results.

V

Vaikuṇṭha—the spiritual world, where there is no anxiety.

Vaiṣṇava—a devotee of Lord Viṣṇu, Kṛṣṇa.

Vaiśyas—farmers and merchants; the third Vedic social order.

Vānaprastha—one who has retired from family life; the third order of Vedic spiritual life.

Varṇa—the four occupational divisions of society: the intellectual class, the administrative class, the mercantile and agricultural class, and the laborer class.

Varṇa-saṅkara—children born of parents who did not follow Vedic rules for procreation or purification.

Varṇāśrama—the Vedic social system of four social and four spiritual orders.

Vedas—the original revealed scriptures, first spoken by the Lord Himself.

Viṣṇu, Lord—Kṛṣṇa's first expansion for the creation and maintenance of the material universes.

Viṣṇu-tattva—personal expansions of the Lord.

Vṛndāvana—Kṛṣṇa's personal abode, where He fully manifests His quality of sweetness.

Y

Yajña—sacrifice; work done for the satisfaction of Lord Viṣṇu.

Yavanas—lowborn persons who do not follow Vedic regulations.

Yogamāyā—internal spiritual potency of the Lord.

Yogī—a transcendentalist who, in one way or another, is striving for union with the Supreme.

Yugas—ages in the life of a universe, occurring in a repeated cycle of four.

Sanskrit Pronunciation Guide

Vowels

अ a आ ā इ i ई ī उ u ऊ ū ऋ ṛ ॠ ṝ
ऌ ḷ ए e ऐ ai ओ o औ au
ं ṁ *(anusvāra)* ः ḥ *(visarga)*

Consonants

Gutturals:	क ka	ख kha	ग ga	घ gha	ङ ṅa
Palatals:	च ca	छ cha	ज ja	झ jha	ञ ña
Cerebrals:	ट ṭa	ठ ṭha	ड ḍa	ढ ḍha	ण ṇa
Dentals:	त ta	थ tha	द da	ध dha	न na
Labials:	प pa	फ pha	ब ba	भ bha	म ma
Semivowels:	य ya	र ra	ल la	व va	
Sibilants:	श śa	ष ṣa	स sa		
Aspirate:	ह ha	ऽ ' *(avagraha)* – the apostrophe			

The vowels above should be pronounced as follows:

a – like the *a* in org*a*n or the *u* in b*u*t.
ā – like the *a* in f*a*r but held twice as long as short *a*.
i – like the *i* in p*i*n.
ī – like the *i* in p*i*que but held twice as long as short *i*.
u – like the *u* in p*u*sh.
ū – like the *u* in r*u*le but held twice as long as short *u*.

ṛ – like the *ri* in *ri*m.
ṝ – like *ree* in *ree*d.
ḷ – like *l* followed by *ṛ* (*lṛ*).
e – like the *e* in th*ey*.
ai – like the *ai* in *ai*sle.
o – like the *o* in g*o*.
au – like the *ow* in h*ow*.
ṁ (*anusvāra*) – a resonant nasal like the *n* in the French word *bon*.
ḥ (*visarga*) – a final *h*-sound: *aḥ* is pronounced like *aha; iḥ* like *ihi*.

The consonants are pronounced as follows:

k – as in *k*ite
kh – as in Ec*kh*art
g – as in *g*ive
gh – as in di*g-h*ard
ṅ – as in si*ng*
c – as in *ch*air
ch – as in staun*ch-h*eart
j – as in *j*oy
jh – as in he*dgeh*og
ñ – as in ca*ny*on
ṭ – as in *t*ub
ṭh – as in ligh*t-h*eart
ḍ – as in *d*ove
ḍha- as in re*d-h*ot
ṇ – as r*na* (prepare to say the *r* and say *na*).

Cerebrals are pronounced with tongue to roof of mouth, but the following dentals are pronounced with tongue against teeth:

t – as in *t*ub but with tongue against teeth.
th – as in ligh*t-h*eart but with tongue against teeth.
d – as in *d*ove but with tongue against teeth.
dh – as in re*d-h*ot but with tongue against teeth.
n – as in *n*ut but with tongue between teeth.

p – as in *p*ine
ph – as in u*ph*ill (not *f*)
b – as in *b*ird
bh – as in ru*b-h*ard
m – as in *m*other
y – as in *y*es
r – as in *r*un
l – as in *l*ight
v – as in *v*ine
ś (palatal) – as in the *s* in the German word *sprechen*
ṣ (cerebral) – as the *sh* in *sh*ine
s – as in *s*un
h – as in *h*ome

There is no strong accentuation of syllables in Sanskrit, only a flowing of short and long (twice as long as the short) syllables.

Index of Sanskrit Verses

This index constitutes a complete listing of the first and third lines of each of the Sanskrit poetry verses of this volume of *Śrīmad-Bhāgavatam*, arranged in English alphabetical order. The first column gives the Sanskrit transliteration, and the second and third columns, respectively, list the chapter-verse reference and page number for each verse.

A

ābādhito 'pi hy ābhāso 15.58 267
abhogino 'yaṁ tava vipra dehaḥ 13.18 101
ācaran dāsavan nīco 12.1 58
acaurāṇām apāpānām 11.30 51
ādāv ante janānāṁ sad 15.57 265

adharma-śākhāḥ pañcemā 15.12 209
adhikaṁ yo 'bhimanyeta 14.8 152
ādhyātmikādibhir duḥkhair 13.31 119
agnau gurāv ātmani ca 12.15 71
agniḥ sūryo divā prāhnaḥ 15.54 263

agni-pakvam athāmaṁ vā 12.18 75
agny-artham eva śaraṇam 12.20 76
ahaṁ ca gāyaṁs tad-vidvān 15.72 284
ahaṁ purābhavaṁ kaścid 15.69 280
ahiṁsā brahmacaryaṁ ca 11.8 30

āhuḥ śarīraṁ ratham indriyāṇi 15.41 242
akṣaṁ daśa-prāṇam adharma-dharmau 15.42 244
amantra-yajño hy asteyaṁ 11.24 45
anarthāya bhaveyuḥ sma 15.29 227
anīhaḥ parituṣṭātmā 13.37 127

anīhānīhamānasya 15.15 213
aniśaṁ tasya nirvāṇaṁ 15.34 234
añjanābhyañjanonmarda- 12.12 69
annādyādeḥ saṁvibhāgo 11.10 31
annaṁ reta iti kṣmeśa 15.51 257
annaṁ saṁvibhajan paśyet 15.6 203

ānvīkṣikyāṁ va vidyāyāṁ 12.27 78
ānvīkṣikyā śoka-mohau 15.22 219
apramattā śuciḥ snigdhā 11.28 48
apsu kṣitim apo jyotiṣy 12.30 82
apsu pracetasā jihvāṁ 12.28 80
apsv asṛk-śleṣma-pūyāni 12.25 79

apy ekām ātmano dārāṁ 14.11 157
arthānarthekṣayā lobhaṁ 15.22 219
arthibhyaḥ kālataḥ svasmān 13.33 123
asaṅkalpāj jayet kāmaṁ 15.23 220

asantuṣṭasya viprasya 15.19 216
āśramāpasadā hy ete 15.39 239
āstikyam udyamo nityaṁ 11.23 44
āśvāghānte 'vasāyibhyaḥ 14.11 157
atha deśān pravakṣyāmi 14,27 174

athānugṛhya bhagavān 10.57 9
athāsau śaktibhiḥ svābhiḥ 10.65 15
ātmanaḥ putravat paśyet 14.9 154
ātmajaṁ yoga-vīryeṇa 15.24 221
ātma-jāyā-sutādīnām 15.65 275

ātmānaṁ ca paraṁ brahma 13.4 88
ātmānaṁ ced vijānīyāt 15.40 240
ātmano 'nyasya vā diṣṭaṁ 10.64 14
ātmānubhūtau tāṁ māyāṁ 13.44 134
ātmany agnīn samāropya 12.24 78

ātma-saṁyamane 'nīhā 15.9 206
ātma-yājy upaśāntātmā 15.55 264
atrāpy udāharantīmam 13.11 96
aupasthya-jaihvya-kārpaṇyād 15.18 215
avākirañ jagur hṛṣṭā 10.68 17

āvartate pravṛttena 15.47 254
avastutvād vikalpasya 15.63 274
avyakta-liṅgo vyaktārtho 13.10 95
ayane viṣuve kuryād 14.20 168
ayanaṁ dakṣiṇaṁ somo 15.50 257

B

bhagavan śrotum icchāmi 11.2 23
bhaktyā kevalayājñānaṁ 13.22 104

bhāvādvaitaṁ kriyādvaitaṁ	15.62	273
bhavān prajāpateḥ sākṣād	11.3	25
bhayād alabdha-nidrāṇāṁ	13.32	120
bhoginām khalu deho 'yaṁ	13.17	100
bhojayet susamṛddho 'pi	15.3	201
bhuñje bhuktvātha kasmiṁś cid	13.38	129
bhuñjīta yady anujñāto	12.5	61
bhūtaiḥ sva-dhāmabhiḥ paśyed	12.15	71
bibharṣi kāyaṁ pīvānaṁ	13.16	100
bibhṛyād upavītaṁ ca	12.4	60
bibhṛyād yady asau vāsaḥ	13.2	87
bimbaṁ bhagavato yatra	14.28	174
brahmacārī guru-kule	12.1	58
brahmādibhiḥ stūyamānaḥ	10.69	18
brahmaṇyatā prasādaś ca	11.22	43

C

candrādityoparāge ca	14.20	168
caran vidita-vijñānaḥ	12.16	73
cared vane dvādaśābdān	12.22	77
catasṛṣv apy aṣṭakāsu	14.21	168
chandāṁsy adhīyīta guror	12.3	60
cittaṁ brahma-sukha-spṛṣṭaṁ	15.35	235

D

dadāha tena durbhedyā	10.67	16
dadarśa lokān vicaran	13.13	97
daive ca tad-abhāve syād	15.2	198
darśaś ca pūrṇamāsaś ca	15.48	256
dattvā varam anujñāto	12.14	70
dehādibhir daiva-tantrair	13.30	116
deśa-kālocita-śraddhā-	15.4	202
deśe kāle ca samprāpte	15.5	203
deśe śucau same rājan	15.31	230
deva-gurv-acyute bhaktis	11.23	44
deva-māyā-vimūḍhāṁs tān	15.39	239
devān ṛṣīn nṛ-bhūtāni	14.15	162
devarṣi-pitṛ-bhūtebhya	15.6	203
devarṣi-pitṛ-siddheśā	10.68	17
devarṣy-arhatsu vai satsu	14.35	182
devāsura-manuṣyādyā	15.80	293
deva-yānam idaṁ prāhur	15.55	264
devo 'suro naro 'nyo vā	10.64	14
dhanur hi tasya praṇavaṁ paṭhanti	15.42	245
dharma-bādho vidharmaḥ syāt	15.13	210
dharma-jñāna-virakty-ṛddhi-	10.65	15
dharmaṁ pāramahaṁsyaṁ vai	13.46	137
dharma-mūlaṁ hi bhagavān	11.7	28
dharmārtham api neheta	15.15	213
dharmas te gṛha-medhīyo	15.74	286
dharmo hy atrehitaḥ puṁsāṁ	14.33	178
dhātavo 'vayavitvāc ca	15.60	270
dikṣu śrotaṁ sanādena	12.27	80
divi dundubhayo nedur	10.68	17
divyaṁ bhaumaṁ cāntarīkṣaṁ	14.7	149
dravya-sūkṣma-vipākaś ca	15.50	257
dravya-yajñair yakṣyamāṇaṁ	15.10	207
dṛṣṭvā teṣāṁ mitho nṛṇām	14.39	188
duḥkhātyayaṁ cānīśasya	13.30	117
durghaṭatvād aindriyakaṁ	15.58	267
durlakṣyāpāya-saṁyogā	10.54	7
dvādaśyām anurādhā syāc	14.23	168
dvaitaṁ tāvan na viramet	12.10	65
dvau daive pitṛ-kārye trīn	15.3	201
dvāv ekaṁ vā yathā buddhir	12.22	77

E

ekadā deva-satre tu	15.71	283
eka eva cared bhikṣur	13.3	88
ekaikaśyenānupūrvam	15.51	257
eke karmamayān yajñān	15.9	206
eko vivikta-śaraṇo	15.30	229
eṣa mākaruṇo hanyād	15.10	207
eṣa vai bhagavān sākṣāt	15.27	224
eṣu snānaṁ japo homo	14.25	172
etad iṣṭaṁ pravṛttākhyaṁ	15.49	256
etair anyaiś ca vedoktair	15.67	278
etān deśān niṣeveta	14.33	178
etat sarvaṁ gṛhasthasya	12.11	67
etat sarvaṁ gurau bhaktyā	15.25	222
ete puṇyatamā deśā	14.33	178
eteṣāṁ śreya āśāse	13.42	132
evam abhyasyataś cittaṁ	15.34	234

evaṁ dagdhvā puras tisro 10.69 18
evaṁ kāmāśayaṁ cittaṁ 11.34 54
evaṁ vidhyāny asya hareḥ sva-māyayā 10.70 18
evaṁ vidho brahmacārī 12.16 73

G

grāmaika-rātra-vidhinā 13.1 86
gṛhaṁ vanaṁ vā praviśet 12.14 70
gṛhastha etāṁ padavīṁ 14.1 140
gṛhasthasya kriyā-tyāgo 15.38 239
gṛhastho yena padavīm 15.74 286

gṛhe 'py asya gatiṁ yāyād 15.67 278
gṛheṣv avasthito rājan 14.2 142
guru-strībhir yuvatibhiḥ 12.8 63
guru-vṛttir vikalpena 12.11 67

H

harir evaika urvīśa 14.34 181
hary ātmanā harer loke 11.29 50
hiṁsraṁ dravyamayaṁ kāmyam 15.48 256
hitvā sva-bhāva-jaṁ karma 11.32 53

I

īhoparamayor nṛṇāṁ 13.21 103
ijyādhyayana-dānāni 11.13 34
ijyeta haviṣā rājan 14.17 165
indriyāṇi manasy ūrmau 15.53 261
indriyāṇi pramāthīni 12.7 62

indriyeṣu kriyā-yajñān 15.52 260
iti dākṣāyaṇīnāṁ te 15.80 293
iti devarṣiṇā proktaṁ 15.78 291
ity akṣaratayātmānaṁ 12.31 83
ity etad ātmanaḥ svārthaṁ 13.28 114

J

jaghanyo nottamāṁ vṛttim 11.17 39
jāgrat-svāpau yathā svapne 15.61 271
jahyād yad-arthe svān prāṇān 14.12 159
jalaṁ tad-udbhavaiś channaṁ 13.29 115
janma-karmāvadātānāṁ 11.13 34
jano yāti na lobhasya 15.20 217
jīva-rāśibhir ākīrṇa 14.36 183

jñānaṁ dayācyutātmatvaṁ 11.21 42
jñānaṁ jñeyaṁ vaco vācyaṁ 15.57 265
jñāna-niṣṭhāya deyāni 15.2 198
jñānāsim acyuta-balo dadhad asta-śatruḥ 15.45 249
jñātayaḥ pitarau putrā 14.6 148
jñātvādvayo 'tha viramed 12.31 83
jñātvā viśva-sṛjas tan me 15.72 284

K

kālaṁ paraṁ pratīkṣeta 13.6 90
kalpas tv evaṁ parivrajya 13.1 86
kalpayitvātmanā yāvad 12.10 65
kāmādibhir anāviddhaṁ 15.35 235
kāmair uccāvaccaiḥ sādhvī 11.27 47

kamaṇḍalv-ajine daṇḍa- 12.21 76
kāmasyāntaṁ hi kṣut-tṛḍbhyāṁ 15.20 217
kāraṇeṣu nyaset samyak 12.24 78
karmaṇākṛtibhir vācā 13.14 98
karmāṇi kāryamāṇo 'haṁ 13.24 106

karmāṇi kurvatāṁ dṛṣṭvā 13.26 111
karma-niṣṭhā dvijāḥ kecit 15.1 197
karmāṇy adhyātmanā rudre 12.29 82
karuṇāḥ sādhavaḥ śāntās 11.4 25
kārya-kāraṇa-vastv-aikya 15.63 274

kasmin karmaṇi devasya 10.52 6
kaviḥ kalpo nipuṇa-dṛk 13.19 102
kavir mūkavad ātmānaṁ 13.10 96
keśa-prasādhanonmarda- 12.8 63
keśa-roma-nakha-śmaśru- 12.21 76

khe khāni vāyau niśvāsāṁs 12.25 79
kim icchan kasya vā hetor 15.40 240
kṛcchrāptaṁ madhuvad vittaṁ 13.36 127
kṛmi-viḍ-bhasma-niṣṭhāntaṁ 14.13 160
kṛpayā bhūtajaṁ duḥkhaṁ 15.24 221
kṛṣṇa-pārthāv upāmantrya 15.79 292

kṣaumaṁ dukūlam ajinaṁ 13.39 129
kṣity-ādīnām ihārthānāṁ 15.59 269
kurukṣetraṁ gaya-śiraḥ 14.30 178
kuryād apara-pakṣīyaṁ 14.19 167
kuryāt sarvātmanaiteṣu 14.24 171
kutas tat kāma-lobhena 15.16 214
kūṭasthe tac ca mahati 12.30 82

kvacic chaye dharopasthe 13.40 130
kvacid alpaṁ kvacid bhūri 13.38 128
kvacid bhūri guṇopetaṁ 13.38 128
kvacit prāsāda-paryaṅke 13.40 130
kvacit snāto 'nuliptāṅgaḥ 13.41 131
kva tadīya-ratir bhāryā 14.13 160

L

labdhe nave nave 'nnādye 12.19 75
lokānāṁ svastaye 'dhyāste 11.6 27
lokasya kurvataḥ karma 13.19 102

M

madhukāra-mahā-sarpau 13.35 126
māghe ca sita-saptamyāṁ 14.22 168
manaḥ-saṁsparśa-jān dṛṣṭvā 13.27 113
mano manorathaiś candre 12.29 82
mano vaikārike hutvā 13.43 133

mano-vāk-tanubhiḥ pārtha 15.64 274
māno 'vamāno 'sūyā ca 15.43 246
martyāsad-dhīḥ śrutaṁ tasya 15.26 223
martyasya kṛcchropanatair 13.31 119
maunena bhaktyopaśamena pūjitaḥ 10.50 4

maunena bhaktyopaśamena pūjitaḥ 15.77 290
māyināṁ paramācāryaṁ 10.53 7
mekhalājina-vāsāṁsi 12.4 60
mṛgatṛṣṇām upādhāvet 13.29 115

mṛgoṣṭra-khara-markākhu- 14.9 154
mṛtaṁ tu nitya-yācñā syāt 11.19 41
mṛtyau pāyuṁ visargaṁ ca 12.27 80
muny-annaiḥ syāt parā prītir 15.7 204

N

nābhinanded dhruvaṁ mṛtyum 12.6 90
na dadyād āmiṣaṁ śrāddhe 15.7 204
nāhaṁ ninde na ca staumi 13.42 132
na hy agni-mukhato yaṁ vai 14.17 165

naimiṣaṁ phālgunaṁ setuḥ 14.31 178
naitādṛśaḥ paro dharmo 15.8 205
na kalpate punaḥ sūtyai 11.33 54
na kṛṣṭa-pacyam aśnīyād 12.18 75

nāmnātīte mahā-kalpe 15.69 280
nanv agniḥ pramadā nāma 12.9 64
nanv asya brāhmaṇā rājan 14.42 192
nārāyaṇa-parā viprā 11.4 25
nārāyaṇāśramo nandā 14.32 178

nāsac-chāstreṣu sajjeta 12.7 91
na saṅghāto vikāro 'pi 15.59 269
na śiṣyān anubadnīta 13.8 93
na syur hy asaty avayaviny 15.60 271
na te śayānasya nirudyamasya 13.18 101

natvā bhagavate 'jāya 11.5 27
na vidanti janā yaṁ vai 13.14 98
na vyākhyām upayuñjīta 13.8 93
na yasya sākṣād bhava-padmajādibhī 10.50 4
na yasya sākṣād bhava-padmajādibhī 15.77 290

na yater āśramaḥ prāyo 13.9 94
nirjitā asurā devair 10.53 7
niṣekādi-śmaśānāntaiḥ 15.52 259
no cec chaye bahv-ahāni 13.37 128

nocet pramattam asad-indriya-vāji-sūtā 15.46 253
nṛṇām ayaṁ paro dharmaḥ 11.11 31
nṛṇāṁ viparyayehekṣā 11.9 31
nyāso daṇḍasya bhūteṣu 15.8 205

O

oṁkāraṁ bindau nāde taṁ 15.53 261

P

padāni gatyā vayasi 12.26 80
paṇḍitā bahavo rājan 15.21 217
paśyāmi dhanināṁ kleśaṁ 13.32 120
paśyan bandhaṁ ca mokṣaṁ ca 13.5 89

paśyed ātmany ado viśvaṁ 13.4 88
pātraṁ tv atra niruktaṁ vai 14.34 181
pitṛ-deva-nṛ-bhūtebhyo 14.25 172
prahrādasya ca saṁvādaṁ 13.11 96

prāṇāpānau sannirundhyāt 15.32 232
praviśya tripuraṁ kāle 10.62 13
pravṛttaṁ ca nivṛttaṁ ca 15.47 254
prāyaḥ sva-bhāva-vihito 11.31 52

preta-saṁsthā mṛtāhaś ca 14.26 173
priyaḥ suhṛd vaḥ khalu māṭuleya 10.49 3
priyaḥ suhṛd vaḥ khalu māṭuleya 15.76 288
pūjayām āsa suprītaḥ 15.78 291
pūjayitvā tataḥ prīta 13.46 137

punantaḥ pāda-rajasā 14.42 192
purāṇy anena sṛṣṭāni 14.37 185
purā rudrasya devasya 10.51 5
pūrtaṁ surālayārāma- 15.49 256
puruṣeṣv api rājendra 14.41 191

R

rāgo dveṣaś ca lobhaś ca 15.43 246
rajaḥ pramādaḥ kṣun-nidrā 15.44 246
rājan yad agra-pūjāyāṁ 14.35 182
rajas-tamaḥ-prakṛtayaḥ 15.44 246
rajas tamaś ca sattvena 15.25 222

rajas-valais tanū-deśair 13.12 97
rājataś cauratah śatroḥ 13.33 123
rājño vṛttiḥ prajā-goptur 11.14 36
rākayā cānumatyā ca 14.22 168
rathaṁ sūtaṁ dhvajaṁ vāhān 10.66 15

rathebhāśvaiś care kvāpi 13.41 131
ṛtāmṛtābhyāṁ jīveta 11.18 40
ṛtam uñchaśilaṁ proktam 11.19 41
ṛte rājanyam āpatsu 11.17 39
rūpāṇi cakṣuṣā rājan 12.28 80
rūpa-peśala-mādhurya- 15.70 281

S

sadā santuṣṭa-manasaḥ 15.17 215
sadasas patayo 'py eke 15.21 218
ṣaḍ-varga-saṁyamaikāntāḥ 15.28 226
sa eṣa bhagavān rājan 10.51 5
sa itthaṁ daitya-patinā 13.20 103
sambhāṣaṇīyo hi bhavān 13.23 105

saṁskāra-kālo jāyāyā 14.26 173
sammārjanopalepābhyāṁ 11.26 47
śamo damas tapaḥ śaucaṁ 11.21 42
saṁskārā yatrāvicchinnāḥ 11.13 34
samyag bhavanti naitāni 15.4 202
sandhye ubhe ca yata-vāg 12.2 59

sa nirmāya puras tisro 10.54 7
sannaddho ratham āsthāya 10.66 15
śāntasya sama-cittasya 13.9 94
santoṣaḥ samadṛk-sevā 11.9 31
santuṣṭaḥ kena vā rājan 15.18 215

santuṣṭālolupā dakṣā 11.28 48
santuṣṭasya nirīhasya 15.16 214
santuṣṭo 'har ahaḥ kuryān 15.11 208
śaraṁ dhanuṣi sandhāya 10.57 9
śaraṁ dhanuṣi sandhāya 10.67 16

sarāṁsi puṣkarādīni 14.30 178
śarkarā-kaṇṭakādibhyo 15.17 215
sarva-bhūta-suhṛc-chānto 13.3 88
sarva-vedamayo vipraḥ 11.20 41
sarve kulācalā rājan 14.32 178

śāstreṇa cakṣuṣā veda 15.56 265
sa teneheta kāryāṇi 15.66 276
sat-saṅgāc chanakaiḥ saṅgam 14.4 144
sattvena cittaṁ kṣetra-jñe 12.29 82
satyaṁ dayā tapaḥ śaucaṁ 11.8 30

satyānṛtaṁ ca vāṇijyaṁ 11.20 41
satyānṛtābhyām api vā 11.18 40
śauryaṁ vīryaṁ dhṛtis tejas 11.22 43
sa vā ayaṁ brahma mahad-vimṛgya- 10.49 3
sa vā ayaṁ brahma mahad-vimṛgya- 15.76 288

sa vai puṇyatamo deśaḥ 14.27 174
sāyaṁ prātar upāsīta 12.2 59
sāyaṁ prātaś cared bhaikṣyaṁ 12.5 61
śeṣe svatvaṁ tyajan prājñaḥ 14.14 161
śete jīvena rūpeṇa 14.37 185

sevejyāvanatir dāsyaṁ 11.12 31
siddhair yajñāvaśiṣṭārthaiḥ 14.14 161
siddhāmṛta-rasa-spṛṣṭā 10.60 11
smaranto nāśayāṁ cakruḥ 10.55 7
smayamānas tam abhyāha 13.20 103

smayan viśokaḥ śokārtān 10.63 13
smṛtaṁ ca tad-vidāṁ rājan 11.7 28
sodyamo bhogavān yathā 13.16 100
śoka-moha-bhaya-krodha- 13.34 124
śraddadhāno yathā-kālam 14.3 144
śrāddhaṁ pitror yathā-vittaṁ 14.19 167

śraddhayā vidhivat pātre	15.5	203
śraddhayopahṛtaṁ kvāpi	13.38	129
śravaṇaṁ kīrtanaṁ cāsya	11.11	31
sravantīndriya-laulyena	15.19	216
śrayeta hima-vāyv-agni-	12.20	76
srag-gandha-lepālaṁkārāṁs	12.12	69
śṛṇvan bhagavato 'bhīkṣṇam	14.3	144
śrutvā kṛṣṇaṁ paraṁ brahma	15.79	292
śrutvehitaṁ sādhu sabhā-sabhājitaṁ	11.1	22
sthiraṁ sukhaṁ samaṁ tasminn	15.31	230
strīṇāṁ ca pati-devānāṁ	11.25	46
strīṇāṁ priyatamo nityaṁ	15.70	282
śūdrasya dvija-śuśrūṣā	11.15	38
śūdrasya sannatiḥ śaucaṁ	11.24	45
sukham asyātmano rūpaṁ	13.27	112
supti-prabhodhayoḥ sandhāv	13.5	89
suśīlo mita-bhug dakṣaḥ	12.6	61
śuśrūṣayānuṣaṅgeṇa	15.73	285
sutām api raho jahyād	12.9	64
sutānāṁ sammato brahmaṁs	11.3	25
sva-bhāva-vihito dharmaḥ	15.14	211
svādhyāye 'nye pravacane	15.1	198
svargāpavargayor dvāraṁ	13.25	108
svātma-vṛttaṁ mayetthaṁ	13.45	135
sva-vṛttyāgata-vittena	14.15	162
svayaṁ ca maṇḍitā nityaṁ	11.26	47
syāt sādṛśya-bhramas tāvad	15.61	271

T

tābhis te 'sura-senānyo	10.55	7
tad-antā yadi no yogān	15.28	226
tadāyaṁ bhagavān viṣṇus	10.61	12
tad-bandhuṣv anuvṛttiś ca	11.25	46
tad vijñāya mahā-yogī	10.63	13
ta enam ātmasāt kṛtvā	15.37	237
ta ete śreyasaḥ kālā	14.24	171
taiḥ spṛṣṭā vyasavaḥ sarve	10.59	10
tais taiḥ kāmair yajasvainaṁ	14.18	166
taṁ natvābhyarcya vidhivat	13.15	99
taṁ śayānaṁ dharopasthe	13.12	97
tān ānīya mahā-yogī	10.59	10
tan-mūlatvād acyutejyā	14.36	183
tapasā vidyayā tuṣṭyā	14.41	191
tapasvino grāma-sevā	15.38	239
tasmād brāhmaṇa-deveṣu	14.18	166
tasmād daivopapannena	15.11	208
tasmāt pātraṁ hi puruṣo	14.38	186
tasyāṁ svatvaṁ striyāṁ jahyād	14.12	159
tathāpi brūmahe praśnāṁs	13.23	105
tatas tata upāhṛtya	15.33	232
tatas te seśvarā lokā	10.56	8
tato 'gni-varṇā iṣava	10.58	9
tato nirīho viramet	13.44	134
tato 'rcāyāṁ hariṁ kecit	14.40	190
tatrāpi dam-patīnāṁ ca	13.26	111
tat sarvam upayuñjāna	14.7	149
tāvad dāsyām ahaṁ jajñe	15.73	285
te dasyavaḥ sahaya-sūtam amuṁ tamo	15.46	253
te 'surā hy api paśyanto	10.63	13
tesv ātma-devatā-buddhiḥ	11.12	31
teṣv eva bhagavān rājaṁs	14.38	186
tisṛṣv ekādaśī vāsu	14.23	168
trāhi nas tāvakān deva	10.56	8
trayīṁ sāṅgopaniṣadaṁ	12.13	70
tretādiṣu harer arcā	14.39	188
triṁśal-lakṣaṇavān rājan	11.12	31
tri-vargaṁ nātikṛcchreṇa	14.10	155
tṛṣṇayā bhava-vāhinya	13.24	106
tṛtīyāyāṁ śukla-pakṣe	14.21	168
tyaktaṁ na liṅgād daṇḍāder	13.2	87

U

upadharmas tu pākhaṇḍo	15.13	210
upahūtā viśva-sṛgbhir	15.71	283
upakrame 'vasāne ca	12.3	60
upāsata upāstāpi	14.40	190
upyamānaṁ muhuḥ kṣetraṁ	11.33	54
uṣitvaivaṁ guru-kule	12.13	70
uttasthūr megha-dalanā	10.60	11

V

vācam agnau savaktavyām	12.16	80
vācaṁ varṇa-samāmnāye	15.53	261
vāda-vādāṁs tyajet tarkān	12.7	91
vairāgyaṁ paritoṣaṁ ca	13.35	126

vaiśyas tu vārtā-vṛttiḥ syān 11.15 38
vaitānikena vidhinā 14.16 163
vakṣye sanātanaṁ dharmaṁ 11.5 27
vākyaiḥ satyaiḥ priyaiḥ premṇā 11.27 47
vānaprasthasya vakṣyāmi 12.17 74

vanyaiś caru-puroḍāśān 12.19 75
vārāṇāsī madhu-purī 14.31 178
varjayet pramadā-gāthām 12.7 62
varjayet tāṁ sadā vipro 11.20 41
varṇāśramācāra-yutaṁ 11.2 23

vārtā vicitrā śālīna- 11.16 38
vartayan svānubhūtyeha 15.62 273
vartmāni mātrā dhiṣaṇāṁ ca sūtaṁ 15.41 242
vase 'nyad api samprāptaṁ 13.39 129
vāsudevārpaṇaṁ sākṣād 14.2 142

vatsaś cāsīt tadā brahmā 10.62 12
veda-dṛgbhiḥ smṛto rājan 11.31 52
vededam asura-śreṣṭha 13.21 103
vicitrām asati dvaite 13.28 114
vidharmaḥ para-dharmaś ca 15.12 209

vikalpaṁ juhuyāc cittau 13.43 133
vilokya bhagna-saṅkalpaṁ 10.61 12
vimuñcen mucyamāneṣu 14.4 144
viprasyādhyayanādīnī 11.14 36
vipra-vṛttiś caturdheyaṁ 11.16 38

virāgaḥ sarva-kāmebhyaḥ 13.36 127
virajyeta yathā rājann 11.34 54
virakto raktavat tatra 14.5 147
vīryāṇi gītāny ṛṣibhir jagad-guror 10.70 18
viśvo 'tha taijasaḥ prājñas 15.54 263

vittaṁ caivodyamavatāṁ 13.17 100
vivitsur idam aprākṣīn 13.15 99
vṛto 'mātyaiḥ katipayaiḥ 13.13 97
vṛttiḥ saṅkara-jātīnāṁ 11.30 51
vṛttyā sva-bhāva-kṛtayā 11.32 53
vyapetaṁ loka-śāstrābhyāṁ 13.45 136

Y

yadākalpaḥ sva-kriyāyāṁ 12.23 78
yad anyatrāpi dṛśyeta 11.35 55
yad brahmaṇi pare sākṣāt 15.64 274
yadi seveta tān bhikṣuḥ 15.36 236

yadṛcchayā lokam imaṁ 13.25 108
yad vadanti yad icchanti 14.6 148
yad yasya vāniṣiddhaṁ syād 15.66 276
ya ete pitṛ-devānām 15.56 264
yāhi tvaṁ śūdratām āśu 15.72 284

yaḥ pravrajya gṛhāt pūrvaṁ 15.36 236
yaiḥ sva-dehaḥ smṛto 'nātmā 15.37 237
yān āsthāya munir gacched 12.17 74
yan-mūlāḥ syur nṛṇāṁ jahyāt 13.34 124
yā patiṁ hari-bhāvena 11.29 49

yarhy ātmano 'dhikārādyāḥ 14.16 163
yaś citta-vijaye yattaḥ 15.30 229
yas tv icchayā kṛtaḥ pumbhir 15.14 211
yasya nārāyaṇo devo 13.22 104
yasya sākṣād bhagavati 15.26 223

yasya yal lakṣaṇaṁ proktaṁ 11.35 55
yathā copacitā kīrtiḥ 10.52 6
yathā-deśaṁ yathā-kālaṁ 14.10 155
yathā hi yūyaṁ nṛpa-deva dustyajād 15.68 279
yathā mayūkha-sandohā 10.58 9

yathā vārtādayo hy arthā 15.29 227
yato yato niḥsarati 15.33 232
yat-pāda-paṅkeruha-sevayā bhavān 15.68 279
yatra gaṅgādayo nadyaḥ 14.29 175
yatra ha brāhmaṇa-kulaṁ 14.28 174

yatra yatra harer arcā 14.29 175
yat svārtha-kāmayor aikyaṁ 15.65 275
yāvad-arthaṁ vyavaharet 12.6 61
yāvad-artham upāsīno 14.5 146
yāvad bhriyeta jaṭharaṁ 14.8 151

yāvād deva-ṛṣe brūhi 14.1 140
yāvan manas tyajet kāmān 15.32 232
yāvan nṛ-kāya-ratham ātma-vaśo- 15.45 248
yeṣāṁ gṛhān āvasatīti sākṣād 10.48 1

yeṣāṁ gṛhān āvasatīti sākṣād 15.75 287
yogāntarāyān maunena 15.23 220
yogeśvarair vimṛgyāṅghrir 15.27 224
yo 'vatīryātmano 'ṁśena 11.6 27

yudhiṣṭhiro daitya-pater mudānvitaḥ 11.1 23
yūyaṁ nṛ-loke bata bhūri-bhāgā 10.48 1
yūyaṁ nṛ-loke bata bhūri-bhāgā 15.75 287

General Index

Numerals in boldface type indicate references to translations of the verses of *Śrīmad-Bhāgavatam.*

A

Ābhāsa defined, **209, 211**
Ābrahma-bhuvanāl lokāḥ
 quoted, 259
Absolute Truth
 as all-pervading, **89,** 90
 education neglects, 71
 features of, three listed, 71, 231
 illusion vs. **89**
 impersonal vs. personal conception of, 3
 as inconceivable, 5
 Kṛṣṇa as, 3,19
 Māyāvādīs misconceive, 95
 for *paramahaṁsas,* 95
 preliminary realization of, **73–74**
 spiritual master embodies, 225
 Vedas reveal, 71, 72
 See also: Supreme Lord
Ācārya. See: Spiritual master
Ācāryaṁ māṁ vijānīyāt
 quoted, 224
Ācāryavān puruṣo veda
 quoted, 265
Acintya-bhedābheda philosophy, defined, 67
Activities
 of devotees, 176, 233
 fruitive. *See:* Fruitive activities
 fruitive vs. devotional, 172
 of Hare Kṛṣṇa movement, 145, 166, 180, 208
 of householders, **236**
 of Kṛṣṇa. *See:* Pastimes of Kṛṣṇa
 as Lord's potency, **15–16**
 pious and impious, 109, 118
 of saints, **5**
 sinful, 49, 145, 157
Activities
 spiritual vs. material, **113–**114
 transcending material, **53**
 in *Vedas,* two types listed, **255**
Activities, material
 brāhmaṇa renounces, **260**
 devotional service stops, 107
 four listed, 111–112
 freedom from, **235**
 futility of, **119**
 Māyāvādīs fall to, 113
 merged in Rudra, **83**
 as miserable, **119–**120
 saintly person renounced, **111, 113**
 spiritual activities vs., **113–**114
 wise man renounces, **135**
 See also: Fruitive activities
Advaita Gosvāmī, Haridāsa Ṭhākura favored by, 199, 200, 201
Advaita-jñānam ity etad
 verse quoted, 67
Age of Kali. *See:* Kali-yuga
Ahaituky apratihatā
 quoted, 172
 verse quoted, 29, 255
Ahaṁ brahmāsmi
 quoted, 146, 238
Ahaṁ sarvasya prabhavo
 verse quoted, 184
Ahaṁ tvāṁ sarva-pāpebhyo
 verse quoted, 262
Ahaṅkāra. See: Ego, false
Ahaṅkāra-vimūḍhātmā
 verse quoted, 110
Air(s)
 as bodily constituent, **79–80**
 in body, ten listed, **245**

Airplanes
Maya Dānava gifted demons with, **8**
Śiva vanquished demons', **17, 18**
Aiśvaryasya samagrasya
quoted, 105
Ājagara-vṛtti, defined, 97
Ajāmila, 211
Ajo 'pi sann avyayātmā
quoted, 27
Akāmaḥ sarva-kāmo vā
verse quoted, 107
Alms
brahmacārī begs, **61**
sannyāsī begs, **88**
Americans as devotees, 126, 200
Anādi karama-phale, padi 'bhavārṇava-jale,
quoted, 91
Anādir ādir govindaḥ
verse quoted, 266
Anāsaktasya viṣayān
verse quoted, 122
Anāśritaḥ karma-phalaṁ
verse quoted, 142–143
Aṇḍāntara-stha-paramāṇu-cayāntara-stham
quoted, 72
verse quoted, 186
Anger
lust causes, 217
renunciation of, **219**–220
"Anglican temple" in Vṛndāvana, 200
Animals
devotees respect, 154–155
evolution to and from, **108**–109, 147
fear slaughter, 207
as God's children, 154–155
human beings above, 33, 52–53, 112, 187
as low birth, 130
nature feeds, 151
people becoming, 112
prasāda to, 167
propensities of, four listed, 147
sense gratification for, 145, 156
as servants, 24
See also: Names of individual animals
Animal slaughter
as abominable, 207
Hare Kṛṣṇa movement forbids, 208
nature punishes, 222
in religion, 207
as "sacrifice," **205, 207**
in society, 155
Annād bhavanti bhūtāni
verse quoted, 150–151
Antavanta ime dehā
quoted, 161
Antyajas
Vedic study optional for, 71
See also: Society, human, mixed marriages in
Ānukūlyena kṛṣṇānu-
quoted, 114, 286
verse quoted, 108
Anulomaja
defined, 51–52
See also: Marriage
Anxiety of materialist, 121, **123**
Anyābhilāṣitā-śūnyaṁ
quoted, 199, 286
verse quoted, 108
Api cet sudurācāro
verse quoted, 200
Appearance of Kṛṣṇa in human society, **19**
Aprāpya māṁ nivartante
verse quoted, 243
Apraviṣṭaḥ sarva-gataḥ
verse quoted, 72
Apsarās
saṅkīrtana by, **283**
Śiva honored by, **17–18**
Ārādhanānāṁ sarveṣāṁ
quoted, 189
Arcanā. See: Deity worship of the Supreme Lord; Devotional service to the Supreme Lord, *arcanā* process in
Arcāyām eva haraye
verse quoted, 177, 189–190
Aries sign in *śrāddha* ceremony calculation, 170

Arjuna
Kṛṣṇa instructed, 4
as spiritual soldier, 114
Arrows of Śiva vanquished demons, **9, 10, 17**
Artha
defined, 156
See also: Economic development
Āruhya kṛcchreṇa paraṁ padaṁ tataḥ
quoted, 113, 236, 251–252
Asaṁśayaṁ samagraṁ māṁ
quoted, 268
verse quoted, 268, 291
Aśocyān anvaśocas tvaṁ
quoted, 4
Aśraddadhānāḥ puruṣā
verse quoted, 243
Āśramas
aim of all, 71, **73–74**
after *guru-kule,* **70,** 71
for spiritual life, 157
three most important, 141
types of, four listed, 24, **35,** 72, 125
See also: Names of individual āśramas (brahmacarya, gṛhastha, vānaprastha, sannyāsa)
Ass
ignorant person compared to, 74
Kali-yuga *gṛhastha* compared to, 145
Association of devotees. *See:* Devotees of the Supreme Lord, association of
Aśuddhāḥ śudra-kalpā hi
quoted, 282
Āśuddheḥ sampratikṣyo hi
quoted, 49
Asuras. See: Atheists; Demons, Nondevotees
Aśvinī-kumāras, **81**
Ataḥ pumbhir dvija-śreṣṭhāḥ
verse quoted, 277
Athāto brahma-jijñāsā
quoted, 147
Atheists
Deity worship opposed by, 176
See also: Demons; Māyāvādīs, Nondevotees
Ātma-mātā guroḥ patnī
verse quoted, 64
Ātmānaṁ rathinaṁ viddhi
quoted, 243
verse quoted, 242
Atom, Lord within, 72, 186
Attachment, material
to body renounced, 161, **162**
to money, **121**–122, 123
to wife renounced, **159, 160**–161
See also: Desires, material
Atyāhāraḥ prayāsaś ca
verse quoted, 125
Austerity
as brahminical symptom, 43
for human beings, 141
as Lord's potency, **15–16**
by Nārāyaṇa, 28
purpose of, 153
by *vānaprastha,* **76**
Authority (Authorities)
cited on temple construction, 218
mahājanas as, 16
paramparā as, 106
Prahlāda as, **137**
śāstra as, 173–174
on Vaiṣṇava philosophy, 16
Vedas as, 106, 109
Avaiṣṇavas. *See:* Atheists; Nondevotees
Avidyā. See: Ignorance
Avyakto 'kṣara ity uktas
verse quoted, 272
Āyur-vedic medicine, Maya Dānava's nectar as, 11

B

Back to Godhead magazine as author's livelihood, 126
Bad and good. *See:* Duality, material
Badarikāśrama
Nārāyaṇa at, 28
as sacred place, **179**
Bahūnāṁ janmanām ante
quoted, 293
Bahutvenaiva vastūnāṁ
verse quoted, 67

Balarāma, Lord, mercy of, as necessity, 252
Bee as spiritual master, **126**, 128
Begging
by *brahmacārī*, **61**, 62
by *sannyāsī*, **88**
Being, living. *See:* Living entities; Souls, conditioned
Bengal followed *Bhāgavata* science, until recently, 143
Bhagavad-gītā
See also: Bhagavad-gītā, cited; *Bhagavad-gītā*, quotations from
Bhāgavatam compared to, 26
as ever fresh, 145, 153
funds for preaching, 153
Hare Kṛṣṇa movement based on, 26
Kṛṣṇa known via, 19
Kṛṣṇa spoke, 26
rascals misinterpret, 211
via spiritual master, 225
value of hearing, 145
Bhagavad-gītā, cited
on Absolute Truth, 3
on demigod worshipers, 212
on Kṛṣṇa's identity, 19
on population pollution, 35
on soul vs. Supersoul, 135
on sun's path, 170
on technology, 157
Bhagavad-gītā, quotations from
on *ācārya's* value, 265
on birth and death, 220
on Brahmā's day, 281
on charity in goodness, 187
on conditioned souls under nature's laws, 110, 118
on demoniac mentality, 152
on devotees, fallen, 243–244
on devotees as pious, 255–256
on devotees as saintly, 200–201
on devotees as transcendental, 134, 223
on devotional service open to everyone, 278, 286
on elevation to higher planets, 109–110
on faith in Kṛṣṇa, 268
on food offered to Kṛṣṇa, 112
Bhagavad-gītā, quotations from
on heavenly planets, falling from, 258
on human society, 42, 55, 158
on knowing Kṛṣṇa's activities, 249–250
on Kṛṣṇa as Absolute Truth, 3
on Kṛṣṇa as birthless, 27
on Kṛṣṇa as origin of species, 150
on Kṛṣṇa as source of everything, 184
on Kṛṣṇa as *Vedas'* goal, 29
on Kṛṣṇa conscious religion, 208
on Lord as creation's resting place, 266
on Lord as enjoyer, 165
on Lord as enjoyer, proprietor, friend, 181–182
on Lord as within and without, 73, 89–90, 270
on Lord in heart, 117–118, 131, 185
on Lord known by devotional service, 291
on Lord supervising living entities, 117–118, 131
on material world vs. spiritual world, 272–273
on modes of nature as *Vedas'* subject, 248
on nature's subsistence plan, 150-151
on nature under Kṛṣṇa, 268-269
on nondevotees, 49, 255
on occupational duties, 52
on offering everything to Kṛṣṇa, 153, 275
on peace formula, 234–235
on population pollution, 46
on preacher, Kṛṣṇa conscious, 191, 193
on renunciation, true and false, 142–143
on sacrifice to Kṛṣṇa, 164, 165
on *śāstra* as authority, 174
on sex life, 68, 111–112
on species according to nature's modes, 110
on spiritual life as essential, 180
on spiritual vision, 66
on Supersoul as intelligence's source, 187
on surrender as salvation, 262
on transcendental happiness, 146, 235–236, 251
on transmigration according to nature's modes, 228
on worship, God vs. demigod, 172
on *yoga* practice place, 231

on *yogīs* in devotion as topmost, 10–11, 233
Bhagavān
defined, 95
paramahaṁsas realize, 95
See also: Supreme Lord
Bhāgavatam. See: Śrīmad-Bhāgavatam
Bhāgavata principle(s)
India followed, until recently, 143
on life's necessities, 158–159
in money matters, 124–126
Bhagavat-kathā
defined, 145
See also: Hearing about the Supreme Lord
Bhaktas. See: Devotees of the Supreme Lord
Bhakti
defined, 30
See also: Devotional service to the Supreme Lord; Kṛṣṇa consciousness
Bhakti-rasāmṛta-sindhu
quoted on pure devotional service, 108
quoted on renunciation, 122, 150
Bhaktisiddhānta Sarasvatī Ṭhākura
āśramas undertaken by, 71
fattiness disliked by, 100
temple construction by, 218
Bhakti-sūtra
author of, 26
purpose of, 26
Bhaktivinoda Ṭhākura
cited on Vaiṣṇava, 189
quoted on material existence, 91
quoted on mind in *mayā*, 262
Bhakti-yoga. See: Devotional service to the Supreme Lord; Kṛṣṇa consciousness
Bhaktyā mām abhijānāti
quoted, 291
verse quoted, 251
Bhogīs defined, 100
Bhoktāraṁ yajña-tapasāṁ
quoted, 165
verse quoted, 181–182, 234
Bhrāmayan sarva-bhūtāni
verse quoted, 118
Bhṛtyānāṁ svāmini tathā
verse quoted, 50
Bhūta-grāmaḥ sa evāyaṁ
verse quoted, 272
Bhūtvā bhūtvā pralīyate
quoted, 91
Bindu-sarovara as sacred place, **179**
Birds sitting in tree, soul and Supersoul in body compared to, 135
Birth
animal vs. king, 130
brāhmaṇa not judged by, 212
death follows, 221
devotees not judged by, 200, 201
freedom from, **264**
Birth and death. *See:* Transmigration of the soul
Bliss
devotee in, **249**
Lord as basis of, **3**
saints seek, **3**
transcendental, 236
See also: Happiness
Blood as bodily constituent, **79,** 80
Bodily concept of life
by conditioned souls, **115**
detachment from, **78–79**
as illusory, 66
living entity in, **245**
merged in Rudra, **83**
See also: Duality, material
Body, material
airs in, ten listed, **245**
chariot compared to, **242–243, 245, 253–254**
cleanliness for, **32,** 33
desire causes, **107, 117,** 118, 120, 131, 154
detachment from, **78–79, 249**
as doomed, **90–91**
elements of, **79–80,** 135
enjoyment according to, 186
as false, **271**
fate of, 161
human, as valuable, 250
living entity limited by, 187

Body, material *(continued)*
living standard according to, 130–131
as Lord's residence, **185, 186–187**
Lord supplies, 117–118, 130–131
as machine, 118, 131, 185–186
as misery, 154
via modes of nature, 110
nature's laws award, 120, 154
occupants of, two listed, 135
as perverted reflection, **66**
as punishment, 112
sannyāsī callous to, **87**
satisfaction for, **28**
sex life needed by, 156
sinful activities produce, 112
as soul's vehicle, 243
soul vs., **84,** 116, 135, 161
time controls, **90–91**
transcendentalist renounces, **78–80**
Bombay, people work like asses in, 145
Brahmā, Lord
as calf, **13**
day of, calculated, 281
dvijas approved by, 35
intelligence sacrificed to, **82**
Kṛṣṇa bewilders, **290**
as Nārada's father, **25, 285**
as Nārada's spiritual master, 26
Pāṇḍavas luckier than, 2, **4–5**
Prahlāda adored by, **23**
as *prajāpati,* **25**
Śiva above, 6
Śiva honored by, **18**
Supersoul above, 187
Brahma-bhūtaḥ prasannātmā
quoted, 238
verse quoted, 146, 235–236, 251
Brahmacārī(s)
brāhmaṇa as, 68
conduct for, **59, 60, 62–64, 69**
dress for, **60–61**
duties for, **59–64,** 157
incorrigible, condemned, **240**
pure parent as, 35
residence for, **59**
Brahmacārī(s)
spiritual master's relationship with, **59–62, 70**
women avoided by, **62, 63**
Brahmacārī guru-kule
quoted, 240
Brahmacarya (student life)
āśrama choices beyond, **70,** 71
defined, 63
sex life forbidden in, 141
in *varṇāśrama-dharma,* 24, **35**
Brahmādi-sthāvarānteṣu
verse quoted, 187
Brahman (impersonal Absolute), 71
as all-pervading, 74
brāhmaṇa knows, 192
Lord as basis of, **3**
merging with, 79, 113
Brahman, Supreme
devotees serve, 192
Māyāvādīs aspire to, 113
realization of, symptoms of, 146, 251
sacrifice for, **262**
See also: Supreme Lord
Brāhmaṇa(s) (intellectuals)
body of, as advanced, 102
as *brahmacārī,* 68
Brahman known by, 192
charity to, 156, 187, **199**
cited on occupational duties, **52**
as dear to Kṛṣṇa, **165, 193**
demigods represented by, 167
as desireless, 124
devotees above, 200
Europeans as, 40
gṛhasthas as, 156
guru-kula for, **70**
Hare Kṛṣṇa movement members as, 42
Hare Kṛṣṇa movement protested by, 40
Lord represented by, **192**
Lord worshiped via, 187
material activities renounced by, 260
Nārada as, **26**
occupational duties for, **35, 36–37, 39,** 40, **42,** 156, **167–168**

Brāhmaṇa(s) (intellectuals)
Prahlāda's saintly friend as, 101–102, 106, 112
prasāda to, 165, **166,** 167, **203,** 208
as preachers, **193**
professions forbidden to, 37
purification of, **260**
by qualification—not birth, **55–56**
as rare in Kali-yuga, 42
rituals performed by, **167–168**
Rūpa and Sanātana ostracized by, 37
as sacred places, **175**
sanctifying power of, **193**
as satisfied, 216
social status of, 187
at *śrāddha* ceremony, **201, 202**
symptoms of, **43, 175, 192**
as tax-exempt, 37
types of, **198**
Vaiṣṇavas above, 187, 192
in *vaiśya* role, **39**
in *varṇāśrama-dharma,* 24, **35**
Vedas studied by, **70,** 71
as worshipful, 192, **193**
Brahmāṇḍa bhramite kona bhāgyavān jīva
verse quoted, 248
Brahmaṇo hi pratiṣṭhāham
quoted, 3
Brahma-saṁhitā, quotations from
on goddesses of fortune worshiping Kṛṣṇa, 50
on Kṛṣṇa as cause of all causes, 266
on Lord as all-pervading, 72
on Lord as *puruṣāvatāra,* 186
Brahma-sampradāya, Hare Kṛṣṇa movement in, 26
Brahma satyaṁ jagan mithyā
quoted, 113
Brahma-vaivarta Purāṇa, quoted on *śrāddha* ceremony on Ekādaśī, 171
Bhrāmayan sarva-bhūtāni
verse quoted, 185
Brahmeti paramātmeti
quoted, 95
verse quoted, 230–231
Brahmins. *See: Brāhmaṇas*
Buddhiṁ tu sārathiṁ viddhi
verse quoted, 242
Buddhist as sectarian designation, 33
Butter pot and fire, man and woman compared to, **65**

C

Caitanya-bhāgavata, quoted on Kṛṣṇa consciousness worldwide, 180
Caitanya-caritāmṛta, quotations from
on Lord Caitanya and Lord Nityānanda, 254
on preachers authorized by Kṛṣṇa, 190
on spiritual master, 137
Caitanya Mahāprabhu
See also: Caitanya Mahāprabhu, quotations from
Hare Kṛṣṇa movement as mission of, 180
philosophy of, 67
as preacher's example, 189
with Rāmānanda Rāya, 147
saṅkīrtana started by, 189
worship of, 208
Caitanya Mahāprabhu, quotations from
on chanting Hare Kṛṣṇa, 231
on devotees as sinless, 49
on devotional service via *guru* and Kṛṣṇa, 248
on Kṛṣṇa consciousness worldwide, 180
on Kṛṣṇa via spiritual master, 250
on living entities as Lord's servants, 24
on Māyāvāda philosophy as dangerous, 204
on spiritual master, 137
Calcutta
Bhāgavata science followed in, until recently, 143
people work like asses in, 145
Calf and cow drank nectar well dry, **13, 14**
Cāṇakya Paṇḍita, quoted on family life, 46
Cancer sign in *śrāddha* ceremony calculation, 170
Caṇḍālas
defined, **158**

Caṇḍālas (continued)
money misused by, 158
Capitalists. *See:* Materialists
Capricorn sign, in *śrāddha* ceremony calculation, 170
Caste system. *See: Varṇāśrama-dharma*
Cātur-varṇyaṁ mayā sṛṣṭaṁ
quoted, 42, 55, 158
Catur-vidhā bhajante māṁ
quoted, 255–256
Celibacy. *See: Brahmacārī; Brahmacarya*
Chanting the Lord's holy names
by *gṛhasthas*, **287**
by intelligent person, 136
in ISKCON centers, 180
Kṛṣṇa consciousness by, 151
mind cleansed by, 33
as nonsectarian, 33
power of, **287**
prosperity by, 151
purification by, 145
rainfall by, 151
See also: Hare Kṛṣṇa *mantra; Saṅkīrtana*
Chariot, body compared to, **242–243**, **245**, **253–254**
Charity
auspicious conditions for, **173**
by *brāhmaṇas*, 36–37
to *brāhmaṇas*, **39**, 156, 187, **199**
to devotees, 199
dvijas give, **35**
in goodness, 187
kṣatriyas forbidden, **36**, 37, 40
to pure people, 37
to Vaiṣṇavas, 187
Children
animals compared to, **154**–155
garbhādhāna purifies, 35
prasāda to, 167
Christian as sectarian designation, 33
Christianity as anti—animal-slaughter, 207
Cities
in passion, 176
See also: Names of individual cities
Citrakūṭa as sacred place, **179**
Civilization, human
ignorance in modern, 110
peace for, 34
Vedic vs. modern, 124, 148
woman's association restricted in, 64
See also: Society, human
Cleanliness
as brahminical symptom, **43**
for human beings, **32**, 33
Clothing. *See:* Dress
Communism, spiritual vs. material, 155
Consciousness
bondage to material, **242**, 243, 244
illusory states of, **89**, **273**
See also: Kṛṣṇa consciousness
Cosmic manifestation. *See:* Material world; Universe
Cow
ignorant person compared to, 74
as mother, 64
protection of. *See:* Cow protection
Cowherd boys as pure devotees, 5
Cow protection
by *brāhmaṇas*, **39**
as *vaiśya's duty*, **38**, **39**, 156

D

Dadāmi buddhi-yogaṁ taṁ
verse quoted, 289
Daivī hy eṣā guṇamayī
quoted, 118
Dakṣa's daughter(s), **28**
universal population generated by, **293–294**
Dampatyoḥ kalaho nāsti
quoted, 46
Daṇḍa for *sannyāsī*, **87**, **94–95**
Daridra-doṣo guṇa-rāśi-nāśī
quoted, 218
Daridra-nārāyaṇa-sevā as word jugglery, 204
Darwin's evolution theory incomplete, 109
Dātavyam iti yad dānaṁ
verse quoted, 187

Death
birth follows, 221
desires frustrated by, 154
freedom from, **264**
life vs., **90–91**
materialist defeated by, **119**–120
Deerskin
for *brahmacārī*, **60**
for *vānaprastha*, **77**
Deity worship of the Supreme Lord (*arcanā*)
atheists oppose, 176
author started, 126
by *brāhmaṇas*, 36–37
chanting Hare Kṛṣṇa vs., 189
by devotees, 176, 177, 180
for Dvāpara-yuga, 164, 188–189
by *gṛhastha*, 208
in ISKCON centers, **179–180**
in Kali-yuga neglected, 189
as Lakṣmī-Nārāyaṇa, 208
as Lord Caitanya, 208
as Lord Jagannātha, 208
for neophytes essential, 190, **191**
prasāda in, 112, **203,** 208
preaching vs., 189, 191
as Rādhā-Kṛṣṇa, 177, **179–180,** 208
as sacrifice, 208
in *śālagrāma-śilā*, 177
by *sannyāsī*, 208
as Sītā-Rāma, 177, 208
society neglects, 175, 177
temple for, 177
Tretā-yuga began, **188,** 189
Vaiṣṇava worship vs., 192
Demigods
brāhmaṇas represent, 167
demons vs., **7–9**
Lord above, **14**
under modes of nature, **83**
prasāda to, **166**
senses and sense objects sacrificed to, **81**
Śiva best among, 6
Śiva honored by, **17–18**
Śiva's protection begged by, **9**
worship of, condemned, 212
Demigods
See also: Names of individual demigods
Demons
demigods vs., **7–9**
Lord above, **14**
Lord's illusory energy baffled, **14**
Maya Dānava as greatest among, **7**
Maya Dānava gifted, **8**
Maya Dānava revived, 11, **12**
mentality of, 152
money misused by, **152,** 153
mystic power misused by, 11
nectar well revived, 11, **12**
Prahlāda ruled, 137
Śiva vs., **9, 10, 16–18**
See also: Atheists; Nondevotees
Deśa defined, 181
Deśe kāle ca pātre ca
verse quoted, 187
Desire of saintly person, 133
Desires, material
body according to, **107,** 117, 118, 120, 131, 154
brāhmaṇas free of, 124
death frustrates, 154
freedom from, **53, 235**
renunciation of, **124, 219**
ritualistic ceremonies for, **257**
suffering caused by, **124**
surrender purifies, 107
See also: Attachment, material; Lust
Detachment. *See:* Renunciation
Devaloka. *See:* Heavenly planets
Devas. See: Demigods
Devotee(s) of the Supreme Lord
activities of, 176, 233
animals respected by, 154–155
Bhaktivinoda cited on, 189
birth irrelevant for judging, 200, 201
in bliss, **249**
above *brāhmaṇas*, 187, 192, 200
charity to, 199
Deity worship by, 176, 177, 180
enlightenment for, 105
fate of fallen, 244

Devotee(s) of the Supreme Lord *(continued)*
goodness accompanies, 34
happiness of, **214**, **215**, 216
as inscrutable, 99
above *jñānīs*, 200, 223
liberation surpassed by, 199, 200
Lord "conquered" by, **159–160**
Lord instructs, **104–105**
Lord protects, **5**, 16
Lord realized by, **290**–291
Lord satisfied by, 143
materialist vs., **214**
Māyāvādīs vs., 113
above nature's laws, 216
neophyte vs. advanced, 189, 190, **191**
nondevotees vs., 49, 105
as pious, 255–256
prasāda to, 166, 167, 200, **203**
public opinion disinterests, **136**
qualifications for, 30
as rare, 199–200
as sacred place, **175**
as *sādhu*, 201
as saintly, 200–201
as satisfied, 216, 218
as sinless, 49
Śiva as topmost, 16
spiritual vision of, 204
as Supreme Brahman's servants, 192
as tax-exempt, 37
temple for, 176
as topmost *yogīs*, 11, 233
as transcendental, 134
worship by, 182
as worshipful, 192, 193
yogīs vs., 223
See also: Pure devotees of the Supreme Lord; *names of individual devotees*
Devotees of the Supreme Lord, association of
hearing about Kṛṣṇa in, **144**, 145–146
value of, 143, 209
Devotional service to the Supreme Lord (*bhakti*)
activities spoiling, six listed, 125
arcanā process in, 208
via disciplic succession, 26
Devotional service to the Supreme Lord (*Bhakti*)
education used in, 164
everyone eligible for, 278, 286
fruitive activities vs., 172
via *guru* and Kṛṣṇa, 248
knowledge by, 105
as liberation, 26
Lord revealed by, 251, 291
material activities stopped by, 107
Nārada expert at, 26
Pāṇḍavas in, **279**
pure, 108, 146, 199
purifying power of, 107
as religion's goal, 29, 30
via religious principles, **24**
as *sanātana-dharma*, 24
as topmost *yoga*, 11
as unconditional, 255
wealth used in, 164
wife given up for, 159–160
for wise men, 184
Dharma
defined, 156
false, **210**, 211
See also: Religion; Religious principles; *Varṇāśrama-dharma*
Dharma Mahārāja, **28**
Dharmaṁ tu sākṣād bhagavat-praṇītam
quoted, 29, 211
Dharmāviruddho bhūteṣu
quoted, 68, 111
Dhenur dhātrī tathā pṛthvī
verse quoted, 64
Dhīra defined, 221
Dhīras tatra na muhyati
quoted, 221
Dhṛtarāṣṭra, 4
Dhyānāvasthita-tad-gatena manasā paśyanti yaṁ yoginaḥ
quoted, 135, 227, 231
Disciples. *See: Brahmacārīs:* Devotees of the Supreme Lord; *Dvijas*
Disciplic succession (*paramparā*)
as authority, 106
devotional service via, 26

Disciplic succession (*Paramparā*)
liberation via, 26
Nārada in, 26
Disease overtakes *vānaprastha*, **78**
Distress. *See:* Suffering
Dogs
householders maintain, **158**
prasāda to, 167
as untouchable, 158
Dream
as illusion, **271**
material life as, 146, 159
Dress
for *brahmacārī*, **60–61**
for Kṛṣṇa conscious preachers, **94–95**
of saintly person, **130**
for *sannyāsī*, **87**
for *vānaprastha*, **77**
Duality, material
conditioned souls afflicted by, **66**
as futile, 132–133
mind concocts, 132
renunciation of, **133**, 143
self-realization free of, 66
sex epitomizes, **66**
as unreal, **274**
See also: Bodily concept of life
Duryodhana, 4
Duty (duties)
for *brahmacārī*, **59–64**, 157
for *brāhmaṇas*, **35**, **36**–37, **39**, 40, **42**, 156, **167–168**
of *dvijas*, **35**
emergencies change, **39**–40, **41**
of householders, 142–174
of human being, 24, 172, **277**, **278**
for *kṣatriyas*, **35**, **42**, 156
perfection of, 277, 278
for *sannyāsī*, **87–96**, 157
for *śūdras*, **38**, 156–157
transcending material, 53
for *vaiśyas*, **35**, **38**, **39**, 156
for *vānaprastha*, **76–78**
varṇāśrama-dharma organizes, 24
for wife, **46**, **48**, 49, **50–51**
See also: Occupations
Dvādaśī defined, 171
Dvandvāhatasya gārhasthyaṁ
verse quoted, 229–230
Dvāpara-yuga, Deity worship for, 164, 188–189
Dvāpare paricaryāyāṁ
quoted, 189
verse quoted, 164, 188–189
Dvārakā as sacred place, **179**
Dvija-bandhu defined, 35
Dvijas
defined, **35**
duties of, **35**
Kali-yuga lacks, 71
mantra chanting by, 45
remunerate spiritual master, **70**
residence for, **70**
Vedas studied by, **70**, 71
See also: Brāhmaṇas; Kṣatriyas; Vaiśyas

E

Earth (element) as bodily constituent, **79–80**
Earth planet
life's necessities from, **149**
as mother, 64
spiritual emergency on, 40
Economic development
for *gṛhasthas*, 156
life wasted on, 153, 162
Education
devotional service uses, 164
for human beings, **32–33**, 74
as Lord's potency, **17–18**
māyā misuses, 164
technological, as incomplete, 71
for wife, **46**
Ego, false
merged in Rudra, **82–83**
under modes of nature, **82–83**
renunciation of, **133**, 134
Ekādaśī day, *śrāddha* ceremony forbidden on, 171
Eko bahūnāṁ yo vidadhāti kāmān
quoted, 162

Eko 'py asau racayituṁ jagad-aṇḍa-koṭiṁ
verse quoted, 186
Elements, material
in body, **78–80,** 135
merged in *pradhāna,* **83**
types of, five listed, **79,** 80, **269**
See also: Energy, material; Nature, material; *names of individual elements*
Energy, material
as illusory, 24
merged in *pradhāna,* **83**
See also: Elements, material; Nature, material
Energy of the Supreme Lord
demons baffled by, **14**
external, 110
illusory, conceals Kṛṣṇa, 19
Enjoyment, material
body for, 186
freedom from, 63
as imaginary, **113**–114
in sex life, **111**–112
See also: Desire, material; Happiness, material; Lust
Entity, individual. *See:* Living entity
Envy
real religion free of, **205, 208**
renunciation of, **219**–220
Etair upāyair yatate yas tu vidvāṁs
verse quoted, 252
Europeans
as *brāhmaṇas,* 40
as devotees, 126, 200
Evam-bhūto yatir yāti
verse quoted, 92
Evaṁ dvi-rūpo bhagavān
verse quoted, 72
Evaṁ trayī-dharmam anuprapannā
verse quoted, 258
Evolution
by fruitive activities, **108**–109
punishment by, 147
as transmigration cycle, 118–119
Vedic vs. Western concept of, **108**–109
See also: Transmigration of the soul

F

Faith
in Kṛṣṇa, 268
in spiritual master reveals knowledge, 227
False ego. *See:* Ego, false
Family life
Cāṇakya Paṇḍita quoted on, 46
detachment from, **144,** 146, **147, 159**
peace for, 46
relatives as rogues in, 123
renunciation of, **229,** 230
ritualistic ceremonies for, **173**
wife's duty in, **46, 48,** 49, **50**
See also: Gṛhastha-āśrama; Gṛhasthas; Marriage
Fasting
by *brahmacārī,* **61**
for human beings, **32,** 33
hunger and thirst conquered by, 219
by *vānaprastha,* 78
Fear
in animals for slaughter, **207**
materialist in, 109, **121, 123**
renunciation of, **219**
Fire
as bodily constituent, **79–80**
brahmacārī's meditation on, **59**
Lord within and without, **72**
woman compared to, **65**
Flower shower for Śiva, **17–18**
Food
for *brahmacārī,* **61**
as God's gift, 155, 162
for human beings, 112
in Kali-yuga scarce, 165, 204
nature provides, 151, 162
python eats available, **128**
saintly person eats available, **129**
sinful society lacks, 151
for *śrāddha* ceremony prescribed, **205**
surplus, as God's grace, 152
for *vānaprastha,* **75, 76**
in Vedic culture, 112
See also: Prasāda

Foodstuffs offered to the Supreme Lord. *See: Prasāda*
Forest
in goodness, 176
for monkeys, 176
for spiritual life, 176
Forgiveness as brahminical symptom, **43**
Form of the Supreme Lord, original, 2
Fruitive activities
body by, **107–108**
bondage to, 117–118
devotional service vs., 172
evolution by, 109
materialist controlled by, 117, 118
ritualistic ceremonies for, **173**
for sacrifice, 165
See also: Activities, material

G

Gambling
Hare Kṛṣṇa movement forbids, 94
as sinful, 49, 145
Gandharva(s)
Nārada as, **281, 282, 284,** 285
saṅkīrtana by, **283**
Ganges River as auspicious bathing place, **173**
Garbhādhāna ceremony
progeny purified by, **35**
spiritual master sanctions, 68
in *varṇāśrama-dharma,* **35**
Gauḍīya Maṭhas, 218
Gauḍodaye puṣpavantau
verse quoted, 254
Gaura-Nitāi, mercy of, 254
Gayā as sacred place, **179**
Gāyatrī *mantra* chanted by *brahmacārī,* **59**
Ghee
India lacks, 165
prasāda with, **203, 205,** 208
Ghee dousing fire, sin dousing desire compared to, **54**
Gītāvalī
quoted on material existence, 91
quoted on mind in *māyā,* 262
Goal of life. *See:* Life, goal of
God
fools pose as, 212
See also: Kṛṣṇa, Lord; Supreme Lord
God consciousness. *See:* Kṛṣṇa consciousness
Goddess(es) of Fortune
family graced by, 46
gopīs as, 50
Lord worshiped by, 50
money as, 122
as wife's ideal, 50
See also: Lakṣmī, Goddess
Godhead. *See:* Spiritual world; Supreme Lord
God realization
human life for, **241**
self-realization accompanies, 116, 135
symptoms of, 146
See also: Kṛṣṇa consciousness
"Gods." *See:* Demigods
Goloka Vṛndāvana. *See:* Vṛndāvana
Good and bad. *See:* Duality, material
Goodness, greed and poverty nullify, 218
Goodness, mode of
charity in, 187
eating in, conquers sleep, **221**
forest in, 176
Gopīs
as goddesses of fortune, 50
as pure devotees, 5
Gosvāmīs of Vṛndāvana, 218
See also: Names of individual *gosvāmīs*
Government
in Kali-yuga corrupt, 127
taxes levied by, 37
wealth restricted by, 152
Greed
as insatiable, **217**
renunciation of, **219**
spiritual life ruined by, 218
spiritual vs. material, 217, 218–219
Gṛhastha(s)
brāhmaṇas as, 156
chanting the Lord's holy names by, **287**
conduct for celibate, **69**
Deity worship by, 208

Gṛhastha(s) (continued)
incorrigible, condemned, **240**
money surplus for Kṛṣṇa by, 152–153
Prahlāda as, 137
sex restricted for, **68**
spiritual master governs, 141
in *varṇāśrama-dharma*, 24, **35**
Yudhiṣṭhira as, **141**
See also: Family life; Householders; Marriage
Gṛhastha-āśrama (household life)
brahmacārīs forego, **63**
Kṛṣṇa as center of, **142**–143
sannyāsa vs., 160, **236–237**
sex restricted in, 141
as voluntary, 71
See also: Family life; Householders; Marriage
Guṇas. See: Modes of material nature
Guru. See: Spiritual master, *all entries*
Guru-kṛṣṇa-prasāde pāya bhakti-latā-bīja
quoted, 250
verse quoted, 248
Guru-kula
as *brahmacārī's* residence, **59**
graduation from, **70**
purpose of, 71
for twiceborn, **70**

H

Happiness
conditioned souls pursue, **116, 117,** 118
of devotee, **214, 215,** 216
goodness essential for, 33
for marriage, 49
materialist lacks, **214**
for society, 29, 47
as soul's nature, 115, **116**
by spiritual activity, 146
spiritual vs. material, **113**–114
by *varṇāśrama-dharma*, 47
See also: Bliss
Happiness, material
futility of, **119**–120
in heavenly planets, 109
Happiness, material
as illusory, 115
See also: Enjoyment, material
Harāv abhaktasya kuto mahad-guṇā
verse quoted, 34
Hardwar as holy place, 177
Hare Kṛṣṇa *mantra*
Deity worship vs. chanting, 189
ISKCON centers enhance chanting, 180
for Kali-yuga, 189
prosperity by chanting, 151
relieves suffering, 222
ritualistic injunctions don't apply to, 231
as topmost sacrifice, 166
See also: Chanting the Lord's holy names
Hare Kṛṣṇa movement. *See:* Kṛṣṇa consciousness movement
Harer nāma harer nāma
verse quoted, 263
Hari-bhakti-vilāsa, quoted, on pure devotees, 200
Haridāsa Ṭhākura
Advaita Gosvāmī favored, 119, 200, 201
as Mohammedan, 199
Harir asmin sthita iti
verse quoted, 50
Hearing about the Supreme Lord
in devotee's association, **144,** 145, 145–146
enlightenment by, 145
by *gṛhastha,* **144**–145, 145–146
Hare Kṛṣṇa movement for, 145, 146
liberation by, 145–146
purifying power of, **19,** 145
sin dispelled by, 145
Vedic culture as, 145
Heavenly planets
elevation to, **108,** 109–110
falling from, **258**–259
happiness in, 109
by *karma-kāṇḍa,* 206
Maya Dānava's demons attacked, **9**
by pious activities, 118
sacrifices for, discouraged, 258–259
Hell, *śrāddha* ceremony abusers bound for, 171

Hetunānena kaunteya
verse quoted, 268–269
Hindu as sectarian designation, 33
Hippies as *varṇa-saṅkara,* 46
Holy name of the Lord. *See:* Chanting the Lord's holy names; Hare Kṛṣṇa *mantra;* Supreme Lord, *appropriate entries*
Holy places. *See:* Sacred places
Honey, money compared to, **127,** 128
Householders
activities of, 236
conduct for, **148–149**
dogs maintained by, **158**
duties for, 142–174
Hare Kṛṣṇa movement benefits, 144–146
hearing about Kṛṣṇa by, **144,** 145–146
in ignorance, 141, 144
in Kali-yuga asslike, 145
laws of God upheld by, 151
sacrifices by, **163–164**
śālagrāma-śilā worship by, 177
sinful activities by, 157
work of, offered to Kṛṣṇa, **142**
worship by, **163–164**
See also: Family life; *Gṛhastha; Gṛhastha-āśrama;* Marriage
Human beings
animalistic, 64, 65, 74
above animals, 33, 52–53, 112, 187
austerity for, 141
cleanliness for, **32,** 33
duty of, 172
evolution to and from, **108–**110, 147
fasting for, **32,** 33
fat, as sense indulgers, **100–**101
food for, 112
heaven awaits pious, 109
Kṛṣṇa consciousness for, 112
Kṛṣṇa played part of, **1, 19**
Lord above, **14**
low-class, misuse money, 158
nature feeds, 151
principles for, listed, **32–33**
sense gratification minimized for, 156
as servants, 24
sex indulgence degrades, 111, 112
Human beings
varṇāśrama-dharma for, 35
See also: Life, human; Souls, conditioned
Human life. *See:* Life, human
Human society. *See:* Society, human
Husbands. *See:* Family life; *Gṛhastha(s); Gṛhastha-āśrama;* Householders; Marriage

I

Idam adya mayā labdham
verse quoted, 152
Idam astīdam api me
verse quoted, 152
Ignorance
conditioned souls in, 116
gṛhastha in, 141, 144
Hare Kṛṣṇa movement dispels, 116
Lord dispels, **104–105**
materialist in, 117
modern civilization in, 110
nondevotees in, 255
unconsciousness as, 89
See also: Illusion
Ignorance, mode of
places in, 176
symptoms of, 247
Illusion
demons baffled by Lord's, **14**
dreaming as, **271**
karmīs in, 133–134
knowledge conquers, **220**
material happiness as, 115
materialist in, 121
material life as, 135
truth vs., **89–90**
types of, two listed, 89
See also: Ignorance; *Māyā*
Imaṁ vivasvate yogaṁ
quoted, 184
Impersonalists. *See:* Māyāvādīs
India
ācāryas in, built temples, 218
Bhāgavata science followed in, until recently, 143

India *(continued)*
ceremonies celebrated in, three listed, 202
ghee lacking in, 165
holy places in, 177
prasāda to devotees from, 200
spiritual life advanced in, 177
temples in, 153
Indra, King, manual prowess sacrificed to, **81**
Indriyāṇi hayān āhur
verse quoted, 243
Intelligence
demigod worshipers lack, 212
duality bewilders, **66**
sacrificed to Brahmā, **82**
Supersoul supplies, **186–187**
surrender requires, 209
International Society for Krishna Consciousness. *See:* Kṛṣṇa consciousness movement
Intoxication
Hare Kṛṣṇa movement prohibits, 94
by lower classes, 52
as sinful, 49, 145
Irreligion, types of, five listed, **209**
Īśāvāsyam idaṁ sarvam
quoted, 150
ISKCON. *See:* Kṛṣṇa consciousness movement
Īśvaraḥ paramaḥ kṛṣṇaḥ
verse quoted, 266
Īśvaraḥ sarva-bhūtānāṁ
quoted, 105, 187
verse quoted, 118, 131, 185
Iti matvā bhajante māṁ
verse quoted, 184

J

Jagannātha, Lord, worship of, 208
Jagannātha Purī as holy place, 177
Jaghanya-guṇa-vṛtti-sthā
quoted, 228
verse quoted, 228
Jana-saṅgaś ca laulyaṁ ca
verse quoted, 125
Janma karma ca me divyam
verse quoted, 249–250
Jātasya hi dhruvo mṛtyur
quoted, 220
Jesus Christ, Lord, Jews' animal "sacrificing" rejected by, 207
Jews, Christ rejected animal "sacrificing" by, 207
Jīva
defined, 186
See also: Living entities; Soul; Souls, conditioned
Jīva Gosvāmī
cited on *saṅkīrtana* and Vedic rituals, 174
cited on *śrāddha* ceremony, 171
Jīva kṛṣṇa-dāsa, ei viśvāsa
quoted, 262
Jīvera 'svarūpa' haya—kṛṣṇera 'nitya-dāsa'
quoted, 24
Jñāna. See: Knowledge
Jñāna-kāṇḍa
devotees reject, 199
life ruined by, 261
Jñānīs
devotees above, 200, 223
perceptive power, 133–134
status of, 133–134
See also: Māyāvādīs
Jñātvā śāstra-vidhānoktam
quoted, 174

K

Kāla defined, 181
Kalau nāsty eva nāsty eva
verse quoted, 263
Kalau śūdra-sambhavāḥ
quoted, 42
Kali-yuga (Age of Kali)
Deity worship neglected in, 189
food scarce in, 165, 204
government corrupt in, 127
gṛhasthas asslike in, 145
Hare Kṛṣṇa *mantra* for, 189
population degraded in, 42, 64, 71
saṅkīrtana for, 164, 166, 174
sannyāsa cautioned in, 125
varṇāśrama-dharma lost in, 42

Kāma
defined, 156
See also: Desires, material; Lust; Sense gratification
Kāma eṣa krodha eṣa
quoted, 217
Kamaṇḍalu for *sannyāsī*, **87, 95**
Kaniṣṭha-adhikārīs defined, 176–177, 190
Kāraṇaṁ guṇa-saṅgo 'sya
quoted, 110
Karma-kāṇḍa
devotees reject, 199
for heavenly elevation, 206
life ruined by, 261
Karma-kāṇḍa, jñāna-kāṇḍa, kevala viṣera bhāṇḍa
verse quoted, 261
Karma-yajña
defined, 206
See also: Activities, material
Karmīs (fruitive workers). *See:* Materialists
Kasmād bhajanti kavayo dhana-durma-dāndhān
quoted, 213
Kaśyapa, Pāṇḍavas luckier than, 2
Kaṭha Upaniṣad, quoted on body as soul's vehicle, 242–243
Kaunteya pratijānīhi
quoted, 16
Kāverī River, Prahlāda and saint at, **98,** 99
Kibā vipra, kibā nyāsī, śūdra kene naya
verse quoted, 137
Killing of animals. *See:* Animal slaughter
King(s)
as high birth, 130
protection by, 37
revenue for, 37
See also: Kṣatriyas
Kīrtana. See: Chanting the Lord's holy names; Hare Kṛṣṇa *mantra; Saṅkīrtana*
Kīrtanīyaḥ sadā hariḥ
quoted, 174
Knowledge
authoritative vs. concocted, 106
as brahminical symptom, 43
by devotional service, 105
Knowledge
by faith in spiritual master, 227
illusion conquered by, **220**
lamentation conquered by, **220**–221
liberation by, 109
as Lord's potency, **15,** 105
renunciation for, **87**
for self-realization, 80
via spiritual master, **249,** 265
Krishna. *See:* Kṛṣṇa, Lord; Supreme Lord
Krishna consciousness. *See:* Kṛṣṇa consciousness
Kṛṣṇa, Lord
as Absolute Truth, 3, 19
Arjuna instructed by, 4
as God, 14, 19, **293**
gopīs worship, 50
with Pāṇḍavas, **1,** 2, 3–4, **288**
See also: Supreme Lord
Kṛṣṇa consciousness
advancement in, 43
by chanting Hare Kṛṣṇa, 151
economic benefits of, 151
greed helps or hinders, 217
human life for, 112, 133, 162, 213, 214
of intelligent people, 136
marriage in, **48,** 49, **50**–51
as necessary, 180
as real religion, 208–211
self-sufficiency of, 213–214
service attitude culminates in, 51
Kṛṣṇa conscious movement
activities of, 145, 166, 180, 208
animal slaughter forbidden in, 208
"*brāhmaṇas*" protest, 40
in Brahma-sampradāya, 26
education used by, 164
eligibility for, 94
for *gṛhasthas,* 144–146
gṛhasthas donate to, 153
for hearing about Kṛṣṇa, 144–146
ignorance dispelled by, 116
Kṛṣṇa provides for, 16, 121, 213–214
as Lord Caitanya's mission, 180
managers of, advised, 125–126
members of, status of, 42

Kṛṣṇa conscious movement *(continued)*
- money surplus meant for, 152–153
- money used by, 121–122, 125–126, 164
- peace via, 42
- people should join, 164, 166
- preachers of. *See:* Preachers, Kṛṣṇa conscious
- purpose of, 19, 24, 55, 95, 110
- regulative principles of, 94
- as *saṅkīrtana,* 164
- *sannyāsīs* in, 95
- scriptural basis of, 26, 40
- society benefits by, 110, 153, 180
- spiritual life advanced by, 175, 177, 180
- temples in, 93–94, 175, **179–180**
- *varṇāśrama-dharma* propagated by, 42, 157
- world prosperity via, 151

Kṛṣṇa Dvaipāyana Vyāsa. *See:* Vyāsadeva

Kṛṣṇas tu bhagavān svayam
- quoted, 19

Kṛte yad dhyāyato viṣṇuṁ
- verse quoted, 164, 188–189

Kṣatriya(s)
- animal food forbidden to, in *śrāddha* ceremony, **205**
- charity forbidden to, **36,** 37, 40
- duties of, **35, 42,** 156
- *guru-kula* for, **70**
- in marriage, 68
- opulence required by, 124
- as rare in Kali-yuga, 42
- revenue for, **36**
- symptoms of, **44**
- in *varṇāśrama-dharma,* 24, **35**
- *Vedas* studied by, **70,** 71
- *See also:* Kings

Kṣīṇe puṇye martya-lokaṁ viśanti
- quoted, 259

Kṣipraṁ bhavati dharmātmā
- quoted, 256

Kṣīrodakaśāyī Viṣṇu, as *puruṣāvatāra,* 186

Kurukṣetra as sacred place, **179**

Kuśa grass, *brahmacārīs* carry, **60**

Kutas tvā kaśmalam idaṁ
- quoted, 4

L

Lakṣayitvā gṛhī spaṣṭaṁ
- verse quoted, 229–230

Lakṣmī, Goddess
- money as, 122
- as Nārāyaṇa's companion, 122
- *See also:* Goddess(es) of fortune

Lakṣmī-Nārāyaṇa worship, 208

Lakṣmī-sahasra-śata-sambhrama-sevyamānam
- quoted, 50

Lamentation conquered by knowledge, **220**–221

Law, true and false, 211

Law(s) of nature
- body awarded by, 120, 154
- devotees above, 216
- ignorance of, 110
- Kṛṣṇa controls, 110
- living entities under, 110
- materialist under, **117,** 118
- punishment by, 147, 153, 154
- transmigration as, 108–110
- *See also:* Nature, material

Laws of the Supreme Lord
- householders uphold, 151
- as religion's basis, 29

Liberation
- devotees surpass, 199–200
- devotional service as, 26
- via disciplic succession, 26
- for forefathers, **199**
- by hearing about Kṛṣṇa, 145–146
- human life for, 145
- by knowledge, 109
- from material life, 146
- from *māyā,* 145–146
- via Nārada, 26
- by spiritual activity, 113–114
- *See also: Jñānīs,* Māyāvādīs

Libra sign in *śrāddha* ceremony calculation, 170

Life
- *āśramas* spanning, 124–125
- death vs., **90–91**

Life
goal of, **24,** 110, 206, 212, **276,** 278
material. *See:* Life, material
materialists waste, 146
necessities of, **149**
perfection of, in Vedic culture, 125
purpose of, 123, 143
real and unreal, **89**
species of. *See:* Species of life
spiritual vs. material, 113–114
Life, human
choices in, 109
conduct for, 147–148
duty of, 172, **277, 278**
economic development wastes, 153, 162
education for, 74
evolution to and from, **108**–110, 118–119
for God realization, **241**
karma and *jñāna* ruin, 261
for Kṛṣṇa consciousness, 213, 214, 249–250
for liberation, 145
principles of, four listed, 156
purpose of, 107
for self-realization, **241**
sense gratification spoils, 145, 147, **241**
success for, 19
value of, 250
See also: Human beings
Life, material
activities of, four listed, 111–112
bondage to, 159, **253–254**
defined, **108,** 109
as dream, 146, 159
as fearful, 109, 112
freedom from, 146, 199
as illusion, **135**
problems of, four listed, 115, 148
renunciation of, **83–84**
as sinful, 112
spiritual life vs., 113–114
as struggle, **107**
as suffering, 109, **119**–120, **255**
See also: Material world
Literature
distribution of transcendental, 189
Literature
Hare Kṛṣṇa movement spread by, 121
transcendental, as ever fresh, 153
transcendentalist rejects material, **92**
Living entity (living entities)
in bodily concept of life, **245**
body limits, 187
as Brahman, **84**
as dependent, 110
duty of, 24
elevation to transcendence by, **263–264**
Lord above, 15, 131, 135, 192
Lord feeds, 162
as Lord's parts and parcels, 115, 150, 185–186, 204
as Lord's servants, 24
Lord "vs.," 246
Lord within and without, 72
in material world, 107, 108–110
māyā above, 131
nature above, 108, 100, 147, 151
as servants, 24
sex life desired by, 111
as spirit souls, 66, **83–84**
on sun, 184
Supersoul supervises, 117–118, **185–186**
under time, **90**–91
transmigration of, 107
universe pervaded by, 184
See also: Soul; Souls, conditioned
Logic, mundane, transcendentalist avoids, 92
Lord Caitanya. *See:* Caitanya Mahāprabhu
Lotus feet of the Supreme Lord
saints worship, **225**
sannyāsī seeks, 93
as shelter, 176
surrender at, 105
Lust
anger from, 217
renunciation of, **219**
See also: Desires, material; Sex life

M

Mad-gatenāntarātmanā
quoted, 11

Mādhavendra Purī, renunciation by, 213
Madhvācārya, quotations from
 on God consciousness, 50–51
 on Lord as background of everything, 269
 on Lord as within and without, 72–73
 on *sannyāsīs'* duty, 93
 on Soul of all souls, 187–188
 on unity in diversity, 67
Mahājana(s)
 defined, 16
 Lord protects, 16
 Śiva as, 16
 See also: Pure devotees of the Supreme Lord
Mahā-mantra. See: Chanting the Lord's holy names; Hare Kṛṣṇa *mantra*
Mahārāja Nanda as pure devotee, 5
Mahārāja Yudhiṣṭhira. *See:* Yudhiṣṭhira, Mahārāja
Maharloka, *vānaprastha* promoted to, **74**
Mahātmā, qualifications for, **161–162**
Mahat-sevāṁ dvāram āhur vimukteḥ quoted, 243
Mahendra Hills as sacred place, **179**
Malaya Hills as sacred place, **179**
Mām ca yo 'vyabhicāreṇa verse quoted, 134
Māṁ eva ye prapadyante quoted, 110
Māṁ hi pārtha vyapāśritya verse quoted, 278, 286
Man. *See:* Human beings
Mandāḥ sumanda-matayaḥ quoted, 282
Man-manā bhava mad-bhakto quoted, 233
Mantra(s)
 dvijas chant, 45
 at *garbhādhāna* ceremony, **35**
 Gāyatrī, **59**
 praṇava, **245,** 246
 at procreation, 35
 See also: Chanting the Lord's holy names; Hare Kṛṣṇa *mantra*
Manu-saṁhitā, quoted on *brāhmaṇa's* duties, 37
Marīci, Pāṇḍavas luckier than, 2
Marriage
 brahmacārīs reject, 63
 happiness for, 49
 husband's duty in, 49, 50
 husband vs. wife in, 49
 Kṛṣṇa conscious, **48,** 49, **50–51**
 kṣatriya in, 68
 mixed, among classes, 51–52
 as sense gratification, 156
 sex indulgence ruins, 111
 spiritual destiny for, **50**
 Vedic vs. modern, 111–112
 wife's duty in, **46, 48,** 49, **50,** 51
 See also: Family life; *Gṛhastha(s); Gṛhastha-āśrama;* Householders
Materialism. *See:* Bodily concept of life; Life, material, Material world
Materialists
 activities of, as self-defeating, **117–118**
 as animallike, 145
 death defeats, **119–**120
 devotee vs., **214**
 as fat, **100–**101
 in fear, **121, 123**
 goodness absent in, 34
 happiness absent in, **214**
 in ignorance, 117
 in illusion, 121, 133
 life wasted by, 146
 as moneygrubbers, **121,** 123, 153
 nature controls, **117–**118
 senses victimize, **121**
 sleep evades, **121**
 suffering of, **121, 123**
 "*yogīs*" cater to, 11
 See also: Atheists; Demons; Nondevotees
Material life. *See:* Life, material; Material world
Material nature. *See:* Nature, material
Material nature, modes of. *See:* Modes of material nature
Material world
 bondage to, 63
 detachment from, 273
 elements in, five listed, **269**

Material world
  fattiness as "success" in, 100–101
  happiness for, 47
  living entity, **107**, 108–110
  Māyāvādīs deny, 150, 267–268
  peace for, 47
  spiritual world vs., 272–273
  time controls, 91
  varṇa-saṅkara ruins, 35–36
Maṭhas
  defined, 126
  Gauḍīya, 218
  See also: Temples
Mathurā as holy place, 177, **179**
Mat-sthāni sarva-bhūtāni
  verse quoted, 73, 90, 270
Mattaḥ parataraṁ nānyat
  quoted, 3
Mattaḥ smṛtir jñānam apohanaṁ ca
  quoted, 187
Māyā
  defined, 24, 110
  education misused for, 164
  liberation from, 145–146
  above living entity, 130–131
  mind in, 262
  miseries from, 147
  money misused for, 164
  philosophers in, 164
  rebellious souls serve, 24
  scientists in, 164
  surrender as salvation from, 262
  See also: Ignorance; Illusion; Life, material; Material world; Nature, material
Maya Dānava
  as demon No. 1, **7**
  demons gifted by, **8**
  demons revived by, **10**, 11, **12**
  mystic power of, 11
  quoted on God's will, **14**
  Śiva baffled, **5, 12**
Mayādhyakṣeṇa prakṛtiḥ
  quoted, 110
  verse quoted, 268–269
Mayānukūlena nabhasvateritaṁ
  verse quoted, 250
Mayā tatam idaṁ sarvaṁ
  verse quoted, 73, 89, 270
Māyāvādi-bhāṣya śunile haya sarva-nāśa
  quoted, 204
Māyāvādīs (impersonalists)
  Brahman sought by, 113
  as dangerous, 204
  Lord Caitanya warned against, 204
  paramahaṁsas excel, 95
  Vaiṣṇavas vs., 113
  world denied by, 150, 267–268
  See also: Jñānīs
Mayy āsakta-manāḥ pārtha
  verse quoted, 268, 291
Meat eating
  celibates forbidden, **69**
  Hare Kṛṣṇa movement forbids, 94
  as sinful, 49, 145
  See also: Animal slaughter
Meditation
  on Brahman unfulfilling, 113–114
  for Satya-yuga, 164, 188
  on Supersoul, 135
  on Supreme Lord, **226**
  by *yogī*, 135
Men. *See:* Human beings
Merchants: *See: Vaiśyas*
Mercy
  as brahminical symptom, **43**
  as human quality, **32**, 33
Mercy of the Supreme Lord
  devotional service by, 248
  living entities at, 185–186
  via spiritual master, 68, 223, 224, 250
Merging with the Supreme. *See:* Brahman, merging with; Māyāvādīs
Miche māyāra vaśe, yāccha bhese'
  quoted, 262
Mind
  brāhmaṇas control, **43**
  cleanliness for, 33
  duality concocted by, **133**
  of materialist disturbed, 121
  in *māyā*, 262
  merged in moon god, **82**
  satisfaction for, **28**

Mind *(continued)*
senses agitate, **63,** 65, 262
technology disturbs, 157
yoga controls, **226**
Misery. *See:* Suffering
Modes of material nature
body according to, 110
conditioned souls under, 110, 118, **247**
demigods under, **83**
devotees surpass, 134
false ego under, **82–83**
occupations according to, **52, 53**
service to spiritual master conquers, **222,** 223
social classes according to, 42
species according to, 110
transmigration according to, 228
types of, three listed, 110
as *Vedas'* subject, 248
See also: Nature, material; *individual modes (goodness, passion, ignorance)*
Moghāśā mogha-karmāṇo
quoted, 180
Mohammedan(s)
Haridāsa Ṭhākura as, 199
Rūpa and Sanātana as, 37
Mokṣa
defined, 156
See also: Liberation
Money
author prudent with, 126
demons misuse, 152
detachment toward, **127**
in devotional service, 164
for Hare Kṛṣṇa movement, 121–122, 125–126
as honeylike, **127,** 128
Kali-yuga government extorts, 127
kṣatriyas require, 124
as Lakṣmī, 122
low-class men misuse, 158
materialist enslaved by, **121,** 123, 153
māyā misuses, 164
minimal, needed, 127, 128
preachers advised on, 121–122
Money
in renunciation, 122
sense gratification misuses, 122, 125
surplus, to Kṛṣṇa, 152–153
in Vedic culture, 124–126
See also: Opulence, material
Monism, perfect and imperfect, 67
Monists. *See: Jñānīs;* Māyāvādīs
Monkeys, forest for, 176
Month
of Āśvina, **167–168,** 168n
of Bhādra, **167**
of Kārtika, **169–170**
of Māgha, **169–170**
Moon
day of, calculated, 170–171
in Vedic ritual calculations, **167,** 168n
Moon-god, mind merged in, **82**
Mothers, types of, seven listed, 64
Mother Yaśodā as pure devotee, 5
Mṛta-sanjīvayitari
as Āyur-vedic medicine, 11
demons revived by, 11
Mṛtyu, rectum sacrificed to, **81**
Mṛtyu-saṁsāra-vartmani
quoted, 244
Muktānām api siddhānāṁ
verse quoted, 199–200
Mukti. See: Liberation
Mumukṣubhiḥ partiyāgo
verse quoted, 122, 150
Muṇḍaka Upaniṣad, quoted on Balarāma's mercy as necessity, 252
Munis
defined, 143
See also: Devotees of the Supreme Lord; Philosophers; Saints
Mūrti as Nārāyaṇa's mother, **28**
Muslim as sectarian designation, 33
Mysticism. *See:* Kṛṣṇa consciousness; Mystic power; *Yogīs*
Mystic power
demons misuse, 11
haṭha-yoga for, 11
of Maya Dānava, 11
Mystic *yoga. See:* Mystic power; *Yoga*

N

Na ca tasmān manuṣyeṣu
quoted, 191, 193
Na codāsīnaḥ śāstrāṇi
verse quoted, 92
Naimiṣāraṇya as sacred place, **179**
Naiva jñānārthayor bhedas
verse quoted, 67
Na māṁ duṣkṛtino mūḍhāḥ
quoted, 49
Na me 'bhaktaś catur-vedī
quoted, 201
verse quoted, 200
Names of God. *See:* Chanting the Lord's holy names; Hare Kṛṣṇa *mantra;* Supreme Lord, *appropriate entries*
Nānā yoni sadā phire, kadarya bhakṣaṇa kare
verse quoted, 261
Nanda Mahārāja as pure devotee, 5
Nandā River as sacred place, **179**
Nāprayojana-pakṣī syān
verse quoted, 92
Nara, "parents" of, **28**
Nārada Muni
See also: Nārada Muni, quotations from
as Brahmā's disciple, 26
as Brahmā's son, **25, 285**
in disciplic succession, 26
as Gandharva, **281, 282, 284,** 285
Prahlāda instructed by, 136
prajāpatis cursed, **284**
scriptures by, two listed, 26
as spiritual master, 26
as *śūdra,* **284, 285**
as Vaiṣṇava, 189
Vyāsadeva instructed by, 26
Nārada Muni, quotations from
on *brahmacarya,* **59–64**
on *brāhmaṇas,* **43, 192, 193, 198**
on Deity worship, **188, 191**
on *dvijas,* **35**
on household life, **142, 144, 147–149, 152, 154, 156, 158–163, 173**
on human life, principles for, **32–33**
Nārada Muni, quotations from
on Kṛṣṇa rescuing Śiva, **15–16**
on *kṣatriya's* qualities, **44**
on life's purpose, 213
on man and woman, **65, 66**
on marriage, spiritual destiny for, **50**
on Maya Dānava & demons vs. Śiva & demigods, **5, 7–10, 12–18**
on mixed marriages, **51**
on occupational duties, **36, 38, 39, 41–42**
on occupation by qualification, **55**
on Pāṇḍavas, **1**
on Prahlāda and saint, 137
on *prajāpati's* curse, **284**
on sacred places, **175, 176, 179–180**
on *sannyāsa,* **87–96**
on *śūdra's* qualities, **45**
on Supersoul (Paramātmā), **185, 186–187**
on Supreme Lord, **3, 4–5**
on *vaiśya's* qualities, **44**
on wife's duties, **46, 48**
on worshiping Kṛṣṇa, **181, 183–184**
Nārada-pañcarātra, purpose of, 26
Nārāyaṇa, Lord, **88**
austerities by, **28**
at Badarikāśrama, **28**
in heart of all, 167
Kṛṣṇa as, **104**
as Lakṣmī's lord, 122
"parents" of, **28**
poor, as misconception, 167, 204
religious principles delivered by, **27**
See also: Supreme Lord
Narottama dāsa Ṭhākura, quotations from
on *karma-kāṇḍa* and *jñāna-kāṇḍa,* 261
on material life, 121
on Rādhā-Kṛṣṇa via Nityānanda's mercy, 252
Na tad-bhakteṣu cānyeṣu
verse quoted, 177, 189–190
Na te viduḥ svārtha-gatiṁ hi viṣṇuṁ
quoted, 245, 276
Nature, material (*prakṛti*)
animal slaughter punished by, 222
body under, **117**–118
food provided by, 151, 162

Nature, material (*prakṛti*) (*continued*)
freedom from, 110
living entities under, 91, 117–118, 147, 151
Lord above, 118, 150, 151, **225**, 268
materialist under, 117
See also: Body, material; Elements, material; Energy, material; Laws of nature; Modes of material nature
Nāty-ucchritaṁ nātinīcaṁ
verse quoted, 231
Na vyākhyayopajīveta
verse quoted, 92
Nawab Hussain Shah, Rūpa and Sanātana employed by, 37
Nāyam ātmā bala-nīnena labhyo
verse quoted, 252
Nāyaṁ deho deha-bhājāṁ nṛloke
quoted, 112, 145
Nectar of Instruction, quoted on activities spoiling devotional service, 125
Nectar well
calf and cow drank dry, **13, 14**
demons revived by, **10, 12**
Nirbandhaḥ kṛṣṇa-sambandhe
verse quoted, 122
Nirdvandvo nitya-sattva-stho
verse quoted, 248
Niṣkāma defined, 53
Nitāi-Gaura, mercy of, 254
Nitāiyera karuṇā habe, vraje rādhā-kṛṣṇa pābe
quoted, 252
Nityānanda, Lord, Rādhā-Kṛṣṇa via mercy of, 252
Niyamitaḥ smaraṇe na kālaḥ
quoted, 231
Nondevotees
devotees vs., 49, 105
goodness absent in, 34
in ignorance, 255
Lord's reciprocation with, 105
as sinners, 49
surrender shunned by, 49
Vedic rituals futile for, **228**
Nondevotees
See also: Atheists; Demons; Materialists, Māyāvādīs
Nṛ-deham ādyaṁ sulabhaṁ sudurlabhaṁ
verse quoted, 250
Nṛsiṁhadeva, Lord, appeared for Prahlāda, 2

O

Occupation(s)
birth irrelevant to, **55**, 56
for *brāhmaṇas*, **36–**37, **39**, 40, **42**
of "dogs," **42**
emergencies change, **39**, 40, **41**
of lower classes, 52
for mixed marriage families, 52
modes of nature determine, **52, 53**
by qualification, **55**, 56
service as eternal, 24
for *vaiśyas*, **38, 39**
varṇāśrama-dharma organizes, 24
See also: Duty; *Varṇāśrama-dharma; names of individual varṇas (brāhmaṇas, kṣatriyas, vaiśyas, śūdras)*
Old age, *vānaprastha* overtaken by, **78**
Old men, *prasāda* to, 167
Old Testament commands nonviolence, 207
Oṁ namo bhagavate vāsudevāya
quoted, 231
Oneness. *See:* Monism
Oneness and difference of the Lord and the living entities, **72**, 73, **83–84**, 204
Opulence, as Lord's potency, **15–16**
Opulence, material
bhogīs misuse, 93
materialists pursue, 153
renunciation of, **219**, 220
for *śrāddha* ceremony restricted, **202**
See also: Money

P

Padaṁ padaṁ yad vipadāṁ na teṣāṁ
quoted, 280

adma *Purāṇa*, quoted on worshiping Viṣṇu, 189
ain. *See:* Suffering
ampā as sacred place, **179**
āñcarātrikī-vidhi, following, recommended, 30
āṇḍavas
  in devotional service, **279**
  good fortune of, **1**, 2, **288**
  as Kṛṣṇa's kinsmen, 3–4, **288, 289**
  as pure devotees, 5
  saints visit(ed), **1**, 2, **288**
  yogamāyā covered, 2
aṇḍita
  defined, 66
  See also: Wise man
āpī tāpī yata chila, hari-nāme uddhārila quoted, 252
arabrahman. *See:* Brahman, Supreme
aramahaṁsa
  Prahlāda as, 137
  as transcendental, 138
aramātmā. *See:* Supersoul
arampará. See: Disciplic succession
aras tasmāt tu bhāvo 'nyo
  verse quoted, 272
arāsya śaktir vividhaiva śrūyate
  quoted, 270
assion, mode of (*rajo-guṇa*)
  cities in, 176
  greed in, 217
  symptoms of, **247**
astimes of Kṛṣṇa
  purifying power of, **19**
  as transcendental, **19**
  value of knowing, 249–250
ātra defined, 181
avarga defined, 109
eace
  for family, 46
  goodness essential for, 34
  via Hare Kṛṣṇa movement, 34
  via *varṇāśrama-dharma*, 42, 47
  for world, 47
enance. *See:* Austerity
People
  Vaiṣṇavas and Viṣṇu as best, 187, 188
  See also: Human beings
Phālgu River as sacred place, **179**
Philosophers
  saints as, 143
  so-called, in *māyā*, 164
  so-called, as useless for spiritual life, 92
Philosophy
  authorities on Vaiṣṇava, 16
  of Lord Caitanya, 67
  of Māyāvādīs dangerous, 204
  Māyāvādī vs. Vaiṣṇavas, 113
Pigs, Kali-yuga workers compared to, 145
Pitās, Śiva honored by, **17–18**
Planets. *See:* Universe
Pleasure. *See:* Bliss; Enjoyment, material; Happiness; Happiness, material
Population
  Dakṣa's daughters generated universal, **293–294**
  lower class, 52
  varṇa-saṅkara, 35–36, 46–47
  under *varṇāśrama-dharma*, 35, 157
  See also: Civilization, human; Society, human
Power
  of chanting the Lord's holy names, **287**
  of providence, **14**
  of Śiva from Kṛṣṇa, 6
  of Supreme Lord, **14–16**
  See also: Mystic power
Prahbāsa as sacred place, **179**
Pradhāna merged in Supersoul, **83**
Prahlāda Mahārāja
  Brahmā adores, **23**
  following, recommended, 2
  as *gṛhastha*, 137
  as Nārada's disciple, 136
  Nṛsiṁhadeva appeared for, 2
  as *paramahaṁsa*, 137
  as pure devotee, 2, **104–105, 136**
  quoted on saintly person, **100–102**
  quoted on sex life, 111
  saint charmed by, 103

Prahlāda Mahārāja *(continued)*
saint discovered by, **98**
saint puzzled, 100, **102**
saint worshiped by, **99, 137**
Śiva adores, **23**
as spiritual master, 137
spiritual vision of, 104
Prahlādo janako bhīṣmo
verse quoted, 138
Prajāpati(s)
Brahmā as, **25**
Nārada cursed by, **284**
sensual pleasure sacrificed to, **81**
Prākṛta-bhakta defined, 177, 190
Prakṛteḥ kriyamāṇāni
quoted, 147, 151
verse quoted, 110
Prakṛti. See: Nature, material
Prakṛtiṁ yānti mām ekam
quoted 266
Praṇavaḥ sarva-vedeṣu
quoted, 231
Prāṇopahārāc ca yathendriyāṇāṁ
verse quoted, 182
Prāpañcikatayā buddhyā
verse quoted, 122, 150
Prasāda (Food offered to Kṛṣṇa), **161**
for *brāhmaṇas,* **203,** 208
in Deity worship, 112, **203,** 208
for devotees, 200, **203,** 208
distribution of, 165, **166,** 167, 200, **203, 204,** 208
with ghee, **203, 205,** 208
for human beings, 112
purifying power of, 112, 145
for saint, **129**
Pratilomaja
defined, 51
See also: Marriage
Pravṛttiṁ ca nivṛttiṁ ca
quoted, 255
Prayāga as holy place, 177, **179**
Preacher(s), Kṛṣṇa conscious
brāhmaṇas as, **193**
in civilian dress, 95
conduct for, **92**
Preacher(s), Kṛṣṇa conscious
Deity worshiper vs., 189, 191
Kṛṣṇa empowers, 190
literature distribution by, 189
Lord recognizes, 191, **193**
money advice to, 121–122
Preaching Kṛṣṇa consciousness
donations for, 153
as *sannyāsī's* duty, 94, 95, 125
temples for, 93–94
Prema-bhakti-candrikā, quoted on *karma-kāṇḍa* and *jñāna-kāṇḍa,* 261
Proprietorship, true and false, 150, 155, **162**
Protection by king, 37
Protection by the Supreme Lord
for devotees, **5,** 16
for Hare Kṛṣṇa movement, 16
for *mahājanas,* 16
for religious principles, **27**
Pṛthivīte āche yata nagarādi-grāma
verse quoted, 180
Pulahāśrama as sacred place, **179**
Punishment
body as, 112
by evolution, 147
for impious activities, 118
by nature's laws, 147, 154
Puṇya-śravaṇa-kīrtanaḥ
quoted, 145
Purāṇas, **176**
following, recommended, 30
subject matter in, **144,** 153
Pure devotee(s) of the Supreme Lord
cowherd boys as, 5
gopīs as, 5
humility of, 2
Lord instructs, within heart, 289, 290
as loyal to Kṛṣṇa, 4
Nanda as, 5
neophytes vs., 189, 190, **191**
Pāṇḍavas as, 5
Prahlāda as, 2, **104–105, 136**
purity of, 105, 200
sannyāsī as, **88**
spiritual vision of, **89**–90
as transcendental, 223

Pure devotee(s) of the Supreme Lord
transcendentalists vs., 5
Vṛndāvana's residents as, 5
Yaśodā as, 5
Purification
of *brāhmaṇa*, **260**
by chanting the Lord's holy names, 145
by devotional service, 107
by *garbhādhāna* ceremony, **35**
by hearing about Kṛṣṇa, **19**, 145
by *prasāda*, 112, 145
via saints, **105–106**
of sex life, 35
of sin, 49
by *varṇāśrama-dharma*, **35**
by Vedic culture, 112
See also: Kṛṣṇa consciousness
Puruṣāvatāra, Lord as, **185**, 186
Puṣkara as sacred place, **179**
Python
living conditions of, **97**
saint living like, **97**, **99**
as self-satisfied, **128**
as spiritual master, **126**, **128**

R

Rādhā-Kṛṣṇa
via Nityānanda's mercy, 252
worship of, 177, **179–180**, 208
Rain
by chanting Hare Kṛṣṇa, 151
from sacrifice, 151
Rājasūya sacrifice
Kṛṣṇa glorified at, **183**, 193
by Yudhiṣṭhira, **183**, 193
Rajo-guṇa. See: Passion, mode of
Rāma, Lord, at Citrakūṭa, **179**
Rāmānanda Rāya
cited on life's goal, 147
with Lord Caitanya, 147
Rāmānujācārya, 218
Rāmeśvara as holy place, 177
Raso 'ham apsu kaunteya
quoted, 116
Rātriṁ yuga-sahasrāntāṁ
verse quoted, 281
Rātry-āgame 'vaśaḥ pārtha
verse quoted, 272
Reincarnation. *See:* Transmigration of the soul
Relationship(s)
of *brahmacārī* to spiritual master, **59–62**
of Pāṇḍavas to Kṛṣṇa, 3–4, **288**, **289**
sannyāsī renounces material, 87
Religion
animal slaughter in, 207
envy absent in real, **205**, **208**
as God's laws, 29
Lord as basis of, **28**, 29, 30
as Lord's potency, **15**
manufactured, condemned, 29
modern, condemned, 30
as necessary, 156
sectarian, as irrelevant, 33
surrender as real, 209, 210
true and false, 30, **209–211**, 212
See also: Devotional service to the Supreme Lord
Religious principles
devotional service as goal of, 29, 30
devotional service via, **24**
as God's laws, 29
Kṛṣṇa consciousness as topmost, 208–211
Lord protects, **27**
Nārada expert on, **26**
Nārāyaṇa delivered, 27
sex life according to, 68, 111–122
for time, place and person, 181
Renunciation
of anger, **219**–220
of bodily attachment, 161
by bumblebee, **127**, **128**
of duality, **133**–134
of envy, **219**–220
of family life, 159, 160, **229**, 230
of fear, **219**
of greed, **219**, 220
for knowledge, 87
as Lord's potency, **15**
of lusty desire, **219**, 220

Renunciation *(continued)*
by Mādhavendra Purī, 213
Māyāvādīs vs. Vaiṣṇava, 113
in money matters, 122, **127**
by saint, **127–132**
by *sannyāsī*, **87–88, 93–95**
of sense gratification, **219**
of sex life, 160, 219
of wealth, **219,** 220
of wife, **159, 160**–161
See also: Sannyāsa
Ritualistic ceremony (Ritualistic ceremonies)
animal killing in, **257**
by *brāhmaṇas*, **167–168**
brāhmaṇas at *śrāddha*, **201, 202**
for family life, **173**
for forefathers, **201**
for fruitive activities, **173**
garbhādhāna, **35,** 68
by Indians, 202
mahālayā, **167–168,** 168n
marriage as, 111
for material desires, **257**
moon calculated in, **167,** 168n, **169–170**
for nondevotees futile, **228**
for procreation, 35
sacred places for, **175, 179–180**
saṅkīrtana required at, 174
for sense gratification, 156
śrāddha, **169–170,** 171, 202
stars calculated in, **169–170**
sun calculated in, **179,** 170–171
time and place important to, **202**
wise men surpass, **206**
See also: Sacrifices
Ṛṣabhadeva, quoted on austerity, 141
Rudra, sacrifices to, **82–83**
Rules and regulations. *See:* Religious principles; Ritualistic ceremonies
Rūpa Gosvāmī
brāhmaṇas ostracized, 37
quoted on activities spoiling devotional service, 125
quoted on renunciation, 122, 150

S

Sacred place(s)
brāhmaṇas as, **175**
in India, 177, **179**
ISKCON centers as, **179–180**
for ritualistic ceremonies, **175, 179–180**
spiritual life advanced by, **180**
temple as, **175, 176,** 177
Vaiṣṇava as, **175**
for *yoga* practice, **230,** 231
Sacred thread, *brahmacārīs* wear, **60–61**
Sacrifice(s)
animal slaughter in name of, **205, 207**
chanting Hare Kṛṣṇa as best, 166
Deity worship as, 208
fruitive activities for, 165
with ghee and grains, 151, **165**
for heavenly elevation discouraged, **258**
by householder, **163**–164
to Kṛṣṇa, 164, 165
pañca-sūnā, **161–162**
prasāda distribution as best, 166
rain from, 151
Rājasūya. *See:* Rājasūya sacrifice
by *saṅkīrtana*, 164, 166
of senses and sense objects to demigods, **81**
for Supreme Brahman, **262**
by *vānaprastha*, **76**
for *yugas*, 164, 188–189
See also: Ritualistic ceremonies
Sādhu
defined, 201
See also: Devotee(s) of the Supreme Lord
Sādhur eva sa mantavyaḥ
verse quoted, 200
Sa guṇān samatītyaitān
quoted, 110, 223
verse quoted, 134
Sahasra-yuga-prayantam
verse quoted, 281
Sahya Mountain, Prahlāda and saint at, **98–99**
Saintly person (Prahlāda's acquaintance)
animals' examples followed by, **126–128**
bodily symptoms of, **102**

Saintly person, quotations from
as *brāhmaṇa*, 102, 106, 112
dress of, 130
as equally disposed, **132**
as fat, **100–102**
fruitive activities renounced by, **112, 113**–114
as inscrutable, 99
Prahlāda charmed, **103**
Prahlāda discovered, **98–99**
Prahlāda puzzled by, **100–102**
Prahlāda worshiped, **99, 137**
in pythonlike state, **97, 99**
renunciation by, **127, 131–132**
as well-wisher, **132**–133
Saintly person, quotations from
on human life, **108, 111**
on materialists, **121, 123**
on Prahlāda, **104–106, 136**
Saints
activities of, **5**
bliss sought by, **3**
as grave, 106
Lord's lotus feet worshiped by, **225**
Pāṇḍavas visited by, **1**, 2, **288**
as philosophers, 143
purification via, **106**
as silent, 106
Śiva honored by, **17–18**
See also: Devotees of the Supreme Lord; Pure devotees of the Supreme Lord
Sākṣād dharitvena samasta śāstraiḥ
quoted, 192, 224
Śālagrāma-śilā worship by *gṛhastha*, 177
Salvation. *See:* Liberation
Samaḥ sarveṣu bhūteṣu
verse quoted, 146, 235–236, 251
Samāśritā ye pada-pallava-plavaṁ
quoted, 280
Sampradāya. See: Disciplic succession
Saṁsāra-biṣānale, dibāniśi hiyā jvale
quoted, 121
Saṁsāra-cakra
defined, 119
See also: Transmigration of the soul
Sanātana-dharma defined, 24
Sanātana Gosvāmī, *brāhmaṇas* ostracized, 37
Saṅkīrtana
by Apsarās, **283**
by Gandharvas, **283**
Hare Kṛṣṇa movement as, 164
for Kali-yuga, 164, 166, 174
Lord Caitanya started, 189
Vedic rituals require, 174
See also: Chanting the Lord's holy names; Kṛṣṇa consciousness movement
Ṣaṇṇāṁ tu karmaṇām asya
verse quoted, 37
Sannyāsa (renounced life)
bogus vs. bona fide, 125
from *brahmacarya* to, 71
household life vs., 160, **236–237**
in Kali-yuga risky, 125
as life's perfection, 125
qualification for, 56
sex life forbidden in, 141
stages of, four listed, 95
symbols of, as optional, **94–95**
in *varṇāśrama-dharma*, 24, **35**
Sannyāsī(s)
bogus vs. bona fide, **93**
conduct of, **88, 96**
Deity worship by, 208
dress of, **87**
duties of, **87–96**, 157
fallen, condemned, **236–237, 238**–239
in Hare Kṛṣṇa movement, 95
identified, **63**
livelihood for, **88**
Māyāvādī vs. Vaiṣṇava, 95
as preacher, 94, 95, 125
as pure devotee, **88**
renunciation by, **87, 88, 92–95**
self-realization for, **89**
spiritual vision of, **88, 89**
as traveler, **87, 88**
women avoided by, **63**
Sarva-dharmān parityajya
quoted, 118, 132, 208–210
verse quoted, 262

Sarvaṁ khalv idaṁ brahma
quoted, 266
Sarvasya cāhaṁ hṛdi sanniviṣṭo
quoted, 117
Sarvatra pracāra haibe mora nāma
verse quoted, 180
Sarva-yoniṣu kaunteya
verse quoted, 150
Sarvopādhi-vinirmuktaṁ
quoted, 245–246
Sa sannyāsī ca yogī ca
verse quoted, 142–143
Śāstras (scriptures). *See: Vedas; names of individual scriptures*
Satisfaction
as brahminical symptom, **43**
as human quality, **32,** 33
Sattva-guṇa. See: Goodness, mode of
Satya-yuga
for meditation, 164, 188
as spiritually advanced, 189
Sa vai puṁsāṁ paro dharmo
quoted, 211
verse quoted, 29, 255
Scientists, material
Bhāgavatam refutes, 184
life misunderstood by, 116
in *māyā,* 164
Secular state as misconception, 33
Self. *See:* Living entity; Soul; Souls, conditioned
Self-realization
advancement symptoms in, 101–102
Brahman realization begins, 74
by chanting Hare Kṛṣṇa, 136
duality absent in, 66
elevation to, **263–264**
God realization accompanied by, 116, 135
human life for, 123, **241**
knowledge for, 80
by *sannyāsī,* **89**
value of, 135
as Vedic culture's goal, 124
See also: Kṛṣṇa consciousness
Semen
as bodily constituent, **79–80**
Semen
value of, 33
Sense control by *brahmacārī,* **59**
Sense gratification
for animals, 145, 156
bondage to, **253–254**
fattiness signifies, **100**–101
human life spoiled by, 145, 147, **241**
marriage as, 156
minimal, needed, 156
money misused for, 122, 125–126
mystic power misused for, 11
renunciation of, **219**
See also: Body, material; Desires, material; Life, material
Senses
bondage to, **215, 216, 253–254**
brāhmaṇas control, **43**
fat people indulge, 100–101
materialist victimized by, **121**
mind agitated by, **63,** 65, **262**
transcendentalist renounces, **81**
Servants of God. *See:* Devotees of the Supreme Lord
Service to God. *See:* Devotional service to the Supreme Lord
Se sambandha nāhi yāra, bṛthā janma gela tāra
quoted, 252
Setubanda as sacred place, **179**
Sevaka-bhagavān, spiritual master as, 225
Sevejyāvanatir dāsyaṁ
verse quoted, 34
Sevya-bhagavān, Kṛṣṇa as, 225
Sex life
āśramas forbidding, 141
as bodily demand, 156
brahmacārīs reject, 63
as distressful, **111**–112
duality epitomized by, **66**
garbhādhāna purifies, 35
good qualities control, 35
for *gṛhastha* restricted, **68,** 141
illicit. *See:* Sex life, illicit
living beings eager for, 111
in marriage, 111–112

Sex life
- for procreation, 35, **68**
- religious principles regulate, 111–112
- renunciation of, 160, 219
- spiritual master sanctions, **68**
- as unnecessary, 141
- Vedic culture minimizes, 63, 65
- *See also:* Attachment, material; Desires, material; Lust

Sex life, illicit
- Hare Kṛṣṇa movement forbids, 94
- by lower classes, 52
- as sinful, 49, 145

Shah, Nawab Hussain, Rūpa and Sanātana employed by, 37

Shower of flowers for Śiva, **17–18**

Siddhas honored Śiva, **17–18**

Simplicity
- as brahminical symptom, **43**
- as human quality, **32,** 33

Sin
- body caused by, 112
- devotees free of, 49
- hearing about Kṛṣṇa dispels, 145
- *prasāda* absolves, 112
- punishment for, 118
- as relative, 52–53
- in society, 157
- types of, four listed, 49, 145
- wine-drinking as, 158

Śiśupāla, Kṛṣṇa killed, 183

Śiṣvāṇāṁ ca gurau nityaṁ
- verse quoted, 50

Śiṣyas te 'haṁ śādhi māṁ tvāṁ prapannam
- quoted, 4

Sītā at Citrakūṭa, **179**

Sītā-Rāma worship, 117, 208

Śiva, Lord
- above Brahmā, 6
- demigods begged protection of, **9**
- demigods honored, **17–18**
- demons' airplanes vanquished by, **17, 18**
- demons vs., **9, 10, 16–18**
- Flower shower for, **17–18**
- Kṛṣṇa above, 6
- Kṛṣṇa bewilders, **290**

Śiva, Lord
- Kṛṣṇa saved, **5, 15–16**
- as Mahādeva, 6
- as *mahājana,* 16
- Maya Dānava baffled, **5, 12**
- Pāṇḍavas luckier than, 2, **4–5**
- Prahlāda adored by, **23**
- as topmost Vaiṣṇava, 16
- as Tripurāri, **18**

Sky
- as bodily constituent, **79, 80**
- life's necessities from, **149**

Sleep
- arrangements for, relative to birth, 130–131
- eating in goodness conquers, **221**
- materialists miss, 121
- purpose of, 112

Society, human
- animal slaughter in, 155
- *brāhmaṇa's* status in, 187
- Deity worship neglected in, 175, 177
- divisions of, four listed, 42, 51, 55, 156
- dogs maintained in, 158
- *dvijas* lacking in Kali-yuga, 71
- food scarce in sinful, 151
- happiness for, 29
- Hare Kṛṣṇa movement benefits, 24, 110, 153, 180
- leaders of modern, condemned, 148
- Lord's appearance in, **19**
- mixed marriages in, 51–52
- modes of nature in, 42
- Nārada teaches, 26
- proprietorship misunderstood by, 150, 155
- *sannyāsī* anonymous in, **96**
- sinful activities in, 157
- spiritual emergency in, 40
- *varṇa-saṅkara* confounds, 47
- *varṇāśrama-dharma* organizes, 24, 46–47, 157
- Vedic culture purifies, 112
- Vedic vs. modern, 124–125
- *See also:* Civilization, human

So 'dhvanaḥ pāram āpnoti
- verse quoted, 243

Soul
body as vehicle for, 243
body vs., **84,** 116, 135, 161
as happy, 115, 116
identification with, 79, 135, 146
living entity as, 66, **83–84**
satisfaction for, **28**
scientists misunderstand, 116
Supersoul above, 135, **186–187**
See also: Living entity
Souls, conditioned
duality afflicts, **66**
happiness eludes, **116, 117**
in ignorance, **116**
under modes of nature, 110, **247**
nature controls, 91, **117–118**
suffering of, **115, 117**–119
surrender frees, 91, 118
under time, **90**–91
transmigration plagues, **90–91**
See also: Living entities; Soul
Species of life
as diseased conditions, 110
lower, as punishment, 118, 147
by modes of nature, 110
number of, 150, 162
origin of, 150
Spirit. *See:* Soul; Spiritual world; Supreme Lord
Spiritualists. *See:* Devotees of the Supreme Lord; *Jñānīs;* Māyāvādīs; Transcendentalists; *Yogīs*
Spiritual life
āśramas in, four listed, 124–125, 138
fattiness hampers, 101
forest for, 176
greed ruins, 218
Hare Kṛṣṇa movement advances, 175, 177, 180
India advances, 177
kaniṣṭha-adhikārīs in, 176–177
marriage in, 111–112
material life vs., 113–114
mealtime for, 101
as necessary, 180
sacred places advance, **180**
Spiritual life
society has abandoned, 40
spiritual master governs, 68
varṇāśrama-dharma advances, 47
whimsical action ruins, 68
women's association restricted in, 63
See also: Devotional service to the Supreme Lord; Kṛṣṇa consciousness
Spiritual master (*Guru*)
Absolute Truth present in, 225
bee as, **126–128**
brahmacārī's relationship to, **59–62, 70**
as captain of the ship, 250
devotional service via, 248
disciple remunerates, **70**
as good as Kṛṣṇa, 192, **223–224**
gṛhastha governed by, 141
knowledge via, 227, **249,** 265
Lord as, **3,** 4
Lord's mercy via, 68, 223, 224, 250, 252
Lord within and without, **72**
material conception of, as doom, **224,** 225–226
Nārada as, 26
as necessary, **249,** 250, 252, 265
Prahlāda as, 137
python as, **126, 128**
service to, conquers nature's modes, **222,** 223
sex sanctioned by, **68**
spiritual life governed by, 68
superexcellent status of, 192
wife of, as *brahmacārī's* mother, 64
Spiritual world
as marriage's goal, **50**
material world vs., 272–273
temple as, 176
Śrāddha ceremony
devotees needed at, 202
on Ekādaśī forbidden, 171
food prescriptions for, **205**
opulence restricted for, **202**
performance time for, **169–170**
worship at, **202**
Śraddhāvān bhajate yo māṁ
verse quoted, 11, 233

Śravaṇaṁ kīrtanaṁ cāsya
verse quoted, 34
Śravaṇaṁ kīrtanaṁ viṣṇoḥ
quoted, 284–285
Śreyān sva-dharmo viguṇaḥ
quoted, 52
Śrīmad-Bhāgavatam
See also: Śrīmad-Bhāgavatam, quotations from
Bhagavad-gītā compared to, 26
cited on false *dharma*, 210
cited on life's necessities, 158–159
communism God-centered in, 155
Hare Kṛṣṇa movement based on, 26, 40
for *paramahaṁsas*, 95
"religion" condemned by, 30
scientists refuted by, 184
subject matter of, 143, **144**
Śukadeva spoke, 26
value of hearing, 143, 145
Śrīmad-Bhāgavatam, quotations from
on Absolute Truth, three features of, 230–231
on authorities on Kṛṣṇa consciousness, 137–138
on desires fulfilled by worshiping God, 107
on devotees as rare, 199–200
on devotional service as unconditional, 255
on goodness in devotees only, 34
on human body as valuable boat, 250
on *kaniṣṭha-adhikārīs*, 177, 189–190
on Kṛṣṇa consciousness for intelligent people, 136
on life's purpose, 213
on occupational duty, perfection of, 277
on religion as devotional service, 29
on religion as God's law, 210–211
on sacrifices for *yugas*, 164, 188–189
on sense gratification unbecoming human life, 145
on Śiva as topmost devotee, 16
on worshiping Kṛṣṇa, 182
Śṛṇvatāṁ sva-kathāḥ kṛṣṇaḥ
quoted, 144
Stars in Vedic rituals, **170**
Strīṣu duṣṭāsu vārṣṇeya
quoted, 46
Striyo vaiśyās tathā śūdrās
verse quoted, 278, 186
Students. *See: Brahmacārīs*; Devotees of the Supreme Lord; *Dvijas*
Subtle body. *See:* Intelligence; Mind
Śucau deśe pratiṣṭhāpya
verse quoted, 231
Śūdra(s)
brāhmaṇa degraded to, 37
duty for, **38**
livelihood for, 124
Kali-yuga population as, 42, 71
Nārada as, **284, 285**
occupations for, 156–157
symptoms of, **45**
technology for, 71
in *varṇāśrama-dharma*, 24
Vedic study optional for, 71
Sudurlabhaḥ praśāntātmā
verse quoted, 199–200
Suffering
of conditioned souls, **115,** 118
Hare Kṛṣṇa *mantra* relieves, 222
material desire causes, **124**
of materialist, **121, 123**
material life as, 109, **119–120, 255**
sex indulgence results in, **111,** 112
soul free of, 115
spiritual activity cures, 113
types of, three listed, **119**
yoga relieves, 222
Suhṛdaṁ sarva-bhūtānāṁ
verse quoted, 181–182, 234
Śukadeva Gosvāmī
Bhāgavatam spoken by, 26
Vyāsadeva instructed, 26
Śukadeva Gosvāmī, quotations from
on depending on Kṛṣṇa, 213
on Nārada and Yudhiṣṭhira, **23**
on Yudhiṣṭhira, **292**
Sun
form sacrificed to, **81**
living entities on, 184
Lord compared to, **104–105**

Sun *(continued)*
path of, 170
in *śrāddha* ceremony calculation, **169,** 170–171
Vivasvān rules, 184
Sunbeams, Śiva's arrows compared to, 10
Sun-god
brahmacārī's meditation on, **59**
See also: Vivasvān
Śuni caiva śvapāke ca
verse quoted, 66
Supersoul (Paramātmā), 71
body as residence of, **185, 186–187**
in heart of all, 117
intelligence supplied by, **186–187**
Lord as, 117–118, **132, 185, 186–187**
matter merged in, **83**
meditation on, 135
as overseer, 117–118
above soul, 135, **186–187**
as supreme person, 187–188
Supreme Brahman. *See:* Brahman, Supreme
Supreme Lord
abode of, 72
as Absolute Truth, 3, 19
as Acyuta, 182, **183–184**
as all-pervading, **72, 73–74, 88, 89**
in atom, 186
Bhagavad-gītā reveals, 19
Bhagavad-gītā spoken by, 26
as birthless, 27
as bliss's basis, **3**
body as residence of, **185, 186–187**
body supplied by, 118
Brahmā bewildered by, **290**
brāhmaṇas dear to, **165, 193**
brāhmaṇas represent, **192**
as Brahman's basis, **3**
as cause of all causes, **181, 183–184,** 266
as cow, **13**
as creator and controller, **14**–15, **72,** **149**–150, 151
as dearmost friend, 182, 235
demigods under, **14**
demons under, **14**
Supreme Lord
desires fulfilled by, 107
devotees "conquer," **159–**160
devotees instructed by, 105
devotees realize, **290,** 291
devotees satisfy, 143
devotional service reveals, 251, 291
energy of. *See:* Energy of the Supreme Lord
as enjoyer, **165,** 181–182, 235
as everything, **266**
expansions of, 14
faith in, 268
food provided by, 155, 162
form of. *See:* Form of the Supreme Lord
as Govinda, 186
Hare Kṛṣṇa movement supported by, 121, 214
hearing about. *See:* Hearing about the Supreme Lord
in heart of all, 117–118, 131, **163,** 164, 167, 185, **214**
human beings under, **14**
human life for knowing, 250
in human role, **1, 19**
ignorance dispelled by, **104**–105
impersonal feature of. *See:* Brahman (impersonal Absolute)
imposters pose as, 11
as inconceivable, 72
as knowledge's master, 105
Kṛṣṇa as, 14, **293**
laws of. *See:* Laws of the Supreme Lord
as life's goal, 133, 276, 278
living entities under, 15, 24, 131, 135, **185**–186, 192
living entities "vs.," 246
lotus feet of. *See:* Lotus feet of the Supreme Lord
material conception of, as foolish, **225**
meditation on, **226**
mercy of. *See:* Mercy of the Supreme Lord
money surplus to, 152, 153
as Nārāyaṇa, **104–105**

Supreme Lord
nature under, 110, 118, 150, 151, **225,** 268–269
offering everything to, 153, **275**
as omnipresent, 72
as one and different, **72,** 73
as origin of species, 150
as Pāṇḍavas' kinsman, **1,** 2, **228, 289**
as Parabrahman, 6, **84, 289**
pastimes of. *See:* Pastimes of Kṛṣṇa
power of, **14–16**
preachers empowered by, 190
preachers recognized by, 191, **193**
as proprietor, 150, 162, 181–182, 235
protection by. *See:* Protection by the Supreme Lord
pure devotees instructed by, in heart, 289, 290
as *puruṣāvatāra,* **185,** 186
Rājasūya sacrifice glorified, **183,** 193
reciprocates one's attitude, 105
as religion's basis, **28,** 29, 30
sacrifice to, 164, 165
as sanctified sex life, 111
satisfying, as life's purpose, 143
Śiśupāla killed by, 183
Śiva bewildered by, **290**
Śiva saved by, **5, 15–16**
Śiva under, 6
as spiritual master, **3,** 4
via spiritual master, 250, 252
spiritual master as good as, 192, **223–224,** 225–226
as Supersoul, 117, 132, **185, 186–187**
as supreme person, 192, 193
surrender to. *See:* Surrender to the Supreme Lord
as sustainer, **88,** 90, **175,** 186
as time, 90
universe pervaded by, 186
varṇāśrama-dharma created by, 42
as Vāsudeva, 143
as *Vedas'* goal, 29
as water's taste, 116
wife less attractive than, **160**
as within and without, **72,** 73, 270
work offered to, **142**
worship of. *See:* Deity worship of the Lord; Worship, of Lord
as Yajña, 114, 118
as *yoga's* goal, 11
Yudhiṣṭhira worshiped, **292**
See also: Brahman, Supreme; Kṛṣṇa, Lord; Nārāyaṇa, Lord
Supreme Lord, quotations from
on Arjuna's falldown, 4
on devotee's activities, 233
on preachers, Kṛṣṇa conscious, 193
on pure devotees, 200, 201–202
on sober philosopher, 221
Supreme Personality of Godhead. *See:* Kṛṣṇa, Lord; Supreme Lord
Suras. See: Demigods; Devotees of the Supreme Lord
Surrender to the Supreme Lord
as brahminical symptom, **43**
desires fulfilled by, 107
enlightenment by, 105
as freedom, 91, 110, 118
intelligence needed for, 209
by nondevotees, 105
nondevotees shun, 49
as real religion, 209, 210
as salvation from *māyā,* 262
by *yogī,* 135
Sva-bhāva-vihito dharmaḥ
quoted, 212
Svāmin kṛtārtho 'smi varaṁ na yāce
quoted, 256
Svāmīs
bogus, 210
See also: Sannyāsīs; Spiritual master; *Yogīs*
Svāṁśa defined, 14
Svanuṣṭhitasya dharmasya
verse quoted, 277
Svargaloka. *See:* Heavenly planets
Svayambhūr nāradaḥ śambhuḥ
quoted, 16

Svayambhūr nāradaḥ śambhuḥ (continued)
verse quoted, 137
Śvetāśvatara Upaniṣad, quoted on Vedic knowledge via spiritual master, 227

T

Tad-vijñānārthaṁ sa gurum evābhigacchet
quoted, 265
Tamo-dvāraṁ yoṣitāṁ saṅgi-saṅgam
quoted, 243
Tamo-guṇa. See: Ignorance, mode of
Tapasya defined, 141
Taranty añjo bhavārṇavam
quoted, 227
Tāsāṁ brahma mahad-yonir
verse quoted, 150
Tasmai deyaṁ tato grāhyam
verse quoted, 200
Tasmāt kenāpy upāyena
quoted, 268
Tasmāt parataraṁ devi
quoted, 189
Tasyaite kathitā hyarthāḥ
verse quoted, 227
Tasyaiva hetoḥ prayateta kovidaḥ
quoted, 151, 213
Tato māṁ tattvato jñātvā
verse quoted, 251
Tatra laulyam ekalaṁ mūlam
quoted, 217
Taxes
brāhmaṇas exempt from, 37
kṣatriyas levy, **36**
Vaiṣṇavas exempt from, 37
Teacher, spiritual. *See: Brāhmaṇas;* Spiritual master
Technology
mind disturbed by, 157
for *śūdras*, 71
Temple(s)
"Anglican," in Vṛndāvana, 200
author founded, 126
construction of, cautioned, 218
for Deity worship, 177
Temple(s)
for devotees, 176
funds for building, 153
Hare Kṛṣṇa, 175, **179–180**
in India, 153
as preaching centers, 93–94
as sacred place, **175, 176,** 177
as transcendental, 176, 177
as Vaikuṇṭha, 176
Tena tyaktena bhuñjīthā
quoted, 150
Teṣāṁ satata-yuktānāṁ
verse quoted, 289
Te taṁ bhuktvā svarga-lokaṁ viśālaṁ
verse quoted, 258
Thief, miser as, 153
Time
body under, **90**–91
conditioned souls under, 91
Lord as, 91
transmigration caused by, **91**
world under, 91
Tithi defined, 170
Tīvreṇa bhakti-yogena
verse quoted, 107
Traiguṇya-viṣayā vedā
quoted, 259
verse quoted, 248
Transcendentalist(s)
bodily conception renounced by, **82–83**
body of advanced, 102
body renounced by, **78–80**
impersonal vs. personal, 3
mealtime for, 101
pure devotees vs., 5
renounces senses, **81**
See also: Devotees of the Supreme Lord; *Jñānīs;* Māyāvādīs; *Yogīs*
Transmigration of the soul
into animal life, 112
conditioned souls plagued by, 90–91
by desire, **107**
knowledge of, conquers lamentation, 220–221
by modes of nature, 228
as nature's law, 110

Transmigration of the soul
time causes, 91
Yamarāja supervises, 29
See also: Evolution
Trayaha-sparṣa defined, 170–171
Trayas te narakaṁ yānti
verse quoted, 171
Tree, universe compared to, **183–184**
Tretā-yuga
Deity worship began in, **188,** 189
sacrifice for, 164, 188
Truth. *See:* Absolute Truth
Truthfulness
as brahminical symptom, **43**
as human quality, **32,** 33
Tuṣyeyaṁ sarva-bhūtātmā
quoted, 227
Tyaktvā dehaṁ punar janma
verse quoted, 251

U

Ugra-karma defined, 157
Unhappiness. *See:* Suffering
Universe
Dakṣa's daughters generated population of, **293–294**
living entities pervade, 184
Lord pervades, 72, **89–90,** 186
Lord sustains, **88**
Maya Dānava's demons ravaged, **8**
as treelike, **183–184**
Upaniṣad
dvijas study, **70**
quoted on human quota, 150
Upāsanā-kāṇḍa, 199
Ūrdhvaṁ gacchanti sattva-sthāḥ
quoted, 248
verse quoted, 228

V

Vadanti tat tattva-vidas
verse quoted, 230–231
Vaikuṇṭha. *See:* Spiritual world
Vairāgya. See: Renunciation
Vaiṣṇavānāṁ yathā śambhuḥ
quoted, 16
Vaiṣṇavas. *See:* Devotees of the Supreme Lord
Vaiṣṇavera kriyā mudrā vijñe nā bhujhaya
quoted, 99
Vaiśya(s)
brāhmaṇa in role of, **39**
guru-kula for, **70**
livelihood for, 124
occupational duties for, **35, 38, 39,** 156
as rare in Kali-yuga, 42
symptoms of, **44**
in *varṇāśrama-dharma,* 24, **35**
Vedas studied by, **70,** 71
Vanaṁ gato yad dharim āśrayeta
quoted, 176
Vānaprastha (retired life)
austerity in, **76**
conduct for, **77**
diet for, **75, 76**
dress for, **77**
duty in, **76–78,** 157
falldown in, **240**
Maharloka rewards rigid, **74**
as optional, **70,** 71
residence for, **76,** 77
sacrifice in, **76**
sex life forbidden in, 141
in *varṇāśrama-dharma,* 24, **35**
Vedas studied in, **78**
Vande śrī-kṛṣṇa-caitanya-
verse quoted, 254
Vārāṇasī as sacred place, **179**
Varṇas
by qualification—not birth, **55,** 56
types of, four listed, 24
See also: Occupations; *names of individual varṇas (brāhmaṇas, kṣatriyas, vaiśyas, śūdras)*
Varṇa-saṅkara
hippies as, 46
in Kali-yuga, 42
society confounded by, 47
wayward women produce, 35, 46
world ruined by, 35–36

Varṇāśramācāravatā
verse quoted, 212
Varṇāśrama-dharma
garbhādhāna ceremony in, **35**
goal of, 43, 212
happiness by, 47
Hare Kṛṣṇa movement propagates, 42, 157
higher classes in, three listed, 177
for human beings, 35
Kali-yuga lacks, 42
Lord created, 42
peace by, 42, 47
purification by, **35**
society organized by, 24, 46–47, 157
See also: Brahmacarya; Brāhmaṇas; Gṛhastha; Kṣatriyas; Sannyāsa; Śūdras; Vaiśyas; Vānaprastha; Vedic culture
Varuṇa, **81**
Vasiṣṭha, Pāṇḍavas luckier than, 2
Vasudeva, 143
Vāsudevaḥ sarvam iti
quoted, 19, 132, 269
Vāyu, touch sacrificed to, **81**
Vedaiś ca sarvair aham eva vedyaḥ
quoted, 29, 132
Vedas
Absolute Truth revealed in, 71, 72
activities in, two types listed, **255**
as authority, 106, 109
brahmacārīs study, **60**
brāhmaṇas study, 36, 37
devotees surpass, 136
dvijas study, **35, 70**
Kṛṣṇa as goal of, 29
modes of nature as subject of, 248
vānaprasthas study, **78**
See also: names of individual Vedic literatures
Vedic culture
dogs in, 158
food in, 112
as hearing about Kṛṣṇa, 145
marriage in, 112
money in, 124
prasāda distribution in, 167
Vedic culture
purpose of, 124–125, 148, 164
sex life minimized in, 63, 65
social divisions in, four listed, 124
society purified by, 112
wealth offered to Kṛṣṇa in, 152–153
See also: Varṇāśrama-dharma
Vedic rituals. *See:* Ritualistic ceremonies; Sacrifices
Vidharma defined, **209, 210**
Vidyā. See: Knowledge
Vidyā-vinaya-sampanne
verse quoted, 66
Vishnu, Lord. *See: Supreme Lord*
Viṣṇu, Lord. *See:* Kṣīrodakaśāyī Viṣṇu; Nārāyaṇa, Lord; Supreme Lord
Viṣṇu Purāṇa, quoted on *varṇāśrama-dharma,* 212
Viṣṇur ārādhyate panthā
verse quoted, 212
Viṣṇu-tattva as Kṛṣṇa's expansions, 14
Viśvanātha Cakravartī Ṭhākura, cited
on Brahmā and Śiva, 6
on *brāhmaṇas* and *kṣatriyas,* 36–37
on Lord "vs." living entities, 246
on material life, 107
on renunciation of sense gratification, 219
Viśvanātha Cakravartī Ṭhākura, quotations from
on neophyte devotees, 190
on overendeavoring, 94
on pure devotee, 105
on spiritual master's status, 192
Visvasvān
sun ruled by, 184
See also: Sun-god
Vomit eater, fallen *sannyāsī* as, **236–237**
Vrajendra-nandana yei, śacī-suta haila sei
quoted, 252
Vṛndāvana
"Anglican temple" in, 200
author in, 126
gopīs worship Kṛṣṇa in, 50
as holy place, 177
as Lord's abode, 72
residents of, as pure devotees, 5

Vyakti-mātra-viśeṣeṇa
verse quoted, 187
Vyāsadeva
Nārada instructed, 26
Śukadeva instructed by, 26

W

War
as animal slaughter's consequence, 222
paraphernalia for, **16**
Water as bodily constituent, **79, 80**
Watering a tree's root, worshiping Kṛṣṇa compared to, 182, 184
Waterpot
for *brahmacārī*, **60–61**
for *vānaprastha*, **77**
Wealth. *See:* Money; Opulence, material
Well of nectar. *See:* Nectar well
Western world
evolution misunderstood in, 109
people work like asses in, 145
Wife. *See:* Family life; Marriage; Women
Wine
celibates forbidden, **69**
lower classes drink, 52, 158
Wise man
devotional service for, 184
duality discarded by, 66
as Kṛṣṇa conscious, 136
life's goal sought by, 206
material desire renounced by, **124**
material life rejected by, **135**
Woman (Women)
association of, given up, 219
association with, restricted, 66–67
brahmacārīs avoid, **62, 63**
chastity for, **46, 48,** 49
devotional service open to, 278, 286
duties for married, **46, 48,** 49, **50–**51
goddess of fortune as ideal, 50
in mixed marriage, 51–52
prasāda to, 167
sannyāsī avoids, 63
varṇa-saṅkara from polluted, 35, 46
Work. *See:* Activities; Activities, material; Fruitive activities; Occupations
World, material. *See:* Material world; Universe
Worship
of *brāhmaṇas* 192, 193
of Deity. *See:* Deity worship of the Supreme Lord
of demigods condemned, 212
by devotees, 182
by *dvijas*, **35**
via Gāyatrī *mantra*, **59**
by goddesses of fortune, 50
God vs. demigod, 172
of Kṛṣṇa by *gopīs*, 50
of Lord and living beings, **163, 166–167, 183–184**
of Lord as protector, **5**
of Lord by householder, **163–**164
of Lord recommended, 107, **181, 182, 183–184**
of saint by Prahlāda, **99, 137**
by saints, **5**
of Śiva by demigods, **17–18**
at *śrāddha* ceremony, **202**
of Vaiṣṇava, 189, 192, 193
of Viṣṇu, 50, 189

Y

Yadu dynasty, Pāṇḍavas luckier than, 2
Yaḥ sa sarveṣu bhūteṣu
verse quoted, 272
Yajanādhyāpane caiva
verse quoted, 37
Yajñād bhavati parjanyaḥ
quoted, 151
verse quoted, 150–151
Yajñaiḥ saṅkīrtana-prāyair
quoted, 136, 151, 164, 166
Yajñārthāt karmaṇo 'nyatra
quoted, 114, 118, 164, 165
Yajña. See: Sacrifice; Ritualistic ceremony
Yajña-śiṣṭāśinaḥ santo
quoted, 112
Yājñavalkya, quoted on sin, 49
Yamarāja
quoted on religion as God's laws, 29, 211

Yamarāja *(continued)*
souls' transmigration supervised by, 29
Yaṁ prāpya na nivartante
quoted, 259
verse quoted, 272
Yamunā River as auspicious bathing place, **173**
Yan maithunādi-gṛhamedhi-sukhaṁ hi tuccham
quoted, 111, 156
Yānti deva-vratā devān
quoted, 109, 172, 259
Yānti mad-yājino 'pi mām
quoted, 172
Yaśodā, Mother, as pure devotee, 5
Yasya deve parā bhaktir
verse quoted, 227
Yasya prasādād bhagavat-prasādaḥ
quoted, 68, 223, 224
Yasyāprasādān na gatiḥ kuto 'pi
quoted, 68
Yasyāsti bhaktir bhagavaty akiñcanā
verse quoted, 34
Yathā jñānaṁ tathā vastu
verse quoted, 67
Yathā taror mūla-niṣecanena
verse quoted, 182
Yat karoṣi yad aśnāsi
verse quoted, 153, 275
Yat tapasyasi kaunteya
verse quoted, 153, 275
Yei bhaje sei baḍa, abhakta—hīna, chāra
quoted, 49
Yei kṛṣṇa-tattva-vettā sei 'guru' haya
verse quoted, 137
Ye kurvanti mahīpāla
verse quoted, 171
Yoga
devotional service as topmost, 11
haṭha, for mystic power, 11
mind controlled by, **226**
place to practice, **230,** 231
purpose of mystic, 11
rules for practicing, **232–233**
suffering relieved by, 222
See also: Kṛṣṇa consciousness; *Yogīs*
Yogamāyā, Pāṇḍavas covered by, 2
Yoginām api sarveṣāṁ
verse quoted, 11, 233
Yogīs
bhakti- vs. haṭha-, 134
bogus, 11, 210
devotees as topmost, 11, 233
devotees vs., 223
meditation by, 135
surrender by, 135
as transcendental, 134
Yudhiṣṭhira Mahārāja
good fortune of, **1,** 2, **288**
as *gṛhastha*, **141**
Kṛṣṇa worshiped by, **292**
quoted on Maya Dānava, Śiva and Kṛṣṇa, **6**
quoted on Nārada, **25, 26**
Rājasūya sacrifice by, **183,** 193
Śukadeva praises, 23
Yugas
sacrifices according to, 164, 188–189
See also: names of individual yugas

Z

Zodiac in *śrāddha* ceremony calculation, 170